The History of History

The History of History
Politics and Scholarship in Modern India

Vinay Lal

OXFORD
UNIVERSITY PRESS

OXFORD

UNIVERSITY PRESS

Oxford University Press is a department of the University of Oxford.
It furthers the University's objective of excellence in research, scholarship,
and education by publishing worldwide. Oxford is a registered trademark of
Oxford University Press in the UK and in certain other countries

Published in India by
Oxford University Press
22 Workspace, 2nd Floor, 1/22 Asaf Ali Road, New Delhi 110002

First published 2003
Oxford India Paperbacks 2005
17th impression 2026

ISBN-13: 978-0-19-567244-2
ISBN-10: 0-19-567244-5

Typeset in Palatine 10/12
by Jojy Philip, New Delhi 110 027
Printed in India by Manipal Technologies Limited, Manipal

for Bernard S. Cohn

scholar extraordinary,
radical democrat,
teacher,
friend

and
for
Ishaan Satej and Avni Sunaina
in the hope that
as they grow up they will
not eschew 'myths' for 'history'

Contents

Acknowledgements

Though much of the substance of the five chapters that comprise this volume has appeared in print before in various journals, some of which are with extreme difficulty if at all available in India, the entire manuscript has been thoroughly revised and much new material has been added. However, it is not the mere inclusion of new information, or the greatly enhanced length of the chapters in their revised form, as well as the new introduction to the volume, which lend to the book, taken as a whole, an entirely different set of characteristics than what is encountered in any of the single chapters, which show their origin as discrete pieces of scholarship. Historiography has not developed as a field of inquiry in India even down to the present day, and I am not aware of its inclusion in courses of study in postgraduate programs in history at Indian universities. Though there have been previous studies of Indian historiography before, they tend to be collections of biographies of leading historians, or enumerative and descriptive in their treatment of historical works. Needless to say, I believe that the singularity of this present study arises from not only the wide scope of my inquiry, which brings together under one rubric widely divergent strands of the study of Indian history, but from the philosophical positions I have adopted and from my insistence on giving full consideration to the politics of knowledge.

This book has been ten years in the making, though the earliest version of Chapter I dates back to an earlier date, more precisely to the spring of 1988. I remember the enthusiasm with which the core of what would later become Chapter I was then received by Ashis Nandy, Roby Rajan, and my brother Anil, and am grateful to them for their critical reading of the text. It was another seven years before I endeavored to bring that paper into print.

An earlier version of Chapter I was first published as 'On the Perils of Historical Thinking: The Case, Puzzling as Usual, of India', *Journal of Commonwealth and Post-colonial Studies* 3, no. 1 (Fall 1995):79–112; a more elaborate version, nonetheless considerably different from the present version, appeared in the *Journal of the Indian Council for Philosophical Research*, Special Issue: Historiography of Civilizations (June 1996):95–137, under the title of 'History and the Possibilities of Emancipation: Some Lessons from India'. Chapter II is a revised version of a chapter that appeared in *India Briefing*, edited by Philip Oldenburg and Marshall Bouton (New York: M. E. Sharpe for Asia Society, 1999), under the title 'History and Politics'; the opening section, in particular, is considerably altered. I am grateful to Philip Oldenburg for his incisive remarks on this chapter in its earlier incarnation, and I have followed many of his concrete suggestions. Dipesh Chakrabarty kindly shared with me some of his thoughts on the political debates over history that took place in India in the 1960s and 1970s.

Chapter III was first published under the title of 'The Discourse of History and the Crisis at Ayodhya: Reflections on the Production of Knowledge, Freedom, and the Future of India', in *Emergences*, nos. 5–6 (1993–4):4–44. I am grateful to my friends, especially Teshome Gabriel, Jim Wilgten, and Patrick Malloy, in what was then the 'Emergences' collective at UCLA, for fruitful discussions on portions of this chapter; and I would also like to express my gratitude to one of the anonymous readers for Oxford University Press who alerted me to the necessity of placing the debates between historians over Ayodhya in their wider context. I would like to thank my student, Mitch Numark, for a careful reading of Chapter IV, an abbreviated version of which was first presented by invitation at an international conference, held in Buffalo in August 1999, on 'Turning Points in Historical Thinking: A Comparative Perspective'. It has since been published as 'Walking with the Subalterns, Riding with the Academy: The Curious Ascendancy of Indian History', *Studies in History* (New Series) 17, no. 1 (2001):101–33, and I am grateful to the journal's editor, Neeladri Bhattacharya, for his comments.

The final chapter first took shape as a paper presented at the annual conference on South Asian studies at the University of California, Berkeley, in February 1999; at the invitation of Stephan Astourian, holder of the William Saroyan Chair in Armenian Studies, University of California, Berkeley, a lengthier version of the paper was presented at a conference at Berkeley on 'Diasporas: Transnational Identity and the Politics of the Homeland', November 1999. I am extremely grateful to David Palumbo-Lin, and in particular Khachig Tölölyan, who offered a learned commentary, for incisive comments on Chapter V. Yossi Shain's enthusiasm for my work on diasporic internet histories is still fresh in my mind. The financial assistance of the Asian American Studies Center, UCLA, which helped in the completion of Chapter V, is gratefully acknowledged.

The intellectual friendship of Frederique Apffel-Marglin has also meant a lot to me in recent years, and she offered a perceptive commentary on the entire manuscript. My friend, Henry Ranjeet of Kolam Travels, Chennai, is an intellectual maverick and iconoclast, and his unflagging interest in my work prodded me to move on with this book. No words are adequate to describe the intellectual support that I have received from Ashis Nandy over the course of the last decade and more. He has always displayed the keenest interest in the arguments put forth in this work. Some of his writings have been critical in helping to shape my thoughts on the enterprise of history in India, and those familiar with his writings will at once recognize the intellectual debt I owe to him. I had been familiar with Gandhi's writings long before I encountered the work of Nandy, but Nandy offered a fresh perspective on Gandhi, one that was immensely desirable in an India where many Gandhians and politicians had succeeded in transforming one of the few great dissenters of our times into a dull, pious, sanctimonious, moralizing 'role model', the very 'Father of the Nation'. Gandhian studies took the politics out of Gandhi. Of contemporary Indian intellectuals, no one has contributed more than Nandy to putting a spark back in Gandhi.

I hope this book will resonate with Shiv Viswanathan, Ramchandra Gandhi, Douglas Lummis, Gustavo Esteva, Claude Alvares, Ziauddin Sardar, and other deprofessionalized academics and dissenting intellectuals whose writings have also been inspirational, or whose friendship has sustained me in the belief that the insights of this book are not without some promise. I am hopeful that this book will endear itself as well to people outside the profession of history, indeed outside the academy, but expect that its demonstrable engagement with a broad swathe of historiography will also persuade professional historians to take its arguments seriously.

Introduction
History in the Ascendant Mode

Almost nothing must appear more remarkable to a student of the social sciences, or of the wider intellectual scene, in India than the recent ascendancy of 'history' and the elevation of historians to a position of public recognition if not eminence. Outside the hard sciences, as well as those disciplines, such as economics, which have self-consciously fashioned themselves after the sciences and mathematics, and in all of which Indian achievements have acquired something of an international dimension, no discipline has gained as much visibility as has history in the course of the previous two to three decades. Its prominence in the public sphere in recent years may be briefly gauged by two developments. Amartya Sen, whose Nobel Prize in Economics conferred on him not merely instant recognition but the kind of celebrity that is generally reserved only for Bollywood stars, cricketing heroes, 'colourful' Indian politicians, and authors of multi-million rupee scams, consented to deliver the keynote address at the annual meeting of the Indian History Congress in early January 2001. Meetings of the Indian History Congress in recent years have not been without some excitement, and it may also well be the case that Sen, who has lately acquired something of a habit of uttering oracular pronouncements on a diverse array of subjects—from the films of Satyajit Ray, the humanism of Tagore, and Indian calendrical systems to secularism, the mode of scientific reasoning, the virtues of reason, and the perils facing democracy—and shows no disinclination to distance himself from the reputation gradually accruing to him as the repository of wisdom, relished the opportunity to speak from yet another platform of authority. But that he would at all consent to give the keynote address for a profession to which he is a relative outsider points to the public visibility of the profession just as much as it suggests the importance that someone such as Sen has come to attach to the discipline of history. Warning against the manipulation of history in the service of sectarian political interests, and the diminishing of India's 'magnificently multireligious and heterodox history' at the hands of bigots, Sen made himself heard: his remarks were reported widely in the press and received profuse circulation in cyberspace.[1]

Only some months before Sen's lecture, the most intense controversy raged over the overt politicization of the Indian Council of Historical Research (ICHR), a national body formed to promote historical thinking and research. Less than a week after Murli Manohar Joshi was appointed Union Minister for Human Resources Development, he promoted B. R. Grover, an historian of no great standing, to the chairmanship of the ICHR. Having previously served in the ICHR for twelve years and then gone into retirement, Grover was plucked from near obscurity and again nominated to its membership in June 1998 after the Bharatiya Janata Party's ascendancy to power. His political predilections, according to one commentator, can be surmised from his voting record at the Indian History Congress, the most prestigious association of professional historians: he apparently opposed a resolution against communal strife in 1984, and likewise voted, in 1987, against a resolution which objected to the politicization of history in the media. Grover only came to be known to a somewhat wider public during the controversy over the Babri Masjid, when he affiliated himself with the position advocated by the VHP and other proponents of what might be termed 'the temple theory'.[2] Thus, considering Grover's background, it cannot have been a complete surprise when the ICHR, with Grover at the helm and the BJP government looking over its shoulder, announced in early 2000 its decision to withdraw from publication two volumes, by the well-known historians Sumit Sarkar and K. N. Panikkar, comprising part of the ambitious multi-volume series under its jurisdiction, entitled 'Towards Freedom'. It was submitted that Sarkar and Panikkar had failed to submit the proofs of the manuscripts to ICHR, and that a review was required by the ICHR. However, as Panikkar has pointed out, the reasons for the withdrawal of the volumes can most likely be traced to the substantive matter found in the volumes, which suggests, among other things, that the Rashtriya Swayamsevak Sangh (RSS), the paramilitary organization which advocates a militant Hinduism and a Hindu polity in modern India, not only played no role in the anti-colonial struggle but actively collaborated with the British. Considering that Prime Minister Vajpayee and L. K. Advani, the Home Minister, are both long-standing members of the RSS, and that the RSS poses as a national volunteer organization committed to the social advancement of Indians, one can begin to understand the acute anxiety generated by such scholarship.

That the 'Towards Freedom' series is intended to tell the Indian side of the story of the critical last few years preceding the attainment of Indian independence in 1947, and so provide a counterpoint to the voluminous series of official records published by the British Government,[3] also tells another tale, which I take up at various places in this book, of the relationship of history to the nation-state, the patronage of history-writing by the state, and the treatment of nationalism by contemporary historians of India. But let me, for the present, stay with the subject of how historical thinking has forged its way into the public consciousness. There are many other signposts. When, in the late 1980s, the dispute over the origins of the sixteenth-century Babri Masjid began to engulf the nation, and culminated in the destruction of the mosque on 6 December 1992, historians were suddenly thrust into the limelight. Hindu militants claimed, much to the chagrin of secular intellectuals, that the Mughal Emperor Babur, or at least some Muslim potentate or aristocrat acting on his command, had ordered the destruction of a Hindu temple which had allegedly been constructed in remote antiquity to honour the deity Rama and mark his exact birthplace; over the rubble of this temple, it was argued, the Babri mosque had been built. Historians were, not unexpectedly, summoned into service to verify or repudiate the claims, but what is truly striking is how the dispute was shifted onto the terrain of historical discourse, with both the 'secularists' and their purported opposites, the 'fundamentalists', choosing to take recourse to notions of historical 'truth' and 'evidence' to stake their positions. The public might have been forgiven for thinking that right belonged to the party which produced the more plausible historical account, and that it was enough to produce compelling 'historical' evidence to settle the vexed questions surrounding the histories of conquest, the politics of memory, the notion of 'historical wrongs' and 'retribution', the communalization of history, the anxieties generated by masculinity, and the emergence of nation-states in the Indian subcontinent which underlay the dispute over the Babri Masjid.

There are many other markers of the unusual importance being ascribed to history by Indians in our times. Among Indians in the diaspora, and most particularly among those in North America who are advocates of a rejuvenated and masculinized Hinduism, and who lend their political support to the Hindu formations that have taken political power in India, the interest in what is taken to be Indian history has grown immensely. One manifestation of this, though this is scarcely a matter of wide public knowledge, is the growth of Indian history as a heritage industry. Over the last decade, the Indian population in the United States grew at a faster rate than any other group, and students of Indian descent are today enrolled in disproportionately large numbers at leading colleges and universities.[4] These second-generation Indians, fed on a diet of Amar Chitra Katha comic books, televised narratives of the Mahabharata and Ramayana, and accounts of India's hoary past imbibed at summer camp, are intensely desirous of learning about India's past or, to invoke the idiom of their thinking, their own 'heritage'. South Asian history professorships at American universities have burgeoned in the last few years; web sites devoted to Indian history have proliferated, and sometimes draw nearly as much attention as web sites chronicling the love affairs and misdemeanours of Bollywood stars.

The debate over the 'Aryan Invasion Theory' is, however, by far a more instructive case in point of history's ascendancy in the affluent Indian diaspora.[5] More so than even the 'natives' back home, Indians in North America have been avid proponents of the preposterous view that the Aryans, far from having migrated to India, dispersed throughout central and west Asia and Europe from India.[6] They have called for a radical revisionism on the grounds that the widely accepted view of an Aryan migration to India from their homeland in the Ural or Caucasian mountains was at first a contribution of colonial scholars, and that India's secular and liberal intelligentsia colluded in this view as it was unable to free itself of its thralldom to colonial learning. It has been argued by these self-nominated historians, the bulk of whom are housed in the United States, when they are not white men settled in India and out-Hinduing the Hindu,[7] that a conspiracy continues to deny the Hindus of India their true designation as the authentic and primordial Aryans. Thus this strand of revisionist Hindu history, which is scarcely familiar with that recent trajectory of historical thinking which describes many purported timeless or ancient cultural and social practices as 'invented traditions',[8] speaks of the entire edifice of Indo-European studies as an invented tradition, and perpetrates a gruesome excess by denying the non-Aryan foundation of early Indian civilization. Nor is this revisionism innocuous or merely inconsequential, judging from the changes in history and social studies textbooks in BJP-ruled states. One such textbook, designed for students in middle school, describes the Aryans unequivocally as 'the most illustrious race in history. They were a tall, fair complexioned, good-looking and cultured people.' One can be sure that the authors of this textbook thought themselves descended from the Aryans. Another book, intended as a world history text, has nothing to say of the holocaust perpetrated upon the Jews by the Nazis, but is instead laudatory in its description of Hitler, since 'he instilled the spirit of adventure in the common people'.[9]

On the other end of the spectrum, India's many left historians are among the country's most distinguished social scientists. For instance, the work of Romila Thapar on ancient India, or that of Irfan Habib on Mughal India, has received unusual accolades. However, it is the ascendancy of the 'subaltern historians' that has, for the first time, earned a school of Indian history a place on the map of international historiography, and even made some Indian historians into academic stars who are feted by the American academy. Their frequent comings and goings from one university department to another are the stuff of intense academic gossip. In 1982, the first volume of *Subaltern Studies* was published by Oxford University Press in Delhi; the next few volumes appeared in rapid succession and to much critical acclaim; and eleven volumes have been published so far.[10] Articles culled from the first four volumes were published by Oxford in New York as *Selected Subaltern Studies* (1988), with a foreword by Edward Said and an introduction by Gayatri Chakravorty Spivak. This was enough to catapult Subaltern Studies—the journal, some of the members of that collective, and the historical enterprise by that name—into fame, and today Subaltern Studies is an inextricable part of the burgeoning and influential field of postcolonial studies. Indeed, a second anthology of subaltern history appeared from the University of Minnesota Press in 1997, accompanied by the curious observation that the 'most famous members' of the Subaltern Studies Collective 'were instrumental in establishing the discipline best known as postcolonial studies'.[11]

Some critics have expressed the view that Subaltern Studies would have been much less noticed had not influential portions of the Anglo-American academy been considerably influenced by the same intellectual movements, such as poststructuralism and post-Marxism, whose presence is so noticeable in subaltern history; others have noted the affinity of Subaltern Studies to what used to be described as 'history from below',[12] and are consequently less inclined to view subaltern history as effecting any radical departure from other resistant modes of writing history. The distinguished anthropologist Marshall Sahlins, while making no reference to *Subaltern Studies*, nonetheless appears to have placed it under his gaze when he remarked that 'Western historians have been arguing for a long time over two polar ideas of right historiography', positing the history of 'communities' against 'elite history'; as he reminds us, Voltaire complained that 'for the last fourteen hundred years, the only Gauls, apparently, have been kings, ministers and generals', and he swore to write instead 'a history of men'.[13] But the inescapable fact is that, whatever the achievements and shortcomings of subaltern history, and howsoever original or predictable their work might be, the collective has not only made a decisive contribution to the writing of Indian history, but also impacted, uniquely for a school of history emanating from the Third World, work in European, African, and Latin American history.[14]

Thus, in its public aspect, the study of Indian history appears to revolve largely around the polarity of Hindutva history and the history associated with left, secular historians. In the most recent controversy that has erupted over the interpretation and, howsoever crude this formulation may sound, the management of Indian history, it is seen to be demonstrably true that history is now viewed as occupying a distinct place in the social order and that both communalists and secularists are alike persuaded that, in Veer Savarkar's remarkable language, 'the holy work of the historians' never terminates.[15] Though the latest chapter in the dispute over the censorship of history textbooks seems to have been written in mid-2001, intimations of the controversy can be traced back to the time of the first non-Congress government in 1977–80 following Indira's Gandhi defeat at the polls in 1977. At that time, as recounted elsewhere in this book, certain history textbooks, used widely in schools around the country, were proposed to be withdrawn from circulation on the grounds that their authors—among them Romila Thapar, R. S. Sharma, and Bipan Chandra—were insufficiently critical of the dark period of Indian history under Muslim rule and the despotism of Aurangzeb, and similarly not appreciative enough of the stellar contributions towards Indian independence of such nationalist stalwarts as Tilak and Aurobindo Ghose (before he became the enlightened Sri Aurobindo). To read about that controversy at this present juncture is to be reminded of how little has apparently changed over the years. As two scholars who have written on the textbook controversy of the late 1970s remark, 'The secularists were convinced that Hindu-oriented historians were *ipso facto* unprofessional. The Hindu enthusiasts thought that professionalism was a cover for the wrong values and interests of the secularists.'[16] On both sides, a similar argument predominates down to the present day.

Yet even in the unchanging India of the Orientalist, everything that occurs is not a minor variation of history that has already been played out. Perhaps Bipan Chandra, a historian at Jawaharlal Nehru University who was among those targeted by the custodians of Hinduism, may have been prescient when, having remarked that the 'communal historical approach has been, and is, the main ideology of communalism in India',[17] he clearly appeared to be implying that history would remain the fundamental backdrop to communalist thinking. Yet in the 1970s history was not nearly as ascendant as it is today; the spectre of Gandhi still loomed large—recall that the nuclear testing at Pokhran in 1974 took the name of a 'peaceful nuclear explosion', the strangest apposition of three words that one can possibly imagine; and though textbooks might seek to have been withdrawn, there were no substantive proposals to have them replaced with complete fabrications. In the flush of independence, the Gujarat government could undertake, in the face of opposition from Nehru, the reconstruction of Somnath, and the claim could be advanced that the injustices of history were being undone and that Somnath was being reclaimed for Hindus. Even then, in the hullabaloo over Somnath, the centrality of historians was nowhere on display, and it is the dispute over the Babri Masjid, as recounted in numerous places in this book, which brought the historians to the proscenium of the nation-state.

The bitter wrangling that has accompanied the present dispute over history textbooks can be traced to the Bharatiya Janata Party's assumption of power in provincial elections and its eventual formation of the central government in 1998. In 1991, the advocates of Hindutva history attempted to capture the Indian History Congress (IHC) at its annual meeting in Ujjain by enrolling 360 of their ilk as 'life members' who would then be able to steer the organization, through their voting privileges, away from its commitment to relatively secular histories. However, the IHC amended its rules of membership, and so prevented the 'takeover' of the organization by communalist historians. To narrate this story is in itself to attribute perhaps more influence to the IHC than it actually exercises, since the

IHC has jurisdiction neither over history textbooks nor over the history curricula at schools and universities. The battle, predictably, shifted to the domain of school textbooks in history and the social sciences. The report of the National Steering Committee on Textbook Evaluation in 1993 warned that the BJP governments in Madhya Pradesh, Rajasthan, and Uttar Pradesh had altered textbooks to reflect a 'communal view of Indian history'. As documented by various researchers, it soon became transparent that at thousands of Vidya Bharati schools, Shishu Mandirs, and Bal Mandirs across BJP-governed states,[18] the textbooks had been amended to reflect such historical 'truths': Iran was settled by Aryans from India; Homer adapted the *Iliad* from the Ramayana; Jesus Christ wandered about the Himalayas and was inspired by Hinduism; Alexander suffered a humiliating defeat at the hands of Porus; the Qutab Minar was constructed by Samudragupta and was previously known as Vishnu Sthambha; and so on.[19]

Today twenty thousand Vidya Bharati schools across the country cater to 2.4 million children.[20] But it is not the books used in these and other similar schools which alone provoke acute anxiety among the defenders of the traditional secular curriculum, since the most recent episode in the history textbooks controversy has extended the dispute to books commissioned by the National Council for Educational Research and Training (NCERT) for use across schools all over the country. In November 2000, the Human Resource Development Minister, Murli Manohar Joshi, released a new National Curriculum Framework for School Education prepared by the NCERT, which proposed to dispense with history altogether in secondary schools by integrating it firmly into the social sciences, and sought to censor and remove certain textbooks at the higher secondary level. As J. S. Rajput, NCERT's new director, who has been the most vocal spokesperson for the proposed changes, and has written widely in English and Hindi newspapers in defence of the new curriculum, was to put it in one of his op-ed pieces, the NCERT was duty bound to provide school children with a curriculum that would 'fit them out with a modern outlook, give them life skills, make them competitive in the 21st century while at the same time lessen the burden of the school-bag and weaken the teacher-private lobby'. Rajput thought it likely that many children who opted out of formal schooling before finishing their studies did so because the curriculum was irrelevant to their needs; moreover, 'the nation needs an educational model rooted to its composite culture and committed to progress'.[21] It was incumbent upon the NCERT to introduce a 'value-based education' system that would instil in children an appreciation for 'truth, love, non-violence and righteous conduct'.[22] The 'fulminations' of a few academics for whom 'history seems to be the most convenient weapon used in their tirade', Rajput opined,[23] could not be allowed to keep school children from their educational entitlements, including an emphasis on 'secular values and religious tolerance'.[24]

It is not in the least remarkable that proponents of Hindutva, who have been the most enthusiastic advocates of the proposed curriculum changes, should be insisting upon 'secular values', non-violence, social justice, and 'religious tolerance'. They have always characterized the secularists as 'pseudo-secularists'; moreover, though neither the secularists nor their opponents are aware of this, opposition must itself be expressed in the idiom of secularism, particularly in view of the fact that in principle the Hindutvavadis are bound to declare themselves in sympathy with an ecumenical and pluralistic conception of Hinduism. Howsoever narrow their conception of Hinduism, they view it as unique among faiths for its manifold expressions of tolerance. Yet the broadly stated objectives of Joshi, Rajput, and others of their ilk could not disguise the articulation of specific 'distortions' allegedly encountered in several history textbooks. Thus, to take a few examples, it was said of Arjun Dev and Indira Arjun Dev's textbook for Class VIII, *Modern India*, that the authors had denigrated the Jats when they wrote of them that from their capital at Bharatpur 'they conducted plundering raids in the regions around and participated in the court intrigues at Delhi'. R. S. Sharma, author of the Class XI textbook, *Ancient India*, is said to have offended on several counts: by putting into question the presumed historicity of Krishna, the Ramayana, and the Mahabharata; by suggesting that the Brahmins were not reconciled to Ashoka's policy of religious tolerance, and that the varna system encouraged the producing and labouring classes to abjure resistance to the upper castes; by suggesting—and this in common with Romila Thapar, author of *Ancient India* for Class VI— that among the early Aryans who settled in India, beef was served to honoured guests, and so on.[25]

That history must be viewed, minimally, as interpretive work rather than as an assemblage of purported facts appears not to have been understood by the critics of the textbooks, as their treatment of Satish Chandra's Class XI history textbook, *Medieval India*, amply demonstrates. In several paragraphs extending over two pages, Chandra sought to furnish an account of the circumstances leading to the martyrdom of Guru Tegh Bahadur, and the condition of the Sikhs in the reign of Aurangzeb. 'The official explanation' for the Guru's execution 'as given in some later Persian sources', Chandra wrote, 'is that after his return from Assam, the Guru ... had resorted to plunder and rapine, laying waste the whole province of the Punjab.'[26] Chandra admits as well the existence of other interpretive traditions: thus 'according to Sikh tradition, the execution was due to the intrigues of some members of his family who disputed his succession, and by others who had joined them'; and, yet again, in the widely accepted and most popular version, Aurangzeb is said to have been 'annoyed because the Guru had converted a few Muslims to Sikhism'. The 'truth', Chandra notes, is not easily sifted 'from these conflicting accounts'.

Writing in vigorous defence of his representation of the Guru, after NCERT director J. S. Rajput claimed that he had offended the Sikh community with his 'adverse and derogatory' remarks about the Guru, Chandra had perforce to note that he had underscored the presence of conflictual oral and written traditions about the life of the Guru. For historians, Chandra argued, the difficulties are paramount: the execution of the Guru is not mentioned in contemporary Persian sources, and the Sikh narratives, mistakenly read by some as contemporary sources, date from the late eighteenth century, or more than a century after the Guru's execution, and rely, it is believed, upon 'the testimony of trustworthy Sikhs'. Far from denigrating Guru Tegh Bahadur, Chandra argues, he stated in his textbook that the Guru had 'begun to be a rallying point for all those fighting against injustice and oppression', and that 'the Guru gave up his life in defense of cherished principles'.[27] It is Chandra's contention, an eminently reasonable one, that in his book *Medieval India* not only was he supremely considerate of the obligations placed upon the historian, but that by delineating the difficulties attendant upon the discernment of historical truth he laid before the students a very model of the interpretive disputes that are central to the enterprise of historical reflection.

The various charges proffered by both sides to the textbooks controversy need not be enumerated at length, nor is it necessary to follow all the intricacies of the dispute, such as the allegation, which appears well-founded, that the historians whose works were sought to be censored appear to have had their contractual rights violated when the modifications to their texts were made without their approval.[28] On 5 October 2001, the NCERT director made it known that he 'would consult religious experts before including references to any religion in the textbooks, to avoid hurting the sentiments of the community concerned', an opinion endorsed by Murli Manohar Joshi, who then went on to characterize the writings of secular historians as 'intellectual terrorism unleashed by the left' and 'more dangerous than cross border terrorism'.[29] The insinuation that left historians should be viewed as a Fifth column, as apostates whose betrayal makes them more dangerous enemies than Pakistani-trained *jihadis*, is extraordinary—even as it is apposite that the Hindutva forces should have understood that they could not have a more enduring impact on Indian society than by transforming the educational infrastructure. One wonders, too, what social reformers would have accomplished in India if they were duty-bound to ensure that religious sentiments of their and other communities—assuming that one can speak at all of Hindus, Sikhs, Muslims, Buddhists, and others as monolithic communities—were not offended? What is a 'community', and do all segments of the 'community' think alike, acting in perfect consistency with each other? Does an individual always speak as a member of a community, and are there not moments when the individual is called to go beyond the community?

If secular commentators advert to the manner in which the Indian Council for Historical Research, the Indian Council for Social Science Research, and other like institutions have been packed with political appointees of the BJP government, they are invariably reminded of the patronage extended to secular scholars for at least three decades after the achievement of independence.[30] Predictably, the Hindutva critics of the old textbooks are met with the rejoinder that their only interest resides in 'talibanizing' education in India, and that the 'saffronization' of education makes 'nonsense of history', besides leading the country down the dangerous path of religious bigotry, intolerance, and bloodshed.[31] Thus, to take as illustrative of the tenor of the common secularist defence the writings of the *Hindu* correspondent Anjali Mody, the Sangh Parivar makes 'nonsense of history writing by getting rid of the critical methodology that separates history from mythology'. The BJP's 'marriage of mythology, fiction and faith does not', we are assured, 'stand up to intellectual scrutiny', and elsewhere it is asserted that the Sangh Parivar's ideological platform for India and the idea of the nation entails various forms of oppression. 'Re-writing school history textbooks to fit this idea of the Hindu Rashtra', in which 'the superiority of Hindus' is taken as axiomatic, 'has always been a top priority' for the Sangh Parivar.[32]

Sometimes the authentic enemy of history in secular or at least anti-communalist writings is described as 'mythology', at other times as 'ideology'; 'mythology', in turn, is construed as fiction, often as fantasy, sometimes as palpable falsehoods and almost always as something opposed to 'truth'. Though the 'talibanization' of education is denounced, commentators have not paused to probe the limits of their representational practices. Did the Taliban propose selective censorship of certain 'offending' texts, or did it largely do away with books except the Koran? If the Taliban is a creation of the Americans, as is often alleged, and was pushed into the limelight in the circumstances eventually arising from the Soviet occupation of Afghanistan in the 1980s, of whom should we say the BJP is a creation? If, as is the customary practice in some scholarly circles, monuments should be read as texts, can we say that the destruction of the Bamiyan Buddhas and the Babri Masjid belong to the same species of criminal acts of wanton destruction of cultural properties? Were the Bamiyan Buddhas as much of a festering wound for the Taliban as the Babri Masjid was held to be for some Hindus?

The present dispute, reduced to a combat between Joshi, Rajput, Arun Shourie, and company on one side, with the secular and 'progressive' historians on the other, echoes the contestation between communalist and secular historians over the affair of the Babri Masjid. I have argued at various places in this book, and will not now dwell on this matter at any length, that this opposition disguises the common and enabling ground for the acrimonious exchanges on witness in recent years. The scholar and activist Gail Omvedt, whose own secular credentials can scarcely be doubted, has pointedly asked whether either the 'secular' or 'saffron' educationists in the country have ever thought much of providing a 'meaningful education for the masses of dalit, bahujan and adivasi students throughout the country', and she submits that the 'secularist' critique of the political maneuvers of the Human Resource Development ministry and the NCERT has been both evasive and inadequate. Neither the 'saffronisers nor the secularisers are really interested in creativity', Omvedt argues, and 'none has said a word against rote learning, against the top-down syllabus; none has questioned why the syllabus should be set in Delhi for such a geographically vast country.' Though evidently not sympathetic to the upper-caste predilections of the Hindutvavadis, Omvedt finds their criticism of the alleged Macaulayite mindset of secularists not entirely pointless, and suggests that the subject of the Indianization of education deserves more careful scrutiny than the secularists are prepared to concede.[33]

One could go further than Omvedt. In the long and heated exchange over textbooks, scarcely a word has been said on either side on the politics and political economy of the *textbook*, and on the sociology of knowledge entailed by the textbook. Why should the textbook be rendered synonymous with learning and education, and what does it mean that a culture allows 'canons of truthfulness' to be set by textbooks? Though textbooks are viewed merely as 'delivery systems' of 'facts', they are, as Michael Apple and Linda Christian-Smith have reminded us, a 'major reference point for what knowledge, culture, belief, and morality really are'; textbooks 'signify—through their content and form—particular constructions of reality, particular ways of selecting and organizing that vast universe of possible knowledge'.[34] What could have been a debate on what Krishna Kumar has termed 'India's textbook culture'[35]—on the restrictions placed on teachers that prevent them from moving outside the parameters set by textbooks, on a system of examinations based wholly on the acquisition of 'knowledge' contained in textbooks, and on the supposition that all history is ultimately the history of the nation-state, requiring uniformity of educational purpose and design, a uniformity best produced by textbooks—was reduced to a controversy where each side charged the other with 'distortion' and 'manipulation' of history.

In the textbooks controversy, as in other disagreements between 'secular' and 'saffron' historians and other scholars, it is indisputable that the Hindutvavadis scarcely have a scholar of any reputation on their side. But if secularists are capable of little more than the argument, as advanced recently in a resolute defence of the maligned textbooks, that these works deserve the same longevity and respect as the economics textbook—'read the world over by generations of students'—of Paul Samuelson, 'a Nobel laureate in Economics',[36] they risk both ridicule and oblivion; nor should one marvel, then, at the immense distance that separates professional historians from the country's wider public. Leaving aside Samuelson's own proclivity towards authoritarianism, it is remarkable that the proliferation of American-style social science should be viewed uncritically, even as a matter of emulation, and that the critical apparatus of Samuelson's admirers in India should not have been brought to bear upon a discussion of how the globalization of social science research, especially in its positivist modes, has impoverished—intellectually, socially, economically—the very countries that were supposed to have been aided by this research.

I have, on more than one occasion in this book, adverted to the failures of academic history in India, and find myself largely in agreement with Sande Cohen's cogent critique of it as part of liberal, bourgeois, reactive culture. His insistence that the 'collapse of the bourgeois–liberal contents of transcendence—progress, knowledge, value, and so on—have been rerouted by much of neo-Marxist historiography into the ethical aspect of transcendence, the obligation to "think historically"', is salutary.[37] What is most germane, from the perspective adopted in the present work, is the ascendancy of history in India as evidenced by the various disputes in contemporary times in which historians have been called upon to play major roles. The politics of history's rise in prominence can be described as one of the chief burdens of my book, and I have sought, for the most part, to track and interpret only those developments in Indian historiography which have a distinct bearing on the growing public importance of historical work in India, as well as on the politics of knowledge in contemporary Indian society. It has not been my ambition, nor is it my interest, to write a full-blown account of historiography in India, but this book should also be viewed as a contribution towards the development of Indian historiography.

The ascendancy of Indian history is all the more astonishing because, as I argue in Chapter I, ahistoricism is one of the defining features of Indian civilization, and even, contrary to the received wisdom, one of its greatest attractions. Though Islamic and Western civilizations have well-developed traditions of historical inquiry, the ancient Indians never bothered much with their history. One cannot insist too rigidly upon the Christian, Western, and monotheistic roots of history,[38] considering as well the place of historical thinking in China, but it is not unimportant to hazard such broad generalizations—especially when the dogmas of academic precision, empiricism, and political correctness encroach upon intellectual life. Certainly it is not too much to say that Indians were supremely indifferent to historical productions, and it is only with the emergence of Islam as a factor in Indian history that the rudiments of a historical sensibility can be discerned in India. The Muslims produced historical chronicles,[39] but the Hindus not even that; and almost nowhere does one encounter any works that betray what might be called historical thinking. If this proposition appears to be framed much too strongly, we might consider at least the fact that discussions of statecraft were generally framed without reference to any particular state, and similarly discussions on law were couched in the most general terms, without reference to specific cases: in other words, discourses in India were stripped of their historicity. In the early nineteenth century, after the British were well-entrenched as the dominant power in most parts of India, James Mill, author of the voluminous *History of British India*, pronounced it as a self-evident truth that Indians were grossly lacking in the historical sensibility, their literature devoid of any historical works, and were consequently not to be considered a rational people. As he stated in no uncertain terms, 'rude' nations were always deficient in historical reasoning. Around this time, Hegel too advanced the idea that India had no history; as Marx was to put in an essay published in 1857, India was vegetating in the teeth of time. In this view, the lack of a historical sensibility was equated with the very lack of history: India was merely a template on which new histories could be written.

Nineteenth-century Indian nationalists agreed that Indians neglected the craft of history and, in Bengal, they set upon creating an agenda to furnish Indians with their own history. Their anguish at what they took to be a serious want in Indian learning comes across in the voice of the novelist and essayist Bankimchandra Chatterji, who (in a much celebrated passage) opined in 1880: 'Bengal must have her own history. Otherwise there is no hope for Bengal. Who is to write it? You have to write it. I have to write it. All of us have to write it. ... Come, let us join our efforts in investigating the history of Bengal.'[40] All great nations had written their own histories; why could not Indians do the same? The enthusiasm with which educated Indian gentlemen set about to study history can be gauged by the fact that at the inaugural meeting of the Society for the Acquisition of General Knowledge in 1838, a discourse was delivered, 'On the Nature and Importance of Historical Studies'.[41] The other part of the endeavour was to argue that India's rich literary traditions could be mined for historical insights; indeed, from here it was not too bold a move to assert that the epic and Puranic literature constituted a tradition of historical inquiry. Historians and nationalists were no longer content to view Krishna as a mythical figure of uncertain origins, as a ludic deity who was at once a shepherd, lover, husband, ruler, village dweller, trickster, moralist, saviour, and more; nor were they prepared to view the Mahabharata merely as an allegorical tale of the struggle, within and outside the self, between knowledge and ignorance, good and evil. Perforce Krishna had to be a historical figure, who in real life had led the 'nation' in arms, and who had the same role to play in the formation of Hinduism that Muhammad did in Islam and Christ in Christianity.

The first chapter, then, not only offers an account of the nationalist obsession with history in the nineteenth century, but a dissenting perspective on the real absence of historical literature and thinking in India until very recent times. No apologies, it is my submission, need be tendered on behalf of Indians' relation to historical knowledge: its absence must be construed not as a lack, but as a form of principled forgetfulness, a disavowal of history as a legitimate form of knowledge. Consequently, I take issue with those scholars who, in their rejection of nineteenth-century colonialist and nationalist interpretations as equally orientalist, but in their simultaneous embrace of historicism, have adopted the view that Indians sustained an engagement with historical reasoning, albeit not of the European variety. These scholars, while well-intentioned, have no place for ahistoricism in their scheme of knowledge.[42] Those among them who translate *itihasa* from Sanskrit traditions effortlessly as 'history' appear to have reflected inadequately on problems of translatability and, even more significantly, overlooked the fact, as some critics well-versed in India's literary traditions are aware, that itihasa can never be divested entirely from its Puranic inheritance and resonances.

With the attainment of independence in 1947, and the emergence of India as a nation-state, historical projects became projects of the state. Chapter II explores, in the first instance, the relationship between nation-building and the making of Indian history. There was a widespread perception that India was no mere nation-state, but one whose destiny had been shaped by the uniquely moral leadership of Mohandas Gandhi. Two generations of Indians who had resisted colonial rule were canonized as 'freedom fighters', and authorized histories, often running into multiple volumes, of the 'freedom struggle' were issued by various state governments. Independence, however, had been accompanied by a bloodbath, and under the Nehruvian dispensation, historical work was seen as playing its part in fostering communal harmony, cementing the nation, and promoting the ideology of secularism. Even then, communal overtones could not entirely be kept out of all histories, and some historians, whose dislike for Gandhi was scarcely disguised, adopted a strident Hindu nationalist view. A project of furnishing a complete historical narrative of Indian civilization was commenced under the auspices of the Bharatiya Vidya Bhavan, and the editorship of *The History and Culture of the Indian People* (11 vols, 1951–69) was entrusted to R. C. Majumdar, whose voluminous histories were the mainstay of college texts for an entire generation. Majumdar was perhaps less of a Rankean than his

Bengali predecessor, Sir Jadunath Sarkar, but he produced histories that, while solidly and usefully empirical, were not much more enlightened. Majumdar subscribed wholly to the distinction between a 'materialist West' and 'spiritual East'; he viewed India as essentially Hindu India, considering the long period of Muslim ascendancy as the 'dark ages' of Indian history; and he stridently adhered to the view that Muslims and Hindus in India were two 'separate' nations.

Following Nehru's death in 1964, the wars between Pakistan and India in 1965 and 1971, the increasing authoritarianism of the political order, the repression of student, working-class, and peasant unrest, and the imposition of an internal emergency in India in 1975, secularism found itself under onslaught and communalism acquired a refurbished legitimacy. There had always been debates about such iconic figures as Aurangzeb, who was reviled by Hindu nationalists as an intolerant but not atypical Muslim ruler, and his political foe Shivaji, who contrariwise was championed as the inspirational figure of Indian nationalism (long before the idea of the 'nation' was born anywhere), but these debates acquired much more visibility in the 1960s and 1970s. These debates are recounted in Chapter II, as is the controversy over those history textbooks which were viewed by communalist historians as offending the sentiments of Hindus. This chapter concludes with a brief assessment of the debate between historians over the origins of the Babri Masjid, recent attempts to communalize such figures as Vivekananda, the attempted legitimization of 'fringe' historical scholarship (such as that which is associated with P. N. Oak, who for nearly four decades has been promoting the theory that all the great Islamic monuments in India were built by Hindu rulers, or were in origin Hindu before they were 'debased' by the invaders), and the revisionism of those who purport to establish Aryanism as the only foundation of Indian civilization. (The emergence of subaltern history is treated in Chapter IV.) It also offers, in a final section, some sobering thoughts on history as the settled terrain on which disputes will henceforth be waged, and interrogates briefly the impoverished readings of 'myth' furnished equally by secular, nationalist, and Hindutva historians. In their disdain for 'myths', historians are united in common cause.

As Chapter III suggests, the effort to render Hinduism into a faith akin to the monotheistic religions continues down to the present day. This chapter focuses, in very substantial detail, on the aforementioned debate over Ayodhya's Babri Masjid, and the manner in which historians allowed themselves to be dragged into the controversy as experts, witnesses, judges, and—most evidently—historians. No one imagines that the 20,000 people who helped to demolish the mosque with their bare hands, shovels, axes, and picks had any respect for the verdict handed down by historians, but nonetheless it is remarkable that both 'secularists' and 'fundamentalists' looked to the verdict of history to validate their positions. Both camps dug deep into the past; both marshalled concrete 'evidence'; both recruited professional historians and archaeologists to lend respectability to their positions. The historians appear to have had the expectation that their expertise, or (as is largely true of the communalist historians) claim to expertise, would receive widespread approbation—and in all this there is more than the mere expression of the thought that in civilized societies, the views of experts and professionals ought to have some meaning for the unlettered. Romila Thapar, at least, has been an unabashed proponent of the view that professional historians in India do not receive the respect due to them, and that the Indian polity would gain much by its embrace of the historical truth that the members of the profession are charged with producing: as she put it in the context of recent disputes, 'What is really at stake in the current row over history textbooks is the right of the professional historian to assert the preeminence of history over myth and fantasy. History in India has been regarded as a soft option: the popular belief is that anyone who has read a few books on a subject can claim to be a historian.'[43]

The secularist historians were not prepared to surrender the ground to their Hindutva adversaries, and insofar as what passes for scientific or objective history is in question, there can be no doubt that they had by far the more compelling account of the origins and history of the Babri Masjid. Indeed, to describe the greater majority of the Hindutva historians as 'historians' appears to be nothing short of mockery. The secularists also had the more ethical position, insofar as they insisted that, whatever the history of the Babri Masjid, the politics of retribution could not be tolerated. However, as I suggest, most striking of all is the common ground shared by those who believed themselves to hold diametrically opposed views. Secularists and the proponents of Hindutva were ironically united in their disdain for religious belief, in their inability to find an argument that would accommodate the Hindu who stood neither for secularism nor for an aggressive religious nationalism; both also failed to unravel the significance of their commitment to modernity and its discourses. Most spectacularly, both secular and Hindutva historians had little use for myth, and both were distinctly uncomfortable with the mythic structuring of Indian civilization. Neither truly understood how they had transformed history into the most eminent and serviceable of the modern myths. And if, in keeping with the maxim that the preservation of the good is attendant with far greater difficulties than the circulation of palpable falsehoods, the greater onus should have fallen upon secular historians and intellectuals, who are not quite the microscopic minority that they are sometimes made out to be, it is also clear that they showed little inventiveness and little ability to step outside the framework of 'historical truth' with its notions of evidence, proof, and what might be called historical reasoning. Secular historians have seldom invested as much time and labour on myths and the Puranic traditions as they have, for example, on the colonial archives and modern commentaries on communalism.

As the dispute over the Babri Masjid loomed large, it must have appeared to observers that historians had, for the first time in the history of the nation-state, arrived on the centre proscenium, even as sanity was departing from the belly of an ancient civilization. Yet most of the subaltern historians, who by the early 1990s had acquired near celebrity status in the Western academy, had very little to say about the Babri Masjid affair: nowhere did subaltern history appear to show more clearly its curious irrelevancy. Chapter IV offers, then, an interpretive history and critique of the subaltern school. It begins with an enumeration of the dispersal and reconstitution of the collective in recent years, recounts some of the broad swipes taken at the subaltern school by neo-imperialist and orthodox left historians alike, and offers some clues about how the achievements and shortcomings of Subaltern Studies as a whole might be viewed. In the delineation of the circumstances under which subaltern history arose, one cannot ignore the precarious political and social conditions of India in the 1970s, and the immense disillusionment generated by the emergency of 1975–7; but just as important is the then dominance of that strand of Indian historiography known as the Cambridge School, which subaltern history set out to contest.

The Cambridge School furnished the immediate backdrop to the emergence of subaltern history, but Ranajit Guha, the founding father of the collective, had a much larger canvas in mind when, in the programmatic note on subaltern history in the initial volume of the series, he instituted an assault upon 'elitist' histories, whether of the imperialist or nationalist variety. While sympathetic to the aspirations of subaltern history, I argue that Guha's opening salvo is riddled with difficulties, anxieties, and various forms of theoretical naiveté, not least of which is Guha's simplistic recourse to the opposition of 'elite' and 'subaltern'. (That such histories are never written for 'subalterns' is not the least of the objections against subaltern history, but this can be argued apropos most of Marx's writings, not to mention the works of his latter-day interpreters such as Gramsci, Althusser, and Balibar.) Even more disturbing is Guha's understanding of what constitutes the true provenance of the historiography of colonial India: 'the historic failure of the nation to come to its own'.[44] Here, again, is the familiar story of India in the metaphors of incompletion, failure, and tardiness.

The practice of subaltern history, I suggest, is far more nuanced and complex than the numerous theoretical articulations of the enterprise, and the bulk of the remaining portions of this chapter are devoted to a detailed analysis of a few of the more influential contributions to Subaltern Studies in the early years, namely Guha's analysis of 'The Prose of Counter-Insurgency', Shahid Amin's brilliant analysis of 'Gandhi as Mahatma', and Gyanendra Pandey's study of the colonial construction of communal riots. Subaltern history, notwithstanding its subtlety, richness of detail, and intellectual sophistication, remains singularly incapable of dealing with religious belief; it has also rendered itself into what I term 'exilic history'. Some of its proponents have gone so far as to argue that it is enough to enter into a 'complex and deep engagement with elite and canonical texts' to do subaltern history:[45] the archives may still matter, though perhaps more peripherally than they have in the past, but the experiences of the subalterns on whose behalf the historians purport to speak are certainly bracketed as insignificant. Yet subaltern historians will not disavow the enterprise of history; they will not concede that history is only one mode of accessing the past, perhaps the one with the least resonance among Indians.

Chapter V of this book extends the discussion of Indian histories to those being generated in cyberspace in the North American Indian and specifically Hindu diaspora. Various claims have been advanced on behalf of cyberspace: its most enthusiastic votaries speak of it as a new frontier, as the gateway to infinite realms of information (and even knowledge), and as the harbinger of more democratic societies. The Chiapas rebellion of recent years has been waged largely by means of the Internet, and the protests in Seattle against the World Trade Organization (WTO) were orchestrated likewise with the help of the Internet: all this is adduced as a sign of the bright future of 'digital Zapatismo'. Its critics, however, suggest that cyberspace has already exacerbated the distinctions between haves and have nots, and that it creates new forms of inequities; it is also hospitable to racists, white supremacists, and others who espouse creeds of hate and authoritarian politics. The critics of cyberspace are alarmed because in the use of cyberspace as much as in activist politics of the conventional varieties, those who subscribe to inegalitarian and avowedly discriminatory ideologies are far more active than those who work for the public good. The politics of cyberspace, in the event, constitutes the backdrop to this chapter, which argues that cyberspace has become, so to speak, the true home of those Indians in North America who imagine themselves as the authentic Aryans. Hindutva or openly militant Hindu histories flourish on the Internet, and they have cornered the market in Indian history.

This concluding chapter on 'Cyber Diasporic Hinduism', moving beyond the initial discussion on the politics of cyberspace, offers a short profile of the Indian community in the United States. It considers the predominance of Indians in Silicon Valley, and the amateurish enthusiasm of Indian computer and software professionals for Indian, and most particularly Hindutva, histories. Hinduism and the Internet, I suggest, were made for each other; but Hinduism on the Internet has been transformed into Hindutva histories, which have a monolithic predisposition, and are equally intent on offering a version of Hinduism which makes it akin to the 'real' faiths found in the West, as well as on conflating 'India' and 'Hindu'. Through a reasonably detailed study of the web sites of the Vishwa Hindu Parishad of America, the Hindu Students Council, the Global Hindu Electronic Network (GHEN), and other like organizations, I show how the work of earlier generations of Hindu nationalist historians has not merely been transposed on to the web, but has acquired a new and dangerous kind of urgency and plausibility. It does not suffice to say that the diasporic practitioners of history remain colonized: arguing from the 'metropole', their histories resonate with a 'Hinduness' that in India is at least contested.

This book, to reiterate, does not propose to offer an exhaustive and chronological account of the history of Indian history, nor is it meant to be a guide, in any conventional sense, to the historiography of colonial and postcolonial India. There are a great many distinguished historians (and historically-minded sociologists) of India—D. D. Kosambi, K. M. Panikkar, A. R. Desai, Irfan Habib, M. Athar Ali, among others—who scarcely receive a mention in these pages. Rather, it narrativizes the engagement of one civilization, and since 1947 of a nation-state, with the historical sensibility and modality, and it puts forth certain propositions that are greatly at odds with the received wisdom about the desirability of historical thinking and the general valorization in nearly every modern culture of the cliched formulation that those who forget history are condemned to repeat it. History has, to deploy the language of the layperson, become something of a 'problem' in the South or the developing world; it is the latest acquisition of the intelligentsia, and India now 'requires' this historical sensibility if it is to achieve a state of completion. In the modern world, those who are without a sense of history are condemned; they belong in the world of children, primitives, and the pre-industrialized.

The uncontested ascendancy of history has dangerously narrowed the possibilities of dissent in our times, and nowhere is this more evident than in India. The argument has all the more poignancy in relation to India, where the imminent hegemony of history also signifies the defeat of India as a civilization and its ignoble triumph as a nation-state. The nuclear explosions of 1998, as I have elsewhere suggested, had everything to do with reclaiming history, and arose as much from the desire to remove the spectre of Gandhi, who never disguised his complete indifference to arguments drawn from history,[46] and so move India on to the road of history, as from geopolitical and expedient considerations.[47] Still, there may well be hope in the fact that the 'native' in India is obdurate, often resistant to clock-time and oblivious of the demands that history has gradually imposed upon the world; history may well be cheated by the non-modern Indian who is an embarrassment to the Indians who now comprise the middle class and inhabit the West long before they have ever arrived at its doors. This book throughout offers suggestions, sometimes more than incipient, that historians (of India in particular), unless they are desirous of enthroning history as the master discourse of late modernity, will have to engage with the mythic, the ahistorical, and the folk if they are committed to the ecological plurality of knowledges.

ENDNOTES

1. Amartya Sen, 'History and the Enterprise of Knowledge', *Frontline* 18, no. 2 (20 January–2 February 2001).

2. My information here is drawn mainly from T. K. Rajalakshmi, 'Agendas and appointments', *Frontline* 16, no. 24 (13–26 November 1999), and Parvathi

Menon, 'The Falsification of History', *Frontline* 17, no. 6 (18–31 March 2000), though the newspaper accounts of the controversy are abundant.

3. N. Mansergh, E. W. R. Lumby, and Penderel Moon, eds, *The Transfer of Power 1942–1947*, 12 vols (London: HMSO, 1970–83).

4. Consider, for example, that at the University of California, Los Angeles (UCLA), there are 1,000 second-generation Indian students; the total student body is in the vicinity of 35,000. At some of the most prestigious private universities, five per cent of the student body is constituted by Indians. Since 1.7 million Indians reside in the US, they constitute much less than one per cent of the total population of the country.

5. As an aside, I might add that no one has cared to speculate on what relationship there may be between affluence and a predisposition towards history. That clichéd observation about victors writing history cannot entirely explain why rich and powerful nations generally appear to have 'more' history—not only more of history books and reflections on history, but more of history as 'events of note'—nor does it tell us what might be the relationship between leisure and the sense of history. Elites appear to be more heavily invested in the enterprise of history, though the wide popularity of history, whether judged, for instance in the US, by the robust sales of biographies or the large memberships of the History Book Club and the Military History Book Club, is not easily reconciled with this observation.

6. The revisionist account is encountered in Navaratna S. Rajaram, *The Politics of History: Aryan Invasion Theory and the Subversion of Scholarship* (New Delhi: Voice of India, 1995), and idem, *Aryan Invasion of India: The Myth and the Truth* (New Delhi: Voice of India, 1993). 'Voice of India' is one of the publishing arms of the Hindu right-wing brigade.

7. I refer here, of course, to David Frawley, an American 'specialist' in Vedic studies, and Koenrad Elst, a Belgian priest who has worked himself into a fervour over the manner in which the world has ridden roughshod over the noble and pliant Hindus over the ages. Then there is François Gautier, *Le Figaro's* correspondent in India over the last 30 years who, though no scholar, defends Hindutva with a vigour encountered only among a few Indians.

8. This is a reference, of course, to *The Invention of Tradition*, eds Eric Hobsbawm and Terence Ranger (Cambridge: Cambridge University Press, 1983; paperback edn, 1984).

9. Cited by Stephen Bates, 'Anger at India Textbook Bias', *Guardian Weekly* (3 February 2000); see also Asghar Ali Engineer, 'Textbooks and communalism', *The Hindu* (16 November 1999), and the account in the *Deccan Chronicle* (30 May 2000).

10. Volumes I–VI of *Subaltern Studies: Writings on South Asian History and Society* were edited by Ranajit Guha (Delhi: Oxford University Press, 1982–9); subsequent volumes have each been edited by other members of the collective. The eleventh volume of *Subaltern Studies* is published by Permanent Black.

11. Ranajit Guha, ed., *A Subaltern Studies Reader 1986–1995* (Minneapolis: University of Minnesota Press, 1997), blurb on back cover.

12. Sumit Sarkar, *Writing Social History* (New Delhi: Oxford India Paperbacks, 1998), pp. 50–108.

13. Marshall Sahlins, 'Other Times, Other Customs: The Anthropology of History', *American Anthropologist* 85 (1983), p. 517.

14. For further discussion, see the first section of Chapter IV.

15. V. D. Savarkar, *The Indian War of Independence* (n.p [London]: n.p., n.d [1910]), p. 1.

16. Lloyd I. Rudolph and Susanne Hoeber Rudolph, 'Rethinking Secularism: Genesis and Implications of the Textbook Controversy, 1977–79', *Pacific Affairs* 56, no. 1 (Spring 1983), p. 17.

17. Bipan Chandra, 'Historians of Modern India and Communalism', in Romila Thapar, Bipan Chandra, and Harbans Mukhia, *Communalism and the Writing of Indian History* (Delhi: People's Publishing House, 1969), p. 36.

18. The network of this schooling is described in part by Tanika Sarkar, 'Educating the Children of the Hindu Rashtra: Notes on RSS Schools', in Praful Bidwai, Harbans Mukhia, and Achin Vanaik, eds, *Religion, Religiosity and Communalism* (Delhi: Manohar, 1996), pp. 237–47.

19. Cf. Anjali Modi, 'History as told by non-historians', *Hindu* (16 December 2001).

20. Saba Naqvi Bhaumik, 'History, Vacuum-Cleaned', reproduced in Delhi Historians' Group, *Communalisation of Education: The History Textbooks Controversy* (Delhi: Delhi Historians' Group, Jawaharlal Nehru University, 2001), unpaginated; Somini Sengupta, 'Hindu Nationalists Are Enrolling, and Enlisting, India's Poor', *New York Times* (13 May 2002).

21. J. S. Rajput, 'Teaching them a lesson', *Hindustan Times* (24 December 2001), p. 10.

22. Quoted in Editorial, 'NCERT new syllabus will promote secular values', *Deccan Herald* (10 January 2002).

23. Rajput, 'Teaching them a lesson'.

24. Editorial, 'NCERT new syllabus will promote secular values'.

25. Just as the objection to the representation of Aryans as beef-eaters was being voiced, it became a matter of public knowledge that D. N. Jha, a specialist in ancient Indian history, was being subjected to death threats for attempting to publish his book, *Holy Cow: Beef in Indian Dietary Traditions*, which demonstrates that the sacrifice of cows and the consumption of beef was very much a part of the culture of pastoral Aryans as well as of indigenous communities. For a defence of Jha, see Ram Puniyani, 'Beef eating: strangulating history', *Hindu* (14 August 2001), p. OB–1. The passages from the 'offending textbooks' are reproduced in Delhi Historians' Group, *Communalisation of Education*, Sec. 4.

26. The critics' command over English is also in question, if the interpretation of 'rapine' as 'rape' by Pramod Mahajan, Union Minister for Parliamentary

Affairs, is a reliable indication. See Anita Joshua, 'Excising the truth', *Hindu* (2 December 2001), p. 14.

27. Satish Chandra, 'Guru Tegh Bahadur's martyrdom', *Hindu* (16 October 2001), p. 10.

28. Anon., 'Breach of contract: historians', *Hindu* (2 December 2001).

29. Cited by Mridula Mukherjee and Aditya Mukherjee, 'Overview' to *Communalisation of Education*, unpaginated.

30. See, for example, anon., 'Delete offensive remarks from history text: L–G [Lieutenant-Governor]', *Hindustan Times* (9 October 2001), p. 2; Sanjay Subrahmanyam, 'How Should History Be Written?', *India-West* (11 January 2002), p. A4. See also the discussion in Arun Shourie, *Eminent Historians: Their Technology, Their Line, Their Fraud* (Delhi: ASA Publications, 1998), and the rejoinder by Vishwa Mohan Jha, *Investigative Journalism or Slander: Do You Have More Questions Mr. Shourie?* (Delhi: SAHMAT, 1998).

31. For example: Vir Sanghvi, 'Talibanising Our Education', *Hindustan Times* (25 November 2001).

32. Anjali Mody, 'Delete and control—the Parivar's mantra', *Hindu* (2 December 2001), p. 14.

33. Gail Omvedt, 'Beyond Saffron and Secular Education', online from BJP Watch at: <*http://www.bjpgovernmentwatch.com*>.

34. Michael W. Apple and Linda K. Christian-Smith, 'The Politics of the Textbook', in Michael W. Apple and Linda K. Christian-Smith, eds, *The Politics of the Textbook* (London: Routledge, 1991), pp. 1–21, esp. pp. 1, 3–4.

35. Cf. Krishna Kumar, 'Origins of India's "Textbook Culture"', *Comparative Education Review* 32, no. 4 (November 1998), pp. 452–64.

36. Mridula and Aditya Mukherjee, 'Overview' to *Communalisation of Education*, n.p.

37. Sande Cohen, *Historical Culture: On the Recoding of an Academic Discipline* (Berkeley: University of California Press, 1986), p. 12.

38. Allan Megill, '"Grand Narrative" and the Discipline of History', in Frank Ankersmit and Hans Kellner, eds, *A New Philosophy of History* (Chicago: University of Chicago Press, 1995), pp. 151–73, esp. pp. 155–7.

39. One scholar of these chronicles has pointed to the 'weakness of the premise that the medieval Indo-Muslim historian and the modern historian inhabit essentially the same world of ideas on historiography'. This caveat is, in my view, not without foundation. See Peter Hardy, *Historians of Medieval India: Studies in Indo-Muslim Historical Writing* (London: Luzac & Co., 1960; reprint edn with new preface, Delhi: Munshiram Manoharlal, 1997), p. 18.

40. Cited by Ranajit Guha, *An Indian Historiography of India: A Nineteenth-Century Agenda and Its Implications* (Calcutta: K. P. Bagchi for the Centre for Studies in Social Sciences, 1988), p. 1.

41. Rev. Krsna Mohun Banerjea, 'Discourse on the Nature and Importance of Historical Studies', in *Selection of Discourses Delivered at the Meetings of the Society for the Acquisition of General Knowledge*, Vol. 1 (Calcutta, 1840), reprinted

in Gautam Chattopadhyay, ed., *Awakening in Bengal in Early Nineteenth Century* (Selected Documents), Vol. 1 (Calcutta: Progressive Publishers, 1965), pp. 1–23.

42. An unfortunate example of the historian's intolerance for ahistoricism, in a book that is not otherwise without some insights, is Peter van der Veer, *Religious Nationalism: Hindus and Muslims in India* (Berkeley: University of California Press, 1994), pp. 138–46.

43. Romila Thapar, 'Do We Need Consensus on History?', *India-West* (21 December 2001), p. A4.

44. Ranajit Guha, 'On Some Aspects of the Historiography of Colonial India', in *Subaltern Studies* I, ed. Ranajit Guha (Delhi: Oxford University Press, 1982), pp. 6–7.

45. Gyan Prakash, 'Subaltern Studies as Postcolonial Criticism', *American Historical Review* 99, no. 5 (December 1994), p. 1482.

46. In 1924, while Gandhi was serving out a six-year prison term for sedition, he read Gibbon. Reflecting on historical and biographical literature, Gandhi observed that 'the dividing line between fact and fiction is very thin indeed' and that 'facts have at least two sides or as lawyers say facts are after all opinions. However I have no desire to engage the reader's attention upon my speculations on the value of history considered as an aid to the evolution of our race. I believe in the saying that a nation is happy that has no history. It is my pet theory that our Hindu ancestors solved the question for us by ignoring history as it is understood today and by building on slight events their philosophical structure. Such is the Mahabharata. And I look upon Gibbon and Motley [author of *Rise of the Dutch Republic*] as inferior editions of the Mahabharata.' See M. K. Gandhi, 'My Jail Experiences—XI', *Young India* (11 September 1924), reprinted in *The Moral and Political Writings of Mahatma Gandhi*, ed. Raghavan Iyer (3 vols), *Volume I: Civilization, Religion, and Politics* (Oxford: Clarendon Press, 1986), p. 187.

47. Vinay Lal, 'Now Are We Men, Not Eunuchs?' *Humanscape* 5, no. 7 (Bombay: July 1998), pp. 6–9; revised version in idem, *Of Cricket, Guinness and Gandhi: Essays on Indian History and Culture* (Kolkata: Seagull Books, 2003), pp. 54–63.

1

The History of Ahistoricity
The Indian Tradition, Colonialism, and the Advent of Historical Thinking[1]

I

One day in 1838, a number of forward-looking Bengali men constituted themselves into a 'Society for the Acquisition of General
Knowledge.' Residents of Calcutta, then the capital of British posses-
sions in India, these founders of the Society perhaps imagined themselves as the vanguard of a native elite that, taking inspiration from
its colonial overlords, would do something to bring European learning to their countrymen. In the prospectus setting forth their aims and
ambitions, these gentlemen admitted with great humility and shame
the truth of the charge levelled by Europeans against Indians, 'that in
no one department of learning, are our acquirements otherwise than
extremely superficial'. The Society aimed to play its part in the elimination of the deficiencies in the knowledge of 'educated Hindus' and
in the revival of learning in an ancient land. The three hundred native
gentlemen gathered together on a morning in March gave their unanimous assent to these lofty goals.[2]

Two discourses on subjects various and sundry were delivered
before members of the Society every month. The very first one,
delivered by the Rev. Krishna Mohun Banerjea, was 'On the Nature
and Importance of Historical Studies'. Its author expounded on the
virtues of studying history and having 'clear views on the subject', for
history—unlike the sciences—addressed itself to 'that principle of
our moral constitution which may be termed faith, belief, or credulity'. The study of history provided intellectual gratification; it taught
men how to distinguish between fact and fiction, truth and falsehood.

The Rev. Banerjea observed that the nations of the West, which once 'groaned under wretched degradation,' had risen by attending closely 'to the lessons of history'. Here was a novel theory to account for the rise of the West, upon which no historian, down to the present day, has bestowed any attention. Indeed, one could not reflect upon the past without imbibing 'important lessons', and the consequent detection of errors would secure 'the next [age] from returning into the same'. Hindus, particularly, were in want of that education which history supplied: their 'early education had a tendency to confound in one mass history and mythology—facts and fables—truth and fiction—receiving them all indifferently as true or else rejecting them all as wholly false—sweeping the gold away from the dross.' Such a situation had been brought about by the 'lamentable want of authentic records in our own [Hindu] literature', and though the mythological legends of India testified to the ancients' keen appreciation of poetry, such legends were not to be confused with 'historical compositions'.[3]

That Hindus were without much of a sense of the past, and prone to intersperse facts with fanciful tales, seems to have been a commonplace from at least the time of Alberuni, an Arab astronomer, mathematician, and geographer who had become a member of the court of Mahmud of Ghazni in 1017 AD, and likely accompanied Mahmud on one or more of his frequent raids into India.[4] In what is doubtless the most famous passage in his voluminous account of Indian life and society, Alberuni observed that 'Mahmud utterly ruined the prosperity of the country, and performed there wonderful exploits, by which the Hindus became like atoms of dust scattered in all directions, and like a tale of old in the mouth of the people. Their scattered remains cherish, of course, the most inveterate aversion towards all Muslims.'[5] Judging from the extreme animus against Mahmud still harboured by many educated Hindus, one might be forgiven for thinking that the historical memory of the atrocities perpetrated by Mahmud, such as they might have been, had persisted among the Hindus for nearly a millennium.[6] However, Alberuni had, most pertinently, noted as well that 'the Hindus do not pay much attention to the historical order of things, they are very careless in relating the chronological succession of their kings, and when they are pressed for information and are at a loss, not knowing what to say, they invariably take to tale-telling.'[7] Had Alberuni known that Mahmud's invasions of India would scarcely find an acknowledgement in Indian writings for centuries thereafter, he would have marvelled at his own prescience. Inattentive to historical discourses, Indians appeared to have relegated Mahmud to relative obscurity. It is only in the nineteenth century that a nascent Indian historiography began to view Mahmud, with much encouragement from the British, as an inveterate foe of the Hindus and as a barbarian who inaugurated the bloodthirsty reign of Muslim monarchs.

Not just India, but large parts of the East, were alleged to lack historical compositions until comparatively recent times. To Gibbon, who opined that 'the art and genius of history has ever been unknown to the Asiatics', it was indubitably certain that no Arab historian had supplied as clear a narrative of the history of the Arabs as was to be found in the pages of his own *The Decline and Fall of the Roman Empire*. Before 'the coming of Mahomet', the Persians had preserved virtually nothing of their history, and as a consequence they were in the dark even about events 'glorious to their nation'.[8] As John D. Rogers has documented, a similar tenor of argument is to be found in early British writings on Sri Lanka. Robert Percival gave it as his opinion in 1803 that 'the wild stories current among the natives, throw no light whatever on the ancient history of the island', and he considered the Portuguese arrival in Sri Lanka in 1505 as furnishing the first authentic piece of information about that island nation, thanks to the documentation of the Portuguese themselves; and similarly a later contemporary, writing in 1821, viewed various Sinhalese chronicles as collections of legends: 'The Singalese possess no accurate record of events, are ignorant of genuine history, and are not sufficiently advanced to relish it.'[9]

Among the scholar-administrator types whose histories of India first emerged in the eighteenth century, and began to proliferate at an alarming rate as larger chunks of India came under their jurisdiction, it was nearly an article of faith to observe that not until the arrival of the Muslims did works resembling historical compositions begin to be written in India. Even then the accounts of the early Muhammadan conquests in India, and of the later Muslim dynasties as well as the Mughal Empire, were authored almost without exception by Muslims.[10] But could these accounts deservedly be designated as 'history'? Sir H. M. Elliot, author of a voluminous history of India during 'The Muhammadan Period' constructed from the writings of Indian 'historians', declared emphatically that the 'Muhammadan histories' could scarcely claim to rank higher than 'Annals'. For the most part they comprised a 'dry narration of events' in strict chronological fashion, without any conception of how events could be grouped 'philosophically according to their relations'. Having had no acquaintance with any political system other than absolute despotism, these 'historians' wrote only about 'thrones and imperial powers', about 'successive conspiracies, revolts, intrigues, murders, and fratricides, so common in Asiatic monarchies'; and they had not the slightest interest in illustrating the conditions under which the common people lived, the state of commerce and agriculture, the 'constituent elements or mutual relations' which characterize any society, the history of religious and social institutions, or indeed any aspect of 'civil history'. Of cause and effect the Muhammadan writers knew nothing; their reflections and suggestions, few to begin with, were of the 'most puerile and contemptible kind'; and, worst of all, the writers displayed an appalling immorality, for they 'sympathize[d] with no virtues', and 'abhor[red] no vices'.[11] If the Muslim histories of India could be dispatched into oblivion with such ease, then one shuddered to think of how entirely preposterous were the writings of the Hindus, who were not even remotely familiar with the conception of history.

'It is allowed on all hands that no historical composition existed in the literature of the Hindus.'[12] This observation, that runs like a refrain through British scholarship on India, acquired in the first half of the nineteenth century a sanctity that was to remain unquestioned until the advent of nationalism at the turn of the century. James Mill, in his *History of British India*, summoned no less than a dozen witnesses to support the contention that the Hindus were 'perfectly destitute of historical records', entirely indifferent to chronology, and not in the least inclined to make statements within the 'sober limits of truth and history'.[13] Mill also drew attention to the lack of any work in Hindu literature on geography that was not patently 'absurd' and 'monstrous', a geography that was not, in the words of his contemporary Thomas Macaulay, 'made up of seas of treacle and seas of butter'.[14] It is certainly the case that Sanskrit lacks a geographical literature. No work gives us any conception of India's neighbours; and despite India's cultural empire or presence in Indonesia, Cambodia, and other parts of southeast Asia, and its role in the Indian Ocean trading network, no Indian traveller left behind accounts that would give us a sense of the history and geography of these places.

Mill's opinions and criticisms of Indian 'literature', if indeed so dignified a word could be used to characterize the fictions of a people belonging to a 'rude age', were not dismissed as the ravings of a madman or as the predilections of a scholar knowledgeable only in the Western classics. In his Preface to the 1858 edition of Mill's *History of British India*, the eminent Orientalist H. H. Wilson, cognizant of the immense influence that the *History* continued to exercise, endeavoured to repudiate Mill's dismissive observations about India with the remark that his characterization of Hindu society 'almost outrages humanity'.[15] Some years later, the compiler of the great Sanskrit dictionary, Sir Monier-Williams, noting that Mill's history was 'still a standard work', expressed regret at the 'infinite harm' it had done by its 'unjustifiable blackening of the Indian national character', and he thought the superciliousness of 'young Englishmen' brought out to govern India owed much to its pernicious influence.[16] Clearly, the *History of British India* had left a deep impression on the minds of Englishmen, and one man who was wholly susceptible to Mill's influence was Thomas Macaulay. As Law Member of the Viceroy's Council, Macaulay in 1835 penned the 'Minute on Indian Education', which had a decisive impact in determining British educational policies in India. Macaulay argued that educational funds would be put to better use in teaching 'sound Philosophy and true History' than Hindu astronomy, 'which would move laughter in girls at an English boarding school', or a history 'abounding with kings thirty feet high, and reigns thirty thousand years long', or a geography full of the most fanciful notions.[17] Henceforth history would not merely comprise a distinct and honoured part of the curriculum in schools and colleges in India, but historical analysis became, as Gauri Viswanathan has suggested, the principal method 'of teaching colonial subjects to identify error in their own systems of thought and, simultaneously, confirm Western principles of law, order, justice, and truth'.[18] While Mill's own history was to 'remain the hegemonic textbook of Indian history' throughout the nineteenth century, Indian classrooms were inundated with numerous other historical texts.[19]

The question remains: why should the absence of historical works in the literature of the Hindus, assuming this to be an observation of some veracity, have struck Mill and other Englishmen as a singularly important fact? To Mill it was demonstrably clear that as people emerge from a 'rude age', and reason begins to exert on human affairs a considerable influence, 'no use of letters is deemed more important than that of preserving an accurate record of those events and actions by which the interests of the nations have been promoted or impaired'.[20] An interest in history was, to the mind of Mill, the eminent mark of reason and culture, of a civilization instituted on rational principles and characterized by intellectual maturity. The Hindus had not yet understood that a 'record of the past' could be used as 'guidance of [sic] the future'. As a Utilitarian, Mill was acutely conscious of the uses and lessons of history, a subject matter on which English and Indian school-children were routinely asked, until perhaps recently, to display their expository and analytical skills. Moreover, Mill, whose intellectual outlook was dictated not only by the Utilitarian ethos, but by the world view of Bacon and Newton, saw poetry and history—dealing with universals and particulars, according to Aristotle—as diametrically opposed to each other. Mill was not loathe to derive moral lessons from this purportedly great divide. 'The rude and untutored barbarian' admired, and wondered at, only those events in the past which could be 'remembered solely for the pleasure of those emotions': 'Exaggeration, therefore, is more fitted to his desires than exactness; and poetry than history.' 'All rude nations,' James Mill averred, 'neglect history, and are gratified with the productions of the mythologists and poets.' The conclusion was inescapable: as Hindus had failed to produce historical works, they were still barbarians.[21] To Mill, as to other European intellectuals, the Greeks provided the needed contrast: whatever their foibles, and they too had indulged in such childish amusements as poetry and mythology, among the earliest luminosities of the Greek world were the historians Herodotus and Thucydides.[22]

Why should, nonetheless, the attention of Englishmen in the period from the end of the eighteenth century to the aftermath of World War I have been riveted, when at all India was within the eye's gaze, upon the lack of historical works in Hindu literature? Why should that have been any more significant than, say, the fact that the ancient Greeks did not produce any grammarians, or certainly no one who would assume in the history of linguistics a place comparable to that occupied by Panini? What animated this predilection for history among Englishmen? The English middle classes in Shakespeare's time had already developed a considerable taste for history, and one historian of this phenomenon has gone so far as to state that the 'reading of history' was regarded by them 'as a virtue second only to an acquaintance with Holy Writ'. History furnished moral examples, and the lessons it provided could be used profitably in the service of the state; the didactic value ascribed to history coincided so 'precisely with the bourgeois conception of the utility of learning that histories were hailed as the perfect literature of the middle class'.[23] If an engagement with history was a measure of England's greatness, the dearth of history-reading in other societies, such as Ireland, was just as surely a measure of their impoverishment, and even of their fitness to be enslaved: as one writer put it in 1578, the Irish were 'baereued of one of the greatest benefites, that giveth light and understanding, which is by reading of histories ...'.[24] The Irish and the Indians were evidently united by more than their common subjugation under the English.

This English interest in history would continue to persist, except that in the England of the seventeenth and eighteenth centuries, history was seen as something entirely divorced from the imagination. The old Aristotelian distinction between poetry and history was very much alive: poetry dealt with what could be, history confined itself to facts. With the ascendancy of the New Science, 'natural knowledge' and especially mathematics were placed in sharp opposition to poetry. The *Philosophical Transactions*, established in 1665, was prepared to publish genuine pieces of knowledge 'free from the colours of Rhetorick, the devices of Fancy, or the delightful deceit of Fables'.[25] In the Augustan Age, even poetry became mathematical in the hands of Pope and Dryden. But the aftermath of the Augustan Age was, from the standpoint of the Evangelicals and the Utilitarians, unpropitious: the Romantic poets restored wicked poetry, unreason, and passion in all its monstrosity to dignity. This distinction, between poetry and history, unreason and reason, fiction and fact, became then the backdrop for Mill's fulminations in India. That Indians lacked a tradition of historical inquiry, and were devoid of respect for facts and reason, was equally illustrative of the degenerate tendencies of the Romantic movement. Observations about India had no necessary intrinsic interest for most Englishmen, but had a great deal to do with the dispute within England between conflicting ideologies; and it is even arguable that Mill's animadversions against India owed a great deal to his animus against Romantic poetry. The passion for facts among utilitarians, social reformers, and evangelicals moved by the spirit of 'improvement' had proceeded so far in the nineteenth century that Dickens was compelled to mock this development: thus Gradgrind, the school inspector in *Hard Times*, would ask for the establishment of Commissioners of Facts, delegated with the responsibility of instituting a regime of fact.[26]

Nineteenth-century English thought, then, would be marked by a passion for facts and history, and this passion can be traced in the historical novels of Sir Walter Scott, in essays by Carlyle ('On History', 1829) and others, and in such massive historical compositions as Macaulay's *History of England* (1849). The study of history was to become institutionalized, and history was to enter Western discourse as an episteme, as the determining principle of all knowledge.[27] History as a formal course of study was introduced into universities, and the transformation of this study into a 'discipline' was marked by the formation of new associations devoted to the study of the 'past', such as The British Archaeological Association (1843), The Royal Historical Society (1868), The Society of Biblical Archaeology (1870), and the Society for the Protection of Ancient Buildings (1877), and the introduction of various scholarly and quasi-scholarly journals, most notably the *English Historical Review* (1886) and *Antiquary* (1880).[28] The *English Historical Review* boldly recommended itself to its readers in the inaugural issue with the observation that 'history, in an even greater degree than its votaries have as yet generally recognised, is the central study among human studies, capable of illuminating and enriching all the rest',[29] and Lord Acton was to assume a similarly elevated tone in his 'Inaugural Lecture on the Study of History', delivered at Cambridge University in June 1895: 'The science of politics is the one science that is deposited by the stream of history, like the grains of gold in the sand of a river; and the knowledge of the past, the record of truths revealed by experience, is eminently practical, as an instrument of action and a power that goes to the making of the future.'[30]

As England showed the way to the future by enshrining the study of history and historical modes of thinking as characteristic of a vigorous and energetic civilization, so India was a pointed reminder of the ill-effects of lacking the historical sensibility. However, the disposition towards history was manifested not merely in the assault upon Indian traditions and the supposed peculiarities of Indians such as their lack of historical works, but also in the creation by the British, from the very outset, of a historical discourse about India and, *pari passu*, in the fixation on 'events', in the privileging of action—history being 'what happened', not what is imagined—over thought. The privileging of action in turn was manifest in the celebration of 'the man on the spot', that intrepid soldier or administrator enacting his role on the field of action, the field of history; conversely, Indians were perceived to inhabit a dream-like world, caught in the stupor of contemplation, averse to action. If this became the received view, how far did it inform the outlook of Indians ruminating about both their own past and the intellectual weaknesses of Hindu civilization? Was the observation about the lack of historical works in Hindu civilization generally accepted by Hindus, and what kind of speculations did they entertain about this embarrassing phenomenon? How did Indian nationalists respond to the charge? Did the nationalist response consist essentially in marshalling data to the contrary, and in establishing, or fabricating, knowledge of the past based upon indigenous sources? Or did the nationalists ground their response in a differing epistemology, an epistemology that, if it did not consider history to be of little consequence, saw no reason to associate organically the spirit of historical inquiry with either the triumph of reason or faith in the idea of progress? Have the nationalist historians' attempts, which prevail to this day, to elevate the so-called *itihasa-purana* tradition to a tradition of historical inquiry conceived partially along scientific principles yielded different principles of historical inquiry, differing conceptions of history? How, finally, are we to interpret the significance of the British charge and, provided there is in it a kernel of truth, the significance of the lacuna itself? If history is full of 'lessons' for the present, which is the predominant popular conception of history, might not the lack of history be a more portentous guide?

II

At an address delivered in the early years of his political career, which spanned the period from 1875 to 1925, the Bengali nationalist Surendranath Banerjea, later viewed by the British as a voice of moderation, observed that anyone wishing to look into the Indian past encountered a 'difficulty of considerable magnitude' at the very threshold of his inquiry. In the whole field of Sanskrit literature, only one historical work, and that too from the late medieval period, was to be found. 'Are we then to conclude', asked Banerjea, 'that our ancestors, the great Aryans of ancient India, were ignorant of the art of historical composition and never wrote histories?' How could it be that 'the great Aryans of ancient India', who produced lasting works of philosophy, religion, poetry, drama, grammar, and law, were so deficient in the production of historical knowledge as not to leave behind a single historical work from the time of antiquity? Was it reasonable to suppose that people who were capable of such supreme achievements in the various branches of human knowledge were wanting in 'the simple art' of recording their past, 'the sayings and doings of their kings and queens'? How could progress have been made in the different branches of knowledge without some progress in the act of historical composition? Indeed, how was one to measure the idea of progress at all without an idea of history? Was it thus not very probable that the Hindus had not been ignorant of historical knowledge? Fortunately to the credit of the country's ancestors, and 'for the good name of India', Banerjea could conclude that such histories had at one time existed, but they could not survive 'the revolutions and convulsions' which India 'had unhappily too often to pass through', the 'carelessness of the Brahmins', and 'the peculiarities' of India's climate.[31]

It is worthwhile dwelling on the reasons adduced by Banerjea for why histories authored by Hindus had not come down to the present age. If James Mill and Macaulay represented one side of Orientalist discourse, the other face of Orientalism, the burden of which in time was assumed especially by the nationalists, consisted in a glorification of the ancient Aryans and correspondingly in the denunciation of the non-Hindu, and particularly Islamic, elements of Indian civilization. Though self-avowedly a nationalist, albeit of the 'moderate' variety, Banerjea was echoing, inadvertently or otherwise, imperialist discourse. He observed that the 'Empire of the Kshatriyas' was followed in turn by that of the Muslims, the Mughals, the Mahrattas, and finally the British: the history of India was an unremitting tale of depredations by foreigners who, enticed to India by the reports of 'her extraordinary wealth', 'grandeur and beauty', thundered down upon 'the fertile plains of Hindustan spreading death, destruction, desolation, on all sides around'. Amidst 'these destructive inroads' all traces of the Hindus' historical literature disappeared.[32] Banerjea's contemporary, Priyanath Mukhopadhyay, was more explicit, and had no difficulty in establishing causation: as he ruminated, 'It is not certain why our ancient countrymen, who were so learned and had achieved so much did not write down any descriptions of the country. Some people say they probably wrote such descriptions, but just in case reading histories of the glorious past should inspire people to rebel, the Muslims destroyed these books together with other good books when they conquered this country.'[33]

This essentially was the hypothesis advanced by Col. James Tod in his *Annals and Antiquities of Rajasthan* (1829–32, 3 vols). Finding it improbable that the Hindus were ignorant of an art which was cultivated in other countries 'from almost the earliest ages', Tod came to the conclusion that 'the paucity of its [Hindustan's] national works on history' could be accounted for by considering 'the political changes and convulsions which [had] happened in Hindustan since Mahmud's invasion and the intolerant bigotry of many of his successors'.[34]

Neither Tod nor Banerjea explained why historical works did not survive the depredations of invaders when a good many number of the sacred and law books of the Hindus did. Sacred books were commonly stored in temples; and if temples, as is generally argued, were the most obvious targets of attack, it is these books which would have been the first objects to have been destroyed or looted. Even if more care was taken to safeguard religious texts, it is not clear why historical records would have had less chance of surviving than other, if one may use what some would deem an anachronism, secular texts.

The reticence that Banerjea genuinely felt in unequivocally placing responsibility upon Muslims for shortcomings in Hindu intellectual traditions was, as we shall see later, not shared by some of his contemporaries. Banerjea was too close to the Orientalist critique of India, and far too enamored of the discourses of modernity and liberalism, to understand that the question is not whether certain discourses are indeed true or false, or whether or not the climate in India is truly inhospitable to the preservation of manuscripts, but rather what are the effects of such discourses. In his observation that the 'carelessness of the Brahmins' contributed to the loss of historical knowledge, Banerjea was voicing a favourite British construction of Indian caste society. No doubt Alberuni too had observed that 'the Indian scribes are careless, and do not take pains to produce correct and well-collated copies'.[35] More attention may have been paid by the Brahmin scribes to the transcription of religious texts than to copying historical works, but this would account more for the inaccuracies present in historical texts, not for their non-existence. This objection is of little consequence, however, and what is rather more arresting is the characterization of the Brahmin as the villain of the piece. When the British sought the reasons for the demise of the ancient culture of the Hindus, and the origins of their degrading practices, their ire fell upon the Brahmins, who had been entrusted from time immemorial with safeguarding the Hindu texts, sacred and profane, passing on knowledge from one generation to another, and regularizing religious customs and practices.

These Brahmins, the British believed, were venerated to the point of idolatry for their supposed learning. The Brahmins, whom one British overlord dismissed as an 'intriguing, lying, corrupt, licentious and unprincipled race of people',[36] would go to any extent to protect their privileges, keep the other castes ignorant, and prevent the British from contradicting their hegemony or attempting to enlighten the common man. All Hindu texts, it was supposed, had been 'systematically Brahmanized for the purpose of bringing all the religious laws and usages of the different races of India into conformity with Brahmanical ideas', and the real nature of Hindu civilization was only to be revealed when the Brahminical overlay had been uncovered.[37] The scholar-administrator who ruled India, first as a servant of the East India Company, and later on behalf of the Crown, railed at the supposed pedantry of the Brahmins, their mindless devotion to the ritualistic act, and their scheming nature. The views of John Gilchrist, who played a not inconsiderable role in determining the shape of Hindustani, may be evoked as a typical instance of the British construction of the Brahmins (and, to a lesser degree, their Muslim counterparts). 'It is not at all improbable', wrote Gilchrist,

that the cormorant crew of Dewans, Mootsuddies, Sirkars, Nazirs, Pundits, Munshis and a tremendous roll call of harpies who encompass power here see with jealous solicitude every attempt in their masters to acquire the means of immediate communication with the great mass of the people who those locusts of the land conceive their lawful prey.[38]

Thus the Brahmins became, at an early date, the hideous monster in the story of India's degradation, in the story of the demise and loss of her traditions. In more recent years, a respected American historian of India, wishing to account for why 'historical thought and scholarship' were not represented in ancient India in greater measure, put forward a theory which resuscitates the image of the Brahmins as a devious, conspiratorial people. Dismissing quite rightly the suggestion that the Puranas, the Jain and Buddhist chronicles, and other genealogical records can be said to furnish historical explanation, the late Burton Stein noted that three factors inhibited, indeed prevented, 'the writing and preservation of good chronicles or histories': the nature of the political system; the role of the Brahmins as custodians and carriers of Indian traditions; and the nature of the transmission of these traditions. Political power in India, argues Stein, was not highly centralized, nor was it exercised by formal political institutions; rather, it was extremely localized and vested in warriors or other elites wielding economic influence. Whatever may have been the prestige of the Kshatriyas, the warrior elite, the full force of their power could not be felt until it had been legitimized by the priestly elite. Stein further contends that as a large proportion of India's rulers came from 'social groups of low ritual status', the legitimizing function performed by the Brahmin priests was central rather than merely marginal to the stability of the political system and the continuation of its traditions.[39] Inscriptions from medieval Andhra, for example, indicate that many local rulers of untouchable or tribal origins were content to refer to themselves as Sudras, members of the fourth estate; others elevated themselves to the rank of Kshatriyas.

The presence of good histories—and we are to remember that even in Europe history was, until comparatively recent times, an account of monarchs and the political and military triumphs and defeats of their reigns—and of reliable chronicles of ruling families, would have exposed both the low origins of the founders of these families and the priests' participation in the perpetuation of fraud. On the one hand, not only would the prestige of the ostensibly warrior elite have suffered, but their authority would have considerably diminished; on the other hand, the process through which the Brahmins, while supposedly acting to ensure political stability, were enhancing their own ritual power, would have become public knowledge. The Brahmin would cease to have a monopoly over ritual power and the transmission of traditions once the sources and modes of his authority had been revealed; and it is hardly reasonable to suppose that the Brahmins would have been willing progenitors and spectators of their own demise. Thus the Brahmins, so continues the argument, chose not to transmit historical knowledge. Their control over the process of transmission of knowledge and tradition was aided by the fact that knowledge was by and large transmitted orally, and this process itself was confined to the relationship between the guru and such male students as he had himself selected. Access to a guru was further restricted to students of ritually pure birth.[40] What knowledge would be transmitted was thus left entirely to the Brahmins' discretion. Stein concludes that 'a conspiracy hypothesis' is warranted to explain why Indians of the 'ancient and medieval periods' did not address themselves seriously to the 'critical study of their past', particularly the production of historical scholarship.[41]

We have returned, with Stein, to the speculations of the early scholar-administrators of India about the conniving Brahmins, to the fixation on caste and the sacred and timeless dichotomy of Brahminical ritual power and the temporal authority of the Kshatriyas. Although Stein brings to bear upon his subject all the paraphernalia of modern scholarship, his argument is not any more tenable. Stein admits that India is unique among 'ancient, literate and continuing civilizations' in that it lacked historically informed views about its own past, and even though his explanation of this anomaly rests upon the unique

Hindu system of controlled transmission of knowledge, in truth what we are offered is a commonplace realpolitik view. Stein's query about the Hindus' failure to produce historical scholarship about their past is not grounded in the attempt to discern whether the indifference to history was rooted in a particular epistemology and style of thinking, and whether the Hindus did, or did not, recognize history as a category of knowledge. Instead we have, doubtless in a more sophisticated form, the banal view that the victorious or dominant elites determine whether, and what kind of, history will be written. Even the more arresting part of his formulation, namely the notion that historical discourses might constitute a betrayal, or that such discourses can be disempowering (and not only a source of power as moderns would like to believe), does not propel him towards a more serious engagement with the politics and culture of historiography as a general field of study.

For Stein, as for some others, the question is not only the lack of a sound historiographical tradition in ancient and medieval India, but of the Hindus' critical awareness of themselves and of their past. The 'quality of social criticism and analysis' began to show a marked improvement, argues Stein, only after the introduction of European values to India and the challenge of European civilization to the Brahminical stewardship of India's intellectual traditions, while another American scholar of India notes with evident pride that India's colonial rulers were the engine of India's intellectual growth, as they 'both historicized the Indian past and stimulated a consciousness of history in the Indian intellectual'.[42] India, on this view, produced many a Plato, the philosopher of the soul; but of the likes of Aristotle, the philosopher of the polis, the body politic, it had no one, nor was there any tradition of political theory. In Hindu India the tradition of analytical or critical inquiry was wanting and the 'lack of an apparatus of social criticism naturally prevented the growth of a tradition of historiography'.[43] The logical outcome of such a view would be the acceptance of an epistemology that allows space for historical inquiry and the historical sensibility and that, while it may not privilege history as a way of knowing, treats it as a distinct and legitimate category of knowledge. Is it not precisely this very accommodation that Hindu India refused to make? Is not the rejection of history as a way of knowing to be grounded in the existence of a different epistemology, indeed a different history, rather than in the quest for power, the reality of politics, and the perpetuation of deceit? Cannot the not-writing of history be a way of writing history, or perhaps more simply be a mode of living with the present, an insistent and urgent reminder that history is another mythography?

III

In the writings of Bankimcandra Chatterji (1838–94), the first great Bengali novelist and a masterful essayist, we move closer to the aforementioned considerations, to an understanding, without being fixated on the categories of 'caste', 'Brahmin', 'Kshatriya', or bound by some theory of the elites or a fanciful 'conspiracy hypothesis', of why Indians produced neither historical literature nor scholarship providing an evolutionary, historical, and sociological view of India's religious and civil institutions. In his own time Bankim was best known as a writer of historical novels, the first practitioner anywhere in India of that genre, and this itself testifies to his interest in history and in reviving the historical sense among Hindus. In the preface to the fourth edition of *Rajsingha* (1893), which Bankim described as his 'first historical novel', he denied having written 'historical novels' previously. But elsewhere Bankim also conceded that the novelist uses his imagination 'to achieve the effects he desires', and though 'the novel cannot always take the place of history', 'occasionally the purposes of history can be accomplished in a novel'.[44] Bankim peopled his novels with characters drawn from history: Aurangzeb, Man Singh and his son Jagat Singh, Raj Singh, the emperor Akbar; but the incidents in which they were described as participants were only remotely, if at all, based on historical events.

In the later years of his life, Bankim turned from writing historical novels to theological treatises, perhaps an apposite shift considering that Bankim extended, as we shall see, the same veneration to history that many extend to theology. Even in the theological tracts, Bankim's interest in history was clearly manifest—indeed, it was paramount. Bankim engaged in the reconstruction of Hinduism from the three-fold perspective of laying the basis for a sound *dharma*,[45] investing the Hindu philosophical tradition and particularly the Bhagavad Gita with a religious and political significance appropriate to the designs of nationalism, and reviving the historical Krishna, the Krishna not of the *gopis* and the Vaishnava *bhaktas*, but that incarnated in the Gita and in India's martial traditions. His programme, if one may call it such, for making Hinduism more historical, *and thereby more mascu-line* and rational, wherein purportedly lay its future, was adumbrated in numerous essays and finally in a trilogy of three historical, philosophical, and theological treatises: *Krsnacaritra*, 'The Life of Krishna' (1886), *Dharmatattva*, 'The Essence of Dharma' (1888), and the posthumously published *Srimatbhagvatgita* (1901).

The origin of Bankim's quest for a masculine Hinduism and a historical Krishna is to be found in the question which no intelligent Indian, and especially not a nationalist, could refrain from asking: why had India been a subject nation for most of its history? Bankim rejected the view, most assiduously propagated by the British, that Indians were weak, effeminate, and childish, averse to fighting. The image of the Bengali was encapsulated in his *dhoti*, which looked to the British like a big diaper, or so at least Robert Orme had thought in the late eighteenth century. In a 'purportedly historical' chapter of his novel *Durgeshnandini*, Bankim in contrast described 'Prithviraj [Chauhan] and other Rajput heroes' as 'resisting with matchless valour' the hordes of 'Mussulman soldierly' who burst upon India 'with new-born fanaticism and in all the pride of strength'. But these brave Rajput warriors, 'instead of combining their strength', 'fell to quarrelling with one another'. By 'virtue of reiterated efforts', the Mussulmans triumphed, and Delhi became the seat of their empire. But the Rajput warriors did not thereby become 'lifeless': they continued to challenge 'the Yavanas [on] the field and on many occasions put them to rout'.[46] Had not the Marathas and the Sikhs, Bankim would ask, contested power well into the first half of the nineteenth century? It was a travesty to describe Indians as a supine people, when in fact the bulk of Hindu people had 'never fought for or against anyone'. 'Hindu kings or the rulers of Hindustan', Bankim wrote in a piece entitled 'Why is the Indian Nation Enslaved?', 'have been repeatedly conquered by alien people, but it cannot be said that the bulk of Hindu society has ever been vanquished in battle, because the bulk of Hindu society has never gone to war.' Bankim affirmed the lack of solidarity amongst Indians as one of the chief causes of their subjection:

For more than three thousand years, Aryans have fought against Aryans, or Aryans against non-Aryans, or non-Aryans against non-Aryans—Magadh has fought Kanauj, Kanauj has fought Delhi, Delhi has fought Lahore, Hindus have battled against Pathans, Pathans against Mughals, Mughals against the English—all of these people have fought against one another and continually stoked the fires of war in this country.[47]

Why had not the vast majority of Hindus fought for their liberty? Did they love liberty less than the Englishman? Or was their inaction attributable to the nature of the caste system, under which the duty of fighting devolved solely upon the Kshatriyas? In the Hindu's attitude towards power, and in his espousal of the ideals of *bhakti* (devotion) and *vairagya* (renunciation) as ethical norms of conduct, Bankim found the second main reason for India's subjection. Although we cannot follow in detail Bankim's historical and philosophical exposition of the Sankhya system of thought, it suffices to note that both other-worldliness and fatalism, considered characteristic of most Hindus' disposition towards life, were described by Bankim as derived from Sankhya, with consequences much too dire: 'It is because of this other-worldliness and fatalism that in spite of the immense physical prowess of the Indians, this land of the Aryans had come under Muslim rule. And it is for the same reason that India remains a subject country till this day.' Social progress was checked and ultimately ceased to take place at all for the same reason. Knowledge was the goal of Sankhya philosophy; but what was the use of knowledge if it were divorced from power? Europeans worshipped at the altar of power, they were its devotees, and that was 'the key to their advancement'; Hindus, in contradistinction, were 'negligent toward power', and that was 'the key to [their] downfall'. As Bankim expressed it in a concise formula, '"Knowledge is power": that is the slogan of Western civilisation. "Knowledge is salvation" is the slogan of Hindu civilisation.'[48]

What was originated by the Sankhya philosophers, and perpetuated over the centuries by all schools of Hindu philosophy and even Buddhism, was given a vigorous new thrust by the advocates of bhakti. The emasculation of India, and the people's ignorance of the martial traditions in which their remote ancestors had been bred, owed as much to the devotional fervour that first swept over India sometime in the ninth century and was prominent throughout Bengal between the fourteenth and the sixteenth centuries, as it did to the 'various divisions' that obtained in that ancient land 'filled with various nations and societies like a honeycomb crawling with bees'.[49] Although Bankim was of the view that the poetry of Chandidasa, Vidyapati, and Caitanya could not anywhere be excelled, and was, along with comparable achievements in theology and philosophy, the hallmark of a Bengali renaissance as mighty as that which was *later* experienced by Europe, he deprecated this poetry for instilling in people devotion to god instead of pride in the nation. As he was to write in his essay on India's subjection, 'for various reasons a sense of devotion to community has been lost in India for a very long time. Because it has been lost, there has never been any national accomplishment executed by Hindu society.'[50] Clearly, it was not devotion itself, imagined as the opposite of intellectual reflection or of action, to which Bankim was opposed: he wished to turn the energy and strength which devotion generates towards the community, the nation-state, and history, away from oneself and God. Without the nation-state there was to be no history; and in the nation-state, Bankim almost seemed to be suggesting, lay the culmination of history.

For Bankim, the contradictory tendencies inherent in the Indian situation were best epitomized in the conflicting interpretations of Krishna that once obtained in India. Both in *Srimatbhagvatgita* and in *Krsnacaritra*, his sketch of the character of Krishna, he set out to establish the historicity of Krishna. If Krishna was not to be an object of contempt and ridicule—and what else could he be if he, one of the most popular of all Indian deities, were shown frolicking on the green with Radha, tantalizing the other gopis, squandering his time and energies in prodigious feats of sexuality, or amusing himself on the fields of Vrindaban with his playmates?—it was essential that the story of Krishna be secured on some historical foundation, be rendered compatible with canons of reason and common-sense, as well as with reasonable notions of divinity, and that Krishna himself be reinstated in his natural state of glory and dignity. Pointing to the predominant representations of Krishna—who 'was a thief as a child— he used to eat stolen cream and butter; as a youth he was a philanderer [who encouraged the milkmaids to commit adultery]; in maturity, a swindler and a knave who slew Drona and others through deception'—Bankim asked with evident anguish, 'Is this the nature of the Divine? He who is immaculate essence, who is the source of all purity, whose name removes impurity and evil; for him to perpetrate all sins on assuming human form: is this appropriate to that Divine Nature?'[51]

The Krishna of Caitanya and Vidyapati was, moreover, effeminate, of sickly pallor and romantic inclination: was this the Krishna that was to be upheld as a model of goodness, not to mention action, for Indians in their state of degradation? Then there was the other, historical Krishna, 'who by the strength of his arms suppressed the enemy, who by the strength of his intellect united the country of the Bharatas, and who in his unique, selfless wisdom promulgated *dharma*'.[52] The mythology of Vrindavan would have to be abandoned for the historical reality of Krishna counseling Arjuna to fight on the battlefield at Kurukshetra; and if the God of Caitanya's Vaishnavism was only Love, the god of a true Vaishnavism would be not only Love but 'Infinite Power'. As the revolutionary sannyasi says in Bankim's novel *Anandamath*, 'Chaitanya's Vishnu is all Love, our Vishnu is all Power.'[53]

The 'original historical account' of the life of Krishna, Bankim believed, was contained in the original text of the Mahabharata, of which the Bhagavad Gita is a part. To uncover this ur-text, a European-like search for the Holy Grail, Bankim adopted formal and textual criteria, such as uniformity of conception and consistency of style, as well as the substantive criterion of rejecting as later accretions all accounts of 'unreal, impossible and supernatural events'. As Partha Chatterjee has aptly stated, it is remarkable that, in order to show how exemplary the character of Krishna was as an ideal for modern man, Bankim should have felt that his discourse '*required* a demonstration of the historicity of Krishna'.[54] Bankim's obsession with the ur-text, and his absolute fidelity to the norms of rationality and scientificity, is a pointed testimony to how far he subscribed to Orientalism, both as style of thinking and as a mode of scholarship. He betrayed an emblematically European anxiety, now widely on display amongst Hindutva ideologues, about origins. Bankim's differences with the Orientalists were not epistemological but empirical: it was not the Orientalist's historicism but his failure to abide by his own standards of scholarship that Bankim attacked with full vigour. It was his opinion that the tendency of European scholars to consider the Mahabharata as an 'unhistorical' work stemmed from their prejudice: if they wished to dismiss it as an admixture of the historical and the mythical, were they not bound to consider the works of Herodotus, Livy, and many other Greek and Latin historians as similarly comprised of the 'true' and the 'false', the 'real' and the 'imaginary'?[55]

His arguments from the historical record of Megasthenes are a more interesting case in point. He adduced evidence from it in support of his hypothesis that even Alexander was intimidated by the military valour of the Ganga-Rary elephant troops and was induced to turn back: 'Whether anyone believes or does not believe that Alexander ceased fighting through fear of the might and valour of the Bengalis, the witness is Megasthenes himself. We are not producing some new witness we have coached.'[56] But when Albrecht Weber pointed out that the Mahabharata could not have existed in the fourth century BC because Megasthenes made no mention of it, and Krishna therefore was not a historical character, Bankim dismissed this remark as 'deliberate fraud' on the part of Weber, who knew that only fragments of Megasthenes' record had survived; moreover, it was fatuous to rely so heavily on Megasthenes, merely because he was European. With a brilliant, if ostentatious, reversal, characteristic of much of his work, Bankim disposed of Weber's objection: 'Many Hindus have visited Germany and written books [about that country]. In none of their works have I seen Mr. Weber's name. Does this then inevitably mean that Mr. Weber never existed?'[57]

The defence of Hindu philosophy; the rejuvenation of India's martial traditions; giving Indians the knowledge of their true character, uncluttered by the fabrications of Muslim or British historians; bringing Indians to an awareness of themselves as Indians; the cultivation of a unitary nationalist consciousness: all of this was to be achieved primarily by reviving the sense of history, uncovering the historical past, digging into archives, and writing history anew. How had the 'Renaissance' come about in Bengal? 'Where did the nation get this sudden enlightenment? ... Why did the light go out? Perhaps it was because of the advent of Mughal rule ... .' There was only one way to ascertain what had happened: 'Gather the evidence and find out all of these things.'[58] Yet, as he was to write elsewhere, 'Indians have no record of their exploits anywhere in writing. There is no chronicle of ancient India. Hence the military achievement of which they could take pride in has been lost.'[59] If chronicles had never been compiled, how was 'the evidence' to be gathered? No doubt written chronicles were not the only guide to the past: but surely the past could be created, invented, fabricated? What else had the Muslims and the British done? Encountering the Bengali in his present state of wretchedness, the British inferred that he had always been effeminate and cowardly; and the entire history of India had been constructed in a similar fashion. 'If a man is declared dead after having been beaten to death', Bankim's argument continues, 'the statement cannot be called a lie. But [he] who says that the Bengalis have always been of this character, that Bengalis were always weak, always cowardly, always effeminate, may lightning strike his head, his words are lies.'[60] The historical novel and the historical essay were Bankim's well-chosen forms to attempt the reconstruction of Indian history: the first allowed him the license to fabricate history, indeed to furnish, even in more exaggerated form, the same arguments that are found in his political and theological works without the kind of scholarly accountability that non-fiction might have demanded; and the essay in turn was his homage to the norms of rationality and objectivity, a medium for presenting 'evidence'.[61]

Bankim never doubted that there is a relationship between historical awareness of the past and pride in one's own country and its accomplishments. 'National pride lies at the root', he wrote in one seminal essay, 'of the creation of indigenous history and the improvement of people; history is the foundation of social science and social betterment. The misery of a people without history is endless.'[62] Bankim would not have been one to agree with Alberuni's assessment of the Hindu as the most conceited of all peoples; rather, the Hindu was self-abnegating to such a degree that he never thought of leaving his mark on history. If one could not leave one's imprint on history, then of what use were historical records? In one remarkable passage Bankim explored this almost symbiotic link between a people's pride in its achievements and historical awareness, contrasting the attitudes of Indians and Englishmen in this respect:

If the English go out to shoot birds, a history is written of the expedition. But Bengal has no history! ... There is a specific reason why Indians have no history. Partly because of the environment, partly the fear of invaders, Indians are greatly devoted to their gods ... . As a result of this way of thinking, Indians are extremely modest:

They do not think themselves the subjects of their own actions; it is always the gods who act through them. It is this modesty of attitude and devotion to the gods which are the reasons for our people not writing their own history. The Europeans are extremely proud. They think that even when they yawn, the achievement should be recorded as a memorable deed in the annals of world history. Proud nations have an abundance of historical writing; we have none.[63]

The other-worldliness and fatalism of Hindu philosophy, on Bankim's view, engendered indifference to the collectivity that was the nation and to history as a guide to action; and once India ceased to have the historical recollection of its former greatness, and began to sing exclusively the praise of God, it became enervated. The vicious circle was not to be broken by standing by idly while the British wrote the history of India for Indians. 'When has the glory of any nation', asked Bankim, 'ever been proclaimed by another nation?' Whatever was known of Roman valor was known from Roman histories; the case for Muslim heroism rested on the records compiled by Muslim historians themselves. How could it be any different for the Hindus? Thus it was to the project of writing history, and thereby reviving an ancient land, that Bankim directed his vision; as he was to put it in a text where Bengal stood for India,

Bengal must have her own history. Otherwise there is no hope for Bengal.

Who is to write it? You have to write it. I have to write it .... Anyone who is not a Bengali has to write it .... It is not a task that can be done by one person alone; it is a task for all of us to do together.[64]

IV

The question of why a tradition of historical inquiry did not exist in ancient and medieval India has been, as we have seen, something of a quandary for students of Indian civilization. Bankim's analysis of why Indians produced no historical records, and the significance he attached to history as a mode of knowledge and as an expression of political and cultural unity, constitutes one kind of response to this question. It is Bankim's view which has triumphed. But I, like many others,[65] have dwelled on Bankim so long because not only was he the most articulate spokesman for the view that historicizing above all leads to 'objective' knowledge, and that a nation is forged and its longevity ensured when its citizens think historically, but also because there is much in his reasoning that is markedly different from other nationalist views. Bankim, for instance, made no half-hearted attempt to argue that a historiographical tradition flourished in India before the advent of Muslim rule or that the climate was not conducive to the preservation of historical manuscripts. Neither can Bankim be made to speak for professional nationalist historians, if we may consider R. C. Majumdar their representative voice. While admitting that 'lack of historical writings is the weakest point in ancient Indian literature', Majumdar stated that 'advanced ideas of historiography were not altogether unknown in India'. The *Rajatarangini*, a twelfth-century chronicle of the kings of Kashmir by Kalhana, a Kashmiri Brahmin, is mentioned in this vein by Majumdar and many others as an example of quite sophisticated historical literature. For Majumdar the problem was why the *Rajatarangini*, which would 'do credit to a historian of the twentieth century', stood in such singular and sinister (or should we rather say splendid) isolation, for Kalhana is 'the only historian that ancient India can boast of'. Elsewhere Majumdar argued that 'the problem we have to solve is not the lack of historical writings, of which we have a fair number of specimens, but the absence of finished products like the *Rajatarangini*.' Noting that Kalhana had four illustrious successors who carried the history of Kashmir down to the reign of Akbar, Majumdar held out the hope that these works, having withstood the test of time, had 'not disappeared' and would one day resurface.[66]

Alongside Majumdar's attempts to argue for the presence of a tradition of historiography in Hindu India before the coming of the British must be placed the rather prodigious effort by nationalist and lately secular and anti-Orientalist historians over a period of over fifty years, and well before them by Orientalist scholars, to have the epics, Puranas, genealogical lists, and chronicles of kings accepted as historical works. The word for history in Sanskrit and the languages derived from it is *itihasa* (iti-ha-asa, 'so it has been'). It is pointed out that the Indian's concern for itihasa is manifest from the fact that the first explicit pronouncement on itihasa can be found in Kautilya's *Arthasastra*, which is dated to the period 321–296 BC, but may be as much as three centuries later. According to Kautilya, 'the three *Vedas*, *Sama*, *Rik*, and *Yajus*, constitute the triple *Vedas*. These together with *Artharvaveda* and the *itihasa-veda* are (known as) the *Vedas*.'[67] The *Satapatha-Brahmana* likewise lists *Itihasa-Veda* among the scriptures to be read on the occasion of the horse sacrifice *(Ashvamedha)*. Kautilya also tells us what constitutes itihasa: '*Purana, itivritta* (history), *Akhyayika* (tales), *udaharana* (illustrative stories), dharmasastra and arthasastra are (known by the name) *itihasa.*' *Itivritta* means occurrence or event; the Puranas are stories; *akhyayika* is a prose composition, 'a connected story or narrative'; and the *dharmasastra* and *arthasastra* denote the two classes of literature dealing with morals and material well-being, respectively. *Udaharana* means both 'narration' and 'stories', as well as 'example', and it is probably the last meaning which is implied, if we consider the conventional reading of history as teaching by example.[68]

The comprehensiveness of the idea of history is further suggested by this well-known definition of itihasa:

> *Dharmartha kamamoksanam upadesa samanvitam*
> *Purvavritta kathayuktam itihasam prachakshate*

[*Itihas* is the narration of the past arranged in the form of stories, and conveying instruction in *dharma, artha, kama* and *moksha*, the four human values.][69]

And Jinasena, the author of the *Jaina Adipurana* (ninth century AD), speaking of itihasa, which 'relates "what actually happened"', and is 'a very desirable subject', says that

it is also called *itivrtta, aitihya,* and *amnaya* (authentic tradition). It is also described as *arsha* for it was composed by the rishis, *sukta* for it instructs through good and pleasant discourses, and Dharmasastra, for it prescribes *dharma.*

If history is narrative, stories, anecdotes, 'what really happened', example, moral instruction, and discourses on morals, wealth, pleasure, desire, and salvation, then what is it not? Far from illustrating how itihasa was privileged among forms of knowledge, or at least placed on an equal footing with the other forms of Vedic literature,[70] the very comprehensiveness of the definitions of history suggests that history was not conceived as a distinct branch of knowledge, encompassing as it did the study of man in relation to society and God and all the conceivable goals of life. There is no suggestion in the texts how the study of itihasa is different from the study of philosophy (*darsana*), religion, law, or a work such as Kautilya's *Arthasastra* itself, which falls within the domain of politics and 'economics', but surely is not history any more than is Machiavelli's *The Prince*.

If the conception of 'history' is itself so broad-minded, we may expect to find history in an equally large number of texts, and it is not surprising that the epics, hagiographies, the biographies of kings, genealogical lists, the Puranas, and various other kinds of texts have been considered, if not something akin to history, quite ripe for the extraction of historical method and historical fact. So, for example, one historian writes that 'the accounts of dynasties and genealogies given in the Mahabharata and the Puranas and the heroic poems composed by the court poets of ancient India do contain elements of historical data', while another has argued that authors of the Sangam age 'were endowed with plenty of historical sense'.[71] The historicity of the Indian epics, as of the *Iliad* and the *Odyssey*, must obviously lie in the fact that it is a later age looking back upon an earlier one, that the written text reflects an oral tradition of greater antiquity which supplied at least the kernel of the story. Almost any work from antiquity, especially an epic, can be mined for historical data, which however cannot substitute for historical explanation. None of the texts said to display the author's 'historical sense' reveal any understanding of causation in history; none demonstrate any familiarity with historical method and the 'rules' of evidence.

Even Herodotus, by contrast, set down his intention in the opening paragraph of *The Histories* 'to preserve the memory of the past ... and more particularly, to show how the two races came into conflict'. Greek and Chinese historical writings point, however minimally by the canons of modern historical scholarship,[72] to conscious human behaviour, to cause and effect, by way of explanation of how a society changes over time. The conception of causation found in the allegedly historical writings from India is of the kind to which even

Gibbon on occasion subscribed, as for instance when, in explaining how an attack of gout prevented Bajazet from marching into central Europe, he observed that 'an acrimonious humour falling on a single fibre of one man may prevent or suspend the miseries of nations'.[73] More often the accidental factor is assimilated to the moral aspect—a kingdom prospers if the king is virtuous and pious; and if he rules the country according to his whim, if he is wicked and irresponsible, he suffers defeat in battles and his kingdom declines. There is also widespread in Indian writings the element of the 'supernatural': because the king is unjust and disrespectful to the gods, they do not come to his assistance; but if he is properly suppliant and god-fearing, they assist him in his battle against evil. It is by the grace of the gods that the world moves; and it because of them that evil is either combated or perpetuated. But with this we are not any closer to a causal explanation of human behaviour. No one can argue from Indian texts that human behaviour was not a subject of interest to their authors, but little in those texts suggest that the authors were critically alive to the historical mode of explanation.

James Mill, whose views of the literature of the Hindus are nothing short of absurd, was however not without reason in his ridiculing of attempts to describe the epics or indeed anything else in Sanskrit literature as tantamount to 'historical records'. 'A more intimate acquaintance with those grotesque productions', Mill noted of the Ramayana and Mahabharata, 'has demonstrated the impossibility of reconciling them with the order of human affairs ... .'[74] The phrase 'human affairs' is in this context indefensible, since, as a work of poetry and of the imagination, as a work with insights into morality and human psychology, the Ramayana is clearly reconcilable with 'human affairs'. Yet the qualifier ('order') preceding 'human affairs' also suggests that Mill, while perhaps even sensitive to the fictional history of the character of Rama, to the fact that the development of Rama in the Ramayana has its own history, could not but think of the Ramayana as lacking in historicity, as a text whose narrative was itself incapable of being located in time and which in fact pointed both to its own ahistoricity and its reliance upon the supernatural.

From Mill's judgment of the epics Kalhana's *Rajatarangini* cannot be exempted, if we consider that one monarch is said to have reigned for 300 years, and that the conquest of Ceylon is attributed to the god Varuna, who provided a passage to the Kashmirian troops by turning the sea into land.[75] While the *Rajatarangini* is more reliable in its genealogy and chronology than other chronicles, it is not essentially different from other chronicles or from the Puranas. Since the Puranas have been made to shoulder so much of the burden of establishing the presence of a historiographical tradition in Hindu India, it would be useful to recall that of the five topics (*pancalaksana*) of which any Purana is constituted—*sarga* (creation of the universe), *pratisarga* (dissolution and recreation of the universe), *vamsa* (genealogies of gods and patriarchs), *manvantara* (the ages of Manu), and *vamsanucarita* (genealogies of the solar and lunar races of kings)—only the last could be said to have any historical content.[76] Although, as Burton Stein observed in 1969, 'the consensus among scholars' who have used the Puranas and other classes of literature with genealogical lists 'is that the useful genealogical information is frequently buried in myth and hopeless exaggeration', the Puranas continue to be mentioned as works embodying 'historical consciousness' even by such well-known historians of ancient India as Romila Thapar.

The vamsanucarita is described by Thapar as the 'historical epicentre of the itihasa tradition'. She argues that 'the genealogical core pertaining to those who were believed to have held power in the past' was carefully preserved because it 'purported to record the past' and would be used to adjudge the authenticity of 'future claims to lineage status'. This is the 'first phase' in the unfolding of Indian history; here 'historical consciousness was embedded and recorded the perception of the ordering lineages'. In the second phase, which begins in the second half of the first millennium AD, north India began to witness the evolution of the state and its gradual assertion to supremacy. There was 'a need for a recognizable historical tradition at this time': there were new claimants to power, not just the monarchs, but also landowners and clan chiefs vested with revenue rights who had to prove their status whenever necessary. That the historical tradition which was preserved had some teeth to it would appear to be demonstrated by the fact that though many ruling families had their claims to power conceded, their *varna* status, in the event that the historical tradition could not authenticate it, was denied to them. Ruling families which could not establish 'kinship links with earlier established lineages' continued to be called *vratya-kshatriyas* (degenerate). Thapar also shows that Stein's thesis, which seeks to ground the lack of a historiographical tradition in the need to hide the lower class origins of many of the ruling houses in India before the coming of the Muslims, is largely without foundation: 'The gradual *increase* [emphasis added] in references to *sudra* rulers would indicate that political power, although in theory restricted to *ksatriyas*, was in fact open to any *varna*.'[77] That ruling families were often of lower social origins was not an unknown fact and, more often than not, this fact could not be hidden. Conspiracies make for good spy thrillers; they are even a delight to the state seeking a warrant to oppress; they rarely make for good history.

Thapar has suggested that the emergence of the state, and the concentration of power in it, produces a need for historical writing. As the state grows, such functions as counting and categorizing come into their own, and similarly the state acquires the paraphernalia of historical writing and scholarship. Here we have a variation of the familiar argument, though Romila Thapar is scarcely an uninformed advocate of the nation-state, that unity of some kind is a prerequisite of historical awareness; and history thus becomes a record of the growth and activities of the nation-state. It is not enough that such unity be the unity of a common culture: it must be embodied in a political entity which gives everyone within its geographical ambit a common or shared identity. Where there is identity, there is also difference: and from the interchange of the two emerges historical awareness. The backdrop to Herodotus is the feeling of the Greeks against the Persians, just as what animates Thucydides is the Athenians' sense of how irreducibly different they are from the Spartans. Did Indians ever experience the feeling of being different from other people, say the Chinese? Well, perhaps not; but almost all historians are agreed, whatever they may think about Indians' feeling of themselves as Indians, that regional identities were strong throughout India's history, as they continue to be today. Bankim with great anguish asked: 'Bengalis, Panjabis, Telugus, Maharashtrians, Rajputs, Jaths, Hindus, Muslims—in all of this, who would be united with whom?'[78] If all these groups and countless others knew themselves only in their difference from others, why did not this situation give birth to multiple historiographical traditions?

But Thapar is not willing to settle for the tendentious argument that in ancient and medieval times India was never one and that Indians never knew themselves as Indians. Both the North and the South fell under Mauryan rule; 'Hindu institutions spread over dominant groups all over India'; and it is 'from this period', she has written elsewhere, that 'a political and social conception of India as a whole came into existence'.[79] Here too the question naturally recurs: if there is, as Thapar herself would argue, a natural connection between the evolution of the state and historical consciousness, or between a people coming into the fullness of their being and the emergence of historical literature, then why do we not have histories from that time? And why must we accept the reduction of history into genealogy, for is that not what we are being offered? More significantly, if historical awareness originates through the forging of a common identity, and the suppression of other identities, might it not be too much of a price to pay? To bring Indians into history, does not Thapar, or for that matter anyone else, have to accept the epistemological primacy of the discourse that the British established for India? This discourse dictated that Indians would be brought into history, and gifted with one, by their imperial masters. The Indian historian like the nationalist is once again compelled to stake a position on the terrain established by that figure so familiar from the colonial dispensation, the scholar-administrator.

What, then, are the substantive differences between James Mill and Surendranath Banerjea, or between Bankimcandra and Romila Thapar or Burton Stein? Far too many, if the histories that comprise their scholarship are in question; and far too few, if their epistemological attachment to historical consciousness and historical truth is in question. To set forth in starkly plain terms the nature of the debate, and the questions that are at issue, we have to only contrast these statements from two professional historians and specialists in historiography of the Indian subcontinent:

It used to be said that Ancient India produced little or no historical literature. It was even suggested that the ancient Indians lacked the 'historical sense' possessed by other peoples: that they were too religious to be interested in such worldly matters. We need not trouble ourselves overmuch with the analysis of such superficial misconceptions [1961].[80]

To say that we had no historic sense would be to court disgrace. But we did lack that sense. I am ashamed to say that we lack that sense today [1962].[81]

Historians have differed over the question of what constitutes a historiographical tradition and what kind of literature can be considered historical. There has been disagreement over whether such a tradition ever existed in India: those who have replied in the affirmative have repaired to some text or the other in justification of their position; others who have been scornful of the proposition have adduced reasons of varying sophistication to account for India's allegedly glaring deficiency in this respect. But nowhere has the value of history been doubted; nowhere has anyone disputed history's claim to be a universally acceptable category of knowledge. It is not doubted that to be anyone one must be in history. Either one is in

history or one is doomed to extinction, stripped of ontological existence. Where for idealist philosophy being has nothing to do with
history, now being cannot be conceived without history. What does
the sound and fury signify?

V

'History may be servitude, History may be freedom.' To invoke these
lines, from Eliot's *Four Quartets*, is not to turn towards the oracular,
nor to substitute poetical truth for historical truth (whatever the
merits of that disposition); indeed, we can be reasonably certain that
they would surely have met with the approval of Bankim, whose
writings suggest no particular propensity for oracular pronouncements. Bankim wanted to turn history into an agent of liberation.
Much like Benedetto Croce and the Cambridge historian J. B. Bury a
few decades later,[82] Bankim subscribed to the idea that history was
the story of man's progress and increasingly consummatory love
affair with liberty. Macaulay's own *History of England* was nothing
other than the history of English liberty under the law, for without
law, as Macaulay and his contemporaries were predisposed to accept, there is neither liberty nor history. India, a lawless country,
subject only to the law of the despot (which is no law), quite 'empty of
law' as the Law Member, Sir Henry Sumner Maine, once put it, was
also without history.

From the standpoint of Bankim, India too had to fall within the
ambit of history as the history of liberty, although here, as elsewhere,
Hindu philosophy no doubt presented formidable obstacles. Where
the Western conception of evolution sees man moving towards a
greater good and an increasingly perfect state of existence, from
original sin to final redemption, Hindu thought postulates that the
current age is the one most devoid of good. The first age, the *satya
yuga*, is characterized by unadulterated truth; in the following two
yugas, *treta* and *dvapara*, truth and goodness decrease in progressively greater amounts; and, finally, in the present age of *kali*, falsehood (*asatya*) and wickedness predominate. History cannot then be
considered as the ascent of man but rather his continuing degenera-
tion. The Hindu schema of four progressively deteriorating ages may
well be dismissed as a mythical construct with no historical reality
and with even less call upon the attention of the historian, but that
would be to ignore the pivotal place of mythic constructions in the
unfolding of history.

The reversal effected by Hindu thought, the characterization of evolution as the progression from authenticity to inauthenticity, is for example unequivocally articulated in the Indian grammatical tradition. 'The chief criterion of validity in the classical Paninian tradition', the linguist and Sanskritist Madhav Deshpande has written, 'is that every explanation must be in consonance with Patanjali's great commentary, the *Mahabhasya*.' Where there is a difference of opinion between classical authorities, the classical Sanskrit grammarians attached a higher value to the views of Patanjali (first century BC) than to the views of his great predecessors, Katyayana (third century BC) and Panini (fifth century BC) himself. But what is truly significant is that where Panini recorded dialectical variations and distinguished between those which were real and those which were optional, Patanjali and the rest of the post-Paninian grammatical tradition declared all dialectical forms to be pure options, and postulated instead 'the doctrine of eternality of language': linguistic usage was 'thought to be eternal and without beginning.' 'What has happened to "history" in this case?', asks Deshpande. '"Historical fact was victimized at the altar of formal consistency."'[83] The same notion of authority is reflected in the dharmasastra literature and, as Sheldon Pollock has argued, in the philosophical system of Mimamsa. Commenting upon the Indian 'tradition's presumed lack of historical awareness', Pollock concedes that there is a 'general absence of historical referentiality in traditional Sanskritic culture', which he seeks to explain by the Mimamsa conception of the Vedas as a 'transcendent' body of literature, emptied of 'referential intention'. For a text to be linked genetically to the Vedas, which perforce was required by the intellectual tradition, it had to suppress the evidence of its own historical existence.[84]

This linguistic eternalism, to return to Deshpande, must be understood 'in the context of the historical situation of the Mauryan era', when Brahminical culture was attempting to reassert its dominance in the face of threats from Buddhism, Jainism, and other non-Vedic and anti-Vedic movements. Brahminical culture and Sanskrit as they then existed were held to have been extant in the same form since the beginning of time: history did not exist. According to Deshpande, the problem of 'existence' was separated from the problem of 'attestation'. That some forms occurred in a particular text while others did not was thus a matter of accident; only 'eternal existence was the fact'. The Sanskrit grammatical tradition, then, embodies, if only in negation, a certain conception of history.[85] Do we thus have a theory of knowledge which refuses to recognize the existence of history?

The theory that there is no history in a real sense was, to follow Deshpande's reasoning, articulated at a time of great change. Brahminical society was burdened with the task of countering various heterodoxies, but it was also 'facing the trauma of the Greek invasion' of India by Alexander. But of this purportedly traumatic event there is virtually no mention in Indian literature, and it is to Western historians, beginning with Arrian and Plutarch, that we must turn for a description of this encounter—an encounter that was, no doubt, multicultural! English historians, in particular, would much later describe Alexander's invasion as an event of monumental significance, a watershed in Indian history; Indian historians, down to the present day, as a very modern history of India concedes, can scarcely be bothered to factor Alexander into their narratives of antiquity.[86] Could Alexander's invasion have been such a 'trauma' for Brahminical culture if the Indian tradition could not be bothered to record even the mere presence of a world conqueror? But it may well be argued that it is precisely because Alexander's incursion into India initiated such a massive rupture in Brahminical society that its representatives and custodians failed to give it even a passing mention. History would purposefully be ignored much as dialectical variations had been ignored.

The question of change—and permanence—assumed a great share in Western and later nationalist explanations of why Indians were without a historical sense and failed to produce a tradition of historical inquiry. The view of India as a static society, with which the figures of Montesquieu, Hegel, Marx, and numerous others, not to mention the scholar-administrators who governed India, are associated is too well-known to require more than a cursory mention. 'Absolute Being is presented here [in India] as in the ecstatic state of a dreaming condition'; and the inhabitants of India, added Hegel, could not wake up from the 'magic somnambulic sleep' into which they had fallen.[87] Marx, in turn, thought India was characterized by an 'undignified, stagnatory and vegetative life'. His verdict on Indian history was that such a thing didn't exist:

Indian society has no history at all, at least no known history. What we call its history is but the history of the successive intruders who founded their empires on the passive basis of that unresisting and unchanging society.[88]

As a later Orientalist scholar, Arthur MacDonell, put it, 'early India wrote no history because it never made any.'[89] In India nothing much happened: invaders came and left, empires were toppled and installed, the arbitrariness of one monarch was replaced and matched by that of another: and underneath this all life in the village communities of which India was composed continued as ever, unchanging, unmoving, oblivious of the passing of time. 'Vegetating in the teeth of time', the natives witnessed, without so much as the blink of an eye, the 'ruin of empires, the perpetration of unspeakable cruelties, and the massacre of the population of large towns'.[90] Change was only illusory, the veneer at the surface: permanence alone was permanent. Where there was no change, what would there be to record? And from whence would spring history?

No explanation that seeks to account for India's lack of a historiographical tradition has had so many adherents than the one which equates history with change. Allied to this cosmic view of unchanging India is the commonly held opinion that Hindu civilization is marked by unworldliness. Where the business of the individual is enhancing her chances of personal salvation, and where the individual is preoccupied with discovering the presence of God within herself or offering devotion to Him to the exclusion of understanding her relationship with other members of her society, a common unity cannot be forged. History is the collective memory of a people, of their common struggle for the achievement of the good, and such history cannot transpire when each person leads an other-worldly life, strangely uninterested in the profane world. The Indologists' India, moreover, reflects the principle of immutability, which is not conducive to historical inquiry, even at the level of interpersonal relationships. It is not just Indian society as a whole which does not show much movement; individuals too stay in their places within a determined and unalterable social order: and so history becomes well-nigh impossible. India's geographical isolation, and her immunity from change, must in the Orientalist view be considered the prime reason why a historiographical tradition was not developed in India before the advent of Islam.

Although the presence in India of Muslim works of history from around 1200 AD onwards is commonly known,[91] the import of this development is perhaps less clear than it should be. Is it too much to conjecture that in the period before the coming of the Muslims, not only the cultural unity of India, but perhaps the very survival of its people was based on a purposeful forgetfulness? In what manner would the people of India have lived with the burden of the knowledge that their country had repeatedly been subjected to the rule of foreigners? Modern man thinks of history as an aid to living in the present, but to the Indian history has the contrary effect of not enabling one to live in the present. Each civilization must find its way to eliminating the suffering that is born of existential dilemmas, of decay from within, and of oppression from within and without; and the latter was, one can perhaps speculate, best achieved by a *wilful amnesia*.

The first significant dent in the wilful amnesia of an entire civilization appeared with the establishment of the Islamic faith on Indian soil. The incursions into India by the Muslims followed that of the Sakas, the Pahlavas, the Kushans, and the Huns, but the Muslims, unlike their predecessors, brought with them a strong monotheistic faith. The sense of history also appears to have been first installed in some meaningful way among Indians with the coming of Islam; or, to advance a less daring claim, the advent of Islam in India and the emergence of historical writing display a certain simultaneity that cannot pass without observation. Among the great continuing world civilizations, the sense of history has generally been most evident in those characterized by a monotheistic faith and a strong proselytizing tendency. The most notable exception here would be China, which in the figure of Ssu-ma-chien produced a great historian as early as the first century BC, and has ever since shown itself fundamentally interested in practices of historical inquiry.[92] If Chinese mythology is scarcely as rich and diverse as that of India, we are obviously tempted to ask whether myth and history were conceived in opposition, or whether mythology suffers when there is an enhanced view of history.

Judaism, Christianity, and Islam, all monotheistic faiths, have been marked by an acute sense of history, and unlike Hinduism these are proselytizing faiths,[93] though the Hinduism of some Hindus, as subsequent chapters demonstrate, has now begun to acquire their characteristics. Where redemption is only possible through the acceptance of The Chosen One, the Saviour, and the rejection both of 'polytheism' and of the possibility of redemption through other avenues, the writing of history must become an imperative task. History records the triumph of that faith, its spread through vast spaces over a period of time, and the acceptance by the conquered peoples of the personal saviour as the redeemer of mankind. There is, for each of these faiths, only one possible history; and the eschatology is not the redemption of man by the Saviour but rather his redemption by history. Does not history, and the development of a historiographical tradition, have something of a natural association with the notion of a personal saviour and with proselytism? Are we not at least pushed towards the thought that monotheistic faiths almost certainly have resorted to the idioms of historical thought and writing, while Hinduism has been indifferent, if not hostile, to the historical enterprise?

Let me, then, speculate further and move us as far away from the arguments conventionally furnished—extending from the hostility of India's climate to historical texts, the conspiratorial character of Brahmins and the intolerance of Muslim conquerors and rulers, to the supposed irrationality of Indians, their animadversion to facts and empirical positivism, and (in Hegelian terms) the stagnation of the Spirit—to explain the lack of historical literature in India until at least the coming of Islam, arguments all predicated on the assumption that to concede this lack is to accept that on the evaluative scale of civilizations, India must fare poorly. The acceptance of history is nothing but the narrowing of man's options, the submission of a people to the reigning ideas of the time, and the renunciation of multiple eschatologies for the exceedingly dubious benefit of being part of the global destiny of the human race. Though histories are increasingly being written in the plural, paradoxically their ascent leads to history in the singular. It is not that 'history may be servitude': history is servitude; and it is this view, which has found its greatest exponent in Gandhi—the real one, not his unpropitiously named namesakes who were bent on bringing India into the orbit of world history—which must principally account for why Hindu civilization chose not to produce a historiographical tradition. As the epistemological clarity of this position is best seen in the writings of Gandhi, and in the style of thinking and mode of action associated with his name, I shall turn to him, here (in the final section of this chapter) and elsewhere in this book, to explore the meaning of this profound indifference to history, and the possibilities of constructing an account of knowledge which allows little or no epistemological space to historical knowledge, historical writing, or even historical consciousness.

VI

For much the same reasons that Bankim was willing to accept history as a guide to action, Gandhi was not. Bankim's interest in history, the historical sense and historical evidence, was derived partly from a desire to demonstrate that the past of India, and particularly of his native Bengal, was one of martial traditions and military prowess. His historical novels set out to establish that the various invaders of India, far from being allowed to enter and pillage the country without contest, were given battle at every turn. But Indians, when at all they had any knowledge of the past, gained that understanding from the accounts of Europeans, for whom non-resistance and cowardice characterized the response of Indians to alien invasions, indeed to the mere threat of violence. As Robert Orme, among the first British historians of India, put it in 1782: if a European sailor 'brandishes his stick in sport, [he] puts fifty Indians to flight in a moment'.[94] Indians had thus been induced to believe that violent resistance formed no part of their past.

Gandhi, on the other hand, displayed a rather more complex and ambivalent attitude to the question of whether violence had constituted a part of the people's response to oppression and injustice, whether inflicted by invaders or indigenous rulers. In Gandhi's Gujarat, various traditional forms of resistance, such as *hartal* (boycott), *hijrat* (migration), and *dharna* (sit-in; fasting; literally, being an 'obstacle'), were still being employed in the nineteenth century.[95] In his treatise of 1909, *Hind Swaraj*, cast in the form of a dialogue between the sceptic ('the reader') and Gandhi ('the editor'), Gandhi showed his awareness that 'passive resistance' had for a very long time been offered by the people to seek redressal of their grievances or to protest against the unjust rule of monarchs.[96] When asked by the imaginary reader whether there was 'any historical evidence as to the success of ... soul-force or truth-force', Gandhi replied that if history meant 'the doings of kings and emperors', then 'no evidence of soul-force or passive resistance was [to be found] in such history'. If history, he added, had the meaning—'it so happened'—given to the word in Gujarati (and other Indian languages), then 'copious evidence' could be supplied.[97] However, later, when he had the experience of many years of satyagraha in India behind him, Gandhi was to describe many of the methods of passive resistance, which he had earlier condoned, as forms of *duragraha* (the grasping on to falsehood) and coercion which were not any less forms of coercion on account of being non-violent. Whatever may have been the forms of resistance in the past, Gandhi knew only too well that his attempt to apply non-violence on a mass scale in India's fight for freedom and thereby to induce the social transformation of Indian society was altogether unprecedented. History could be no guide to action in the present; indeed, the very idea that battle had to be given to the opponent non-violently required that history be ignored, or else the burden of the past would have been so overpowering as to render futile the enterprise at the very moment of conception. Gandhi rejected the notion, widespread even today, that there are 'lessons' to be learned from history. Perhaps the only lesson was that history itself had to be unlearned.

As history had serviced imperialism, so it could be wielded as an ideological weapon by nationalism. The study of history received its first impetus from nationalist sentiment, though, as Partha Chatterjee and Ranajit Guha among others have documented, in Bengal the writing of history can be dated to the middle of the nineteenth century, to a time when nationalist feeling was at best merely incipient. The brutal suppression of the revolt of 1857–8 must have played some part in generating historical reflection. The study of history by Hindu nationalists and historians predictably began in earnest in the last quarter of the nineteenth century, when nationalism was first emerging in force. Gandhi's rejection of the nationalist use of history is once again seen best by way of contrast with the historicism of Bankim. To Bankim's mind there was no doubt, as we have seen, that Krishna was a real, historical figure, and the Mahabharata a text with a historical core. The vast majority of Indian nationalists, and virtually all of the most important Hindu leaders with the exception of Gandhi, were of one mind with Bankim on this question. The mammoth interpretation of the Bhagavad Gita by Bankim's renowned contemporary, Tilak, can be adduced as evidence of this tendency; and neither is it surprising that the Gita, wherein Krishna induces Arjuna to accept the creed of the Aryan warrior, was the favoured text of Indian 'terrorists' or 'extremists'.[98]

Gandhi, however, was just as firmly indisposed towards treating the Mahabharata as a historical record and accepting the historicity of Krishna. 'The Mahabharata', he wrote in 1924, 'is not to me a historical record. It is hopeless as a history. But it deals with eternal verities in an allegorical fashion.'[99] The original core of the Mahabharata was just as allegorical as the accretions; there was nothing historical about it. Gandhi developed his interpretation of the Mahabharata as an allegory, and of the war between the Kauravas and the Pandavas as the fight within the soul between the forces of darkness and the forces of good, in an extended commentary on the Gita.[100] As for the Krishna of the Mahabharata, there was not enough knowledge to warrant the conclusion that he 'ever lived'. 'My Krishna has nothing to do with any historical person', affirmed Gandhi.[101] His secretary and close personal associate, Mahadev Desai, describing Gandhi's attitude towards the Gita, was certain that 'no textual discovery' would 'affect by a jot the essence or universality of that message. The same thing may be said about questions of the historical Krishna.'[102] Thus Gandhi distanced himself from interpretations of the Mahabharata which sought to establish its historicity and resuscitate Krishna as a historical figure who not only urged Arjuna to use his arms but was also not above using some chicanery to defeat the forces of evil.

Gandhi would have considered the resort to history as another facet of the attempt of educated Indians, and particularly of the modernizing and urbanized elite which constituted the vanguard, to enter into a race with the West. He saw very clearly how the programme to rewrite history, to turn Krishna into a historical figure and depict the Bhagavad Gita as a historical record of Krishna's teachings to Arjuna, had a hard, even cold-blooded, edge to it, a natural link with realpolitik and an exaggerated masculinity. Gandhi alone among Indian nationalists and thinkers recognized not merely that women have been evicted from history, but also that history has been a masculinist enterprise, and that history produces no notable truths about humanity, but rather *man's* truth.[103] Is it surprising that Veer Savarkar, a noted Hindu chauvinist who was suspected of having masterminded the conspiracy to murder Gandhi, first made his presence as a nationalist known by rewriting the history of the so-called 'Sepoy Mutiny' of 1857, terming it instead 'The First War of Indian Independence', and that he was an addict of history? As Savarkar was to say of the word that he has made (in)famous, 'Hindutva is not a word but a history. Not only the spiritual or religious history of our people as it is sometimes taken to be by being confused with the other conjugate term Hinduism, but a history in full.'[104] The assassin of Gandhi, likewise a history buff who understood Gandhi better than all those who dubbed him 'mad', felt compelled to extinguish the life of Gandhi because the old man, by introducing such fads as 'fasting' and obedience to the 'inner voice' into politics, was emasculating the nation; moreover, Gandhi's creed and policy of non-violence was an affront to history, which in 'a thousand years' had never been prey to a 'more stupendous fiction' than that fostered by Gandhi when he led Indians and the world to believe that non-violence was anything other than 'suicidal'.[105]

Whereas the nationalists chose to exploit history for their own ends, Gandhi shunned it altogether: what was corrupt at the source was irredeemable. Almost nowhere else did he reveal himself to be so characteristically Indian. In terms both epistemological and practical at once, the implication of this rejection of history was the abandonment of the notion that history has 'lessons' to offer to human beings and of the idea of progress, or at least progress as it was conceived by Enlightenment thinkers, colonial policy planners, and (though Gandhi did not live to encounter this breed) 'development experts'. History as it was practised when Gandhi was writing was still mainly political history, the history of kings and of the wars which they periodically fought, the history of cities sacked and rebuilt only to be sacked again. This no doubt deepened Gandhi's indifference to history. But how could doing history one way rather than another way, when the very idea was oppressive, have made a difference? Would the advent of social and cultural history, the explosion of women's history and the history of other marginalized and oppressed people,[106] and the quest (following Foucault) for the archaeologies of knowledge, have made history more palatable to Gandhi? History with a capital 'H' has enough detractors, and they have almost entirely wound up on the side of history with a small 'h'. And we must also ask apropos of these new developments in history: do they suggest that whatever may have been the reasons which induced Indians to forgo the creation of a historiographical tradition, such reasons do not exist any more? If history once oppressed, does it now liberate?

Gandhi would have welcomed the sentiments behind recent developments in historiography and the good intentions of their proponents. In his own, howsoever limited, way he tried to bring women into the public arena and into political life. He decried the use of history to propagate a hyper-masculinity; indeed, he consciously strove in the other direction of attempting to feminize Indian politics, as the introduction of both fasting and spinning, which came to acquire a complex web of meanings, into politics amply demonstrates.[107] Women were 'out of history'; but was Gandhi seeking, as are modern feminists, to write them back into history? Similarly he set up the untouchables and the lower castes against the higher—and if he didn't, as his more stringent critics would claim, it is remarkable that his Brahmin foes have generally viewed Gandhi with extreme hostility as a person whose conduct and social thinking were alike destructive of the social order. But it was not Gandhi's intent in challenging the authority of Brahminism that equality should come about by everyone being treated as a Brahmin: true equality would obtain when every Indian felt himself or herself to be an untouchable, and untouchability consequently lost its force in Indian society. The political parity he sought to win for Indians 'was not done in the name of restructuring traditions but in the name of strengthening Indianness, Hinduism or dharma, all of which are supposedly collectivist-hierarchical in spirit'.[108] But where there is something almost profoundly ahistorical about how Gandhi set out to restructure Indian society and yet strengthen Hinduism and the *sanatana-dharma* (the eternal religion), the project of Bankim, Tilak, and others in achieving precisely the same ends entailed the glorification of a hyper-masculinity, the imitation of the West, and the fabrication of history.

I began with the query as to why India lacked a tradition of historical inquiry. In concluding with Gandhi I do not mean to suggest that there is a linear history to this ahistoricism at the end of which stands the Absolute Spirit, reincarnated not as Hegel but as Gandhi the Prophet. The past can be read from many objects; there can be many kinds of 'texts'. But it must be candidly admitted that the past of India cannot be read from historical records. A tradition of historical inquiry and writings has not existed in India until very recent times, and did not exist for very good and compelling reasons. Perhaps I have not sufficiently indicated that some contemporary historians, who can scarcely be accused of supporting either nationalist or colonialist interpretations of history, take strong exception to the characterization of pre-modern India as a civilization which lacked the historical sensibility, but their denunciation of a positivist conception of history is nonetheless itself contingent upon a positivist embrace of history, howsoever non-positivist and non-Eurocentric their conception of history may be. Thus Nicholas Dirks asks, following a quotation from a pronouncement in 1800 by a British official declaring that Indians are inattentive to 'History, or tradition', 'if it is true that India had no sense of history until the British introduced it', and why this assumption had not faced more 'critical scrutiny'?[109] Dirks points to the importance of caste histories and family chronicles, but his own study of Indian society and its notions of kingship relies on chronicles from the time *after* the British had made known their presence in India for several decades. Peter van der Veer similarly finds 'ridiculous' the notion that Indians should have 'lacked' a sense of history, but his mere assertion has no value beyond the expression of an anti-Indological sentiment, and significantly enough, he ends up admitting, following the argument of Pollock, that 'Hindu discourse often tried to avoid historical referentiality'.[110] Neither can envision the possibility that a people may choose to opt out of history, or—the softer version—that they may not desire to possess the sense of history. Agreement with the Orientalist argument that Indians did not produce a historical literature need not signify one's assent to the proposition that this must perforce be construed as a debilitating and unacceptable 'lack'.

In post-Independence India, and more particularly in the last couple of decades, a tradition of historical inquiry has developed in significant ways. The growth of such a tradition, with which this book is in substantial part concerned, is not necessarily a propitious development, and we have only to look at the revival of history in its crudest forms among the advocates of the Rama Janmabhoomi movement to understand how the aspiration to be possessed of a history has now entered the public domain and wrought havoc.[111] I have summoned Gandhi as an instance of why we should believe that the absence of historical inquiry suggests an acute presence of mind and why this lack, an allegedly grave fault, must be revalourized and turned to advantage. If it is claimed that universal history has given way to local and particular histories, that claim provides no relief when we consider that the discourse of history has become the new universal discourse of our times, supplanting even the long period of the hegemony of science. Science, however, was never without its detractors, and Europe had to suppress its own traditions of dissent. Now, at the dawn of the twenty-first century, the race around the entire non-Western world to catch up with the scientific West does not nearly have the unanimous appeal it once did, and perhaps this race matters less today than it did even a few decades ago, when modernization theory prevailed, and the West, despite the anti-colonial struggles, could only be emulated for its achievements. However, we are now witnesses to the universal enthronement of history. Is there an educational system where history is not part of the curriculum, and is there a country where history textbooks are not the subject of acute debate and unrest? No sooner is a people faulted or pitied for having no history, for not having been part of history, than one of them sets out to write that glorious history of his or her people. Is there a people that does not want a history?

Contemporary narratives suggest that the civilization of the West is now largely postmodern and 'post-industrial'; it has entered the age of 'late capitalism', and at some point so will the rest of the world, unless that world has a suicidal intent to become history. What is transnational is not so much the leviathan corporation which pays scant respect to history and to the nation-state but certain categories of knowledge, most particularly 'history'. Science never achieved the conquests which history is now positioned to accomplish. History is the new dogmatism; and as a dogma, as well as a mode of conquest, it is more unremitting and total than science, which has had its detractors from the very beginning. What better instance of the totalizing tendency of history do we have than the manner in which Gandhi, who dismissed history to the periphery of human knowledge, has in turn been dismissed by history to the periphery of human knowledge? If Indian intellectual and cultural traditions, of which Gandhi was supremely emblematic, present something of an anomaly, that appears to be perfectly apposite for a civilization that has chosen to burn, not bury, its dead. To use the historian's jargon, the only 'lesson' history has to offer is that as the Indian tradition did without this historical sense, so might we. In a world where the most radical theories are sold on the market, and revolutions are managed by financiers and corporate executives, the abandonment of history may well be the only heresy that remains to us, for that defiance is nothing other than the defiance of the categories of knowledge which have become the most effective and insidious means of oppressing humankind today. This might be taken as a philosophical plea; but perforce the rest of the book will be conjugated in the historical tense.

ENDNOTES

1. A word of explanation is required for my use of the word 'history' in this chapter. By that term I seek to designate, least of all, 'what happened'; I am much less interested in the past as history. As the very title of this book, *The History of History*, suggests, I am largely concerned, in speaking of history, with historical writing and historical thinking, and thereby also a certain method of investigating the past, and with what is generally conveyed when we speak of the 'sense of history'. I also intend to suggest by this usage the ability to reason historically and to ground one's arguments in a historical sociology. In short, I am most interested in those usages of history which designate what is often termed the 'historical consciousness', or the historical sensibility.

2. See Gautam Chattopadhyay, ed., *Awakening in Bengal in Early Nineteenth Century* (Selected Documents), Vol. 1 (Calcutta: Progressive Publishers, 1965), pp. lv–lix.

3. Rev. Krishna Mohun Banerjea, 'Discourse on the Nature and Importance of Historical Studies', in *Selection of Discourses Delivered at the Meetings of the Society for the Acquisition of General Knowledge*, Vol. 1 (Calcutta, 1840),

reprinted in Chattopadhyay, *Awakening in Bengal*, pp. 1–23; see esp. pp. 4, 7–8, 22–3.

4. For details, not always reliable, about Alberuni's life, see Sir H. M. Elliot, *The History of India As Told by Its Own Historians: The Muhammadan Period*, ed. (and continued) by John Dowson, 8 vols (reprint edn, Allahabad: Kitab Mahal, n.d.), 2:1–13. The introduction by Ainslee Embree to the abridged 1-volume translation by Edward Sachau, *Alberuni's India* (New York: W. W. Norton, 1971), pp. v–xix, is useful.

5. Edward C. Sachau, trans. and ed., *Alberuni's India* (London: Routledge & Kegan Paul, 1888; reprint edn, Delhi: S. Chand & Co., 1964, 2 vols in 1), 1:22.

6. Cf. K. M. Munshi, *Somnath: The Shrine Eternal* (Bombay: Bharatiya Vidya Bhavan, 1953), p. 89.

7. Sachau, *Alberuni's India*, 2:10–11. The translation of Sir H. M. Elliot, working from a French version which he compared with the Arabic text, appears to be less adequate: 'The Indians attach little importance to the sequence of events, and neglect to record the dates of the reigns of their kings. When they are embarrassed, they are silent.' See Elliot and Dowson, *The History of India*, 2:10.

8. Edward Gibbon, *Decline and Fall of the Roman Empire*, ch. li and x, p. 442, cited by James Mill, *History of British India*, ed. with notes by Horace Hayman Wilson, 10 volumes, 5th edn (London: James Madden, 1858), 2:48 n. 2. John Malcolm, in his *History of Persia*, 1: 273, wrote of the ancient Persians that he had never heard of any work by them 'in the ancient Pehlavi that could be deemed historical'. See James Mill, ibid., 2:49.

9. R. Percival, *An Account of the Island of Ceylon* (London, 1803), pp. 4–5, and J. Davy, *An Account of the Interior of Ceylon* (London, 1821), p. vi, both cited by John D. Rogers, 'Historical Images in the British Period', in Jonathan Spencer, ed., *Sri Lanka: History and the Roots of Conflict* (London: Routledge, 1990), p. 88.

10. See Mill, *History of British India*, 2:47–8.

11. Elliot and Dowson, *The History of India*, Original Preface by Sir Henry Elliot, pp. xviii–xxi.

12. Mill, *History of British India*, 2:47.

13. Ibid., 1:114–5. Mill cited, among others, one Captain Wilford: 'The mythology of the Hindus is often inconsistent and contradictory, and the same tale is related many different ways. Their physiology, astronomy, and history, are involved in allegories and enigmas, which cannot but seem extravagant and ridiculous ... .' ('Discourse on Egypt and the Nile', *Asiatic Researches* III.29). Another of Mill's 'authorities' was Major Rennel, a naval officer who served as a major in Clive's army, and went on to become Surveyor General of the East India Company Territories of Bengal: 'There is no known history of Hindoostan (that rests on the foundation of Hindu materials or records) extant, before the period of the Muhammedan

conquests' (*Rennel's Memoir*, Introduction, p. xl). Similarly Scott Waring, whom Mill described as an 'Oriental scholar of some eminence', said of 'Hindu mythology and history' that they appear to be buried in 'impenetrable darkness' (see Mill, *History of British India*, 1:116 n. 2 and p. 117 n. 1). H. H. Wilson, in his notes to the fifth edition of Mill's history, made a brave and well-intentioned but, as I shall argue later, fruitless and misdirected attempt to counter Mill's assertions about the poverty of Hindu literature, whether historical or otherwise. James Mill and H. H. Wilson represent the two faces of Orientalism, and as Ronald Inden has so aptly remarked, romantics like Wilson constituted a 'loyal opposition' to positivists like Mill. See Inden, *Imagining India* (Oxford: Basil Blackwell, 1990), pp. 41–8.

Captain Wilford's allegation that among the Hindus 'the same tale is related many ways' is striking. It is extraordinary that 'the Hindus' should have had to defend themselves against such a charge. The supposition that there is, or ought to be, only one way of telling a tale is one that only 'Enlightenment' Europe was capable of harbouring. It is this hyper-rationality that induced, within European thinking and action alike, a singularity of purpose that, on the one hand, led to European colonialism and a display of self-aggrandizement such as had never been witnessed before, and on the other hand to a conception of knowledge that had no room for plurality of opinions, or for a plurality of modes of apprehending the world. After Akira Kurosawa's *Rashomon*, no one can insist that there must be one way of telling a tale, and it is just as clear that the decentring of narratives, which one can accept as the principal contribution of postmodernism, is also one of the central strategies deployed in Indian texts. But this is a matter that I cannot take up here.

14. Mill, *History of British India*, 2:51; Thomas B. Macaulay, 'Minute on Indian Education', *Selected Writings*, ed. John Clive (Chicago: University of Chicago Press, 1980), p. 243 (para 13).

15. Mill, *History of British India*, Preface by Wilson, 1:xii.

16. Sir Monier Monier-Williams, [Address to the National Indian Association], *Journal of the National Indian Association* (January 1878), p. 30.

17. Macaulay, *Selected Writings*, pp. 242–3.

18. Gauri Viswanathan, *Masks of Conquest: Literary Study and British Rule in India* (New York: Columbia University Press, 1989), pp. 100–01.

19. Inden, *Imagining India*, p. 45.

20. Mill, *History of British India*, 2:46.

21. Ibid., pp. 46–7.

22. It is not my claim here that Thucydides, and much less Herodotus, were 'historians' in the sense in which that might be understood today: the intricacies of any such assessment, in the event, fall far outside the purview of this book. Even from the standpoint of a Mill, there was too much of 'myth' in the writings of these Greeks, and indeed Herodotus was full of fanciful and absurd notions, but no one would have been willing to allow that Herodotus

and Thucydides were *not* historians, albeit of widely varying calibre. The problems of claiming the Greeks as their true intellectual ancestors, as the fount of their civilization, is one that Europeans have scarcely addressed, and the emotional and intellectual disruptions that this enterprise would create are not such that Europeans are equipped to handle with equipoise. This appears to be demonstrated by the sharp controversy aroused by the publication of Martin Bernal's *Black Athena: The Afroasiatic Roots of Classical Civilization, Volume I: The Fabrication of Ancient Greece 1785–1985* (London: Free Association Books; New Brunswick, NJ: Rutgers University Press, 1987); see also Mary R. Lefkowitz and Guy MacLean Rogers, eds, *Black Athena Revisited* (Chapel Hill: University of North Carolina Press, 1996).

23. Louis B. Wright, 'The Elizabethan Middle-Class Taste for History', *The Journal of Modern History* 3, no. 2 (June 1931), pp. 175, 179.

24. Ibid., p. 177, citing Barnabe Rich, *Allarme to England* (1578).

25. Thomas Sprat, *The History of the Royal Society of London* (1st edn, 1667; 4th edn, London: J. Knapton, J. Walthoe, etc., 1734). See also Richard Foster Jones, 'Science and English Prose Style in the Third Quarter of the Seventeenth Century', *PMLA* 45 (1930):977–1009, esp. p. 1002.

26. Charles Dickens, *Hard Times* (Harmondsworth: Penguin Books, 1983), pp. 48–9.

27. Cf. Michel Foucault, *The Order of Things: An Archaeology of the Human Sciences* (New York: Vintage Books, 1973), pp. 367–73.

28. For an exhaustive study of the institutionalization of history, see Philippa Levine, *The Amateur and the Professional: Antiquarians, Historians, and Archaeologists in Victorian Britain, 1838–1886* (Cambridge: Cambridge University Press, 1986).

29. Cited by Christina Crosby, *The Ends of History: Victorians and the 'Woman Question'* (New York and London: Routledge, 1991), p. 4.

30. Quoted in Stefan Collini, Donald Winch, and John Burrow, *That Noble Science of Politics: A study in nineteenth-century intellectual history* (Cambridge: Cambridge University Press, 1983), p. 183.

31. S. N. Banerjea, 'The Study of Indian History', *Speeches of S. N. Banerjea, 1876–1880* (n.p.; n.d.), pp. 2–3.

32. Ibid.

33. P. Mukhopadhyay, *Balya Shiksha Banglar Itihas* [*A Children's History of Bengal*] (Habra, 1891), p. 20, cited by Indira Chowdhury, *The Frail Hero and Virile History: Gender and the Politics of Culture in Colonial Bengal* (Delhi: Oxford University Press, 1998), p. 52.

34. See comment by K. S. Ramaswami Sastri, in K. A. Nilakanta Sastri et al., 'Historiography: India and the West', *Bulletin of the Institute of Traditional Cultures* [hereafter *BITC*] (Madras), Part 1 (1962), p. 299.

35. *Alberuni's India*, ed. Sachau, p. 18.

36. Mountstuart Elphinstone, *Report on the Territories Conquered from the Peshwa* [1821], excerpted in George W. Forrest, ed., *Selections from the Minutes*

and Other Official Writings of the Honourable Mountstuart Elphinstone, Governor of Bombay (London: R. Bentley, 1884), p. 260.

37. J. Talboys Wheeler, *The History of India from the Earliest Ages* (London: Trubner, 1869; reprint edn, Delhi: Cosmo Publications, 1922), p. 6, cited by Viswanathan, *Masks of Conquest*, p. 125.

38. John B. Gilchrist, 'Preface', *A Dictionary, English and Hindoostanee* (Calcutta, part I, 1786; part II, 1790), p. xxvi, cited by Bernard S. Cohn, 'The Command of Language and the Language of Command', *Subaltern Studies* IV, ed. Ranajit Guha (Delhi: Oxford University Press, 1985), p. 302. Gilchrist was of the opinion that Sanskrit was a 'cunning fabrication' of the 'insidious Brahmans', an artificial language derived from 'Hinduwee' (see Cohn, pp. 304–05).

39. Burton Stein, 'Early Indian Historiography: A Conspiracy Hypothesis', *Indian Economic and Social History Review* 6 (1969):41–60, esp. pp. 48–51. But cf. Romila Thapar, 'Society and Historical Consciousness: The *Itihasa-Purana* Tradition', in Romila Thapar and Sabyasachi Bhattacharya, eds, *Situating Indian History—for S. Gopal* (Delhi: Oxford University Press, 1986), pp. 353–83, esp. pp. 366–67.

40. Although undoubtedly the transmission of knowledge from a guru to a male student was a purely Brahminical affair, our understanding of this very process hinges upon the definition of a 'Brahmin'. There is no reason to suppose, as Stein does, that a 'Brahmin' necessarily signifies membership in a *jati* or *gotra* of ritually pure birth. The story of Satyakama [seeker of truth] in the *Chandogya Upanishad* (IV.4) is illustrative in this respect. Seeking to live the life of a student of sacred knowledge, Satyakama asked his mother of what family he was descended. She replied that she begat him in her youth when she 'went about a great deal serving as a maid', and did not know who had fathered him. When Satyakama came before Haridrumata Gautama and asked to be admitted as his student, he was queried about his family, whereupon Satyakama relayed the exact words spoken to him by his mother. The guru accepted Satyakama as his student, for he had not deviated from the truth, and no non-Brahmin (*a-brahmana*) would have done the same. There are other famous instances of Hindus of low social origins and even non-Hindus such as Kabir being accepted as students of sacred knowledge. The point is that, in principle, a Brahmin was a Brahmin not by virtue of birth but by his steadfast devotion to truth and the purity of his character. But by and large it is true, if the Dharmasastras be our witness, that the injunction against the Sudras learning, reciting, and hearing the Vedas was very strong. Manu said that the Brahmin who explained the sacred law to the Sudra would, along with the latter, sink into hell (*The Laws of Manu*, IV. 80; cf. III. 156 ff.); and Sudras would gain merit if they 'imitate[d] the practice of virtuous men without reciting sacred texts' (X. 127; translation of G. Buhler). The cultural politics of staking the definition of Brahminhood on conduct and behavior is scarcely unproblematic; from one standpoint, it is more

oppressive than the conventional and circumscribed meaning of 'Brahmin', which restricts this appellation to persons of certain birth, for on the more generous reading every person of good moral conduct must perforce be a Brahmin. This would, needless to say, not be acceptable to certain sections of Indian society, such as the Dalits or others harbouring anti-Brahminical sentiments.

41. Stein, 'Early Indian Historiography', pp. 41, 58–9. On traditions of Indian learning, see the collection edited by Alex Michaels, *The Pandit*: *Traditional Scholarship in India* (Delhi: Manohar, 2001).

42. Ibid., pp. 55–6, and David Kopf, *British Orientalism and the Bengal Renaissance: The Dynamics of Indian Modernization 1773–1835* (Berkeley: University of California Press, 1969), p. 275.

43. Comment of N. Subramaniam, in K. A. Nilakanta Sastri et al., 'Historiography: India and the West', *BITC*, pp. 266–7.

44. See T. W. Clark, 'Bengali Prose Fiction Up to Bankimcandra', in T. W. Clark, ed., *The Novel in India: Its Birth and Development* (Berkeley: University of California Press, 1970), p. 65; and Vera Novikova, *Bankimchandra Chattopadhyay: His Life and Works*, trans. Nishitesh Banerjee (Calcutta: National Publishers, 1976), p. 169.

45. I might note here that Sanskrit words occur in this chapter, and indeed elsewhere in the book, without diacritical marks; secondly, a number of words appear in two or more forms: within a quotation, the word is reproduced from the original without any alterations, but my own usage of that word may reflect the more common or modern transliteration.

46. Bankim Chatterjee, *Durgesa Nandini* or *The Chieftain's Daughter* (1880), trans. Charu Chandra Mookerjee, 2nd edn (Calcutta: The Classic Press, 1903), pp. 15–16. 'Yavanas' may be translated as 'foreigners' or 'barbarians'; it is a corruption of the word 'Ionian'.

47. 'Bharatvarsa paradhin kena?' *Bankim Racnabali* [henceforth *BR*], ed. Yogesh Chandra Bagal, Vol. 2 (Calcutta: Sahitya Samsad, 1965), p. 239.

48. 'Sankhyadarsan', *BR* II:222–6, cited by Partha Chatterjee, *Nationalist Thought and the Colonial World: A Derivative Discourse?* (London: Zed Books, 1986), pp. 56–7.

49. Bankim Chatterjee, 'Bharatvarsa Paradhin Kena?', *BR* II:239.

50. Ibid., p. 240.

51. Bankim Chandra Chatterjee, *Krishna-Charita*, trans. with introduction by Pradip Bhattacharya (Calcutta: The M. P. Birla Foundation, 1991), p. 21.

52. Bankim Chatterjee, *Dharmatattva*, *BR* II.

53. *Anandamath*, translated as *The Abbey of Bliss* by Nares Chandra Sengupta (Calcutta: Padmini Mohan Neogi, 1904), p. 97.

54. Chatterjee, *Nationalist Thought*, p. 59.

55. Bankim Chandra Chatterjee, *Krishna-Charita*, p. 29.

56. 'Pracar', *BR* II:334, cited by Rachel R. van Meter, 'Bankimcandra's

View of the Role of Bengal in Indian Civilization', in *Bengal Regional Identity*, ed. David Kopf (Lansing, Michigan: Asian Studies Center, Michigan State University, 1969), p. 62.

57. Bankim Chandra Chatterjee, *Krishna-Charitra*, p. 35.

58. 'Bangalar itihas sambandhe kayekti katha' ('A Few Words Concerning the History of Bengal'), *BR* II:339, cited by Chatterjee, *Nationalist Thought*, p. 79.

59. Quoted in Novikova, *Bankimchandra Chattopadhyay*, p. 91.

60. 'Pracar', *BR* II:333, cited by van Meter, 'Bankimchandra's View of the Role of Bengal', p. 69.

61. Notwithstanding the unnecessary, even absurd, stabs at Ashis Nandy and Partha Chatterjee, the essay by Tanika Sarkar, 'Imagining Hindurashtra: The Hindu and the Muslim in Bankim Chandra's Writings', in *Making India Hindu*, ed. David Ludden (Delhi: Oxford University Press, 1996), pp. 162–84, offers some useful insights into Bankim's novels and essays, and has the virtue of treating them together while suggesting modes of differentiating between the polemical strategies of the two genres (see esp. pp. 167, 172–81.

62. 'Bangalar itihas sambandhe kayekti katha', *BR* II:330.

63. 'Bangalar itihas sambandhe kayekti katha', *BR* II:330, cited also by Chatterjee, *Nationalist Thought*, p. 82 n. 9.

64. Cited by Ranajit Guha, *An Indian Historiography of India: A Nineteenth-Century Agenda and Its Implications*, S. G. Deuskar Lectures on Indian History (Calcutta: K. P. Bagchi & Co., 1988), p. 1.

65. The literature on Bankim, some of it specifically devoted to his views on history, is burgeoning. Other than the essays of Partha Chatterjee, which are largely different versions of the same theme, there is the book-length study of Sudipta Kaviraj, *The Unhappy Consciousness* (Delhi: Oxford University Press, 1995), as well as Henry Schwarz's *Writing Cultural History in Colonial and Postcolonial India* (Philadelphia: University of Pennsylvania Press, 1997). When Bankim wrote of Bengal, particularly in a nationalist vein, he generally meant India; on the other hand, by 'India' Schwarz really means 'Bengal', and the figures under scrutiny are Vidyasagar, Romesh Chandra Dutt, Bankim, Aurobindo, Dinesh Chandra Sen, J. C. Ghosh, Susobhan Sarkar, Ranajit Guha, Sumit Sarkar, and a few other intellectuals, all Bengalis. This conceit, which allows scholars to speak of India when their only interest resides in Bengal, or when their material is drawn exclusively from Bengal, has not been sufficiently addressed in the modern historiography of India. The omission of Jadunath Sarkar and R. C. Majumdar, perhaps the two most widely read historians in the country during their respectively long careers, from Schwarz's considerations tells another story of postcolonialism's selective (and generally predictable) engagement with texts, histories, and scholars. I myself take up Jadunath Sarkar and Majumdar in Chapter II.

66. See R. C. Majumdar, *Historiography in Modern India* (London and Bombay: Asia Publishing House, 1970), p. 5; 'Ideas of History in Sanskrit

Literature', in C. H. Philips, ed., *Historians of India, Pakistan and Ceylon* (London: Oxford University Press), esp. pp. 27–8; and *Seminar*, no. 39 (1962), p. 15.

67. Kautilya, *Arthasastra*, trans. R. Shamasastry (8th edn, Mysore: Mysore Printing and Publishing House, 1967), p. 6; the subsequent quote is from pp. 9–10.

68. See V. S. Apte, *The Practical Sanskrit-English Dictionary*, 4th revised and enlarged edn (Delhi: Motilal Banarsidass, 1977), v. itivrrtta and itihasa (p. 245), akhyayika (p. 202), udaharana (pp. 269–70).

69. Ibid., v. itihasa, p. 245; the translation into English is by Chidambara Kulkarni, *Studies in Indian History* (Bombay: Shri Dvaipayana Trust, n.d.), p. 3.

70. This is the view of R. C. Majumdar, 'Ideas of History', p. 13 and Buddha Prakash, 'The Hindu Philosophy of History', *Journal of the History of Ideas* 16, no. 4 (October 1955), p. 495.

71. F. E. Pargiter, *The Ancient Indian Historical Tradition* (London, 1922), cited in *BITC*, p. 258; and comment by one Mr. Sanjivi, in *BITC*, p. 294.

72. Even Thucydides, whose value as an historian is seldom questioned, has been accused by F. M. Cornford in *Thucydides Mythistoricus* of having no clear conception of causation. See E. H. Carr, *What is History?* (New York: Vintage Books, 1961), p. 114. How much more palpable is this 'flaw' in Kalhana, writing well over 1,500 years after Thucydides? It is not impertinent to note that at least a few modern thinkers have stressed the absence of any sense of 'historicity in general' in Greek thought: see Alisdair MacIntyre, *After Virtue*, 2nd edn (Notre Dame: University of Notre Dame Press, 1984), p. 159.

73. Gibbon, *Decline and Fall of the Roman Empire*, chap. lxiv, cited by Carr, *What is History?*, p. 128.

74. James Mill, *History of British India*, 2:48–9: 'An inclination at first appeared among the warm admirers of Sanscrit to regard the poems Mahabharat and Ramayan, as a sort of historical records.'

75. *The Rajatarangini*, trans. R. S. Pandit (New Delhi: Sahitya Akademi, 1953; reprint edn, 1968), Book III, verses 470 and 171.

76. No one Purana can be described as exhibiting in fine (or even coarse) detail all five of these distinguishing traits, but sometimes the *Vishnu Purana* is thought to most closely resemble the traditional definition. The Puranas can be described as a form of sectarian literature: some exhibit devotion to Vishnu; in others the devotion to Shiva predominates. Two introductory anthologies of Puranic literature are Cornelia Dimmitt and J. A. B. van Buitenen, eds and trans., *Classical Hindu Mythology: A Reader in the Sanskrit Puranas* (Philadelphia: Temple University Press, 1978), and Wendy Doniger O'Flaherty, ed. and trans., *Hindu Myths: A Sourcebook* (Harmondsworth: Penguin Books, 1975). Of recent critical studies, the most insightful is Kunal Chakrabarti, *Religious Process: The Puranas and the Making of a Regional Tradition* (Delhi: Oxford University Press, 2001).

77. All quotations in this paragraph are from Romila Thapar, 'Society and Historical Consciousness', pp. 365–7.

78. 'Bangadarsan', BR II:240, cited by Van Meter, see note 48 at p. 69.

79. R. Thapar in *Seminar* (1962), no. 39.

80. A. K. Warder, in Philips, *Historians of India, Pakistan and Ceylon*, p. 44.

81. K. K. Pillay, in *BITC*, p. 289.

82. Benedetto Croce, *History as the Story of Liberty* [1938] (London: George Allen & Unwin, 1941); J. B. Bury, *The Idea of Progress: An Inquiry into Its Growth and Origin* [1932] (New York: Dover Books, 1955).

83. Madhav Deshpande, 'History, Change and Permanence: A Classical Indian Perspective', *Contributions to South Asian Studies* I, ed. Gopal Krishna (Delhi: Oxford University Press, 1979), pp. 6–8; the last line is quoted from Siddheshwar Varma, 'Scientific and Technical Presentation as Reflected in the *Mahabhasya* of Patanjali', *Vishveshvarananda Indological Journal* 1, no. 1 (1966).

84. Sheldon Pollock, 'Mimamsa and the Problem of History in Traditional India', *Journal of the American Oriental Society* 109, no. 4 (1989), pp. 603, 607–9.

85. Deshpande, 'History, Change and Permanence', pp. 8–9.

86. Cf. John Keay, *India: A History* (New York: Grove Press, 2000), pp. 70–1: 'Alexander the Great's Indian adventure, though a subject of abiding interest to generations of classically-educated European historians, is not generally an episode on which historians of Indian nationality bother to dwell. They rightly note that it "made no impression historically or politically on India", and that "not even a mention of Alexander is to be found in any [of the] older Indian sources".' The quotations are from Romila Thapar, *A History of India*, Vol. 1 (Harmondsworth: Penguin, 1966), p. 59.

87. Hegel, *The Philosophy of History*, trans. J. Sibree (reprint edn, New York: Dover, 1956), pp. 139–40.

88. Marx, 'The British Rule in India', in *The First Indian War of Independence 1857–1859* (Moscow: Foreign Languages Publishing House, n. d.), p. 20 and, in the same volume, 'Further Results of British Rule in India', pp. 32–8.

89. Arthur MacDonell, *A History of Sanskrit Literature* (New York: Haskell, 1966 [1900], p. 11.

90. Marx, 'The British Rule in India', in *The First Indian War of Independence*, pp. 15–22.

91. Peter Hardy, *Historians of Medieval India: Studies in Indo-Muslim Historical Writing* (London: Luzac & Co., 1960; reprint edn with new preface, Delhi: Munshiram Manoharlal, 1997), remains the principal study on Muslim historiography of medieval India.

92. My intent is scarcely to enter into a discussion of comparative historiography or the historical traditions of different civilizations. I am aware, for example, of the remarkable utilization of African oral traditions as history following the pioneering work of J. Vansina, *Oral Tradition: A Study in Historical Methodology* (Chicago: Aldine, 1961) and *Oral Tradition as History* (Madison:

University of Wisconsin Press, 1985). The results of this strand of work have been more productive for East and Central Africa than for South Africa, perhaps because the written histories for South Africa, which came under European domination earlier than the rest of sub-Saharan Africa, are richer. In some contexts, certainly, writing and orality may have an inverse bearing on the production of histories or what might pass for histories. See Paul la Hausse, 'Oral History and South African Historians', in Joshua Brown et al., eds, *History from South Africa: Alternative Visions and Practices* (Philadelphia: Temple University Press, 1991), pp. 342–50. In a somewhat similar vein, though much less narrowly empiricist, is Peter Nabokov, *A Forest of Time: American Indian Ways of History* (Cambridge: Cambridge University Press, 2002). But we must persist in asking: why should history remain the mountain-top? Is it enough that more climbers are permitted to take the stride, and that more routes are created, and kept open for longer periods? Does the repudiation of history take us straight to structural-functionalism?

93. As I point out elsewhere in this book, some scholars, such as Achin Vanaik and Sumit Sarkar, are not inclined to accept the description of Hinduism as a non-proselytizing faith; but that seems no reason to preclude, at least for the present, the more commonly accepted understanding of Hinduism as a religion that is generally inhospitable to the idea of conversion.

94. Robert Orme, 'Effeminacy of the Inhabitants of Indostan', *Historical Fragments of the Mogul Empire ...* (London: F. Wingrave, 1805; reprint edn, New Delhi: Associated Publishing House, 1974), p. 299.

95. Cf. Howard Spodek, 'On the Origins of Gandhi's Political Methodology: The Heritage of Kathiawad and Gujarat', *Journal of Asian Studies* 30, no. 2 (Feb. 1971), pp. 361–72.

96. M. K. Gandhi, *Hind Swaraj or Indian Home Rule* (reprint edn, Ahmedabad: Navajivan Publishing House, 1962), p. 83. Gandhi himself initially rendered satyagraha as 'passive resistance', but later, realizing that the English phrase did not do the word justice, that there was nothing passive about non-violent resistance, he used the phrase 'non-violent resistance' and, more often, the word satyagraha itself to describe his method, teachings, and movement.

97. *Hind Swaraj*, p. 77.

98. There is no systematic treatment of the place of the Gita in nationalist writings; a small beginning, however, has been made in Dilip Bose, *Bhagavad-Gita and Our National Movement* (Delhi: People's Publishing House, 1981).

99. 'My Jail Experiences—XI', *Young India*, 4 Sept. 1924, reprinted in Raghavan Iyer, ed., *The Moral and Political Writings of Mahatma Gandhi, Volume 1: Civilization, Politics and Religion* (Oxford: Clarendon Press, 1986), p. 183.

100. See Iyer, ibid., 1:77–100; Mahadev Desai, *The Gita According to Gandhi* (Ahmedabad: Navajivan Publishing House, 1946); and M. K. Gandhi, *Discourses on the Gita* (Ahmedabad: Navajivan, 1960).

101. 'Sikhism', *Young India*, 1 October 1925, reprinted in Iyer, ibid., 1:484–5.

102. Desai, *The Gita According to Gandhi*, p. 6.

103. Christina Crosby has addressed the intricate ties between the Victorian passion for history and the interest in the 'woman question' in *The Ends of History* (see note 29). My frequent use of 'man' in this chapter has been, thus, less unreflective than what some readers may have supposed.

104. Cited by T. C. A. Raghavan, 'Origins and Development of Hindu Mahasabha Ideology: The Call of V D Savarkar and Bhai Parmanand', *Economic and Political Weekly* 18, no. 15 (9 April 1983), p. 597.

105. Tapan Ghosh, *The Gandhi Murder Trial* (New York: Asia Publishing House, 1976), see especially pp. 15, 212–36. Godse's speech in his defense, which took over five hours to deliver, was proscribed by the Government of India for well over twenty years. The text is available as Gopal Godse, *May It Please Your Honor: Statement of Nathuram Godse* (Poona: Vitasta Prakashan, 1977). The literature on the assassination, which has been growing rapidly over the years, is in the main devoted to enumerating the details of the conspiracy to murder Gandhi. Ghosh's sensitive study is an exception in this regard; more exceptional still is Ashis Nandy's article, 'The Final Encounter: The Politics of the Assassination of Gandhi', in *At the Edge of Psychology: Essays in Politics and Culture* (Delhi: Oxford University Press, 1980), chap. 4.

106. For some of the current trends in history, and a brief account of the significant developments—such as women's history, microhistory, and postmodern histories—over the last twenty years, see the succinct monograph by Keith Jenkins, *Re-thinking History* (London: Routledge, 1992); also useful, though slightly dated, is Juliet Gardiner, ed., *What is History Today ...?* (London: Macmillan, 1988). Jenkins' parochialism, more evidently on display in his *The Postmodern History Reader* (London: Routledge, 1997), is breathtaking: no one would receive the slightest hint from his collection that practitioners of postmodern history exist outside the fields of European and American history, or that the work of postcolonial critics, working on histories of colonialism, might have some bearing on postmodern histories. It may have been of interest to Jenkins that one of subaltern history's most vigorous critics charges the practitioners of this school of Indian history with having drifted too far in the direction of postmodernism; but all this is quite foreign to Jenkins, who opts rather for the inclusion of such pedestrian pieces as an excerpt from Joyce Appleby, Margaret Jacob, and Lynn Hunt, *Telling the Truth About History* (New York: W. W. Norton, 1995), which is at best an uninspiring defence of multicultural and inclusive histories. Put *Reader's Digest* and Benetton together and one gets Appleby and Company's totalizing history. I have discussed subaltern history in Chapter IV (see below); critiques of subaltern history from orthodox Marxist, feminist, and even postmodern positions, while not without interest, nonetheless share in the enthusiasm for 'history'. An interesting rumination on what many of these developments portend is to be found in Dipesh Chakrabarty, 'Minority Histories, Subaltern Pasts', *Postcolonial Studies* 1, no. 1 (1998), pp. 15–29.

107. On the question of fasting and the feminization of politics, see Vinay Lal, 'Gandhi's Last Fast', *Gandhi Marg* 11, no. 2 (July–September 1989), pp. 171–91.

108. Ashis Nandy, 'From Outside the Imperium: Gandhi's Cultural Critique of the "West"', *Alternatives* 3, no. 2 (June 1981), p. 184. The same paper, in a revised version, appears in Ashis Nandy, *Traditions, Tyranny, and Utopias: Essays in the Politics of Awareness* (Delhi: Oxford University Press, 1987), pp. 127–62.

109. Nicholas B. Dirks, *The Hollow Crown: Ethnohistory of an Indian Kingdom*, 2nd edn (Ann Arbor: The University of Michigan Press, 1993), pp. 55, 97.

110. Peter van der Veer, *Religious Nationalism: Hindus and Muslims in India* (Berkeley: University of California Press, 1994), pp. 140–1.

111. See Chapter IV, and also Gyanendra Pandey, 'Modes of History Writing: New Hindu History of Ayodhya', *Economic and Political Weekly* 29, no. 25 (18 June 1994), pp. 1523–8. Pandey fails to reflect, however, on how it is that the 'new Hindu history' was able to come into place and gain the assent of many Hindus. Though he recognizes that the discourse of the Rama Janmabhoomi movement is postulated on ascribing a divine importance to Ayodhya (and in particular the contested spot) as the supposed birth-place of Rama, he does not take into consideration the epistemological and political consequences of staking a claim on the notion of 'place' rather than 'space'. It was the function of colonial discourse to collapse the notion of 'place' into the notion of 'space', and the renewed emphasis on 'place' constitutes a discursive challenge to the notion of 'space', though—as in the case of the Rama Janmabhoomi movement—this particular ascendancy of the notion of 'place' is hardly propitious. There are other similar problems in Pandey's important paper: Hindutva discourse is described as exemplifying a nationalist 'excess', as seen in the fixation on numbers and statistics, on grotesque figures as in the '1,74,000 Hindu lives' said to have been sacrificed before the supposed temple was brought down by Mir Baqi. Pandey implies that such narratives are quite unbelievable; and though they may well be unbelievable, the question is whether such numbers are to be taken seriously, and if so, whether the only way to take them is to consider them as reflective of some 'real' conditions. If kings can be described in the Puranas as ruling for 600 years, or there can be 330 million gods and goddesses, or if the Kauravas can be described as being 100 in number, is this also the 'excess' of 'nationalist' narratives? What kind of interpretive strategy is required to understand the cultural logic of such 'excess'? What are the hazards of imposing upon the authors of the pamphlet literature on Ayodhya standards of veracity which bear a distinct relationship to different regimes of representation and truth?

2

Contours of the Past, Shape of the Future
The Politics of History in Independent India

In the fifty-some years since independence, Indian historians have undoubtedly assumed charge of their own history. Though historians—more so than archaeologists, anthropologists, professional philosophers, or linguists—can everywhere be public figures, in few countries have they acquired such a prominent public presence as they have in India. In the controversy surrounding the Babri Masjid, historians found that they had become ascendant among the class of intellectuals, called upon to verify or dispute the claims of both militant Hindus and their opponents; and in the aftermath of the destruction of the mosque in December 1992, they were transformed into editorialists, pamphleteers, and activists.[1] At issue was not merely the 'authentic' history of the mosque, but Hindu-Muslim relations in India and the rest of South Asia, the future of India as a democratic polity, and the idea of India as a composite culture. In the meantime, the advent of the 'subaltern school' of Indian history, comprised mainly of Indian historians clustered at a few universities and research centres in Delhi, Calcutta, and elsewhere, was to give Indian history not only an unprecedented international respectability, such as has ordinarily been reserved for developments in French or English history,[2] but an important place in various debates in postcolonial theory, postmodernism, and what is termed 'cultural studies'. Historians and scholars around the world have turned to the writings of the subaltern historians to pose questions about the politics of knowledge, the nature of 'elitist' history, the apparently frequent congruence between nationalist and imperialist models of history-writing, and the various voices through which history is interpreted.

These developments in Indian history appear all the more remarkable against the backdrop enumerated in the previous chapter. We have only to recall that as late as 1925, the English historian and 'friend of India', Edward Thompson, was able to write, with all the supreme arrogance that a ruling class everywhere is capable of, that 'Indians are not historians, and they rarely show any critical ability. Even their most useful books, books full of research and information, exasperate with their repetitions and diffuseness, and lose effect by their uncritical enthusiasms. ... So they are not likely to displace our account of our connection with India.'[3] Indian nationalists, as I have argued, were determined to prove Thompson and his ilk wrong, and Bankim was giving expression to the sentiments of many nationalists and modernizers who agonized over India's enslavement and the lack of a historical literature, and who saw in those twin deficiencies, which had to be overcome, an inescapable connection. Bankim's near contemporary, the revered Punjabi nationalist Lala Lajpat Rai (1865–1928), similarly deplored his countrymen's want of 'love of history': 'They read Shakespeare, Milton and Dante and obtain degrees. But they do not know anything about even important things relating to their country. They have no idea of the deeds of their forefathers.'[4]

These clarion calls were not issued in vain: within a little over a generation after his death, the study of history had acquired respectability to the point that at a professional gathering of Indian historians in 1939, it was admitted that 'no subject is perhaps studied in Indian universities of the present day with the same assiduity as the history of India'.[5] Taking their cue from Bankim, the nationalists were to mine the past for heroes, and otherwise seek to historicize legendary figures from Indian mythology; and at least the first generation of historians such as R. C. Dutt (1848–1909) and R. G. Bhandarkar (1837–1925) was to devote its labours largely to the study of ancient India, which was already being envisioned as the high point of Indian civilization. With the knowledge gleaned of remarkable achievements in the past across a wide array of subjects, the degradation of the present was more acutely perceived; and as nationalists engaged in the social reconstruction of Indian society, so the reconstruction of Indian history would be attempted, acquiring with the rapid political changes leading to the end of colonial rule a degree of urgency.

INDEPENDENCE AND HISTORICAL
PROJECTS OF THE STATE

With the advent of independence in 1947, the creation of an Indian history, for and by Indians, became something of a national imperative. Since at least the time of Bankim, nationalist Indians were firmly of the opinion that imperialist history was irredeemably contaminated, and that British accounts of the Indian past existed for no other reason than to serve colonial interests, establish the purported superiority of Western civilization, and create rifts between various Indian communities, whether constituted on grounds of religion and caste (as was most common), ethnicity, or linguistic affiliation. Indians had only to recall that the British historian who had offered them their own history had hoped that his eight-volume set would 'make the native subjects of British India more sensible of the immense advantages accruing to them under the mildness and equity of [our] rule'.[6] In colonial histories, nationalists argued, Indians were invariably represented as a supine people who had truly never offered resistance, and whose destiny (until the enlightened British came along) condemned them to the eternal acceptance of a merciless Oriental despotism. By a perverse twist of logic, the genius of Indians (and by this was meant Hindus) was construed as residing in their capacity to submit, almost without distinction, to all invaders and to absorb them in turn. Bankim had argued that India's indifference to history had created the grounds for its repeated conquest by foreign powers, as Indians had become oblivious of the greatness of their own past, the valour of their soldiers, and the eminent justness of their kings. It was entirely unreasonable to suppose that anyone else would sing of the glories of Bengal or India: perforce Indians must accomplish this task themselves. Let us recall again his plea, in a text where Bengal stood for India as well, 'Bengal must have her own history. Otherwise there is no hope for Bengal. Who is to write it? You have to write it. I have to write it ...'[7] So long as India remained under colonial rule, however, its aspirations to represent its own history and acquire something of an intellectual autonomy would be thwarted. Indeed, the most insidious aspect of British writings on India, as nationalists were to maintain, was that the British had posited themselves as a transcendent power, alone capable of keeping the peace between communities and factions that had, as the British alleged, historically always been at war with each other.

Thus, on the attainment of independence, no intellectual task, other than that of ushering India into the scientific era and ensuring that the country acquired a pool of scientific talent, acquired a greater sanctity and urgency than creating new histories of India. In a speech given shortly after attaining the highest office of the land, Rajendra Prasad, the first President of the Republic of India, underscored the importance of the 'role of history' in nation-building. In his inaugural address before the All-India History Congress, Prasad emphasized that 'India needs a true and exhaustive history of its distant and glorious past, no less than of its unique and unprecedented struggle which has succeeded in placing it, once again, on the map of the world.'[8] Prasad did not doubt that history taught by example, and provided 'guidance for the future'; and summoning the authority of Greek and Roman historians such as Polybius, Cicero, and Livy, he suggested that the historian was bound to the highest standards of 'truth'. Had Prasad said no more, he would have been confined to the conventional pieties about the lessons of history; but rather uncommonly, he advanced the argument that history would be inadequate if it did not go beyond 'an account of kings and nobles' to a consideration of the achievements of the 'common man'. More particularly, pointing to the apotheosization of the warrior in European culture, as manifested in war memorials and monuments of conquerors and soldiers, Prasad hoped that historians of India would be cognizant of the unique importance of the new technique of resistance forged by Gandhi and attentive to the history of the non-violent armies raised by him. Here the task of the historian, as Prasad appeared to imply, was to demonstrate that 'non-violence has victories more glorious than war'.[9]

Fortuitously for those who wished to advance the study of history in India, the mantle of political and intellectual leadership had fallen upon Jawaharlal Nehru, who was not only possessed of a fine historical imagination but had also made a considerable name for himself as the author of historical works. Being openly partial to the enterprise of history was only one manner in which Nehru displayed a sensibility quite at odds with that of his political mentor Gandhi, who in a characteristic moment had written, 'I believe that a nation is happy that has no history'.[10] In a remarkable and extended series of letters to his daughter Indira collected in *Glimpses of World History* (1934), Nehru confessed, 'I do not claim to be a historian', but nonetheless he hoped that these letters would offer her glimpses of the past and awaken her curiosity.[11] Quite unlike most world histories, which were scarcely more than accounts of the development of Western civilization, the narrative of Nehru displayed an exemplary ecumenism and genuine attempt to give a parity to nearly all the principal civilizations. In this respect, *Glimpses of World History* foreshadowed Nehru's propensity toward nonalignment, and his stated policy of cultivating South–South relations and paying close attention to India's relations with other colonized parts of the world. Nehru was not inclined to the view that as the West had been preeminent in world affairs since the late fifteenth century, it ought to command centrestage in history books. He sought even his daughter's indulgence in being, perhaps, somewhat more attentive to India: as an Indian, he was more fully conversant with Indian history and culture; moreover, as he wrote to her, 'If we are to understand India as she is, we must know something of the forces that went to make her or mar her. Only so can we serve her intelligently, and know what we should do and what path we should take.'[12]

Nehru continued his exploration of Indian history in his autobiography (1941), which purported to trace his own mental development rather than offer a survey of recent Indian history,[13] and in *The Discovery of India* (1946), in which he painted a broad canvas of India's multifarious and tumultuous past.[14] India appeared to him as akin to some 'ancient palimpsest on which layer upon layer of thought and reverie had been inscribed, and yet no succeeding layer had completely hidden or erased what had been written previously'. While Nehru may even have accepted many of the assumptions of colonialist histories, he rejected the narrative which sought to render India's past as little more than a tale of invasion, conquest, bloody warfare, Oriental despotism, and fratricide, and most of all he strenuously repudiated the view that there never was an India, or Indian civilization, until the British came along and welded together disparate and quarrelsome communities into one people. 'Though outwardly there was diversity and infinite variety among our people,' wrote Nehru, 'everywhere there was that tremendous impress of oneness, which had held all of us together for ages past, whatever political fate or misfortune had befallen us.' The 'essential unity' of India, which he had comprehended through his extensive travels in India in 1936–7 not only as an 'intellectual conception' but as an 'emotional experience', had been 'so powerful that no political division, no disaster or catastrophe, had been able to overcome it'.[15]

Having gone far beyond the commonplace nationalist view that India had been united under the reign of powerful monarchs such as

Ashoka, Chandragupta Maurya, Harsha, and Akbar, Nehru was also prepared to undertake a postmortem on India's inability to preserve its political integrity. In a clear demonstration of his readiness to give his historical sensibility a public face and allow his historical understanding to pervade the contours of his political thought and economic policies, Nehru embraced the view that the cultural and emotional unity of India would not suffice in the age of the modern nation-state to furnish India with secure borders and political integrity. India had almost fatally succumbed to British rule, and modern political arrangements had an intractability that even the most resilient civilizations might find taxing. The decentralization that had been the strength of India as a civilization was disempowering to India as a nation-state, and while tempted to experiment with federalism, Nehru resolved that India would now be governed from a strong centre. Just as his view of centre-state relations was historically (mis)informed, so Nehru looked to the contemporary history of the Soviet Union, whose practical achievements he was to describe as tremendously impressive, in formulating plans for India's economic development. If the 'Soviet Revolution had advanced human society by a great leap ... and had laid the foundations for that new civilization toward which the world could advance',[16] then there could be no doubt that India's future likewise lay in centralized economic planning and investment in industrial infrastructure.

In an analogue to the dams and steel mills that Nehru had characterized as the future 'temples' of India, the new nation-state proceeded to initiate large projects of history-writing. These were designed to edify and instruct the public just as industrial schemes were intended to develop the country. At the very first meeting of the Indian Historical Records Commission held after the end of colonial rule, it was resolved to prepare an 'authentic and comprehensive' history of the 'freedom struggle'.[17] As a consequence, a committee was appointed in 1950, at the behest of the Government of India, to supervise the collection of material 'throwing light on the various phases and technique' of the 'freedom struggle' around the country, and so highlight its 'unique' character.[18] India had not merely achieved its 'independence': as the chairman of the committee, the distinguished historian and educational adviser Tara Chand put it, 'Independence is a negative concept. Its implication is absence of dependence; it has no positive connotation; it does not indicate the quality and character of the society which achieves political sovereignty after throwing off alien domination'.[19] Tara Chand could not have been unaware of the fact that in some circles India's attainment of freedom was prone to being characterized as a 'gift' from the British; moreover, the largely non-violent nature of the engagement, owing to Gandhi's leadership of the movement, had created the illusion that British rule in India had been, on the whole, a mild and gentlemanly affair.

It was, perforce, necessary to inject into the understanding of India's resistance to colonial domination the sense that Indians had to wage a 'struggle', that they had striven to be free: non-violent resistance can be active and aggressive, and so too violence is often the resort of the weak and the passive. 'Independence' spoke to the idea of accomplishment; 'freedom struggle' had in it something of the Promethean endeavour that every people must undertake to realize their full potential and confer dignity on the entire human race. 'Freedom is more than the mere absence of foreign control', Tara Chand noted, 'for it implies a society possessing certain positive attributes—a capacity to order its affairs in accordance with the will of the people, and a democratic way of life guaranteeing liberty and equality to all its members.'[20] It is as a 'freedom struggle' rather than as an 'independence movement' that the Indian state sought to enshrine the resistance to British rule in official histories; and it is as 'freedom fighters' that opponents of British rule are still celebrated in Indian histories and entitled to pensions from the state.

Over the next three decades, numerous state-sponsored histories of the freedom struggle were to make their appearance. Authorized to collect material and take other steps necessary for the preparation of an official history, the committee under Tara Chand created a Central Board of Editors under the chairmanship of Dr Syed Mahmud, a high-ranking official in the Ministry of Foreign Affairs. As the Board numbered among its members politicians and civil servants besides professional historians, it was soon recognized that the writing of a 'unified history' would be better entrusted to a single hand. The choice fell upon Tara Chand, whose name was associated with the 'Allahabad School'. The first volume of Tara Chand's *History of the Freedom Movement in India* appeared in 1961, and was followed by three other volumes. Moreover, realizing the enormous scope of its work, the Board itself passed a resolution at its first meeting in January 1953, requesting state governments to appoint committees to assist the Board in its collection of material. It is these state committees, and the organizations created in their wake, that were to generate official histories, which were often little more than compilations of source material, of the freedom struggle in those states. Most notable among these were multi-volume histories of the freedom struggle in Bihar, Madhya Pradesh, Uttar Pradesh, Andhra Pradesh, Hyderabad, and Bombay; in subsequent years, more modest efforts in this direction were made by other governments, such as Maharashtra (which had been created by the division of the old Bombay Presidency) and Orissa.[21]

Not unexpectedly, the official histories took on a largely hagiographic tone, with homage being rendered in reverential language to the martyrs of the revolution. This enterprise was, on occasion, no easy task, considering that in some parts of India the 'freedom struggle' had not been received with enthusiasm by Indians, while in others native rulers had even worked to suppress the nationalist movement. In writing the foreword to *Who's Who of Freedom Struggle in Andhra Pradesh*, a publication of the State Committee for the Compilation of the History Struggle in Andhra Pradesh, Channa Reddy, the Chairman of the aforementioned committee, was at pains to demonstrate that even Hyderabad, which under the Nizam had offered unstinting support to the British both during the Rebellion of 1857–8 and throughout the years of the nationalist movement, had contributed immeasurably to the freedom struggle since 'the people were considerably agitated' and had 'led an attack against the British Residency'. As Reddy was to note, 'It is a matter of common knowledge that the Telugu-speaking areas of the erstwhile Madras State were the foremost in the struggle in the South against the British imperialism. ... Perhaps, I may not be wrong if I were to venture to state that next to U.P., Andhra contributed the largest contingent of women Satyagrahis who willingly entered jails braving great hardships.'[22]

More belaboured still was the attempt of the author of the official history of the nationalist movement in Orissa, who was to note that the 'freedom struggle in Orissa began as far back as 3rd century BC when the Maurya Emperor Asoka invaded Kalinga in 261 BC. The Kalingan army faced the invader with grim determination and laid down their lives in thousands to save the freedom of their motherland.'[23] It was scarcely necessary, on this logic, to examine what freedom could have meant in third-century Kalinga, what (if any) place the idea occupied in India political philosophy, and whether the political structures were hospitable to the idea of freedom. Nor did the notion of an unbroken history of 'Oriya nationality' over three millennia appear to pose any problems for the author. Much like the English, who were prone to represent themselves as a people naturally imbued with the spirit of freedom, the Oriyas thought of 'being free' as their 'very life blood'; and the history of Orissa was, consequently, none other than the story of the Oriyas' continuing attempts, in true Enlightenment fashion, to retain their freedom: 'That sense of freedom has been all along with the Oriyas and Orissa was the last province in the country to come under the Mughal subjugation. It was, therefore, not unusual that these people should be fighting hand in hand and shoulder to shoulder with their brothers in other parts of the Country to free India from the British.'[24]

It is under the auspices of the Advisory Board for the History of [the] Freedom Movement in Uttar Pradesh that six volumes of *Freedom Struggle in Uttar Pradesh* were published between 1957 and 1961. Not coincidentally, all the volumes appeared on August 15 (Independence Day), January 26 (Republic Day), or October 2 (Mahatma Gandhi's birthday). Despite the blatantly nationalist tone of the undertaking, the intellectual agenda of the compilers and authors was more complex, as the endeavour was to dispel the notion that the Rebellion of 1857–8 was merely the aggregate of sporadic and spontaneous uprisings, lacking any coherence, direction, and the potential to be transformative. Indeed, the entire set was to be devoted to making available material pertaining to the Rebellion of 1857–8. The author of the foreword to Volume I gave it as his considered opinion that 'to those who have been prone to belittle the 1857 struggle as a mere sporadic mutiny of sepoys and a few disgruntled princes this material is bound to prove an eye-opener'. It was Uttar Pradesh, then the United Provinces, that 'constituted the principal theatre of the Struggle', and 'the emotions and aspirations that inspired her fighters' were the mainstay of the 'entire process of revolt and its organisation'.[25] Though it was well-known that histories of the freedom struggle had not been written by Europeans, who had been inclined only to record 'the achievements, trials and tribulations' of such of their countrymen as had come to 'carve out an Empire for their mother country', the editor thought that 'contemporary Indian scholars' had, in the matter of the Rebellion of 1857–8, 'done greater injustice to the historical truth' and 'intentionally suppressed the national character of the movement'. By striving to prove that the movement was the handiwork of 'a limited number of disloyal and mean wretches', they had succeeded even in contradicting the work of those English scholars 'who believed willingly or unwillingly that the upsurge was a national one'.[26] Though refraining from the observation that Indian history was, at this time, wholly derivative, the editor meant to imply all too clearly that Indian historians were themselves profoundly colonized.

While work on compilation of regional histories of the freedom struggle continued unabated, the Government of India sought to fulfill a yet more sacred task when it established an office to collect all the known works and speeches of the 'Father of the Nation'. This was doubtless a way of rendering homage to Gandhi, preserving the records of a large chunk of the history of the independence movement (at the helm of which Gandhi had stood for over two decades), and perhaps even keeping alive his name when he was already appearing as something of an embarrassment and anachronism to those elites who rendered craven submission to the West; more pointedly, it was also a way of asserting that Gandhi ought to occupy in the Indian imagination the place reserved in the Soviet Union for Marx and Lenin, the publication of whose collected writings in uniform volumes had become a matter of not only great state prestige, but a way of aiding communist revolutions around the world. The first volume of the *Collected Works of Mahatma Gandhi*, published with a massive state subsidy, made its appearance in 1958; and though it was presumed that Gandhi's writings would run to some sixty volumes, it is only in 1994 that the project was brought to a close with the publication of Volume 100 of the series.[27] Nothing as ambitious as this enterprise was to be attempted in respect to other principal figures of the nationalist movement, though many historians would be employed, as they still are today, in preparing volumes of selected writings, usually sponsored by regional governments, of numerous national heroes. Among those so honoured were Vallabhai Patel, one of Gandhi's principal associates and the man chiefly responsible for the integration of Indian states after partition; B. R. Ambedkar, the chief architect of the Indian constitution and venerated as the leader of the Dalits; and G. B. Pant, a principal leader of the nationalist movement in the United Provinces.

NATION-BUILDING AND
THE MAKING OF INDIAN HISTORY

Though histories of the freedom struggle were to instil in Indians a sense of pride in those of their countrymen and women who had devoted their lives to the attainment of freedom, and make them aware of the 'unique' nature of the struggle under the leadership of Gandhi and his associates, the pressing task of presenting a comprehensive account of Indian civilization, from remote antiquity to the end of British rule, remained. Until well into the late nineteenth century, Mill's *History of British India* (8 volumes), which Macaulay astonishingly described as the 'greatest historical work which has appeared in our language since that of Gibbon', had retained its paramount importance as a textbook in Indian universities and as a tool for training civil servants.[28] Though Mill, who did nothing to ingratiate himself with Indians with his numerous aspersions about them, such as the observation that 'in truth, the Hindu like the Eunuch, excels in the qualities of a slave',[29] was an easy target for attack by Indian intellectuals, the consensus of nationalist historians was that the work of most other British historians was only slightly less offensive to the sentiments of Indians, being just as rooted in palpable falsehoods. If Mill was animated by anti-Hindu feeling, other histories were inclined to view Muslims as, in the words of John Malcolm, the 'scourge of the human race'.[30]

No doubt some British historians and archaeologists had distinguished themselves by their devotion to learning, and on a rare occasion by their love, albeit paternalistic, for India. James Prinsep (1799–1840), who decoded the Brahmi script, was warmly remembered; likewise, James Tod's *Annals and Antiquities of Rajasthan* (2 volumes, 1829–32), would continue to evoke the admiration of Indian historians, since Tod's description of Hindus as a people who were 'affable, courteous to strangers, cheerful, enamoured of knowledge, lovers of justice, able in business, grateful, admirers of truth and of unfounded fidelity in all their dealings' was sufficient to endear him to Indians who had grown up with nothing else but Mill and his breed.[31] Nonetheless, British writers were, on the whole, perceived as having highly derogatory views of India, while to a considerable extent the energies of the two generations of Indian historians before 1950 were expended either on merely combating the British view of India, or on staking various political positions.

The supposition that India before the advent of British rule was altogether lacking in democratic institutions, or that the Hindu polity was irredeemably despotic, was keenly contested. Thus the early nationalist historian K. P. Jayaswal (1881–1937), in his *Hindu Polity* (1924), advanced the view that 'democratic and republican states were experiments of the Hindus themselves'; his contemporary, Radha Kumud Mookerji (1880–1964), while firmly rejecting the image of 'stagnant' Indian village communities, made a strong case for the presence of local self-governing institutions of a socialist variety in ancient India.[32] Many Indian historians were drawn to the study of ancient Indian culture: here, it was supposed, Hindu India was to be witnessed in its pristine glory, and here indubitably the essence of Indian civilization was to be discerned. The lives of Indian emperors began to appear as exemplary in their policy and conduct, and it required little encouragement to depict Ashoka, Chandragupta, or Harsha as paragons of wisdom, patrons of learning, and—most significantly—architects of Indian unity. As Mookerji, who was to write monographs on all these figures, besides more general accounts of *Nationalism in Hindu Culture* (1921) and *Hindu Civilization* (1957), put it in his study of Harsha, he provided 'one of the few examples in our ancient annals of a king who by his conquests made himself a king of kings and achieved the political unification of a large part of India as its paramount sovereign'.[33] In the lives of these early 'nationalists', as they had now become, there was inspiration enough for the present generation of nationalists labouring to achieve once again the sovereignty of India under Indian hands.

At the dawn of independence, then, though Indian historians appeared to have made considerable strides, particularly in the interpretation of ancient India, the prospects of a comprehensive history of India appeared rather unpromising. Yet it was altogether an intolerable thought that such a project should not be attempted, since no nation-state in our times can rest contented until it can produce a master narrative that documents the people's triumph over adversity, the nation-state coming into its own, and the fulfilment of a people's destiny. It is through history that a nation proudly occupies its place among the pantheon of nations. Secondly, there remained the vexatious question that no history could be construed as comprehensive or complete until it contested the British interpretation of the history of Islam in India, the logical outcome of which, at least on the nationalist reading, had been India's partition and the creation of Pakistan. As British writers (beginning with James Mill) had, following the example of European history itself, parcelled the history of India into three periods—ancient, medieval, and modern, which by sleight of hand became transformed, respectively, into Hindu, Muslim, and British (rather than Christian)—it remained to subject 'medieval' history to a thorough reinterpretation. Finally, there was also the consideration that, with the publication of the multi-volume *Cambridge History of India* (6 volumes, 1922–32), whose contributors with few exceptions were British, a nationalist rejoinder to that enterprise, which bore all the marks of authority and imperial fervour that

Cambridge histories carry, seemed imperative. Little in that history would have then suggested to the reader that the British were about to be stripped of their most formidable possession and consequently be reduced to a second-rate power.

As far back as 1937, Rajendra Prasad was to float a plan for the publication of a 20-volume history of India, but the scheme was abandoned after the publication of one volume.[34] The following year, the Indian History Congress, the first national association of Indian historians, was founded. At the 1940 annual session of the Indian History Congress, it was resolved to produce a 12-volume comprehensive history of India. When it became known that the Bharatiya Itihas Parishad [Indian History Organization] was planning on a similar undertaking, the two bodies decided to collaborate in a single venture. But this enterprise was similarly stalled: the first volume was not released until 1957, and another volume made its appearance only in 1970.[35] Meanwhile, the novelist, dramatist, and scholar of Gujarati culture, Kanaiyalal Maneklal Munshi, had founded the Bharatiya Vidya Bhavan, an educational institution dedicated to the promotion of Indian, and particularly Hindu, spiritual and cultural history.[36] Much like Bankim in Bengal, Munshi, who had an immensely successful career as a lawyer, turned to historical fiction, and his first three novels, *Patan-ni Prabhuta* ('The Greatness of Patan', 1916), *Gujarat-no Nath* ('Lord of Gujarat', 1918–19), and *Rajadhiraja* ('King of Kings', 1922–3), sought both to bring Gujaratis to an awareness of the 'greatness of their ancestors' and, contrariwise, of the demise of their culture under the Muslims. In his novel, *Jaya Somanatha* ('Victory to Somnath', 1937), Munshi dramatized Mahmud of Ghazni's destruction of the Somnath temple in or around 1026 AD. 'Desecrated, burnt, and battered', Munshi was to write of the temple which he visited in 1922, 'it still stood firm—a monument to our humiliation and ingratitude. I can scarcely describe the burning shame which I felt on that morning as I walked the broken floor of the once-hallowed *sabhamantap* littered with broken pillars and scattered stones.'[37] Munshi then resolved, one imagines, to restore Somnath to its previous glory.

Restoration and recovery were to figure prominently in Munshi's designs, which also envisioned a grand place for historical narratives, for a rejuvenated India. As he was to write a few years following independence, he had 'long felt the inadequacy of our so-called Indian histories', and from the very inception of the Bhavan in 1938 he started planning 'an elaborate history of India in order not only that India's past might be described by her sons, but also that the world might catch a glimpse of her soul as Indians see it'.[38] This scheme, like its predecessors, might well have foundered, but for the fact that the wealthy industrialist, G. D. Birla, decided to give it his financial support. The services of Ramesh C. Majumdar, who by then had made a considerable name for himself as a historian not only of India but of India's relations with neighbouring portions of the world that were once under its cultural orbit, were secured as general editor of the series, and by 1951 the first of eleven projected volumes of *The History and Culture of the Indian People* had been released. Subsequent volumes, published by the Bhavan itself, appeared in relatively quick succession, and with the publication in 1969 of the ninth volume on the *Struggle for Freedom*, Munshi could declare with satisfaction that his 'long-cherished ambition of preparing and publishing a comprehensive history and culture of the Indian people by Indians' had been nearly realized.[39] Most certainly, Majumdar and Munshi were able to attract contributions from what were then India's most prominent historians, Sanskritists, philosophers, and philologists; and perhaps the eminence with which the enterprise was to be regarded is borne out by the fact that it was to receive, some years after its commencement, the financial support of the Indian government.

As *The History and Culture of the Indian People* remains the most ambitious history of India by Indians ever attempted, it merits some critical attention. Munshi, who was to write a foreword to every volume, defined the political contours of the study at the outset. He noted that generations of Indians 'were told about the successive foreign invasions of the country, but little about how we resisted them and less about our victories'. Indeed, Munshi was inclined to the view that the 'role of alien invasions in the history of India' had been greatly 'exaggerated': the Aryan and Turko-Afghan conquests had, over time, 'lost their character of foreign military occupation', and only during the British period was the country 'governed essentially by foreigners from a foreign country and in foreign interests'. Though the 'Hindu social system' had been loudly decried as an execrable remnant of India's past, Munshi pointed to its role in protecting life and culture 'in times of difficulty by its conservative strength', and its vitality in enabling 'the national culture to adjust its central ideas to new conditions'.[40] During the entire period of India's occupation by conquering forces, the 'vitality of the race and culture' expressed itself 'with unabated vigour in resistance movements, military, political, and cultural'. What most of all vitiated the true understanding of Indian history, Munshi observed, was that the canons of modern historical research had been shaped by the attitude European scholars held towards 'ancient Egypt, Greece, and Rome, which have a dead past and are, in a sense, museum exhibits'.[41]

It is certainly no exaggeration to suggest—as only one instance of the consequences of deploying European history as a template for understanding India—that influenced by the continuous history of internecine religious warfare in Europe, British scholars took it for granted that a similar history characterized relations between Hindus and Muslims. At the same time, however, Munshi's own profoundly disturbing turn towards communalism cannot remain uncontested: what remains striking about his trajectory of thought is the manner in which he takes it as axiomatic that 'national culture' is nothing other than 'Hindu culture'. In the short manifesto outlining the principles for which the Bharatiya Vidya Bhavan stood, Munshi had stated that the 'ultimate aim of Bharatiya Shiksha [Indian education]' is 'to teach the younger generation to appreciate and live up to the permanent values of Bharatiya Vidya [knowledge] which is flowing from the supreme art of creative life-energy as represented by Shri Ramachandra, Shri Krishna, Vyasa, Buddha and Mahavira', and which in modern times manifested itself in the lives of Sri Ramakrishna, Vivekananda, Aurobindo, Dayanand Saraswati, and Gandhi.[42] Though the inclusion of the Buddha and Mahavira might appear to stand as testimony to Munshi's ecumenism, this is quite unremarkable, as Hindus with great ease assimilate the Buddha and Mahavira into the fold of Hinduism. Indeed, Munshi himself remarked that the 'Buddha made no break in [the] cultural continuity' of Hindu civilization, and 'the process of absorption was completed when Buddha became an *avatara* of Vishnu, and Mahayana Buddhism was absorbed in Vaishnavism and Saivism'.[43] For Munshi, the contours and texture of Indian civilization had been set by the ancient Hindus, long before civilization emerged elsewhere in the world, and most certainly before Islam, as he was wont to argue, disturbed the social fabric of Indian life.[44] It is in the crucible of this civilization that all that is good and just was shaped, before barbaric foreigners sought to leave their imprint: thus, on Munshi's account, women were honored in ancient India, and distinguished themselves even as queens and warriors; but this harmony was shattered: 'About the beginning of the Christian era, however,—perhaps it was under the influence of the foreigners— the spiritual disenfranchisement of women began', and no doubt under the Muslims, the position of women was further eroded.[45]

If Munshi had specified the broad parameters of the multi-volume history, Majumdar was to delineate more sharply the specific tenor of the arguments. As one might reasonably surmise, he objected to the pervasive narrative of Oriental Despotism present in British histories of India, and shared Munshi's view that attempts to model one's understanding of Indian history on the basis of the experience of European nations, or other ancient civilizations, were bound to be unproductive. In the 'continuity of her history and civilization' lay one distinguishing feature of India, since ancient Persia, Egypt, Greece, Babylon, Assyria, and Sumer had all perished; no less important was the fact that one had perforce to 'adopt a different scale of values in order to appraise her culture and civilization', since in India it was not the rise and fall of empires, or the development of political ideas and institutions that mattered, but rather 'philosophy, religion, art, and letters, the development of social and moral ideas, and the general progress of those humanitarian ideals and institutions which form the distinctive feature of the spiritual life of India and her greatest contribution to the civilization of the world'.[46] However, while purporting to critique the Orientalist framework of knowledge, which had made impossible any 'authentic' history of India, Majumdar was himself replicating a cardinal feature of the Orientalist's epistemology, namely the distinction between a 'materialist West' and 'spiritual East'.

Just as problematic was to be Majumdar's view about the place of Islam in Indian history. His remarks in *The Vedic Age* made unmistakably clear his view of Islam as a religious force that, whatever its other merits might be, led to the utter degradation of Indian civilization; and transposing the equation, common among European scholars, of the European middle or dark ages with superstition, magic, and religious bigotry, to the Indian scene he arrived at the reading that the medieval or Islamic period represented the dark side of Indian history. As he was to write, in obvious contradiction of the view he had espoused about the *sui generis* nature of Indian history, and in just as obvious emulation of European categories of experience, 'the onslaught of Islam, accompanied by a marked decadence of culture and the disappearance of the creative spirit in art and literature, seems to mark AD 1000 as the beginning of the Medieval Age'.[47] In explaining the basis for the organization of the series, Majumdar noted that the Vedic Age represented 'the dawn of Hindu civilization'; the period from 600 BC to 750 AD, the subject of volumes 2 and 3, marked the 'full morning glory and noonday splendour' of that civilization, just as in the period from 750 AD to 1300 AD, the subject of volumes 4 and 5, were to be seen the 'shadows of the declining day' and the advent of 'dusk'.

Islam arrived in India in the eighth century, and had become dominant in parts of north India by the eleventh century; and it was in 1296 that Allaudin Khilji captured the Delhi Sultanate, thereby establishing its imperial phase: in Majumdar's words, 'Then follows the darkness of the long night, so far as Hindu civilization is concerned, a darkness which envelops it even now.'[48] In all this, Majumdar chose to remain oblivious to well-established facts or opinions about Khilji, from his marriages to Rajput women and friendships with Jain ascetics to, more significantly, his insistence on placing the state above Islam.[49] Though resentful of India's subjection to foreign rulers over a long period of time, Majumdar should, one thinks, have been more admiring of Allaudin's repeatedly successful repulsion of the Mongol invasions of India between 1297 and 1303, but perhaps he saw little to distinguish between what he took to be two forms of barbarism. True, Ziya al-din Barani, the most important chronicler of the early history of the Delhi Sultanate, admitted that Allaudin had issued instructions that Hindus were to be so suppressed as to make them incapable of fomenting rebellion, but by the same token Allaudin rejected the idea that strict Islamic injunctions were to guide him in the task of governance. Indeed, the authors of a modern history of India opine that Allaudin was 'rather impartial in his oppression, his measures being aimed at Muslim courtiers just as much as against Hindu notables and middlemen'.[50] In all his actions, Allaudin appears to have been guided by the consideration that he would take whatever measures, 'lawful or unlawful', that he thought 'to be for the good of the State'.[51]

If darkness appeared to Majumdar to envelop Hindu civilization even after independence, it is worthwhile probing how, in the latter volumes, Majumdar represented the quest for freedom from British rule. In most respects, the arguments of Volume 11, *The Struggle for Freedom* (1969), a massive tome to which Majumdar was almost the lone contributor, had been foreshadowed in his *History of the Freedom Movement in India* (3 volumes, 1962–3), a work undertaken by him to signal his differences with the official view. Here he had suggested that Hindus lost their freedom, long before the arrival of the Europeans, when they submitted to Muslim rule; and that though Hindus and Muslims had lived together, they did so as separate nations.[52] Elsewhere he openly decried, as an offence against canons of historical truth, the 'distinct and conscious attempt to rewrite the whole chapter of the bigotry and intolerance of the Muslim rulers towards Hindu religion'.[53] This, in turn, bound Majumdar to the view that the events of 1857–8 could in no manner be construed as a nationalist uprising in which Hindus and Muslims joined forces to evict the British, and the attempt to argue otherwise, from the expedient political motive of creating communal harmony, seemed reprehensible to him. Majumdar agreed with the colonial view that Indian nationalism was itself a consequence of the introduction of Western ideas in India; likewise, while acknowledging Gandhi's services to the nation, he was inclined to the view that the extremists contributed as much to the cause of Indian freedom, which in the last instance was made possible by the demise of British power.[54]

In the *Struggle for Freedom*, which carries the history of India from the partition of Bengal in 1905 to the attainment of independence, Majumdar was to press these points further. What is striking, and yet almost imperceptible, is the manner in which he represents Islam. In the chapter on religion, Majumdar reviewed developments in Hinduism, such as the activities of the Arya Samaj, the Ramakrishna Mission, and the Hindu Mahasabha, as well as developments in Sikhism. But the pages on Islam are relegated to an appendix,[55] as an afterthought, and as though its history forms only an incidental, peripheral, and certainly unfortunate part of the history of India. Majumdar insisted on taking the 'realistic', rather than 'idealistic',[56] approach to Hindu-Muslim relations, and it is in the application of this criterion that he found Gandhi truly wanting, deficient in political realism. Gandhi's controversial support of the Khilafat movement,[57] Majumdar maintained, was to be explained principally on the 'grounds of expediency',[58] though he seems to have little understood that Gandhi, alone of all the political leaders of our times, repudiated the principle of reciprocity. Gandhi did not cave in to repeated offers from Muslim leaders that the Muslim abnegation from cow-slaughter would be the reward for support of the Khilafat movement: rather, his support was given unreservedly in an attempt to endow the Muslim community with political meaning and intent, and to draw Muslims into the political life of India following a long period of marginalization. (Gandhi also had, though this observation takes us far afield, an extraordinarily expansive and magnanimous conception of the 'gift'.) Again, it is argued by Majumdar that the Quit India movement of 1942 was not predominantly non-violent, and that no credit should be given to Gandhi for carrying out what purports to be a 'glorious revolution which led us to our goal of freedom'.[59] Indeed, with the 'failure' of the Quit India movement, Gandhi ceased to be at the helm of affairs, and henceforth, in Majumdar's view, the battle was to be fought mainly by Subhas Chandra Bose. Yet Majumdar in no way deems Bose's actions as expedient, though he struck an agreement with the Japanese and the Nazis on the grounds that any enemy of Britain was a friend of India.[60] Majumdar's account of the political negotiations leading to independence and the partition of India ends with the observation that Gandhi and other 'Hindu leaders' allowed themselves to believe that the slogan of 'Hindu-Muslim Brotherhood' was a reality, something more than merely an empty vessel which Muslim communalists would exploit to their own ends.[61]

COMMUNALISM AS AN EMERGING FORCE IN INDIAN HISTORY

Throughout the 1950s and 1960s, Majumdar was the most prolific of all Indian historians, and in India he remained supremely influential. Few historians anywhere in the world had been active for as long as six to seven decades. Yet his readings of Indian history have little for which to commend themselves, and not only because they are characterized by a virulent anti-Muslim sentiment. His animus towards Gandhi is quite unremarkable, since among a class of historians and scholars, most prominently in Bengal, it had become a matter of honour to regard Gandhi not only as ineffective and misguided, possibly even as the author of the great 'sin' of partition, but as one who betrayed the possibilities of the Bengal Renaissance. Though critical of the British historiography of India, Majumdar never disguised his admiration for the British for having ushered India, as he thought, into the era of modernity, enabling Indians to free themselves of the onerous burden of age-old superstitions and oppressive customs, and in this matter as in all others he subscribed to the most conventional view of the Indian past. Moreover, on his view, the British rid India of the tyranny of Muslim rule, a signal achievement in itself. He wholly endorsed the view of the nineteenth-century Bengali historian, Sir Jadunath Sarkar (1870–1958), that the Bengal Renaissance, as initiated by Rammohun Roy, whose efforts in part led to the official abolition of sati in 1829, was 'truly a Renaissance, wider, deeper, and more revolutionary than that of Europe after the fall of Constantinople'.[62] While incapable of understanding the subtlety of Gandhi's thought, Majumdar could sense that Gandhi appeared to be repudiating all the strides that had been taken in Bengal with his critique of science and modernity.

It is in his pedestrian attachment to 'facts', however, that Majumdar most came to represent the dominant strand of Indian historiography from 1947 until at least the mid-1970s. In setting forth the historical agenda of the *History and Culture of the Indian People*, Majumdar asked the 'student of Indian history' to suspend judgment, repudiate 'false doctrines', be prepared to face hostility, and 'follow the modern method of scientific research'. The data had to be sifted through 'by all rational methods', and the mind had to be applied 'fearlessly and without prejudice and preconceptions to the study of all available evidence'. The historian was bound to respect only one aim, 'the discovery of the truth, and nothing but the truth'.[63] This ambition is scarcely surprising, considering that the Indian historian that Majumdar and his generation admired the most was the prodigious Jadunath Sarkar, most recognized for his works on the Mughal Empire in the age of Aurangzeb. Sarkar was often likened to the German historian Leopold von Ranke and became known as the principal expositor in India of 'modern scientific historiography'. The attitude of Ranke, whose plodding works aimed at an exactness of detail, can be judged by the aphorism for which he is remembered, namely that the task of the historian is 'simply to show how it [the past] really was', though as has been argued recently, Ranke was himself a thoroughgoing idealist.[64]

In his Presidential Address to the History Section of the Bangiya Sahitya Sammelan [Bengali Literature Conference] in 1915, Sarkar declared that the 'best method in historical studies is the scientific method', by which he meant little more than the necessity for the historian to disavow fictions and embrace the truth. Truth could be unpalatable, opposed to popular notions: 'But still I shall seek truth, understand truth and accept truth. This should be the firm resolve of an historian.' Recalling Aristotle's distinction between history and poetry, Sarkar reminded his audience that the historian had to be aware that 'history is not poetry', and that the 'shining examples' of truth discovered from the past would 'throw light on our future path. This is the greatest achievement of historical studies ... .'[65] Writing in 1937 to Rajendra Prasad, who had invited him to become the become the chief editor of the aborted 20-volume history of India, Sarkar described 'national history' as a worthwhile endeavour only when it was 'true as regards the facts and reasonable in the interpretation of them'.[66] That truth might be polysemic, speaking in numerous voices, was not a possibility that Sarkar or Majumdar would have entertained; and neither did they ruminate over their easy recourse to the British empiricist tradition, with its clear separation of subject and object, and consider how it is that facts get constituted as facts.

Though Sarkar had set up 'reasonable' interpretations as the desirable end of the fetish with facts, debates in Indian history suggest that criteria for what is 'reasonable' are, to put it mildly, not so easily established. It is possible to argue that the first decisive shift in modern Indian historiography occurred in the late 1950s, following the publication of D. D. Kosambi's *An Introduction to the Study of Indian History* (1956), which helped to move historical discourse towards an engagement with questions pertaining to class conflict, social transformation, and the economic structures of society.[67] Certainly by the early 1970s, the focus of contemporary Indian historians was beginning to shift from the obsessive concern with the 'freedom struggle' to a wider array of questions in political, cultural, and social history. The 1971 war with Pakistan brought to the fore questions of ethnicity, language, and nation-formation, just as the Pakistani army's massacre of Bengali intellectuals brought an awareness of the precariousness of intellectual life in South Asia. The unrest of the mid-1970s, leading to the declaration of an internal emergency in 1975, the arrest of thousands of political figures, and the regime of censorship (some of it self-imposed) politicized many teachers and researchers, many of whom had hitherto been content to practice what they considered to be 'objective' scholarship. The virtually unchallenged supremacy of the Congress party had been seriously fractured, and the ascendancy of numerous other parties, including what was then the Jana Sangh, which championed the interests of Hindus, was to introduce new factors into Indian politics. The state's commitment to secularism was no longer to seem so secure. Meanwhile, the special relationship, as it was imagined, with the Soviet Union no doubt served to strengthen ties to Marxist scholars, and a very considerable strand of 'left scholarship' was soon to leave its imprint upon the study of Indian history. The establishment of Jawaharlal Nehru University (JNU), an institution almost exclusively for graduate studies where (it was rumoured) only scholars with pronounced left inclinations could expect to be hired, certainly gave Marxist historians a boost, and it is from JNU that nationalist and communalist historians alike have since received some of the most concerted resistance.

While a constellation of factors pointed to the emergence, in the 1970s, of newer forms of history writing, communalism was to assume a heightened importance in historical narratives. As I shall dwell on this subject at various points in this book, it is desirable to etch the broad contours of communalism in the writing of Indian history at this juncture, as many of the developments in Indian history, and in those narrative forms which have drawn upon history, must otherwise remain unintelligible. In the communal view of Indian history, which was to become one of the bedrocks of the British construction of Indian society and an eminent instrumentality of governance, the primordial and fundamental element of an Indian's identity is religion. Though it can readily be conceded that religion has played an important (and perhaps even pivotal) role in every society, and that it—along with class, ethnicity, gender, and linguistic affiliation—provides a modality for determining identity, the communalist view insists on the exceptional place of religion in the constitution of identity in India. Once it is recognized that an Indian is a Muslim, Hindu, or Sikh before he or she is anything else, community-formation is also seen to proceed along the lines of religion. Thus, in the communalist view, Indians have always constituted themselves pre-eminently into religious communities, where other people, such as Americans, might be seen as constituting themselves into communities of homosexuals, sports-lovers, gun-owners, so on. Finally, to follow the seemingly implacable logic of the communalist view, in India it so transpires that these religious communities must invariably be at war with each other, howsoever attenuated the hostilities may be at any time. As one British official put it in his book, *Dawn in India* (1930), 'the animosities of centuries are always smouldering beneath the surface'.[68] Partly such animosity arises from the nature of religion itself and the rigid attachment to beliefs that it induces; partly it arises from the 'fanaticism' of the Muslim and the absurd 'superstition' of the Hindu; and partly it is the consequence of the juxtaposition of two faiths that, as British (and later Indian) writers were prone to argue, are wholly or largely incompatible.

A communalist reading of Indian history, then, can take many forms. A class conflict, say between a Hindu landlord and Muslim landless labourer, is likely to be represented by the communal-minded historian as a religious conflict; and the same historian, taking the communal argument to more absurd lengths, might be predisposed to argue that north Indian classical music, in some *gharanas* (schools) of which Muslims have been preeminent for a very long time, is 'Muslim', while south Indian classical music, a domain from which Muslims are almost entirely absent, is 'Hindu'. The communalist generally finds 'south Indian' culture to be a true repository of the Hindu sensibility, since Muslim influence was considerably less pervasive in most of the south, and of little consequence in the Tamil heartland, though the non-Aryan features of the south are often cause for alarm. Communalist historians, when they have not taken the view that adherents of different faiths were often at war with each other, have usually adopted the view that Muslims and Hindus had little in common, and lived largely separate existences; on the other hand, those historians who subscribe to the view that India had a largely syncretistic past emphasize the customs in common between Hindus and Muslims, the various forms of mixed culture—from cuisine and everyday practices to architecture and music—that emerged from their proximity to each other, and even the forms of religious worship shared by them, such as the devotion offered at the *dargahs* (tombs) of Sufi *pirs* (religious teachers).

ARYANS AS BEEF-EATERS, MUGHALS AS FOREIGNERS: ICONIC DEBATES IN INDIAN HISTORY

In the debates over Indian history, the syncretistic and communalist viewpoints have conventionally been represented, to take one case in point, by offering a contrast between the lives of the two emperors under whom the Mughal Empire was at its zenith, Akbar (reigned 1556–1605) and Aurangzeb (reigned 1658–1707). Akbar is often adduced as an example of the tolerant ruler, whose policies demonstrate that though he himself was a Muslim, the state under him was not Islamic. Some have even pointed to Akbar as a 'secular' ruler, when scarcely any monarch in Europe was such, and his advocacy of a new faith, the *Din-i-ilahi*, which combined elements from various religions, exemplifies the ecumenism with which he is associated. 'He looked upon all religions alike', writes Tara Chand, 'and regarded it his duty to make no difference between his subjects on the basis of religion. He threw open the highest appointments to non-Muslims.'[69] Though it is admitted that Akbar may have forged political and military alliances with Hindu rulers from considerations of expediency, other historians allude to more enduring signs of his real commitment to religious harmony and interest in different faiths, such as his marriage to Rajput women, his scholarly interest in epics such as the Ramayana, and his zeal in promoting Hindu learning. Historians point to Akbar's elimination of the *jizya* (poll-tax) usually levied on non-Muslims and his assumption of final authority on religious questions on which there might have been conflict of opinion among Muslim theologians, thereby undermining the authority of the *ulama* (Muslim clergy). Describing Akbar's success as 'astonishing', Jawaharlal Nehru gave it as his opinion, in a work that places him among the ranks of historians, that Akbar 'created a sense of oneness among the diverse elements of north and central India'.[70]

The commonplace view of Aurangzeb, on the other hand, is that he repudiated Akbar's policies of religious toleration, and by alienating Hindus he undermined the very empire whose tremendous expansion he masterminded. Nehru maintained that Aurangzeb had 'put the clock back', undoing what his predecessors had achieved by working against the 'genius of the nation' and ignoring the common culture that had been forged among the different elements of the Indian population. 'When Aurangzeb began to oppose this movement [of synthesis] and suppress it and to function more as a Moslem than an Indian ruler', Nehru argued, 'the Mughal Empire began to break up.' But where Nehru saw Aurangzeb as a 'bigot and an austere puritan' whose policies were instrumental in creating unease and dissent, and Tara Chand deplored his 'misdirected efforts' which caused 'irreparable damage' to the 'great edifice of the empire',[71] many Indian historians have been inclined to take a much harsher view of Aurangzeb's conduct. In this they were to follow the lead supplied by Jadunath Sarkar, whose 1928 biography of Aurangzeb in four volumes bequeathed the view of Aurangzeb that still predominates in the popular imagination. Sarkar suggested that Aurangzeb intended nothing less than to establish an Islamic state in India, an objective that could not be fulfilled without 'the conversion of the entire population to Islam and the extinction of every form of dissent'; and to render this scenario more complete, he proposed that the jizya on non-Muslims, which Aurangzeb had re-instituted in 1679, was aimed at forcibly converting Hindus to Islam, though he was unable to marshal evidence to substantiate this view.[72]

Doubtless, Sarkar's view is held by some modern historians as well,[73] but to suggest that inducements were held out to convert, as they are in modern political cultures with diverse objectives in mind, seems to be rather different from the proposition that there was an official policy beyond mere encouragement which aimed at conversion. Then, as now, conversion would have been more attractive to the vast number of Hindus living under the tyranny of caste oppression, though this raises other ethical considerations which historians, of whatever political persuasion, have largely disavowed. Recent historical scholarship, however, has complicated some of the common assumptions with which conversion is viewed, and Sarkar's argument is not easily reconciled with Richard Eaton's finding that 'in the subcontinent as a whole there is an inverse relationship between the degree of Muslim political penetration and the degree of Islamization'.[74] The entire discussion on conversion in twentieth-century historical literature has, moreover, rested on the usually unstated assumption that if Islam's penetration into the Indian countryside is to be explained as a consequence of forcible conversion of the lower castes and captives of war, that stands in diametrical opposition to Hinduism's repudiation of proselytization. Discourses that hover around the relationship of Islam and conversion are, in the Indian context, just as much discourses about Hinduism's allegedly unique disavowal of conversion.[75]

If Aurangzeb was so ferocious a communalist, why is it, some historians have asked, that the number of Hindus employed in positions of eminence under Aurangzeb's reign rose from 24.5 per cent in the time of his father Shah Jahan to 33 per cent in the fourth decade of his own rule? They suggest, moreover, that Aurangzeb did not indiscriminately destroy Hindu temples, as he is commonly believed to have done, and that he directed the destruction of temples only when faced with insurgency.[76] This was almost certainly the case with the Keshava Rai temple in the Mathura region, where the Jats rose in rebellion; and yet even this policy of reprisal may have been modified, as Hindu temples in the Deccan were seldom destroyed. The image of Aurangzeb as an idol-breaker may not withstand scrutiny, since there is evidence to show that, like his predecessors, he continued to confer land grants (*jagirs*) upon Hindu temples, such as the Someshwar Nath Mahadev temple in Allahabad, Jangum Badi Shiva temple in Banaras, Umanand temple in Gauhati, and numerous others.[77] On the other hand, one might argue, if Akbar was so dedicated to the principle of religious harmony, why is it that none of the Mughal princesses were ever allowed to marry into Rajput households? And while he may have propagated a new syncretistic faith, how was it received by ordinary Muslims? Moreover, do not both the supporters of Akbar and critics of Aurangzeb presume that relations between Hindus and Muslims are to be inferred by studying the lives of rulers, or at best members of the ruling class? What, in any case, is really conceded when it is admitted that Akbar was tolerant towards other faiths to the same extent that Aurangzeb was only solicitous of the welfare of his Muslim subjects? As the historian Harbans Mukhia has argued, 'Once one accepts that the liberal religious policy of Akbar was only the reflection of his own liberal outlook, the conclusion becomes inescapable, for instance, that the fanatic religious policy of Aurangzeb flowed from his fanatic disposition.'[78] If Aurangzeb sought to convert members of important Hindu families to Islam, all the more to ensure the preservation of his empire, why should that serve as a basis for the presumption that a wholesale conversion of Hindus was a matter of state policy? By what method of transference is it possible to construe that conflicts among the ruling elite are conflicts at the broader social level? Why, moreover, should Aurangzeb's annexation of Mawar be viewed as indicative of his desire to crush Hindu resistance, as an episode in Hindu-Muslim relations, rather than as an aspect of Mughal-Rajput relations?[79]

In the debate over the nature of the Indian past, particularly with respect to Hindu–Muslim relations, Akbar and Aurangzeb were to become, as they still are, iconic figures. No less important has been the Maratha leader Shivaji (1627/30–80),[80] who offered tenacious resistance to Aurangzeb, and was raised to the eminence of a 'freedom fighter' and 'nationalist' by nineteenth-century Indian nationalists in search of martial heroes. The Indian nationalist Lala Lajpat Rai, known to school children as the 'Lion of the Punjab', published a biography of Shivaji in Urdu (1896), and commended him to the attention of the youth with the observation that 'Shivaji protected his own religion, saved the cow and the Brahmin but he did not disrespect any other religion. This is the highest praise that can be bestowed on a Hindu hero like Shivaji in the days of Aurangzeb.' Shivaji's life demonstrated that 'during any time [sic] in Muslim rule Hindus did not lose any opportunity to show their valour and attain freedom nor did they quietly suffer oppression'.[81] So long as Indian nationalists persisted in portraying Shivaji as a Hindu leader who withstood Aurangzeb's attempts to impose his tyrannical rule upon the Deccan, they were given no hindrance by the British; but when the nationalist Bal Gangadhar Tilak (1856–1920) invoked Shivaji's name and courage to rouse Indians to resistance against British rule, he was convicted on the charge of sedition. The emergence of Gandhi, and the adoption by the Indian National Congress of non-violence as its official policy, did little to erode the popularity in which Shivaji was held. His name was kept alive by armed revolutionaries and by a nation, stung by charges that it was effete and incapable of offering resistance, eager to flaunt a martial past; and the emergence of communalism in the 1920s, leading eventually to demands for the creation of a Muslim state, again made it possible to urge resistance to Muslim demands in the name of Shivaji.

While Shivaji's name could not so easily be invoked after the assassination of Gandhi in January 1948 by Marathi-speaking Hindus, he had already been partly divinized as one of those martial heroes who kept the banner of Hindu India floating despite adversity and India's enslavement under 'foreign' rule. With the creation in 1960 of the new state of Maharashtra, carved out of the old Bombay presidency, Shivaji became canonized as the creator of the Marathi nation, and the celebration in 1974 of the 300th anniversary of his coronation was to furnish ripe opportunities for consolidating the view that he was a 'national' leader. To take any other view was to invite retribution, as one Marathi historian at Marathwada University found out in 1974 when he was dismissed from his position for disputing the hagiographic view of Shivaji.[82] One volume of contributions, mainly by historians, was entitled *Chhatrapati Shivaji: Architect of Freedom* (1975). Its editor states that Shivaji 'laid the foundation of a nation-state, the state of the Marathas, on a firm, secular basis'. But what is this nation-state of the Marathas,[83] and of what 'freedom' was Shivaji the architect? Though for the greater part of the eighteenth century the Marathas would be the dominant power in the Deccan, and keep the Mughal Empire at bay, the argument of Maratha sovereignty cannot easily be sustained—as the defeat of the entire Maratha army at the hands of the Afghan chief, Ahmad Shah Abdali, on the historic battlefield of Panipat in 1761 so amply suggests.

It was to mark his independence from the Mughals, and to repudiate his formal relation to them of a feudatory, that Shivaji had himself crowned, but that very gesture of defiance points to the fact that he recognized the overwhelming power of the Mughals. Moreover, as a lower-caste person, Shivaji had perforce to enact some ceremony by means of which he could be raised to the status of a *kshatriya* or traditional ruler: thus, in every respect, his coronation pointed to his anxieties about his origins and subservience. His successors, taking advantage of the weakness of the later Mughals, would play more the role of plunderers and marauders than kings while still acting as the tax-collectors for the Mughal emperors; by the second half of the eighteenth century, they were also contending with the military strength of the East India Company's forces, though they were nonetheless able to capture Delhi and Agra, the nerve centers of the Mughal Empire, in 1770-1. But there never was much of a 'Maratha nation-state'.

Similarly, it is only possible to characterize Shivaji as the 'architect of freedom' on the presumption that Hindus were labouring under severe disadvantages and were suffocated by Muslim tyranny before Shivaji freed them from their woes. One historian, taking this view, put the matter rather dramatically in another volume commemorating the tercentenary of Shivaji's coronation when he described Shivaji as having liberated the Marathas from three centuries of 'alien rule' which had 'turned the natives fatalistic': 'It was Shivaji who emancipated them from this terrific mental torpidity. He created in them self-confidence ... . He gave them back their dearly loved religious freedom.'[84] Yet this assessment appears almost moderate, when we consider Majumdar's opinion that in the whole history of India, there was no Hindu other than Shivaji 'who made such a pious resolve in his mind to save his country and religion from foreign yoke and oppression'. Dismissing with utter contempt the position of 'modern Hindu politicians and pseudo-historians' who insist on 'a complete assimilation between the Hindus and Muslims after the first fury of intolerance and oppression was over', Majumdar remarked: 'But Shivaji was in any case free from such ideas. He looked upon the Muslims as oppressive rulers and the Hindus as long-suffering subject peoples.'[85] It is a chilling fact that the most celebrated act of Shivaji's life should be his killing of Afzal Khan, a Mughal commander who is described as having attempted the murder of Shivaji but who evidently received a fatal dose of his own medicine before he could fulfill his treacherous designs. As the Khan's dagger struck at Shivaji's side, the Maratha passed his arm around the Khan's waist and 'tore his bowels open with a blow of steel claws' that were hidden in the palms of his hand. The 'Afzal Khan affair', exulted one scholar amidst the euphoria of the celebrations in 1974–5, 'marks the most glorious event in the history of the Marathas'.[86]

To substantiate the Hindu communalist reading of Shivaji as the architect of Hindu freedom requires that Hindu–Muslim conflict be seen as the backdrop of his own times, just as it turns him into an inveterate foe of Muslims. The communalist interpretations, for instance, usually ignore the telling fact that following his coronation, Shivaji struck a military alliance with the Muslim leader, the Qutb Shah Sultan, and together they waged a campaign against Shivaji's own half-brother, Vyankoji Bhonsle. Nehru's pointed remark that 'Shivaji, though he fought Aurangzeb, freely employed Moslems', should be viewed in a similar vein, as an attempt to contradict the communalist interpretation.[87] There is little documentary evidence to warrant the conclusion that Hindus in present-day Maharashtra, before Shivaji apparently arrived to liberate them from their yoke, were being systematically persecuted, either by way of outright discrimination, the destruction of their temples, or forcible conversions; quite to the contrary, many Muslim dynasties in the south retained a catholic attitude towards Hinduism. Few historians in the 1970s, as communalism was becoming an important force in the writing of Indian history, were prepared to reflect on how far it is possible to infer from Shivaji's encounters with Afzal Khan and Aurangzeb that people belonging to various social strata similarly felt their lives to be bounded by oppositional religious feelings. Yet, just as Aurangzeb and Akbar had become symbolic figures in the emerging dispute between secularists and communalists, so Shivaji was to become an iconic figure in the struggle to define the 'authentic' history of India.[88]

One of the most hotly contested terrains of dispute was to be history textbooks, which, with respect to schools affiliated to the Central Board of Secondary Education (CBSE), come under the purview of the National Council for Educational and Research Training (NCERT), an autonomous institution that nonetheless owes its existence to government funding. The debate over textbooks since the advent to power of the BJP in 1998 appears to have been largely anticipated in the textbook controversy of 1977–9, which makes it something of more than mere historical interest. In May 1977, a few months after the Janata had been swept into power, V. Shankar, the principal secretary to Morarji Desai, made it known in a memorandum to the Education Minister that the Prime Minister was unhappy about certain history textbooks with 'controversial and biased material', and he thought it probable that the Education Ministry could have them withdrawn from circulation. Desai seemed to be keen that 'readers do not get wrong ideas about various elements of our history and culture', and the memorandum submitted to the Prime Minister identified four works, three of them textbooks[89]—Romila Thapar's *Medieval India* (1957), Bipan Chandra's *Modern India* (1970), and *Freedom Struggle* (1972) by Amales Tripathi, Barun De, and Bipan Chandra—as unacceptably soft on Islam's bloody history in India, unnecessarily critical of nationalists such as Tilak and Aurobindo, and not sufficiently appreciative of the unique tenor of Hindu civilization. No sooner had the controversy commenced than R. S. Sharma's *Ancient India* was published, and it likewise came under scrutiny. The three books on which the controversy came to centre, on ancient, medieval, and modern India, were published by NCERT for use in high schools. What was also said to be common to these works was their left and aggressively secular orientation to Indian history.

A Professor of History at JNU, Bipan Chandra had come to be identified with a left-nationalist view of Indian history. Unlike his fellow Marxist scholars, who were often prone to dismiss the nationalist movement under the Congress as a bourgeois enterprise, Bipan Chandra submitted that the nationalist movement was the only substantial nationalist movement that India had, and that it was critical for the 'nation-in-the-making'. While embracing Marx's theory of social relations, he found that Marx himself subscribed to a largely colonialist interpretation of India. Chandra objected forcefully, moreover, to the communalist view of Indian history, and saw communalism as a divisive force, which the British did everything to promote, that tunneled the energies of the nationalists into unproductive and ultimately disastrous channels. 'To declare Akbar or Aurangzeb a "foreigner" and [Rana] Pratap or Shivaji a "national" hero', he wrote in obvious rejection of communalist history, 'was to project into past history the communal outlook of 20th century India. This was not only bad history; but was also a blow to national unity.'[90] Chandra's reference to the 'communal outlook of 20th century India' suggested to his detractors that he had a rather romantic idea of India's supposed composite culture in the medieval period, and that his very critique of communalism was based on a distortion of the historical record.

Chandra's colleague in JNU's Centre for Historical Studies, Romila Thapar, stood similarly charged of pandering to Muslim sentiments and overlooking the history of Muslim oppression. Her handling of facts was not, as Shankar's memorandum stressed, in question; but her interpretive strategies, and ideological predilections, made her gloss over, in the name of a false secularism, the blatant oppressions of Muslim rulers. 'For example', wrote Shankar, 'Mahmud Ghazni's destroying of Hindu temples has been justified on the ground that he wanted to plunder them. His proud claim as breaker of idols has been almost ignored.' Similarly, the note pointed to the 'subtle manner' in which 'Aurangzeb's religious intolerance' was not merely tolerated but 'defended', and it objected to Thapar's unwillingness to attribute the decline of the Mughal Empire in part to policies pursued by Aurangzeb which alienated his subjects and depleted his treasury.[91]

More strenuous still were to be the objections to Sharma's book on ancient India. A very prominent Marxist scholar, Sharma was then

Professor of History and Dean of the Faculty of Social Sciences at Delhi University. The memorandum submitted to the government claimed that 'communist' intellectuals had infiltrated 'important national building Ministries and allied organisations', and were promoting, with grants to 'fellow travellers', their 'own way of thinking on their favourite subjects which presented a completely different view of the image of the country far removed from our traditional and cultural and scientific values'. Adverting to NCERT's vital role in building up the character of youth through their textbooks, Shankar's note expressed concern that 'the greatest casualty' of the alien way of thinking represented by Marxist scholars was 'in the highly important subject of history'.[92] One suspects that with the India of antiquity being the repository of everything that was imagined to be good and beautiful in Hindu civilization, and with textbooks routinely highlighting the Guptas as the golden age of Indian history, Sharma's book, *Ancient India*, was bound to be the target of the most sustained onslaught. Indeed, the attack upon him was stepped up with printed Hindi pamphlets, denunciations of his scholarship by the archaeologist S. P. Gupta, and public meetings, demanding a ban on his book, called by Hindu communal organizations such as the Arya Samaj and the Rashtriya Swayamsevak Sangh (RSS). Later in the year, Sharma, who had already been relieved of his directorship of the ICHR, was denied permission, on various other pretexts, to go to the Soviet Union to partake in an international symposium on 'Ethnic Problems of the Early History of the Peoples of Central Asia in the Second Millennium BC'. As the mandarins in the Janata Government correctly surmised, this would be a conference on the early history of the Aryans, a matter on which, as we shall see, Sharma's views were less than welcome.

Of the numerous objections voiced against Sharma's book, two might be considered briefly for the light they shed on the interpretive nature of all historical exercises and the politics of historical knowledge in contemporary India. Sharma stated in *Ancient India* that the ancient Aryans were beef-eaters; as he was to explain in his defence of the book, 'it is because of the prominence of pastoral life that beef-eating prevailed in Vedic times'. The practice would continue among certain sections of the population, particularly 'artisans and agricultural labourers', even after agriculture had been introduced.[93] Sharma had said nothing exceptional, and had the weight of much Indological scholarship behind his work: thus P. V. Kane, whose multi-volume *History of Dharmashastra* remains authoritative six decades after its first publication, had averred that the *Rig Veda* made frequent reference to the cooking of the flesh of the cow. What was remarkable, from his point of view, was how the beef-eating Aryans of India became, over the course of the centuries, converts to vegetarianism.[94] Though himself prone to view the carcass of a cow as an 'unedifying spectacle', the sociologist Atindra Nath Bose, in his 1942 study of the economy of North India, likewise observed that 'in the Vedic and Buddhist classical literature, there is no dearth of allusions to cow killing or the taking of cow's flesh', and he pointed to the evident relish with which the sage Yajnavalkya was described, in the *Satapatha Brahmana*, consuming beef.[95] Indeed, even K. M. Munshi had noted, without a trace of embarrassment, that 'in spite of Jainism and Buddhism, fish and meat, not excluding beef, were consumed extensively by the people'.[96]

Sharma's remarks were nonetheless construed—indeed, they still are, if one considers the severe animadversions passed upon his work by Arun Shourie and the controversy, recounted in the introduction, over references to beef-eating among the Aryans in school textbooks[97] —as conveying his advocacy of non-vegetarianism, and particularly beef-eating; and so Sharma was charged with deliberately offending the sentiments of Hindus among many of whom the consumption of beef would, sometime after the Vedic Age, become strictly prohibited. A local Hindu leader demanded the 'immediate banning of Prof. R. S. Sharma's *Ancient India*' for his references to beef-eating in Vedic India. Though Sharma was ably defended by professional historians and much of the print media, his supporters—in a foreshadowing of the later debates on Ayodhya—insisted principally that scientific and objective history was not to be sacrificed to political and much less communal ends, and that the objections of Sharma's critics were 'completely baseless on historical grounds'.[98] It was scarcely recognized that the ferocious objections to Sharma's argument quite likely disguised a profound anxiety among communalists about the thin line that divides Hindus from Indian Muslims, for a beef-eating Hindu, by virtue of the transgression that is implied in that act, might be inferred as becoming akin to a Muslim. If a circumcised penis remained one of the few ways to distinguish Hindu and Muslim men during the horrendous killings accompanying the partition,[99] the all-consuming anxiety over beef-eating is better understood. Where substantive differences are minimal, and certainly subservient to common cultural practices, symbols are the preeminent way in which differences are exaggerated in order to permit the drawing of boundaries.

Sharma also reasonably maintained, following the almost over-whelming international scholarly consensus on this question, that the Aryans had come to India from outside. He was consequently a tacked for supposing that so glorious a civilization as that of Vedic India had emanated from foreign soil. As in recent years a strenuous effort, recounted elsewhere in this book as well, has once again been made to revive the argument that there was never any Aryan migra-tion to India, this brazen attempt to rewrite Indian history from the point of view of establishing India as the original homeland of the Aryans and the fount of all civilization cannot be allowed to remain uncontested. The argument first appears as early as the late nine-teenth century, and though K. M. Munshi was one of its supporters, the *History and Culture of the Indian People* volumes preferred to en-dorse the widely received view of an Aryan migration to India.[100] According to one of its more vocal proponents, the crux of the prob-lem is that while the Aryans, 'the so-called invaders', left behind a vast and complex literature consisting of the Vedas, *Brahmanas, Sutras, kavyas,* and Puranas, there are no archaeological remains or historical works testifying to their existence; on the other hand, the Indus Valley civilization people, whom the Aryans, according to the con-ventional view, displaced, are known only by the remains of their urban settlements at Harappa, Mohenjo-daro, Lothal, and a few other places, as they appear to have produced no literature. This purported 'paradox' is further deepened, it is suggested, by the anomaly that the invading Aryans are supposed to have been barbarians, while the Harappans are represented as a people who were literate: and yet it is the former who bequeathed a great literature to the world.[101] Can it not then be supposed that the Harappans and the Aryans were one people, that the epicentre of this common civilization was the Sarasvati basin, and that India furnishes evidence of one continuous civiliza-tion from remote antiquity? And if the Aryans of India did originate elsewhere, asks the historical novelist Bhagwan S. Gidwani, why is it that the region that was their supposed homeland 'itself showed no evidence of such philosophic development or artistic achievement or spiritual heritage' as is commonly associated with ancient India?[102]

Proponents of the view that India is the true homeland of the Aryans must nonetheless still explain how it is that Sanskrit, their language in India, is cognate with various other languages in Europe and Asia that now comprise what is called the Indo-European family of languages. Not surprisingly, given the strand of their thinking, it is argued that the Aryans, rather than moving eastward from the Russian steppes towards Iran and India, moved westwards from India and settled at least as far away as Europe. Could it 'not have been Sanskrit', proposes Gidwani, 'that moved out to those countless lands instead of the reverse?'[103] Far from there being any proto-Indo-European language, as linguists agree, it is argued that Sanskrit itself is the prototype for all Indo-European languages, which has the effect of making Western civilization itself derivative of Aryan civilization. But there is an absurd confusion here, as advocates of the Aryan immigration would argue, between language, culture, and race.[104] The admission that Sanskrit is only one, albeit among the oldest, of languages which all derive from another language need not lead to the presumption that Indian civilization is of 'foreign' vintage.

The 'invasion' theory is, in any case, something of a red herring, since most historians, while they firmly adhere to the idea that the Aryans emigrated to India, long ago rejected the theory of an 'invasion': [105] Merely because there were invasions of India by Turks or Afghans, or because the characteristic pattern of European interaction with much of the rest of the world has been one of invasion and conquest, is no reason to assume that the Aryans came into India as plundering or invading hordes. While those who insist on inverting the 'Aryan invasion theory' are easily answered,[106] the question that remains is why so much has been invested in attempting to establish that India is the original Aryan homeland, and why there should be so much umbrage at the thought that Aryans were at one point 'foreigners' in India. There is of course the unpalatable fact that the major sites of Harappan civilization are largely in Pakistan, which might explain why, as D. N. Jha puts it cryptically, 'the Hindu revivalists are busy locating the epicentre of this culture in the elusive Sarasvati valley'.[107] Least of all can proponents of Hindutva countenance the thought that the origins of Indian civilization should now lie in present-day Pakistan! Nor can the Brahminical, certainly uppercaste, origins of the proponents of the 'India as Aryan Homeland' theory be disguised, with ramifications that the Hindutva lobby has never fully been able to control. In an age of electoral politics, when every vote counts, it is expedient to broaden the definition of 'Aryan' and include within its orbit all those, including the pre-Aryan descendants of the Harappans, who would ordinarily be excluded from the category of the nobles.[108]

When one understands that the revival of the 'India as Aryan Homeland' theory has again occurred at a time of heightened communal tension, the other subtext of the dispute begins to emerge. For militant Hindus and their xenophobic supporters among the ranks of historians and other scholars, the argument that the Muslim in India is a 'foreigner', whose loyalty to India is consequently suspect, and who did nothing to contribute to the essential features of Indian civilization, remains decisive in their endeavour to draw the boundaries of an 'authentic' Indian civilization and even to give birth to a Hindu state. Yet there is an apprehension that the argument cannot be sustained if their own (real or imagined) ancestors themselves came to India and displaced the 'original' inhabitants. Any such concession, militant Hindus believe, renders the meaning of 'home' or homeland unacceptably flexible, and deflates the possibility of construing Indian civilization as a civilization that is Hindu in its most essential and fundamental aspects. On the one hand, the two-nation theory which led to the creation of Pakistan is accorded credence, since the idea of a 'homeland' to which they must eventually repair is held out before Indian Muslims as their ultimate destiny (unless they should wish to live by Hindu norms in a Hindu state); on the other hand, the dream of a united India is intrinsic to the conception of India as the original Aryan homeland (*Aryavarta*), and the vivisection of India is attributed to the malicious designs of India's colonial rulers and the cowardice and effeteness of much of the Hindu leadership. It is on the horns of this dilemma that 'Hindu history', which is poor history to begin with, irreversibly falters.

DISPUTES OVER MONUMENTS:
HISTORIANS IN THE NATION-STATE

On 6 December 1992, Hindu militants and their supporters reduced to rubble a sixteenth-century mosque, known as the Babri Masjid, standing in the ancient and venerable town of Ayodhya in central Uttar Pradesh. The Babri Masjid is thought to have been constructed in 1528–59 at the orders of Babur (1483–1530), the founder of the Mughal Empire, though this is far from certain.[109] Militant Hindus claim that a temple was destroyed to make room for the mosque; however reprehensible that may be, the crime is said to have been infinitely compounded by the 'fact', as they call it, that the temple commemorated the birth of Lord Rama, who is alleged to have been born on that very spot several thousands of years ago. They maintain that Hindus have recognized Ayodhya's sacredness since remote antiquity. While Rama is worshipped as a deity by most of his devotees, to others he is the exemplar of the just and noble king, the hero be churlish to pretend that the crisis generated in and around Ayodhya does not continue to pose critical questions about the future of secularism in India and the notion of 'Indianness', questions to whose explication if not resolution a good deal of the debate is and will continue to be directed. It is not only the future of the nation-state that has been called into question, and indeed if that were so, there might—besides the lament—be considerable cause for celebration as well, for India as a nation-state remains but a pale shadow of the richer entity it has been in history; moreover, as the pieces by Pandey, Tharoor, Khair, and innumerable others suggest, there are many other larger moral, existential, and epistemological questions, located around the issues of identity, cultural difference, hybridity, otherness, and moral conduct, that must necessarily impinge upon our consciousness. Nonetheless, there is at least one other critical question suggested by much of the commentary to which we must direct our attention if we are to emerge from the debacle at Ayodhya not with an incapacitating sense of defeat and loss, but with the hope that from the wreck of Ayodhya and its aftermath we might still be able to salvage not only some sense of good, but a real possibility of emancipation from the forces that have made a blasphemous mockery of a civilizational ethos that has always recognized and paid homage to the plurality of cultural and religious traditions. This 'critical question' that I refer to is, of course, none other than the appeal to history, the resort to the historical mode of inquiry and persuasion, by all the parties to the debate in an attempted justification of their respective positions. Ayodhya marks, for the first time in the history of post-independent India, the ascent of the historian to the proscenium of the nation-state; it signifies the indubitable importance of the historian to the nation-state, and the presumed indispensability of historical thinking and an historical consciousness to a nation-state that seeks recognition as a member of a world community bound together by a commitment to modernity and norms of rationality.

Where dharma and law once constituted the court of justice, today history appears as the tribunal before which proponents of conflicting representations must wage their struggle. As I shall suggest towards the end of this chapter, after having established the unrepentant attraction to history that the shakers and movers of Indian society have displayed, perhaps the most salutary insight we can imbibe from the destruction of the Babri Masjid and the deplorable loss of life in its wake is that historical consciousness and the awareness history is altogether to the contrary. In the early 1960s, the self-professed historian, P. N. Oak, constituted himself and several other gentlemen into an organization described as the 'Institute for Rewriting Indian History', which by the mid-1970s had over 200 members. Oak and his friends took it as their divine brief to demonstrate that all major monuments associated in India with the Muslim faith are Hindu in origin, which was meant to imply not merely that they had been built with the remnants of Hindu edifices, but that they had been converted from Hindu to Muslim places of worship. The further implication was that Muslim rulers do not have the capacity to construct architectural masterpieces. 'Our Institute is pledged, among other things', wrote Oak in 1976, 'to rid Islamic history of the silly notion that Muslim rulers and courtiers who built no palaces built majestic and massive mosques and tombs. The world must know that those buildings are all pre-Islamic.' Oak put foreign scholars on notice 'that all historic buildings in India are captured Hindu buildings', and students of the 'Islamic period of Indian history' were admonished to recognize the 'basic fact that every temple, mansion and fort overrun by Muslim invaders was advertised as a mosque tomb or citadel "built" by them'. By this time, Oak had been able to publish a score of books, the titles of many of which adequately convey the gist of his claims: *The Taj Mahal is a Temple Palace*; *Fatehpur Sikri is a Hindu City*; *Agra Red Fort is a Hindu Building*; *Delhi's Red Fort is Hindu Lalkot*; and *The Taj Mahal is Tejo Mahalaya: A Shiva Temple*. In his efforts to leaven his claims with the nectar of popular devotion, Oak went so far as to characterize, in his pamphlet *Lucknow's Imambaras are Hindu Palaces*, the famous mosques from the time of the Nawabs of Oudh as 'conclusively proved in our research volume to be of holy and hoary Ramayanic origin'.[111]

The presence of great Islamic architecture outside India does not appear to have been disconcerting to Oak, since he was prepared to argue that 'his findings in history have a worldwide application': all great Islamic building complexes, whether in Iran, Central Asia, or elsewhere, were 'earlier Hindu palace complexes'.[112] Oak's arguments are so evidently preposterous that he may justifiably be described as a crank, and likewise his claims assuredly do not deserve the dignity of rebuttal. Nonetheless, his very popularity, which can be gauged partly by the controversy over his claims carried out in the 'Letters to the Editor' column of the English-language daily *Indian Express* over a period of four months in 1987–8, has compelled historians to issue detailed rejoinders to his work. R. Nath, a historian at Rajasthan

University who has devoted many years of his life to the study of the Taj Mahal, has shown conclusively that Oak does not have a shred of evidence to support his various allegations that the Taj Mahal was earlier a temple devoted to Shiva, or—as though the inconsistency of these charges was of no consequence—at least a palace built or owned by one of Akbar's generals, Raja Mansingh (1550–1614).[113]

That some mosques were built with the remnants of Hindu temples is, however, amply documented and beyond question. Parts of destroyed temples were carted away as plunder and a new use was found for them as building material in mosques: this no doubt signified to some the triumph of the believers over the infidel. But it is just as reasonable to infer that Muslim architects forged with Hindu materials a new style, and even that the use of such material was a testimony to their appreciation of Hindu aesthetics, such as was revealed in patterned pillars or geometrical designs. Plunder may not always have been as such; in other words, Hindu material in mosques must be interpreted, like other material objects, along a semiotic register. No less important a consideration is that places of worship, not unlike other monuments and institutions, change ownership when political power passes into other hands. Both Hindus and Muslims worship at the dargahs of Sufi pirs: yet, when Hindu kings were in power, some dargahs would take on signs more characteristic of the Hindu faith, just as they would assume a more Muslim ambiance under Muslim rule. Though it is tempting to construe some of this history preeminently as a sign of religious conflict, such change of ownership marks also the ascendancy of different political regimes. The art historian Michael Meister has written that the 'state cathedrals of Latin America were often built on the ruins of Meso-America's sacral remains. Mexico City's Xocolo establishes the primacy of a colonial government by levelling the sacred centre of one people and replacing it with another.' An inscription at Delhi's 'Might of Islam' mosque records the 'fact' that it was built with the remains of 27 temples, but as Meister notes, the number 27, which reflects the 27 *Nakshatras* (asterisms) of India's lunar calendar, may have been chosen for its 'symbolic value'. He suggests that broad (and loud) claims in Muslim sources about the levelling of temples and the punishment of idolaters 'should be read with a sensitivity to the value of verbal virtue',[114] to which one might add that the rhetorical claims may have been all the more exaggerated to disguise the degree to which Muslim rulers *desisted* from the destruction and plunder of Hindu temples.

Such sensitivity as Meister asks for was not much on display as historians were brought to the fore to help resolve questions about the history and status of the Babri Masjid. The very long and complex history of negotiations surrounding the mosque need not detain us, since what is most germane is the manner in which historical evidence and discourses were mobilized by Hindu militants and their opponents to stake their respective positions. An anthology of critical articles on the dispute establishes that around the mid-1980s, certain historians and others with pretensions to the historical craft began to publish 'evidence' which, as they argued, indubitably proved the presence of a temple, built to Lord Rama, on the very spot on which then stood the Babri Masjid.[115] The author of one Hindi pamphlet gave it as his considered opinion that 'it is an undisputed *historical fact* that at Ramjanmabhumi there was an ancient mandir' [emphasis added], while another supporter of the RSS, writing in its official weekly *Organiser*, felt that 'there is no room for any doubt that the Babri Masjid was constructed after demolishing Shri Ramjanmabhumi temple and on the very spot. This *fact* has been clearly recorded in many *authentic history* books [emphasis added].'[116] As their own writings and those of other proponents of the temple theory were to make clear over the course of the next few years, by 'authentic history books' the authors meant mainly European accounts of Ayodhya, as though the weight of those alleged 'authorities' was enough to establish the 'facts'. Nor did these authors pause to reflect on the anomaly that while they habitually deplore European histories and accounts of India as irredeemably contaminated, prejudicial to Indian civilization and contemptuous of the 'Hindu way of being', European histories were now being canonized as offering an 'authentic' account of Ayodhya's past.

As historical evidence had been enlisted in the cause of the temple theory, professional historians were now bound to intervene. The first systematic rejoinder came in the form of a pamphlet, entitled 'The Political Abuse of History', authored by 25 historians at Jawaharlal Nehru University. While recognizing that behind the controversy lay issues of 'faith, power and politics', they felt pressed, in view of the fact that 'beliefs [laid] claim [to] the legitimacy of history', to demarcate between 'the limits of belief and historical evidence.' The authors rejected the assumption, as not warranted by 'historical evidence', that 'Muslim rulers were invariably and naturally opposed to the sacred places of Hindus'. The brunt of the evidence indeed points to the generous patronage of Muslim Nawabs, which led not only to the construction of new Hindu temples, but turned Ayodhya into an important pilgrimage centre; and they could have added that, to this day, the flowers used for worship in Hindu temples are grown almost exclusively by Muslims. The military forces of the Nawabs were, it is argued, 'dominated by Shaivite Nagas', and at times of religious conflict, the rulers did not always support their own religious brethren. In the dispute between Sunni Muslims and Naga Sadhus over a temple in 1855, the Shiite Nawab, Wajid Ali, eventually took the side of the Hindus and resorted to force to suppress the resistance offered by the Sunnis.[117]

On more specific questions of the ancient history of Ayodhya and the architectural features of the Babri Masjid, the JNU historians were to be joined by R. S. Sharma, whom we have encountered previously as the author of *Ancient India* (1977). Sharma enumerated, in a short monograph called *Communal History and Rama's Ayodhya* (1990), the gaping holes in the historical evidence offered by the proponents of the temple theory; along with two other historians and an archaeologist, he was also to offer a 'Historians' Report to the Nation'. Together, these various documents, which represent the views of many of the most prominent members of India's historical fraternity, were able to establish, among other things, that the Ayodhya of the Ramayana, assuming its historicity to begin with, is not the present-day Ayodhya; that Ayodhya was not particularly associated with the worship of Rama in antiquity; and that Ayodhya, contrary to the claims of the temple advocates, was most likely not an important pilgrimage site for Hindus in the ancient or middle periods. Only in the beginning of the nineteenth century was it first asserted that a temple had been destroyed, but the historical veracity of British sources in which the claims appear has never been investigated.[118]

The overwhelming evidence was such as to render the arguments of the temple proponents altogether improbable. Nonetheless, as the dispute spilled over into major newspapers, the 'communalists' and the 'secularists', as the two camps came to be known in India's urban centres and in the media, continued to marshal evidence in support of their various positions. The only point of agreement among the secularists and communalists appeared to be their readiness to deploy the discourses of history, though the appropriate disclaimers were issued. The secular historians stated, quite rightly, that irrespective of the historical evidence, the proposed destruction of the mosque could never be justified; the communalists, while claiming to disavow the place of history in helping to resolve conflicts where the religious beliefs of people weighed heavily, nonetheless conducted their campaign predominantly in the language of history. The memorandum on the Babri Masjid-Rama Janmabhoomi issue presented by the Vishwa Hindu Parishad (VHP), an organization created to do the work of Hindu cultural nationalism in India and abroad, to the Government of India on 6 October 1989 set aside questions of religious belief, and adverted to the 'historical evidence' in support of its claim. Subsequent talks held between the VHP and the Government of India in December 1990 and January 1991 were published by the VHP under the significant title *History versus Casuistry*,[119] and the reader is never left in doubt that 'history' belongs on the side of the Hindutvavadis, just as the evidence and scholarly apparatus of their foes is 'casuistry'. Yet, as I have been endeavouring to suggest, it is not any less remarkable that secular historians could issue a 'Report to the Nation', as though they had a mandate to do so from the people. Never before had the services of professional historians and archaeologists been recruited in this manner; never before were they placed so directly under the gaze of the nation.

On 6 December 1992, the Babri Masjid came crumbling down. The historians had arrived on the proscenium of the nation-state, but sanity had departed from the belly of an ancient civilization. One is tempted to snatch those memorable words from Auden's testimony to Yeats, 'poetry makes nothing happen', and say: 'history makes nothing happen'.

BABRI MASJID: THE RUIN(S) OF HISTORY

I have gestured briefly at the politics of history entailed in the dispute over the Babri Masjid, and the following chapter takes up the matter in earnest. But the narrative of how historians entered into the fray, and what that might mean for the study of history as well as for the future of Indian civilization, has an obvious place in this chapter as well. As violence engulfed some of India's urban centres after the destruction of the mosque, and women, children, and men were left to bemoan their fate, India's historians and intellectuals began to ponder over the nature of Hindu-Muslim relations, the soundness of the political arrangements, and the future of the country. They deplored the fact that 'myth', which is how they understood communalist history, had triumphed over (real) history: in the cliched phrase, history was the greatest casualty. The other notable lament was about the passing of an age, the end of Nehruvian secularism: this was no mere affectation, as many Indians had been strongly committed to the principles of secularism.[120] The ideals for which Gandhi and the 'freedom fighters' stood had been betrayed, and even the communists, who since the 1930s have derived immeasurable pleasure from deriding Gandhi as a bourgeois leader who placed too excessive a reliance upon Hindu religious idioms, suddenly found in the Mahatma the model of sanity, tolerance, and religious ecumenism. Having witnessed the Hinduism of VHP and RSS stalwarts, the Hinduism of Gandhi now seemed positively healthy and inspiring, a mild affair of the soul and a balm for the wounded.[121] Yet there was almost no ceflection on how it transpired that historians had become involved in the dispute, what their proposed solutions portended for the future of India, and what it meant for them to accept the call to offer estimony. Almost the sole voice of dissent from among the secular historians, and perhaps all the more poignant considering its source, was that of Majid Siddiqi, a Muslim intellectual at JNU who did not ppend his name to the document on the 'Political Abuse of History' eleased by his colleagues. Siddiqi asserted that it was not for historians to 'prove' or 'disprove' various claims made in the public realm: ad they to enter the debate, they should have done so after discard[ing] their personae as historians'. As he advised his colleagues, historians 'must exhibit intellectual self-confidence in their iscipline and determine their own agenda in terms of their own uestions and not allow the existence of communalism in this society to force its agenda upon them'.[122]

As one sifts through the writings of secular historians and intellectuals on the Babri Masjid affair, four considerations come to the fore trying to understand the uses and politics of history in India in cent years. First, their proposed solution to the problem had little to mmend itself to the attention of Indians, having in it more than a int touch of the otiose and the comic, before the destruction of the osque altogether foreclosed the options. As the status of the mosque as 'disputed', they proposed it be handed over to the Archaeologi-l Survey of India (ASI), on the supposition that it would thereafter in safe and neutral hands. Yet it is these very secularists who point the indifference of Indians to their architectural and cultural heri-ze, the neglect of monuments, and even the ASI's poor handling d management of the monuments under its care.[123] The Babri asjid would most likely have gone to seed under the ASI.

Yet by far the more objectionable aspect of the proposal is the anner in which it makes itself obeisant to the dead weight of colonial thinking and notions, widely prevalent in the Western world, of museumized cultures. Since religious worship has no attraction for secular intellectuals, it is of little consequence to them that religious edifices placed under the ASI's care *generally* are no longer used for worship: yet both Hindus and Muslims have at various times offered prayers at the Babri Masjid. Moreover, there are some who would like to see India develop, in the manner of the developed nations, a 'heritage industry', which would no doubt be a source of employment for 'culture management specialists', traffickers in tourism, and even historians. But India, to our good fortune, is still far from reaching that stage where its culture will be reduced to giant amusement parks, historic homes, national monuments, museums, and other sanitized and bracketed spaces. By turning over 'disputed structures' to the ASI, we commit the greater folly of substituting for modes of cultural negotiation and social practices of pluralism, the authority of impersonal and transcendent institutions presumed to embody neutrality.

Secondly, secular historians sometimes seem to rely a little too excessively on the *quid pro quo* form of argument, and not only with reference to the Babri Masjid affair. They have often asserted that if Muslims are to be charged with destroying Hindu temples and idols, it should not be forgotten that both Jains and Buddhists were the victims of Hindu bigotry, and that Hindu temples were at times built with the remains of Buddhist stupas. 'The large scale persecution of Buddhists by followers of Sankaracharya', one historian has written, has passed into 'convenient oblivion', while the authors of a pamphlet (called 'Black Sunday') published after the destruction of the Babri Masjid state that 'destruction of places of worship was not done exclusively by Muslim rulers'.[124] They adduce a number of examples, and point, as has almost everyone else, to the Hindu king Harshadeva, who as the eleventh-century ruler of Kashmir not only looted temples to fill his treasury, but appointed a special officer whose duty was to collect plunder from temples.[125] In the sectarian warfare between Saivites and Vaishnavas of which there is ample evidence, temples were not infrequently destroyed. Insofar as it is true that no one culture or people has a monopoly on goodness, and that barbarism recognizes no cultural or religious boundaries, their argument can scarcely be faulted; and it is certainly just as reasonable to suggest that the destruction of religious edifices and places of worship was an activity in which the ruling classes engaged as an aspect of their quest for political power. Nonetheless, the attempt to establish equivalencies of evil has little ethical value, and a great deal more thought must be given to the political consequences and socio-cultural effects of this mode of historicization. There is, in this form of argument, even a remarkable and uneasy similarity to the apologetics often encountered on behalf of Western imperialism, where the presumption is that Western powers did nothing to the people they conquered that they, the indigenes, had not previously done to themselves or others.

Thirdly, secular historians, and indeed historians of every hue and colour, must unravel the meaning of their relationship, and commitment, to modernity. The authors of 'Black Sunday', a pamphlet released within days of the destruction of the mosque by the Sampradayikta Virodhi Andolan [Movement Against Communalism], recognize that 'the destruction of places in medieval and ancient times' was 'an integral part of political power', and that consequently the destruction of such edifices should not invariably be construed as a sign of religious conflict. Yet a great deal more is implicated in their analysis, for as they go on to say, the attack on the Babri Masjid 'is reminiscent of the barbaric politics of ancient and medieval rulers that defies all modern, democratic, and civilised institutions of our society'. The historian Neeladri Bhattacharya of JNU, in like fashion, has expressed the considered opinion that it was 'medieval logic' that was 'at work behind the struggle for the Ramjanmabhumi'.[126] Considering that in Indian history, which James Mill fatally periodized into the Hindu, Muhammadan, and British periods, the 'medieval' period is itself taken to be congruent, howsoever absurdly, with Islam, the argument has the wholly unintended effect of suggesting that in their present-day barbaric conduct, the Hindus are following the example set by Muslims.

The equation of the 'medieval' with the 'barbaric' betokens an extraordinary faith in conventional narratives of the progress of history, while it ignores the remarkable plurality of pre-modern India. It is the 'modern' Hinduism of Hindu militants that has insisted on homogenizing the faith, divesting it of the diverse, and often contradictory, strands of worship, conduct, belief, and thought. Though Indians in the 'medieval' period were able to live comfortably with multiple versions of the Ramayana, the modern advocates of the temple theory decry this plurality. The Babri Masjid stood for nearly 500 years, through all the turmoil and 'barbarism' of pre-modern India, until it fell on account of the enthusiasm of the modern advocates of Hinduism, the same advocates who are fixated on historical evidence and on the desirability of establishing the historicity of

Rama, Krishna, and other Indian deities and mythological figures. The pre-modern world, one gets the striking impression, may have been more modern than our own, though Indian historians, on the whole, are a long way from arriving at this recognition. They fear the derision with which those who critique modernity are met and their characterization as hopelessly 'romantic', the favourite word of abuse among hard-nosed realists and Marxists for all those who have held out alternative interpretations of the past and visions of the future.

Fourthly, to take up briefly an argument advanced towards the end of the previous chapter, secular historians and intellectuals are not only indisposed towards what they call 'myth', but appear to be wholly incapacitated in their ability to negotiate with discursive forms that are hostile, opposed, indifferent, or merely complementary to history. They have argued that the communalist writers engage in the 'mythification of history', since the entire edifice of their argument appears to be constructed on myth. Thus various myths, such as 'the myth of ancient Ayodhya, the myth of its loss and recovery, the myth of the destruction of the temple and the construction of the mosque', are sought by the communalists to be converted or transformed into history.[127] One historian deeply committed to the secular ethos recognizes that the Hindutvavadi conception of the 'right Ramarajya' consists in nothing else but 'retelling history'. But his conclusion betrays the positivist conception of history and myth alike held by this historian: 'Having translated mythical lore into modern mobilizing metaphors and ideology, Hindu communalists transform the resultant frenzy into retaliative corrective measures. ... The Hindutva forces' interpretation of Hinduism and history, and their understanding of "greatness" and "regeneration" are all deceitful and opportunistic. In sheer desperation, they misappropriate Indian heritage, misrepresent Indian legends, and manipulate the people.'[128] In a word, history and myth are deliberately confounded, a charge analogous to the often heard secular complaint that the admixture of religion and politics is enough to make Hindu militancy unacceptable.

On this reading, then, myths are false, distorted, or bad history. 'History' and 'myth' are analytically separate, it is suggested, and to reinforce this point, the authors of 'Black Sunday' place myths in black boxes, with text repudiating a given myth following each box. Myths are statements that 'have no support in any historical evidence', but that is a scarcely helpful formulation, considering that the 'historical evidence' is itself held to be in dispute. Another writer says of the VHP that it 'Digs Up Myth, Buries History'; elsewhere, he rues that 'the method Indians appear to have found to deal with their past is to mythologise it. Fact is at a discount .... Thus, while myths move millions, the actual and complex historical reality is ignored.' The problem, to follow this logic, is not of the VHP alone: millions of Indians betray the same inability to confront the 'complex historical reality' as do members of the VHP, so they too must harbour similarly communalist and fascist tendencies.[129] An entire people needs to be rescued from its childlike dependency on myths—an argument encountered in the writings of several generations of British administrators of India. If we had better history, the people would not be led astray by myths; and so the historians must constitute the vanguard that will deliver us from the communal malaise. It is with this thought that R. S. Sharma concludes his brief study of the Babri Masjid dispute: 'Only patient and sustained efforts of right thinking writers, researchers and educators can foil the communalist attempt to use the past as a wedge to divide the people into warring camps.'[130]

Myth, in these formulations, is everything that history is not: as history is (or ought to be) fact, myth is not-fact. If this is the impoverished reading of myth to which secular historians and intellectuals hold, does it not substantially impair their reading of history? While secular historians view the debacle at Ayodhya as arising partly from attempts at the 'mythification of history', we should perhaps wonder if it is not the historicization of myths which has contributed to the increasing communalization of Indian politics, the emphasis on the nation's Aryan 'heritage', and the rise of aggressive nationalism. Though the story of the Ramayana, to take one instance, has been circulating in India for at least two millennia, and no one bothered much with the attempt to turn Rama into a historical personage, a man of flesh and bones, in recent years some Hindus have felt that their lives as Hindus could not be fulfilled until they were able to demonstrate the historicity of Rama. These are the Hindus who feel that a date must be assigned to Rama, who would like to push back the origins of Indian (by which they mean Hindu) civilization to at least as far back as 10,000 BC, and who have engaged in a search for the precise dates of the war described in the Mahabharata.[131] They have now promised, in their language, to 'liberate' the *Janmasthan* or birthplace of Krishna in Mathura, which is also, as they maintain, now occupied by a mosque. Their liberation of Krishna is not unlike the liberation which Bankim desired, who sought to free the historical

Krishna from the shackles of the mythical Krishna and so inaugurated the modern phase of Indian nationalism.[132]

HISTORY IN THE NATION-STATE, MYTH IN THE CIVILIZATION

As the most far-reaching critique of the contours of Indian nationalism was to emanate from Gandhi, who is also the initiator of the critique of modernity, it once again behooves us to consider that no one embodied more the ahistoricity of Indian civilization than Gandhi. In his first and most seminal tract, *Hind Swaraj or Indian Home Rule* (1909), an exploration in the form of a dialogue—calling to mind a Sunday School catechism, the philosophical exchanges in the Upanishads, and the Platonic dialogues—on the epistemological evils of modern civilization and the fatal attraction of Indian nationalists to such a civilization, Gandhi sought also to defend the practice of nonviolent resistance. When asked by the imaginary reader whether there was 'any historical evidence as to the [previous] success of ... soul-force or truth-force', Gandhi replied that insofar as history meant (as it mainly did then) the 'doings of kings and emperors', then 'no evidence of soul-force or passive resistance was [to be found] in such history'. Gandhi certainly was not going to allow the verdict of history to deter him from his chosen path, as he had little use for cliches about the 'lessons of history'; and as he matured his indifference to historical discourses became more pronounced. If Bankim was certain that the Mahabharata had a historical core and that Krishna was a real, historical figure, Gandhi was just as certain that no such interpretation was required. 'The Mahabharata', he wrote in 1924, 'is not to me a historical record. It is hopeless as a history. But it deals with eternal verities in an allegorical fashion.' A year later he affirmed, 'My Krishna has nothing to do with any historical Krishna.'[133] Though the Government of India may not have understood Gandhi's philosophical defence of ahistoricity, apparently they put up numerous banners around railway stations in the centenary year of his birth, one of which attributed a saying to Gandhi: 'I am not interested in history, I am interested only in getting things done.'[134]

It is quite apposite, then, that the most radical and perceptive analysis of the meaning of what transpired at Ayodhya has come from Gandhi's grandson, Ramachandra Gandhi, who has similarly gone far beyond the parameters of historical discourse. He has been less interested in assigning culpability than many others, and has sought to understand the meaning of Ayodhya in Indian categories. Ramachandra Gandhi has been the first observer to take serious cognizance of a building, known as 'Sita-ki-Rasoi' or Sita's Kitchen, adjoining what used to be the mosque and standing within the complex. Though India's honour is as important to him as it is to any secular historian, he experienced no moral anguish in recognizing, when he first visited the mosque, that 'sacred components of a Hindu temple (or a cognate Buddhist or Jaina shrine) had been used in the construction of the mosque in the sixteenth century'. Turning his attention to Sita-ki-Rasoi, he ponders about its proximity to the Babri Masjid, its origins, and the manner in which it acquired its name. From this musing Ramachandra Gandhi goes on to spin a radical account of the architectural complex's association with Buddhism, and Sita-ki-Rasoi is itself described as a grove of 'aboriginal spirituality' and 'sacred fertility' from where Sita fed Rama and his kin and from where, after her severance from Rama, she descended into the bowels of the earth. How is it that the Babri Masjid and Sita-ki-Rasoi stood together, cheek by jowl, for several centuries, and is their severance not like the separation of Rama and Sita, a violent ecological disruption of the order of the world? Is a Hindu or a Muslim complete any more without the other?[135] Indeed, is there any definition of Hinduism that is complete without Islam, and contrariwise can (at least South Asian) Islam find its moorings without turning to Hinduism?

Unless we can entertain some radical scepticism towards the discourses of history, there will surely be other Ayodhyas. My argument is substantially contrary to the regnant assumption behind the secularist discourses of historians and their intellectual allies, which insist that fidelity to the historical record, and the repudiation of 'mythified history', will prevent communal mischief, violence, or other political fiascoes. The Hindu militants have already identified 2,000 religious edifices which are described as being held in captivity under Muslim jurisdiction, but the terrains of dispute are still more numerous. The VHP and its friends have designated themselves, to take one example, as the true inheritors of the legacy of Swami Vivekananda, who came to the United States to represent India and Hinduism at the World Parliament of Religions in Chicago in 1893 and made a profound spiritual impression upon Americans. The government of Rajiv Gandhi, in particular, put Vivekananda before the youth of India as an example of a nationalist devoted to the revival of India who was at the same time an 'internationalist' and a spiritual leader. It is in Vivekananda's life, to follow his hagiographers, that we can witness the mode in which the spiritual and the material, reason and faith, works and devotion all judiciously coexist. Vivekananda had spoken of organizing Hindus, just as he sought to rejuvenate the faith and reinterpret it for the modern age; and yet there is little in his writings, as I argue again in the closing chapter, which sustains the view which the VHP has promulgated about Vivekananda as a zealous and xenophobic crusader for the faith. The interpretive circles cannot be closed by mere enumeration and rigorous defence of 'facts'.

Needless to say, all contestations in Indian history do not posit 'Hindus' against 'Muslims', nor is religion necessarily the decisive factor in the debates being shaped around Indian history today. Tamil anti-brahmanical histories have a long trajectory, and they too resist the Aryanization of Indian history in their own way, though here, too, the impulse towards 'manifest destiny' has sometimes been irresistible. How else can one explain the tendency in some Dravidian histories to insist that the Lanka of the Ramayana is modern Sri Lanka, when the work of many reliable scholars suggests otherwise? Dalit histories are slowly coming into their own, but the predominant voices in that literature have been those of the poet, polemicist, and pamphleteer.[136] Similarly, histories (and not only in the multicultural mode of consumption) will emerge from secessionist and insurrectionary movements in Kashmir, Punjab, Assam, Nagaland, and elsewhere. These developments, and numerous others, might perhaps help move Indian history away from the Bengali, Hindu, and modernist strands in which it has been trapped. It is the congruence of these latter strands that shaped the minds of Jadunath Sarkar and his admirer R. C. Majumdar, who between them wrote for 100 years, and of the legion of those historians who flourished under their tutelage. One shudders to think what the Assamese, for example, must think of this history, when we consider the dedication that appears in one of Majumdar's smaller books on Bengal: 'To the Memory of BENGAL THAT WAS by One who Has the Misfortune to Live in BENGAL THAT IS While the CROAKING AHOM FROGS Kicked with Impunity the DYING BENGAL ELEPHANT And the PEOPLE AND GOVERNMENT OF INDIA Merely Looked On.'[137]

The point here has not been to enumerate all the significant developments in the writing of Indian history in the last decade or so, since then one would perforce have to turn to those areas where some of the more insightful work has been done, such as subaltern history (which is taken up elsewhere in this book) and women's history. Rather, it has been to trace, through selected chapters of Indian historiography and iconic debates, the trajectory of the politics of history from shortly before the end of colonial rule until the debacle at Ayodhya, and to engage in some further considerations as we contemplate the future of history and knowledge in the nation-state.[138] While one may be epistemologically indisposed towards discourses of history, perhaps they cannot be disavowed in the late twentieth century without surrendering what is now unquestionably one of the tools of citizenship. However, that the destruction of the Babri Masjid was at all possible, despite overwhelming 'evidence' suggesting that the mosque did not take the place of a temple that was claimed to have stood on the same spot, points not merely to the ineptitude of the state, or even to its encouragement of communalist tendencies, but to the fact that historical discourses largely do not address the world that Indians inhabit. The secular historians remained oblivious to the twin considerations that many Indians were not prepared to have the dispute resolved by recourse to some notion of historical truth, and that the invocation of historical veracity has not much resonance among a people who have imbibed from the Mahabharata the notion that dharma (right conduct, law, justice) is a slippery concept.

History is only one way of accessing the past, and in India it is still a novel way of doing so, since Indians remain more at ease in accessing the past through non-historical modes such as folktales, customary practices, epic literature, proverbs, and myths. Thus, for example, while historians turn to the intellectual history of the Mughal court under Akbar to find examples of syncretism, or to the bhakti poets to understand the nature of anti-clerical sentiments, they could also engage themselves with folktales and proverbs. Though the jokes of Birbal, a courtier closely associated with Akbar, constituted an entire genre with which schoolchildren grew up in India in the 1960s and 1970s, historians have relegated such literature to the margins. Similarly, Brahmins, *maulvis* [Muslim priests], and *pandits* [Hindu priests] are the brunt of jokes and abuse in Indian folktales, but the supposition appears to be that the provenances of the folklorist and the historians have little in common.[139] Indian historians should not surrender the use of this huge repository of non-historical modes to nationalists and communalists. Rather than berating Indians for their neglect of the past, their indifference to historical truth, their invocation of myths and puranic stories, and for contaminating 'authentic' histories by use of 'myths', Indian historians must enter into a more fruitful engagement with Indian myths and other non-historical modes. They may not be able to win the battle that is fought on the terrain of history, but they could perhaps enliven Indian myths with fresh readings. Myths should no longer remain the exclusive preserve of the Hindutva historians; they belong to Indian civilization more than they do to the Indian nation-state. Were secular Indian historians to turn to myths, it is just possible that history might take care of itself. Otherwise, as the remaining chapters of this book suggest, they would have collaborated with the Hindutvavadis in turning history into the only true religion of India.

ENDNOTES

1. For a discussion of this phenomenon, see Chapter III.

2. The obvious reference here is to the work of Ladurie, Braudel, and others of the annales school, and to the 'history from below' associated with English social historians such as E. P. Thompson.

3. Edward Thompson, *The Other Side of the Medal* (London: Hogarth Press, 1925), pp. 27–8.

4. Cited by J. C. Srivastava, 'Lala Lajpatrai's Urdu Biography of Shivaji', in *Chhatrapati Shivaji: Architect of Freedom*, ed. Narayan H. Kulkarnee (Delhi: Chhatrapati Shivaji Smarak Samiti, 1975), p. 73.

5. Subodhkumar Mukherji, 'The Cultural History of India—An Apology', *Proceedings of the Indian History Congress*, 3rd session (Calcutta: Calcutta University Press, 1939), p. 107.

6. Elliot and Dowson, *The History of India*, 1:xxii.

7. Cited by Ranajit Guha, *An Indian Historiography of India*, p. 1. For a discussion of Bankim's enchantment with historical discourses, see Chatterjee, 'Claims on the Past', pp. 2–4.

8. Rajendra Prasad, 'The Role of History', in *Speeches of Rajendra Prasad 1952–1956* (New Delhi: Government of India, Ministry of Information and Broadcasting, Publications Division, 1958), p. 103.

9. Ibid., pp. 104–08. It is useful to remember that Prasad spoke not only in his capacity as President of India, but as someone who, since 1917–18, had witnessed in close proximity to Gandhi the triumphs of non-violence on the battlefield. Prasad played an important role in the struggle over peasants' rights at Champaran, an obscure place in Bihar where Gandhi launched his political career in India, and he authored perhaps the first authoritative study of the Champaran Satyagraha.

10. M. K. Gandhi, 'My Jail Experiences—XI,' *Young India* (11 September 1924), reprinted in *CWMG* 25:128.

11. Jawaharlal Nehru, *Glimpses of World History: Being Further Letters to his*

Daughter, Written in Prison, and Containing a Rambling Account of History for Young People (London, 1934; reprint edn, Delhi: Oxford University Press, 1982), pp. viii, 94. For an extended discussion of this work, see Vinay Lal, 'Nehru as a Writer', *Indian Literature*, no. 135 (January–February 1990), pp. 20–46.

12. Nehru, *Glimpses of World History*, p. 429.

13. *Toward Freedom: The Autobiography of Jawaharlal Nehru* (Boston: Beacon Press, 1958), Preface.

14. Jawaharlal Nehru, *The Discovery of India* (1946; reprint edn, Delhi: Oxford University Press, 1988).

15. Ibid., p. 59.

16. Ibid., p. 29.

17. Foreword by Humayun Kabir to Tara Chand, *History of the Freedom Movement in India*, 4 vols (New Delhi: Government of India, Ministry of Information and Broadcasting, Publications Division, 1961–72), 1:vii.

18. Foreword by Jugal Kishore, Minister of Information (1961), to *Freedom Struggle in Uttar Pradesh*, ed. S. A. A. Rizvi, 6 vols (Lucknow: Government of Uttar Pradesh, Information Department, Publications Bureau), 6:vii; see also Preface by Kamalapati Tripathi, Minister of Information (1957), to Vol. I, p. iii.

19. Tara Chand, *History of the Freedom Movement*, 1:xi.

20. Ibid.

21. See K. K. Datta, ed., *History of the Freedom Movement in Bihar*, 3 vols (Patna: Government of Bihar, 1957–8); *The History of the Freedom Movement in Madhya Pradesh* (Nagpur: Government Printing, 1956); Mamidipudi Venkatarangaiya, ed., *The Freedom Struggle in Andhra Pradesh* (Hyderabad: Andhra Pradesh Committee Appointed for the Compilation of a History of the Freedom Struggle in Andhra Pradesh, 1965–74); K. K. Choudhari, *Maharashtra and Indian Freedom Struggle* (Bombay: Government of Maharashtra, 1985).

22. See Sarojini Regani, ed., *Who's Who of Freedom Struggle in Andhra Pradesh* (Hyderabad: Ministry of Education and Cultural Affairs, Government of Andhra Pradesh, 1978), 1:v.

23. Sushil Chandra De, *Story of Freedom Struggle in Orissa* (Bhubaneswar: Orissa Sahitya Akademi, 1990), p. 1.

24. Ibid., introductory note by Surendranath Satapathy, pp. i–ii.

25. Foreword by Sampurananda to *Freedom Struggle in Uttar Pradesh*, p. i.

26. *Freedom Struggle in Uttar Pradesh*, pp. vii, xiv.

27. *The Collected Works of Mahatma Gandhi*, 100 vols (New Delhi: Government of India, Ministry of Information and Broadcasting, Publications Division, 1958–94). Vols 91–7 are supplementary volumes; Vols 98–9 provide a comprehensive index of subjects and persons; and Vol. 100 reprints the introductions to all the previous 99 volumes, thereby providing a resume of the entire series. A Hindi edition, though not of the entire set at this time, is

also available; there are also editions in other Indian languages. *The Collected Works* remain the indispensable source for any serious study of Gandhi's life and thought.

28. Cited by George Peabody Gooch, *History and Historians of the Nineteenth Century* (London: Longmans, Green & Co., 1913), p. 306, and by John Clive in his introduction to the abridged one–volume edition of James Mill, *History of British India* (Chicago: University of Chicago Press, 1975), p. viii. The importance of Mill's history is underscored by Ronald Inden, *Imagining India*, pp. 45–6.

29. Mill, *History of British India*, 2:365.

30. Cited by R. C. Majumdar, *Historiography in Modern India* (London and Bombay: Asia Publishing House, 1970), p. 15. Sir John Malcolm rose to high office in India, becoming the Governor of Bombay. He is one of the four early administrators described as having a 'romantic' view of India: see Eric Stokes, *The English Utilitarians and India* (Oxford: Clarendon Press, 1959). Malcolm was also one of the administrator-scholar types who displayed a flair for history, as evidenced by his influential *Political History of India*, 2 vols (London: J. Murray, 1826). For a discussion of British administrators and their historical works, see E. T. Stokes, 'The Administrators and Historical Writing on India', in *Historians of India, Pakistan and Ceylon*, ed. C. H. Philips (London: Oxford University Press, 1961), pp. 385–403.

31. Cited by S. C. Mittal, *India Distorted: A Study of British Historians of India*, Volume 1 (New Delhi: M.D. Publications, 1995), p. 96.

32. Kashi Prasad Jayaswal, *Hindu Polity: A Constitutional History of India in Hindu Times* (Calcutta: Butterworth, 1924), 1:189, cited by Inden, *Imagining India*, p. 189; Radha Kumud Mookerji, *Local Government in Ancient India* (Oxford: Clarendon Press, 1919).

33. Radha Kumud Mookerji, *Harsha* (1925; 3rd edn, Delhi: Motilal Banarsidass, 1965), p. 1.

34. See Majumdar, *Historiography in Modern India*, p. 56.

35. K. A. Nilakanta Sastri, ed., *A Comprehensive History of India, Volume 2: The Mauryas and Satavahanas, 325 BC–AD 300* (Bombay: Orient Longmans, 1957), see 'Note on the Volume'. Vol. V, on the Delhi Sultanate, appeared in 1970. Another four volumes have since been published.

36. For a short account of Munshi's promotion of Indian scholarship, see P. G. Shah, 'Munshi in the Field of Research', in *Munshi Indological Felicitation Volume*, eds Jayantkrishna H. Dave et al. (Bombay: Bharatiya Vidya Bhavan, 1963), pp. 1–4.

37. Cited by Richard H. Davis, *Lives of Indian Images* (Princeton, New Jersey: Princeton University Press, 1997; Delhi: Motilal Banarsidass, 1999), p. 210.

38. Foreword to *The Vedic Age*, Vol. 1 of *The History and Culture of the Indian People* [hereafter *HCIP*], ed. R. C. Majumdar, 11 vols (London: George Allen & Unwin, 1951), p. 7.

39. Foreword to *Struggle for Freedom*, Vol. 11 of *HCIP*, ed. R. C. Majumdar (Bombay: Bharatiya Vidya Bhavan, 1969), p. vii. Vol. 11 was the ninth to be published.

40. This point is reinforced by Munshi in subsequent volumes: in his foreword to *The Age of Imperial Unity*, Vol. 2 of *HCIP*, Munshi wrote of the *sanatan dharma* [eternal religion] of the Hindus, as represented in the *Manu Smriti* and other law books, that it 'laid down a code of social conduct; while it made society slow-moving, it prevented chaos; while foreigners were after some time absorbed and their ways adopted, it provided a firm foundation to social institutions and ensured the continuity of cultural values' (p. xxi).

41. Foreword to *The Vedic Age*, Vol. 1 of *HCIP*, pp. 7–12.

42. This manifesto, called 'What Bharatiya Vidya Stands for', appears on the front inner covers of every book appearing under the logo of 'Bhavan's Book University', an ambitious publishing programme that includes Indian classics, lives of the saints, philosophers, and religious teachers, and studies of Hindu culture. See, for example, Radha Kumud Mookerji, *Hindu Civilization* (1957; 4th edn, Bombay: Bharatiya Vidya Bhavan, 1977).

43. Foreword to *HCIP*, 2:xv.

44. Ibid., p. xii.

45. Ibid., p. xxiv.

46. *HCIP*, 1:38–39, 43. Munshi's foreword to Vol. 11, published in 1969, or 18 years after the appearance of *The Vedic Age*, resolutely reinforces this point: as he notes, 'Even in the present century when political thought and scientific approach dominate the destiny of man', the 'great names of Indian history' are those of its seers and religious teachers, men such as Ramakrishna, Gandhi, Ramana Maharshi, and Vivekananda. If we fail to recognize this 'fact of history', we are unable to understand, so Munshi argues, 'that the science and methodology of history, as developed in the West, being based upon the Graeco–Roman history and that of Europe in the middle and modern ages, may bypass special features and accomplishments of Indian history, when it differs from the established notion, as irrelevant or obscurantist'. See *HCIP*, 11:vii.

47. *HCIP*, 1: 24.

48. Ibid., p. 29.

49. For a different view of the Delhi Sultanate under Allaudin Khilji, see I. H. Qureshi, *The Administration of the Sultanate of Delhi* (4th rev. edn, Karachi: Pakistan Historical Society, 1958), and Mohammad Habib and Afsar Umar Salim Khan, *The Political Theory of the Delhi Sultanate* (Allahabad: Kitab Mahal, 1961).

50. Hermann Kulke and Dietmar Rothermund, *A History of India*, 3rd edn (London: Routledge, 1998), p. 164.

51. Cited in ibid., p. 163.

52. Majumdar appears to be a proponent of the two-nation theory, but this should not be construed to imply that he was agreeable to the partition of

India. Quite to the contrary, he held to the view that the essential features of Indian civilization were Hindu, and that Muslims would reside in undivided India as a separate race. Throughout, he insisted that Hindus and Muslims had not forged common bonds of culture; as he wrote in one of his lesser-known books, 'There is a general impression, deliberately created by the politicians of the early twentieth century, that the close contact between the Hindus and Muslims during the long period of six or seven centuries resulted in such a transformation of both that each lost its individual character and a new culture was formed by the fusion of both, which was neither exclusively Hindu nor purely Muslim. This is not, however, borne out by the actual state of things in India. A fundamental and basic difference between the two communities was apparent even to a casual observer.' See his *Glimpses of Bengal in the Nineteenth Century* (Calcutta: Firma K. L. Mukhopadhyay, 1960), p. 5.

53. Majumdar, *Historiography in Modern India*, p. 48.

54. R. C. Majumdar, *History of the Freedom Movement in India*, 3 vols (1st edn, 1962–3; 2nd rev. edn, Calcutta: Firma K.L. Mukhopadhyay, 1971–2).

55. See Majumdar, *Struggle for Freedom*, Vol. 11 of *HCIP*, pp. 981–2, 1069–73.

56. Ibid., p. 792.

57. The Khilafat movement was designed to persuade the British government not to dismember the Ottoman empire, so that the Ottoman sultan would continue to exercise spiritual and temporal authority as the chief custodian of Islam. See Gail Minault, *The Khilafat Movement: Religious Symbolism and Political Mobilization in India* (New York: Columbia University Press, 1982).

58. Majumdar, *Struggle for Freedom*, Vol. 11 of *HCIP*, pp. 318–9.

59. Ibid., p. 673.

60. Ibid., pp. 682–93.

61. Ibid., p. 792.

62. Majumdar, *Glimpses of Bengal in the Nineteenth Century*, p. 5.

63. Majumdar, *HCIP*, 1:40.

64. For an interesting discussion of Ranke and his canonization, for the wrong reasons, in the American academy, see Peter Novick, *That Noble Dream: The 'Objectivity Question' and the American Historical Profession* (Cambridge: Cambridge University Press, 1988), esp. pp. 26–31.

65. See appendix to Subodh Kumar Mukhopadhyay, *Evolution of Historiography in Modern India: 1900–1960* (Calcutta: K. P. Bagchi & Co., 1981), pp. 162–4.

66. Cited by Majumdar, *Historiography in Modern India*, p. 56.

67. See, for example, Harbans Mukhia, 'Historical Wrongs', *Indian Express* (27 November 1998).

68. Francis Younghusband, *Dawn in India: British Purpose and Indian Aspiration* (London: J. Murray, 1930), p. 144.

69. Tara Chand, *History of the Freedom Movement*, 1:111–12. In like fashion,

Akbar forged a new synthetic solar calendar in 1584, discussed briefly by Amartya Sen, 'India through Its Calendars', *The Little Magazine* 1, no. 1 (May 2000).

70. Jawaharlal Nehru, *The Discovery of India* (Calcutta: Signet Press, 1946; reprint edn, Delhi: Oxford University Press/Jawaharlal Nehru Memorial Fund, 1981), p. 270.

71. Ibid., pp. 265, 271; Tara Chand, *History of the Freedom Movement*, 1:112.

72. J. Sarkar, *History of Aurangzib, Based on Original Sources*, 5 vols in 4 (Calcutta: M. C. Sarkar, 1924–52), 3:249–50, cited by Satish Chandra, 'Reassessing Aurangzeb', *Seminar*, no. 364: *Mythifying History* (December 1989), p. 35. The view that the jizya was imposed on the Hindus in an effort to gain their conversion to Islam was first aired by Niccolao Manucci, who was resident in India during much of Aurangzeb's reign. He argued that 'the personal tax paid by the Hindu traders every year in advance nearly ruined them, to the great delight of Aurangzeb who expected their imminent conversion to Islam.' Cited by Tapan Raychaudhuri, 'The Mughal Empire', in Tapan Raychaudhuri and Irfan Habib, eds, *Cambridge Economic History of India* (Cambridge: Cambridge University Press, 1982), Vol. I, p. 188.

73. The historian John F. Richards opines, quite candidly, that 'Aurangzeb's ultimate aim was conversion of non-Muslims to Islam. Whenever possible the emperor gave out robes of honor, cash gifts, and promotions to converts. It quickly became known that conversion was a sure way to the emperor's favor.' See his *The Mughal Empire*, New Cambridge History of India, I:5 (Cambridge: Cambridge University Press, 1993; Indian edn, Delhi: Foundation Books, 1995), p. 177.

74. Richard M. Eaton, *The Rise of Islam and the Bengal Frontier, 1204–1760* (Delhi: Oxford University Press, 1997), p. 115. In the heartland of Muslim rule in the upper Gangetic Plains, Eaton argues, the Muslim population ranged from 10 to 15 per cent, while in eastern Bengal and western Punjab, where the reach of the sword of Muslim rulers was the weakest, nearly 70 to 90 per cent of the Hindus converted.

75. In writing about the contemporary debate on conversion, Sumit Sarkar is doubtless right in suggesting that there is a 'semantic ploy' insofar as the frequent outrage expressed against conversion also becomes the pretext for asserting Hinduism's unique disposition against conversion and consequently its vulnerability to more aggressive religions. On the other hand, both Sarkar and his ideological soul-mate, Achin Vanaik, who has also been agitated by Hindutva's ideological deployments, furnish little evidence which would make it plausible to think of Hinduism as a proselytizing religion. Both mention the *shuddhi* or 'purification' campaigns of the late nineteenth century, and Sarkar adverts to the VHP's advocacy of *paravartan*, 'turning back'; but the nineteenth century does not take us back to Hinduism across the centuries. Vanaik has offered some wild observations to the effect that since 'Hinduism' at one time prevailed in much of Southeast Asia, it must have

done so through various regimes of conversion, though in a work laden with lengthy notes, not a single source is cited in support of this claim. Similarly, to Sumit Sarkar it is transparent that terms such as 'Sanskritization' and 'cultural integration' are merely anodyne terms for what 'other religious traditions' would have 'termed "conversion"'. This cavalier approach to the relationship between language and society requires little commentary. See Sumit Sarkar, 'Hindutva and the Question of Conversions', in *The Concerned Indian's Guide to Communalism*, ed. K. N. Panikkar (New Delhi: Viking, 1999), pp. 73–106, esp. p. 81; and Achin Vanaik, *The Furies of Indian Communalism: Religion, Modernity and Secularization* (London: Verso, 1997), p. 147.

76. Richard Eaton has advanced this argument more generally in reference to various allegations about the widespread destruction of temples by Muslim invaders and rulers. See Richard Eaton, 'Temple desecration in pre-modern India', *Frontline* 17, no. 25 (9–22 December 2000).

77. This paragraph draws upon M. Athar Ali, *The Mughal Nobility Under Aurangzeb* (Bombay: Asia Publishing House, 1968), pp. 30–2; Chandra, 'Reassessing Aurangzeb', pp. 35–8; and B. N. Pandey's comments in *Parliamentary Debates, Rajya Sabha*, Vol. 102 (29 July 1977), col. 127. See also Sita Ram Goel, 'Some historical questions', *Indian Express* (16 April 1989), p. 8.

78. Harbans Mukhia, 'Medieval Indian History and the Communal Approach', in Romila Thapar, Harbans Mukhia, and Bipan Chandra, *Communalism and the Writing of Indian History* (New Delhi: People's Publishing House, 1969), p. 29.

79. See Robert C. Hallissey, *The Rajput Rebellion Against Aurangzeb: A Study of the Mughal Empire in Seventeenth-Century India* (Columbia, Missouri: University of Missouri Press, 1977).

80. Earlier historians furnished 1627 as Shivaji's birth date, but 1630 is now generally agreed upon as the more accurate date. See Stewart Gordon, *The Marathas 1600–1818, New Cambridge History of India* II.4 (Cambridge: Cambridge University Press, 1998), p. 59.

81. Cited by J. C. Srivastava, 'Lala Lajpatrai's Urdu Biography of Shivaji', pp. 72–4.

82. See Vijay Chandra Prasad Chaudhary, *Secularism Versus Communalism: An Anatomy of the National Debate on Five Controversial History Books* (Patna: Navdhara Samiti, 1977), p. 104.

83. Stewart Gordon has argued that many writers, especially Maharashtrian Brahmin historians of the twentieth century, would have us believe that 'Shivaji was creating a Hindu state, something fundamentally different and in opposition to the Muslim states that surrounded it', or at least some state based on 'Maharashtra Dharma'. His own position on this claim is expressed unequivocally: 'The only articulation of a "Maharashtra Dharma" is in a text that predates Shivaji by four hundred years. Further, it details only the relations between castes, not any sort of a Hindu political program.' See *The Marathas*, pp. 65–6.

84. B. K. Apte, ed., *Chhatrapati Shivaji: Coronation Tercentenary Commemoration Volume* (Bombay: University of Bombay, 1974–5), introduction, pp. vii–viii.

85. R. C. Majumdar, 'Shivaji's Relevance to Modern Times', in Kulkarnee, *Chhatrapati Shivaji*, pp. 2–3.

86. The description of the murder is drawn from his admiring biographer Jadunath Sarkar, *Shivaji and His Times* (Calcutta: M. C. Sarkar and Sons, 1919), p. 66; the quote following is from R. V. Herwadkar, 'Historicity of Shivaji-Afzal Khan Confrontation', in Apte, *Chhatrapati Shivaji*, p. 127. At the annual gathering in Pune in 1897 to celebrate Shivaji's birthday, a lecturer at Fergusson College, Chintaman G. Bhannu, adverting to Afzal Khan's death, stated that 'every Hindu, every Mahratta must rejoice' in it. See Richard I. Cashman, *The Myth of the Lokamanya: Tilak and Mass Politics in Maharashtra* (Berkeley: University of California Press, 1975), p. 114.

87. Nehru, *Discovery of India*, p. 272.

88. Since Shivaji occupied so preeminent a place in Marathi folk culture, twentieth-century scholars and public figures with divergent political views were able to deploy the figure of Shivaji for quite diverse ends. See Rosalind O'Hanlon, 'Maratha History as Polemic: Low Caste Ideology and Political Debate in late Nineteenth-Century Western India', *Modern Asian Studies* 17, no. 1 (1983).

89. The fourth was a very short monograph, *Communalism and the Writing of Indian History*, with three separate pieces by Romila Thapar, Harbans Mukhia, and Bipan Chandra, published privately by the People's Publishing House (New Delhi) in 1969. See Lloyd I. Rudolph and Susanne Hoeber Rudolph, 'Rethinking Secularism: Genesis and Implications of the Textbook Controversy, 1977–79', *Pacific Affairs* 56, no. 1 (Spring 1983), pp. 15–37, esp. pp. 16, 26.

90. Bipan Chandra, *Modern India* (New Delhi: NCERT, 1971), p. 253.

91. Rudolph and Rudolph, 'Rethinking Secularism', p. 27.

92. Cited by Chaudhary, *Secularism Versus Communalism*, pp. 4–5. The identification of the author of the memorandum or note as V. Shankar is made by the Rudolphs.

93. R. S. Sharma, *In Defence of 'Ancient India'* (New Delhi: People's Publishing House, 1978), pp. 20–1.

94. P. V. Kane, *History of Dharmashastra*, 5 vols (Poona: Bhandarkar Oriental Research Institute, 1968–77), Vol. II, Part II, pp. 772–6.

95. A. N. Bose, *Social and Rural Economy of Northern India* (Calcutta: Calcutta University Press, 1942), Vol. I, p. 76, cited by Prodipto Roy, 'Social Background', *Seminar*, no. 93 [Special Issue: 'The Cow'], p. 19.

96. Foreword to *HCIP*, 2:xxiv–xxv.

97. Arun Shourie, *Eminent Historians: Their Technology, Their Line, Their Fraud* (New Delhi: ASA Publications, 1998).

98. The controversy surrounding Sharma's book is discussed, though

with shocking shoddiness, in Chaudhary, *Secularism Versus Communalism*, pp. 47, 67–110, passim; for references to beef-eating, see pp. 83, 91, 110.

99. See the chilling fragment by Saadat Hasan Manto, 'Islaah (Correction)', in his 'Black Margins', in *Inventing Boundaries: Gender, Politics and the Partition of India*, ed. Mushirul Hasan (New Delhi: Oxford University Press, 2000), p. 294.

100. Majumdar made note of the argument without offering it his support: see *HCIP*, 1:25, 215–17.

101. The argument is summed up in Navaratna S. Rajaram, *The Politics of History: Aryan Invasion Theory and the Subversion of Scholarship* (New Delhi: The Voice of India, 1995), pp. 28–9 and is again recounted in N. S. Rajaram, 'Historical divide: archaeology and literature', *Hindu* (22 January 2002). The same author's *Aryan Invasion of India: The Myth and the Truth* (New Delhi: Voice of India, 1993) offers a briefer account of the Aryan invasion theory and its purported refutation. His most recent full-length 'study', co-authored with Natwar Jha, *The Deciphered Indus Script: Methodology, Readings, Interpretations* (New Delhi: Aditya Prakashan, 2000), not only claims to have deciphered the Indus Valley script, but alleges to have explained the supposed mystery of the loss of a massive literature from the Harappan period. Michael Witzel and Steve Farmer, in 'Horseplay in Harappa', *Frontline* 17, no. 20 (30 September–13 October 2000), demolish Rajaram's arguments. Witzel's more recent rejoinders, which similarly savage Rajaram, can be read in the pages of the *Hindu*: 'Indus Civilisation and Vedic Society' (29 January 2002) and 'Harappan horse myths and the sciences' (5 March 2002).

102. Bhagwan S. Gidwani, *Return of the Aryans* (Delhi: Penguin Books, 1994), p. xiii.

103. Ibid.

104. Max Müller, whose writings in the late nineteenth century set the parameters for the debate on Aryans and India, himself could not steer clear of the rampant confusion between race, language, and culture. 'Ram Mohan Roy was an Arya', Müller informed an audience in 1883, 'belonging to the south-eastern branch of the Aryan race and he spoke an Aryan language, the Bengali'; and, apropos Ram Mohan Roy's visit to England, where he died, Müller recognized in that event 'the meeting again of the two great branches of the Aryan race, after they had been separated so long that they had lost all recollection of their common origin, common language and common faith'. Cited by Romila Thapar, 'The Theory of Aryan Race and India: History and Politics', *Social Scientist* 24, nos 1–3 (January–March 1996), p. 6.

105. This point is addressed by Romila Thapar, *Ancient Indian Social History: Some Interpretations* (New Delhi: Orient Longman, 1978), and reiterated briefly in a very recent piece, 'Hindutva and history', *Frontline* 17, no. 20 (30 September–13 October 2000), pp. 15–16. The firm evidence for multiple Aryan migrations to India is reviewed by R. S. Sharma, *Advent of the Aryans in India* (Delhi: Manohar, 1999).

106. For a devastating critique of Rajaram and his ilk (note 100), see Shereen Ratnagar, 'Revisionism at work: A chauvinistic inversion of the Aryan inversion theory', *Frontline* (9 February 1996):74–80. There is, on the whole, more scholarly consensus on the issue of an Aryan migration to India than on any other subject: among historians and archaeologists of India, one could consult the works of H. D. Sankalia, R. S. Sharma, F. R. Allchin, Suvira Jaiswal, D. N. Jha, and Romila Thapar.

107. D. N. Jha, *Ancient India in Historical Outline*, rev. and enlarged edn (New Delhi: Manohar, 2001), p. 30.

108. Cf. Thapar, 'Theory of Aryan Race and India', p. 10.

109. Sushil Srivastava, *The Disputed Mosque: A Historical Inquiry* (New Delhi: Vistaar Publications, 1991), finds it probable that a Buddhist stupa stood at the site of the mosque (pp. 113–24). Arvind Das, 'Cut-Price Culture: VHP Digs Up Myth, Buries History', *Times of India* (11 December 1990), p. 6, takes the same view in a favourable review of the book. The little-noticed book by Surinder Kaur and Sher Singh, *The Secular Emperor Babar: A Victim of India's Partition* (New Delhi: Genuine Publications, 1991), a victim of the authors' poor knowledge of English and scholarly conventions, not to mention the gutter-press culture of much of modern Indian publishing, disputes whether Babar ever constructed the mosque named after him.

110. The Golden Temple was, in the summer of 1984, seriously damaged by military action in the attempt to weed out Sikh terrorists holed up in the famous Sikh shrine, but it was *not* under government protection.

111. Institute for Rewriting Indian History [hereafter IRWI], *Annual Report* (New Delhi: IRWI, 1976), pp. 8–9, 11, 18.

112. Ibid.

113. R. Nath, 'The Taj: A mausoleum', *Seminar*, no. 364: *Mythifying History* (December 1989):28–34.

114. Michael W. Meister, 'Mystifying monuments', *Seminar*, no. 364: *Mythifying History* (December 1989):24–7.

115. Sarvepalli Gopal, ed., *Anatomy of a Confrontation: The Babri Masjid-Ram Janmabhumi Issue* (Delhi: Penguin Books, 1991). In the enumeration of the role played by historians in this affair, I am drawing heavily upon, and anticipating, Chapter III (see below).

116. Both citations are from Gopal, *Anatomy of a Confrontation*, p. 138 notes 6–7.

117. Sarvepalli Gopal et al., 'The Political Abuse of History', as reprinted in *Social Scientist*, nos 200–01 (January–February 1990):76–81, esp. pp. 76, 80. See also Ashis Nandy et al., *Creating a Nationality: The Ramjanmabhumi Movement and Fear of the Self* (Delhi: Oxford University Press, 1995), pp. 2–3. The poet Aḳbar Allahabadi, who hailed from the Awadh region, was reportedly asked by his maid if he was a Sunni or a Shia. His response,

Mazhab ka haal mujhse kya poochtee ho Munni
Shia ke saath Shia, Sunni ke saath Sunni

[Why do you ask from me the state of religion Munni?
I am a Shia with a Shia, Sunni with a Sunni],

speaks volumes about the syncretic histories of places such as Lucknow, which neither secular nor Hindutva histories are able to capture. Cited by Amaresh Mishra, *Lucknow, Fire of Grace: The Story of the Renaissance, Revolution and the Aftermath* (New Delhi: HarperCollins, 1998), pp. 300–01.

118. I have drawn upon: Gopal, 'The Political Abuse of History'; R. S. Sharma, M. Athar Ali, D. N. Jha, and Suraj Bhan, *Ramjanmabhumi-Baburi Masjid: A Historians' Report to the Nation* (New Delhi: People's Publishing House, 1991); and R. S. Sharma, *Communal History and Rama's Ayodhya* (New Delhi: People's Publishing House, 1990).

119. *History Versus Casuistry: Evidence of the Ramajanmabhoomi Mandir Presented by the Vishwa Hindu Parishad to the Government of India in December–January 1990–91* (New Delhi: Voice of India, 1991).

120. Something of this lament over the decline of Nehruvian secularism is found in two recent ruminations over India's history and future: Shashi Tharoor, *India: From Midnight to the Millennium* (New York: HarperCollins Publishers, 1997), pp. 51–4, and Sunil Khilnani, *The Idea of India* (New York: Farrar Straus Giroux, 1997).

121. See, for example, A. B. Bardhan, *Sangh Parivar's Hindutva versus The Real Hindu Ethos* (New Delhi: Communist Party of India, 1992), esp. pp. 5–7.

122. Majid H. Siddiqi, 'Ramjanmabhoomi-Babri Masjid Dispute: The Question of History', *Economic and Political Weekly* 25, no. 2 (13 January 1990):97–8.

123. See, for example, Arvind Das, 'When History Causes Ennui', *Times of India* (11 July 1993), p. 17.

124. Ratnabali Chatterjee, 'The Rulers and the Ruled in Medieval India and VHP's Myth', in *The Nation, the State and Indian Identity*, eds Madhusree Dutta, Flavia Agnes and Neera Adarkar (Delhi: Samya, 1996), p. 33; 'Black Sunday', issue of *Manas* (Delhi: Sampradayikta Virodhi Andolan, 1992), p. 2.

125. 'Black Sunday', p. 2; Harbans Mukhia, 'Medieval Indian History and the Communal Approach', p. 34. The passages in question in the *Rajatarangini* are from Book VII, Verses 1082–91. There are two complete translations into English: one by M. A. Stein, dated to 1900, is available in a reprint edition of two volumes (New Delhi: Motilal Banarsidass, 1979); the more recent translation is of R. S. Pandit (New Delhi: Sahitya Akademi, 1953; repr. edn 1968).

126. 'Black Sunday', p. 2; Neeladri Bhattacharya, 'Myth, History and the Politics of Ramjanmabhumi', in Gopal, *Anatomy of a Confrontation*, p. 129.

127. Bhattacharya, 'Myth, History and the Politics of Ramjanmabhumi', pp. 132–7

128. S. P. Udayakumar, 'Historicizing Myth and Mythologizing History: The "Ram Temple" Drama', *Social Scientist* 25, nos 7–8 (July–August 1997), pp. 21, 23.

129. Arvind Das, 'Cut-Price Culture'.

130. Sharma, *Communal History and Rama's Ayodhya*, p. 32.

131. For a perceptive analysis of neo-Hindu history, see Gyanendra Pandey, 'Modes of History Writing: New Hindu History of Ayodhya', *Economic and Political Weekly* 29, no. 25 (18 June 1994):1523–8; see also Shriram Sathe, *Search for the Year of Bharata War* (Hyderabad: Navabharati Publications, 1983).

132. I would refer the reader to the discussion in Chapter I, as well as to Bankimcandra Chatterjee, *Krishna-charitra*.

133. M. K. Gandhi, *Hind Swaraj or Indian Home Rule* (reprint edn, Ahmedabad: Navajivan Publishing House, 1962), p. 77; idem, 'My Jail Experiences—XI', *Young India* (4 September 1924), reprinted in Raghavan Iyer, ed., *The Moral and Political Writings of Mahatma Gandhi, Volume 1: Civilization, Politics and Religion* (Oxford: Clarendon Press, 1986), p. 183; and idem, 'Sikhism', *Young India* (1 October 1925), reprinted in Iyer, ibid., 1:484–5.

134. My source for this information is Ashis Nandy.

135. Ramchandra Gandhi, *Sita's Kitchen: A Testimony of Faith and Inquiry* (New Delhi: Penguin Books, 1992), pp. 14–15, 110, passim. For another perspective on Sita-ki-Rasoi, inspired by Ramachandra Gandhi, see Phyllis Herman, 'Relocating Ramarajya: Perspectives on Sita's Kitchen in Ayodhya', *International Journal of Hindu Studies* 2, no. 2 (August 1998), pp. 157–84.

136. Two important works that tackle some questions in Dalit history do so from very different positions: see D. R. Nagaraj, *The Flaming Feet: A Study of the Dalit Movement in India* (Bangalore: South Forum Press, in association with Institute for Cultural Research and Action, 1993), and Kancha Ilaiah, *Why I Am Not a Hindu: A Sudra Critique of Hindutva Philosophy, Culture and Political Economy* (Calcutta: Samya, 1996). Ilaiah's embrace of the historical mode can be reasonably inferred from his critique of 'Brahmin' rites of death: 'Cremation is an unscientific method of dealing with dead bodies because it leaves no history in the form of fossils. If the whole world had done what the Brahmin rituals require, the whole fossil history of human bodies would not have been available' (p. 112). Ilaiah observes, quite rightly, that the practice of cremation allows the state to dispose of the bodies of its victims with complete impunity, and moves from there to the inference that 'Brahminism must have evolved this practice [of cremation] in ancient India as the Hindus killed several Dalitbahujans who had revolted against them to destroy evidence of torture and murder'. For all his celebration of the historical consciousness, Ilaiah's own fidelity to historical practices appears to be negligible.

137. R. C. Majumdar, *Glimpses of Bengal in the Nineteenth Century*. I am grateful to Dipesh Chakrabarty for drawing my attention to this work.

138. For an elaboration of directions we might choose to pursue, see as well my 'Discipline and Authority: Some Notes on future histories and epistemologies of India', *Futures* 29, no. 10 (December 1997), pp. 985–1000.

139. For good examples, see *Folktales from India: A Selection of Oral Tales from Twenty-two Languages*, selected and edited by A. K. Ramanujan (New York: Pantheon Books, 1991), pp. 203–04, 273–4, 319–20.

3

History as Holocaust
Ayodhya and the Historians

I

On 6 December 1992, the Babri Masjid, a mosque in the city of Ayodhya in the Gangetic Plains, was brought down by a large crowd numbering in the thousands. While a police force of nearly 20,000 looked on, the crowd set to work on demolishing this (in the words of the Indian state) 'disputed structure' with axes, shovels, picks, and their bare hands. In the immediate aftermath of the destruction of the mosque, violence broke out across the length and breadth of India, in which the casualties were overwhelmingly of the Muslim faith.[1] The Babri Masjid, which takes its name from the Mughal Emperor Babur, at whose command the mosque was most likely constructed in 1528–9, is said by the 'fundamentalist' or militant Hindus to have been built at the very spot at which supposedly stood a temple dedicated to the Hindu deity, Lord Rama. On the 'fundamentalist' view, which finds, as adumbrated earlier, its cultural voice embodied in the Vishwa Hindu Parishad (VHP), its political expression in the activities and pronouncements of the Bharatiya Janata Party (BJP) and the Shiv Sena,[2] and its brute strength in the armed support rendered to it by the paramilitary organizations known as the Rashtriya Swayamsevak Sangh (RSS) and Bajrang Dal (BD)—not that these divisions of duty are at this juncture entirely meaningful—the temple also marked the exact place at which took place the birth of Lord Rama. Thus reparation to the Hindus, for the offence caused to their religion, could only be achieved by the destruction of the mosque, so that the way might be paved for the construction of a temple dedicated to Rama, which would then stand as a monument to Hindu pride.

The destruction of the Babri Masjid has, it is likely, occasioned more comment in Indian newspapers and magazines than any other 'communal' event since the nation achieved its independence in 1947 amidst the bloodshed and carnage of the partition. Only the recent killings in Gujarat, which have an obvious relation to the events of 6 December 1992, have perhaps been the subject of more intense scrutiny—and this ten years later, in the age of the Internet and satellite television. A great deal of the discussion on the debacle at Ayodhya hovered around several sets of questions. In the first instance, what was the role of the state in perpetuating this crisis, and to what extent did the demolition of the mosque represent the abnegation by the state of its duties? More pointedly, how could the single-minded demolition of the mosque have been wrought when the state had furnished guarantees about the safety of the mosque, and provided an armed force of several thousand policemen as an assurance of its commitment to live by those guarantees? To political scientists, these questions resolve themselves into more precise queries about the respective roles of the central and state governments and their relationship to each other. Was the relationship inimical or, on the contrary, conducive to the resolution of the crisis?

A second set of considerations that loomed large in the press and media pertained to what is habitually referred to as the 'law and order' aspects of the crisis. When the Supreme Court itself had forbidden any party from encroaching upon the mosque, with what impunity could militant advocates of the Hindu faith, acting with the blessing of a parliamentary party sworn to uphold the constitution and the law of the land, have arrogated to themselves the right to take the law into their own hands? Did the destruction of the mosque signal the complete erosion of the 'rule of law', and if so, would the imperative to retain 'law and order' necessitate more advanced techniques of repression? Is India moving, editorialists on 1 January 1993 were wont to query, towards chaos and lawlessness, towards the anomie that signifies a structural failure in the economy, the breakdown of civil society, and the inefficaciousness of the political arrangements by which a nation was sought to be governed? Thirdly, and here again the political scientists with their penchant for positivism and party politics talk found the situation ripe for the display of their 'expertise', there was much speculation about what the future portended for the Congress, whether the Bharatiya Janata Party would be able to steal victory and return India to the fold of an authentic Hinduism, and how the country would divide at the time of the next general election. What would be the coalitions by which India would be governed?

Finally, and most poignantly, there was a great deal of soul-searching about the future of secularism in India and the nature of its purported opposite, 'communalism' or (though this word was then much less in vogue) 'fundamentalism'. This element of the commentary, far more ponderous in tone, continues down to the present day, except that in the immediate aftermath of the destruction of the Babri Masjid it was etched in the language of mourning. It is as a lament that we must read the movingly eloquent piece by Gyanendra Pandey, one of India's most well-known historians, in the *Times of India* on 10 December 1992 mourning the demise of Indian secularism and the betrayal of the ideals which informed his childhood and in which the grand experiment of nationhood was sought to be nourished; and likewise is the reflection on the struggle for India's soul that the Indian novelist and international civil servant, Shashi Tharoor, penned for the 11 December edition of the *New York Times*. The India in which Tharoor and Pandey grew up could not be spoken of in the singular: it was emphatically not 'Hindu' India, and as Tharoor put it poignantly, 'the singular thing about India is that you can speak of it only in the plural'. Tharoor went on to say, by way of illustration, that 'Our National leaders and heroes were Muslim, Parsi, Christian, Sikh, as well as Hindu. When my Brahmin mother-in-law visited us in Europe, she was most anxious to light a candle at Lourdes.' And yet in the India that his sons stand to inherit, the fear of symbols, 'the mark on a forehead or the absence of a foreskin', appears to rule the lives of its inhabitants.[3] If this is not the India that Tharoor would like his children to claim as their own, it is most decisively not the India of Tabish Khair, who found that the destruction of the Babri Masjid had stripped him of his Indian identity, an identity that had perforce already been problematic. Growing up as an Indian, Khair had been relegated to that special sub-species that went by the name of 'Secular Indian Muslim'; as the years went by, that designation had all but been evacuated of the term 'Indian', and on 6 December the remainder of his 'historical, social and legal identity was systematically demolished'.[4] The 'average Hindu' had suddenly discovered a Muslim in people like Khair; to the 'average Muslim', the non-religious, liberal Muslim could, after Ayodhya, scarcely flaunt his secular credentials. 'Most Muslims look at me and see red. Most Hindus look at me and see green.' Would anyone paint him as an Indian?

All these considerations are undoubtedly significant, and it would be churlish to pretend that the crisis generated in and around Ayodhya does not continue to pose critical questions about the future of secularism in India and the notion of 'Indianness', questions to whose explication if not resolution a good deal of the debate is and will continue to be directed. It is not only the future of the nation-state that has been called into question, and indeed if that were so, there might—besides the lament—be considerable cause for celebration as well, for India as a nation-state remains but a pale shadow of the richer entity it has been in history; moreover, as the pieces by Pandey, Tharoor, Khair, and innumerable others suggest, there are many other larger moral, existential, and epistemological questions, located around the issues of identity, cultural difference, hybridity, otherness, and moral conduct, that must necessarily impinge upon our consciousness. Nonetheless, there is at least one other critical question suggested by much of the commentary to which we must direct our attention if we are to emerge from the debacle at Ayodhya not with an incapacitating sense of defeat and loss, but with the hope that from the wreck of Ayodhya and its aftermath we might still be able to salvage not only some sense of good, but a real possibility of emancipation from the forces that have made a blasphemous mockery of a civilizational ethos that has always recognized and paid homage to the plurality of cultural and religious traditions. This 'critical question' that I refer to is, of course, none other than the appeal to history, the resort to the historical mode of inquiry and persuasion, by all the parties to the debate in an attempted justification of their respective positions. Ayodhya marks, for the first time in the history of post-independent India, the ascent of the historian to the proscenium of the nation-state; it signifies the indubitable importance of the historian to the nation-state, and the presumed indispensability of historical thinking and an historical consciousness to a nation-state that seeks recognition as a member of a world community bound together by a commitment to modernity and norms of rationality.

Where dharma and law once constituted the court of justice, today history appears as the tribunal before which proponents of conflicting representations must wage their struggle. As I shall suggest towards the end of this chapter, after having established the unrepentant attraction to history that the shakers and movers of Indian society have displayed, perhaps the most salutary insight we can imbibe from the destruction of the Babri Masjid and the deplorable loss of life in its wake is that historical consciousness and the awareness of historical thinking, far from being the mode in which India shall be delivered from the throes of communal violence, arguably represent the nemesis of any reasonable attempt to find solutions that would enable Indians to live in comparative harmony.

II

The Babri Masjid was, as an inscription on the now-destroyed mosque stated, built in 1528–9 by the Muslim nobleman Mir Baqi on the order of the Emperor Babur, whose victory at arms over Sultan Ibrahim Lodi in 1526 at Panipat paved the way for the creation of the Mughal empire in India.[5] Only the date of the erection of the mosque appears to be beyond dispute; everything else, as the voluminous writings in Indian newspapers, magazines, journals, and other polemical and scholarly literature amply suggest, is contested. As the most well-known scholarly compilation on the 'Babri Masjid–Rama Janmabhoomi Issue' demonstrates, certain historians and others posing as practitioners of the historical craft began to put forth 'evidence' from the mid-1980s onwards that purportedly would prove, beyond any reasonable doubt, that a temple dedicated to Lord Rama, marking the very site where the Hindu king and deity was born, was demolished and the mosque built in its place.[6] Pratap Narain Misra's *Kya Kahati Hai Sarayu Dhara? Sri Ramjanmabhumi ki Kahani* [*What Says the River Sarayu? The Story of Ramjanmabhumi*], which appeared in 1985, was perhaps the first work of its kind with its appeal to historical evidence as the supreme arbiter; it was followed in quick succession by a number of other works, largely penned in Hindi and emanating from Lucknow, Allahabad, Ayodhya, and other principal Hindi literature-producing centres of the so-called cow belt.[7] These works and other sundry pieces, many of them published in the *Organiser*, the organ of the RSS, sought to establish, as an incontrovertible fact, the existence of a temple at the very spot where stood the Babri Masjid: as the author of one article put it, 'There is no room for any doubt that the Babri Masjid was constructed after demolishing [the] Shri Ramjanmabhumi temple and on the very spot. This fact has been clearly recorded in many authentic history books.'[8] In a similar vein, with just as much of an emphasis on the supposed historical irrefutability of certain alleged 'facts', Deoki Nandan in his historical and legal review of the controversy surrounding Ayodhya gave it as his opinion that 'it is an undisputed historical fact that at Ramjanmabhumi there was an ancient mandir since the time of Maharaja Vikramaditya'.[9]

Once purportedly historical evidence had been invoked in support of the view that a Rama temple—and no ordinary Rama temple at that, for the claim was that the temple marked the place where Rama was born—was destroyed to make way for a mosque that heralded the triumph of the Muslim faith over Hinduism, historians who could not share in this view were compelled to enter the fray. As S. Gopal and over twenty other scholars associated with the Centre for Historical Studies at Jawaharlal Nehru University were to argue, the historian, when faced by beliefs camouflaging under the 'legitimacy of history', must attempt a 'demarcation between the limits of belief and historical evidence. When communal forces make claims to "historical evidence" for the purposes of communal politics, then the historian has to intervene.'[10] Accordingly, they issued the first rejoinder in the form of a pamphlet entitled 'The Political Abuse of History: Babri Masjid-Rama Janamabhumi Dispute', and shortly thereafter a smaller group of four scholars, of whom three are historians, entered the dispute by way of another pamphlet entitled 'Ramjanmabhumi Baburi Masjid—A Historians' Report to the Nation'.[11] In like fashion, the authors of the latter report lamented the fact that the Government of India, by initiating negotiations with the Vishwa Hindu Parishad (VHP) and the Babri Masjid Action Committee (BMAC), should have allowed disputes over 'facts of history' to be decided by clearly partisan 'litigants' instead of turning the matter over to an 'independent forum of historians'. 'This seemed to us, as professional historians,' the authors further noted, 'a very unhappy procedure.'[12] There will be time enough to ruminate over the peculiar circumstance whereby historians, much like public policy or scientific 'experts', are called to furnish a 'report to the nation', or in any case do so at their own behest; and similarly we need only note, for the time being, the manner in which 'professional historians' are presumed to represent transcendence, an ethical force of 'neutrality' and 'objectivity'.

The authors of the two pamphlets, which complement each other neatly, gave it as their considered opinion that the debate over the 'disputed structure' could be framed around several sets of considerations which are amenable to serious historical investigation. First, is it the case that Hindus have 'always, and certainly over a long period before the construction of the Baburi Masjid', believed that Ayodhya is a sacred place, sacred by virtue of its association as the *janmabhumi* (birth-ground) of Lord Rama? In a detailed assessment, Sharma and his fellow authors noted that no ancient Sanskrit text could be cited in support of the claim that 'there has been an ancient Hindu belief in Rama Janmasthan at Ayodhya'. One might ask just how ancient is 'ancient', but the writings of the Hindutvavadis leave no doubt that they have in mind a period dating back to remote antiquity, to many centuries before the supposed destruction of the Rama temple in 1528 or thereabouts. The only Sanskrit text that the VHP has put forth in substantiation of its claim, the *Skanda Purana*, appears to be rather unreliable, for the 'Ayodhya-mahatmya', or that portion of the Purana which recites the merits of visiting Ayodhya [mahatmya=eulogy], was most probably an eighteenth-century interpolation; moreover, the core of the Purana itself was evidently not compiled before the second half of the fourteenth century, and indeed may even bear a much later date, for there is a reference in it to the fourteenth-century Bengali poet, Vidyapati.[13] The inference is clear: Ayodhya did not occupy a central place in the religious imagination of Hindus,[14] and was endowed with a rare importance sometime after the establishment of Muslim hegemony in North India in the sixteenth century. Just as pointedly, the *janmasthan* does not appear in the itinerary of pilgrimage spots mentioned in the 'Ayodhya-mahatmya';[15] to the contrary, the relative insignificance of the janmasthan is suggested by the fact that the *Skanda Purana* devotes a mere eight verses to the description of the janmasthan, while lavishing a hundred verses on the *Svargadara*, or the site from where Rama is supposed to have ascended to heaven. Neither of the two Svargadara sites, moreover, bears any relation to the 'disputed structure'.

Sharma further argues that the location of Rama's birth enumerated in the 'Ayodhya-mahatmya' and other texts does not tally with the geographical location of where the Babri Masjid stood until December 1992; indeed, if we are to follow Gopal and his colleagues, that discrepancy should scarcely surprise us, for it is more than probable that the present-day Ayodhya is not the capital of the Iksvaku dynasty described in Valmiki's *Ramayana*, or even the Ayodhya identified in many later texts. The Ayodhya of today is on the banks of the river Sarayu; the Ayodhya that was a city in Koshala, and which is claimed to be the ancestor of the present-day Ayodhya, was located on the banks of the Ganga and was known to early writers as Saketa. There is also a controversial argument, advanced by Hans Bakker among others, that the Gupta rulers who in the fifth century AD sought to link their rule to the traditions associated with the name of Rama renamed the site known in Buddhist and Jain texts as Saketa to Ayodhya; indeed, to follow Bakker further, the Ayodhya of epic literature has no reference to any real city, but rather to an idealized city constructed from cities of a later period.[16] Historicity, as Bakker evidently suggests, is not the most productive way of understanding the scared geography of the Ramayana.

But it is more than in this confusion of names that the local tradition recognizes the ambiguous history of the origins of Ayodhya; as Gopal's brief recounting of the mythic origins of the present-day Ayodhya suggests, an attempt has been made to confer the city with a 'sacred lineage' that it never possessed or was endowed with only most ambiguously. Ayodhya was, so the story goes, lost after the Treta Yuga; while in search of Ayodhya, the Emperor Vikramaditya met Prayag, 'the king of tirthas' or pilgrimage sites, who guided the king to Ayodhya. Vikramaditya marked the spot, but could not find it later: an act of forgetting, wilful or otherwise, that would unleash its own consequences. A yogi whom Vikramaditya then encountered 'told him that he should let a cow and a calf roam. When the calf came across the janmabhumi milk would flow from its udder. The king followed the yogi's advice. When at a certain point the calf's udders began to flow the king decided that this was the site of the ancient Ayodhya.' Gopal concludes, 'even in the myths the process of identification of the sites appears uncertain and arbitrary.'[17]

What, then, of the more specific claim that the spot where the Babri Masjid stood until recently was the very spot where a temple existed in commemoration of the birth of Lord Rama, and that this temple was demolished to make room for the mosque? It is with respect to this question that scholars, commentators, journalists, and others on either side of the divide have most fully and self-consciously resorted to the idiom of history in substantiation of their respective positions. Consider, for example, the debate as it appeared in the pages of the *Indian Express*, a national newspaper then openly sympathetic to the VHP/RSS position. Pursuant to a response by Professor A. R. Khan to the pamphlet by Gopal and his associates in the pages of the *Indian Express* on 25 February 1990, Abhas Kumar Chatterjee on 26 March offered 'more evidence' to 'further remove', as he confidently put it, 'the unwarranted doubts harboured in some quarters' about the historicity of Ayodhya and the destruction of a Rama temple. Chatterjee noted that Joseph Tiffenthaler, a Jesuit priest who travelled extensively in the Oudh region between 1766 and 1771, wrote a detailed account of his impression of Ayodhya. On Tiffenthaler's account, 'The emperor Aurengzeb destroyed the fortress called Ramkot, and built at the same place a Mohammedan temple with three domes. Others say that it has been built by Babar.' Tiffenthaler went on to describe certain pillars, fourteen in number, twelve of which supported the inner arcades of the mosque, that bore non-Islamic designs and were reputed to have been brought from Lanka by Hanuman. The complex also bore signs of destruction, for a hollow space marked the place where stood the house in which Rama was born.

Either Babar or Aurangzeb, Tiffenthaler surmised, had 'destroyed the place in order to prevent the heathens from practising their superstition'. But the faith of a people is not so easily arrested; indeed, the destruction of the temple may have spurred Hindus in the ardent profession of their belief, for 'they continued to practise their religious ceremonies in both places [i.e., the mosque and the courtyard in front of it] knowing this to have been the birthplace of Rama'.[18] To Chatterjee this account appears as decisive a piece of evidence as one could summon of the association of the site with a Rama temple, and if the only point of uncertainty in Tiffenthaler's narrative is whether the act of villainy should be attributed to Aurangzeb or Babar, for Chatterjee this doubt is easily resolved by the inscription that was in the mosque. The position, then, as it appears to Chatterjee is that

The holy Janmabhoomi temple, which once stood in Ramkot disappears. Pillars of a destroyed Hindu temple are used to construct a mosque under Babar's orders in Ramkot at a spot surrounded by scores of other shrines associated with Ram. Hindus claim all along that this was the site of the temple. In spite of the efforts of Mughal rulers to keep them out, they reoccupy the site and continue to offer worship there. Great gatherings of people continue to be held here to celebrate Ram Navami. They defend the shrine against Muslim attacks in violent clashes as in 1853, when 70 Muslims making a bid to recapture the temple, are killed and are buried in the nearby 'ganj shaheedan'.

If this is not 'evidence', asks Chatterjee, then what would avail to satisfy the detractors of the Rama Janmabhoomi movement, unless it be the tarnished 'evidence' of 'their other exercises of history'?[19]

It has been pointed out that the inscription, over which a great deal of ink and blood has been spilled, says nothing whatsoever about a mosque having been constructed at the site of a temple; moreover, according to the historian Sunil Srivastava, the line *Bafarnmada-i-Shah Babur*, which was rendered by the English translator of Babur's memoirs as 'By the order of the Emperor Babur', means equally 'By the desire of the Emperor Babur'.[20] The claim that Hindus had all along considered the complex the site of the original Rama temple has been, as we have seen, contested; likewise, no undue significance can be attached to the fact that the complex is surrounded by 'scores of other shrines associated with Ram', for many of these shrines are of recent vintage, built to enshrine the importance of Ayodhya when it became politically expedient to do so. If there are many snrines in the area, there are not a few mosques as well.

But let us suppose that the inscription offers irrefutable testimony to the construction in 1528–9 of a mosque at the disputed site; and let us also concede that the presence of innumerable shrines offers evidence of the Hindus' devotion to Ayodhya as the birthplace of Rama. Is that evidence enough that, in order to pave the way for a mosque, a temple was desecrated and demolished? If the Muslim is enjoined, as Hindus are asked to believe, to celebrate the defeat of the infidel and the destruction of idolatry, why did not Mir Baqi, whom the inscription states as having built the mosque, mention the destruction of the temple, a deed for which he would have acquired merit? Why is it that the great *bhakta* of Rama, Tulsidas (1532–1623), who was a contemporary of Akbar (1556–1605) and an inhabitant of the Awadh region, said nothing about the destruction of a temple devoted to his venerable God?[21] Would not the destruction of a temple marking the janmasthan of Rama have evoked the anger of Rama's greatest devotee? Or could it be that, since Tulsidas had no firm attachment to the Ayodhya of history, an Ayodhya of stone embedded firmly in the ground—as he says in the *Ramacaritmanas* (2.74.3), '*Avadh tahan jahan Rama Nivasu*' ('Wherever Rama resides, there is Awadh')—he refused to concern himself with the destruction of Rama's temple?[22] But does that not make the position of Rama's self-professed devotees, who seek to be militant guardians of his memory, even more fraught with difficulties? Do they think that their devotion is superior to that of Tulsidas? If it is the sign of a bhakta that he or she is not moved to anger, must we not conclude then that those masquerading as the protectors of Hinduism today are least filled with the nectar of devotion to Rama? Or is there nothing, in their perspective, to be learned from Tulsidas?

These questions do not, however, square well with the enterprise of invoking historical evidence, and so we return to the question: was a temple demolished to make way for a mosque? Apart from the aforementioned inscription, the archaeological data has provided the grounds for much of the contestation, and indeed an entire work in a relatively recent series of political tracts has been devoted to this question.[23] The 'archaeological evidence' may not have assumed such importance were it not the case that it is now, in the words of Romila Thapar, 'the single most significant new source for the writing of early Indian history', and thus the ramifications of how the archaeological data is employed in the interpretation of the Rama Janmabhoomi dispute may well extend to the study of the entire Indian past.[24] According to proponents of the Rama Janmabhoomi movement, archaeological research has provided 'conclusive evidence' of the existence of an eleventh-century Vaishnava temple at the site of the Babri Masjid[25]; with just as much positivist certainty, scholars critical of the movement appear convinced that their work 'totally demolishes the theory of the mosque having been erected on the ruins of a large temple'.[26]

No one has denied that the Babri Masjid had fourteen pillars bearing non-Islamic motifs, but to understand the possible relationship of these pillars to the mosque, the extent of other excavations in and around the site, and finally the politics of these findings, we have to traverse briefly some historical ground. Excavations in Ayodhya go back to 1969–70, when an archaeological team from the Benares Hindu University began digging in three separate localities. Their results were first announced in the pages of *Indian Archaeology—A Review*, the principal organ of the Archaeological Survey of India. The history of Ayodhya was described as going back to the NBP (Northern Black Polished Ware) Period, 'which is generally accepted as covering the sixth to perhaps the first centuries BC'.[27] This is of more than incidental significance, for Rama is described in the Valmiki Ramayana as having been born in the Treta Yuga, or thousands of years before the present-day Kali Yuga, which itself began in 3102 BC. Yet there is no archaeological evidence to support the view that Ayodhya was inhabited at that time; and it is much less likely then that the Ayodhya of today could have been the large urban settlement, replete with palaces and buildings on a grand scale, that the Ayodhya of the Valmiki *Ramayana* purports to be. As Gopal and others would have it, and as I have previously stated, the Ayodhya of the epic poem is 'fictional', and what is later taken to be Ayodhya is none other than Saketa, which—as noted before—the king Skanda Gupta (also known as Vikramaditya) renamed Ayodhya, no doubt because 'he was trying to gain prestige for himself by drawing on the tradition of the Suryavamsi kings, a line to which Rama is said to have belonged'.[28]

It is agreed that habitation in Ayodhya continued after the NBP period into the end of the Gupta period; between the sixth and the eleventh centuries, Ayodhya appears to have been abandoned. Following the first round of excavations, in 1975 B. B. Lal, who had just retired as Director-General of the Archaeological Survey, initiated a project on the archaeology of the 'Ramayana sites'. In the reports that he submitted to the Archaeological Survey in 1976–7 and 1979–80, he acknowledged this 'break in occupation', and the rehabitation of the disputed site 'around the eleventh century AD'. Lal not only made no mention of any pillar-bases, he went so far as to say that though 'several later-medieval brick-and-kankar lime floors [had] been met with', 'the entire late period was devoid of any special interest'.[29] Is not the 'late period' the very time when the temple is supposed to have been demolished? Notwithstanding these reports, B. B. Lal was much later, towards the end of 1990, to submit that certain brick bases he had excavated in the 1970s were meant to support pillars and thus suggested 'the existence of a temple-like structure in the south of the Baburi Masjid'.

B. B. Lal's extraordinary delay in making known his 'findings', particularly when they contradict the earlier published results, has of course been questioned, but that is the least of the objections that have been raised by historians and archaeologists opposed to the Rama Janmabhoomi movement. Turning first to the carvings on the pillars, it has been argued that they are far from offering any irrefutable association with Vaisnavism: they lack the emblems through which Vishnu is known, such as the *shankha* (conch shell), *chakra* (wheel), *gada* (mace), and *padma* (lotus). The motifs on the pillars suggest varying dates between the ninth and the eleventh centuries; to be more precise, 'eight of them are dissimilar, the pattern of carvings or decorative sculptures being quite different from each other', while the remaining four, though carrying similar motifs, 'do not necessarily occur in a particular grouping'. The predominant motifs are floral, conventionalized or stylized lotuses, and the female figure. All these motifs, while common to much 'Hindu' art, are also found in early Buddhist art originating from places like Sanchi and Bharhut, as well as in Jain and Shaivite architecture. As one scholar has argued, 'the only pillar (doorjamb?) which has anything that may be called a religious motif is the one found in the Sita-ki-Rasoi [literally, "Sita's Kitchen"]', a structure that stood apart from the Babri Masjid though in the same complex. 'On its lower part it has a figure with a *trishula* in its left hand', but the trishula most emphatically suggests a Shaivite association, 'for no Vaishnava *dvarapala* [door keeper] can be and has ever been shown with the *trishula* as an attribute'.[30]

The pillars themselves, Lal and his supporters have claimed, were sustained by pillar bases that he is said to have excavated. Sharma and his colleagues observe that the site notebook that Lal as a professional archaeologist would have had to keep, as well as the register of antiquities connected with the Ayodhya excavations, have not been made available to other archaeologists. Nor has a full report of Lal's supposed findings, which should have followed the preliminary report, been published. As Sharma puts it bluntly, the 'failure to make available the relevant material raises not only questions of ethics in using archaeological material, but also makes it doubtful whether Professor Lal's new interpretation is really borne out by the actual record and material of his excavations'.[31] But let us, once again, suppose that Lal did excavate some pillar bases, and let us hear the voice of his supporters first. Is there agreement that the black pillars and the bases said to support them are structurally akin, and that both can be dated to the eleventh century?[32] This is certainly not the considered opinion of many professional archaeologists. Thus D. Mandal, in his monograph *Ayodhya: Archaeology after Demolition*, argues in considerable detail that it is 'highly probable that the so-called pillar bases are actually the remnant portions of walls of different structural phases'. He concurs with Sharma et al. that the so-called pillar bases would have been unable to sustain the 'vertical load of large-sized stone pillars', which must be construed as being decorative rather than load-bearing pillars. In short, in Mandal's view, 'the contention that a "pillared building" was raised in the eleventh century AD is absolutely baseless'.[33]

Similarly, Mandal makes short shrift of alleged 'new archaeological discoveries' at the Babri Masjid site of a 'hoard' of sculptures and other stone fragments bearing figures of Vishnu's incarnations, on the basis of which a team of eight archaeologists and historians were able to claim that their finds 'prove that there did exist at this very site a magnificent temple, from at least the 11th century, which was destroyed to build a mosque-like structure over the debris of the temple in the 16th century'.[34] A panel depicting incarnations of Vishnu did not, as Mandal notes, appear in the 'dig photo'; other objects, such as an image of Shiva-Parvati, 'were found some distance away', and in general the 'stratigraphic position and locus of discovery' of various 'finds' have not been specified. From the point of view of an archaeologist with professional training, 'archaeological finds acquire the status of evidence when situated in their context', and 'context' in archaeology is 'the concerned stratigraphy, the sequence of soil deposits and the cultural material that is found in the various deposits'.[35] Mandal made then the pointed observation that 'not a single photograph showing the sequential stages of the unearthing of the pieces of the "hoard" has so far been published', and this neglect of stratigraphy marred the entire digging operation.[36] The haphazard manner in which the digging was conducted did not merely ignore the stratigraphy of the site, in relation to which both the structural remains and the objects found there must be assessed, but in fact destroyed the stratigraphic evidence. Romila Thapar describes the recent operations in Ayodhya as 'wilful destruction':[37] those who have pilloried sixteenth-century Muslims as pillagers are shown to be accused of the crime themselves.

The so-called archaeological evidence proffered in support of the hypothesis about the existence of a temple at the site of the Babri Masjid has thus been put forth on the problematic supposition that the stratigraphically unassociated structural pieces—the pillar-bases, pillars at the Babri Masjid and in trenches at some remove from the mosque, and a door jamb built of the same blackstone found at a mound—are 'an integral part of one and the same structure, namely, a "Hindu Temple"'.[38] As one might expect, proponents of the Rama Janmabhoomi movement have also been described as being selective in their use of 'evidence', a charge that is the most transparent reason for debates in the historical profession anywhere in the world. In the case of Ayodhya, it has been noted by more than one archaeologist and historian that excavations at Ayodhya have yielded Islamic glazed ware pottery pieces; all these pieces 'are securely dated', in the words ironically of one of the protagonists of the Rama Janmabhoomi movement, to a period between the thirteenth and fifteenth centuries, and on stylistic and comparative grounds, that is in relation to West Asian pieces, they are determined to be Islamic in origin.[39] The archaeological evidence, in other words, indicates not a temple but rather the distinct possibility 'of a Muslim settlement' at or in the proximity of the mosque 'from the 13th century onwards'.[40]

It is the contention, then, of credentialled critics of the Rama Janmabhoomi movement that the entire archaeological enterprise to demonstrate the existence of a temple, more particularly an eleventh-century Vaishnava shrine dedicated to Rama, at the Babri Masjid site has been marked by scholarly incompetence and ignorance, exceedingly questionable motives, violation of professional ethical codes, and even—it would not be too far-fetched to say—downright dishonesty. Such work, argue some professional archaeologists, cannot withstand professional scrutiny; and indeed the temple theory stands, on their view, completely contradicted. 'The available information is quite adequate to support the categorical statement', states Mandal, 'that there was no temple, either of stone or of brick or of both materials, lying below the mosque at the site during the three centuries (the thirteenth to the fifteenth) which preceded the construction of the mosque.'[41] Archaeological evidence in itself may not have furnished sufficient grounds for establishing the prior existence of a Hindu temple, but given that the historicity of the temple was sought to be proven by the use of archaeological data, archaeology had perforce to become a contested terrain. As Romila Thapar puts it simply, 'Whereas anyone has a right to his or her beliefs, the same cannot be held for a claim to historicity.'[42] The great transgression, one might say, consists in having shifted the dispute from the domain of 'belief' to the realm of 'history', and it is to an interrogation of this transgression, and the collusion of both the proponents and antagonists of the Rama Janmabhoomi movement in propelling history as the idiom in which the dispute is likely to be understood and resolved, that we shall now turn.

III

Insofar as one accepts that historical and archaeological evidence can establish or effectively contradict the theory that a Hindu temple was demolished to make way for a mosque in 1528–9, and further that the awareness of the 'truth' provided the grounds for a resolution of the problem, and does so perhaps even today when the Babri Masjid no longer exists, it is quite certain that the proponents of the temple theory have fared poorly in the debate. Again, if one were to accept, as indeed one must, that there are certain standards for historical knowledge and scholarship, then it is just as clear that the standards by which the antagonists of the temple theory abide are far more stringent and in congruence with standards that are accepted within the historical profession worldwide. Of course one might well ask, and with perfectly good reason, why we should allow the notion of what constitutes acceptable historical scholarship to come down to us from the West, or why 'history' should be none other than what 'history' has been in the West. But given that both the proponents and critics of the temple theory have given their implicit, and often explicit, consent to the notion of historical knowledge, craft, and understanding inherited from the West, the question within these parameters is one of assessing how far either party has adhered to the canons of historical scholarship.

The promoters of the Rama Janmabhoomi movement have, as a whole, not merely displayed poor scholarship and an impoverished understanding of the nature of the historical enterprise; they have not been above fabricating 'evidence' or other material that would support their position. Thus, for example, the public was one day in December 1990, not long after the kar sevaks ['workers in the cause of Hinduism'] breached the defences placed around the Babri Masjid and placed a saffron flag atop one of its domes, informed through the newspapers that the Bharatiya Janata Party (BJP) had urged the Prime Minister to accept 'Mahatma Gandhi's formula' in an attempt to achieve a resolution to the Rama Janmabhoomi-Babri Masjid dispute. Writing to the Prime Minister, the general secretary of the BJP apprised him of an article purportedly written by Gandhi and published in the *Harijan Sevak* on 27 July 1937, wherein Gandhi had said:

It is a very heinous sin to forcibly take over any place of religious worship. During Mughal times many places of worship, which were sacred to Hindus, were looted and destroyed. Many of them were converted into Masjids. *Although both temples and masjids are places of worship of God and there is no difference between the two, yet the way of prayers and traditions of both Hindus and Muslims worship are quite different.*

From the religious point of view, a Muslim will never tolerate a Hindu placing an idol in a Masjid where he had been praying for long. Similarly, a Hindu will never be able to bear where he has been worshipping Rama, Krishna, Shankar and Devi, is converted into a masjid. As a matter of fact such events, wherever they occur, are a symbol of religious slavery. Both Hindus and Muslims should try to settle such disputes among themselves. Places of Muslim worship which are under the control of the Hindus should be returned to the Muslims. Similarly, Hindu religious places which have been taken over by the Muslims should be handed over to Hindus voluntarily ... .

There is, in this letter, at least something—such as the portions that I have placed in italics—that one can imagine might justifiably be credited to the Mahatma had he written the letter, but one must wonder at the audacity entailed in pushing forth a forgery, and that too in the name of the 'Father of the Nation', in an attempted resolution of the dispute. Queries revealed that the news weekly in which the article supposedly appeared, the *Harijan Sevak*, was not published on 27 July 1937, and the *Collected Works of Mahatma Gandhi*, which runs into over ninety hefty volumes, does not carry the letter, certainly not under that date. The BJP could not produce a copy of the letter, and its general secretary, when interrogated about the matter, insisted that 'it is for the Prime Minister to deny its authenticity'.[43]

It is always possible to argue that in questions of faith, the evidence that history can furnish has no place, and to some variant of this position we shall return in due course. It bears reiteration, however, that the proponents of the Rama Janmabhoomi movement have placed themselves entirely within the problematic established by historicism, and thus display all the signs of confusion and anxiety attendant upon those who, while having accepted in principle the standards of interrogation and 'truth' set by an alien culture, then reject those very standards as woefully inadequate and yet simultaneously claim on their own behalf a more rigid and exact adherence to those standards.[44] While critical if not contemptuous of history, the proponents of the temple theory have been the most ardent advocates for the historicity of the temple, and have relentlessly pursued a historical line of inquiry. The contradictions of seeking to set 'faith' apart from 'history', and yet seeking validity by the invocation of historical authorities (or by attempting to demonstrate, as is quite common, the compatibility of 'science' with Vedic religion), are well-exemplified in much of the literature, such as Abhas Chatterjee's article in the *Indian Express*, a daily newspaper that then unabashedly advocated Hindutva history. 'To take first things first,' writes Chatterjee, 'the question whether Lord Ram was born at this spot, or was born at all, is irrelevant. Items of religious belief are essentially matters of faith and not of history, in Hinduism as much as in other religions of the world.'[45]

Nothing in what Chatterjee says is likely to incite disagreement; indeed, as we have seen, the brunt of the argument from the critics of the temple theory has been that history ought never to have been implicated in an attempt to resolve the dispute. As Gopal and his associates wrote, 'Each individual has a right to his or her belief and faith. But when beliefs claim the legitimacy of history, then the historian has to attempt a demarcation between the limits of belief and historical evidence.'[46] On Chatterjee's view, every faith rests on certain 'myths' which its adherents hold sacred and beyond interrogation, and the Hindu should not be put to tests which we would not think of applying to Christians or Muslims. 'Can any of these', asks Abhas Chatterjee of Christian beliefs such as Christ being born of a virgin mother, or his rising from the grave after three days, 'be proved by historical evidence?' Can it be doubted that the interrogation and violation of such beliefs induces, judging from the anger with which

Muslims the world over reacted to Salman Rushdie's mere suggestion that the Koran may not be a work of revelation, extreme feelings of 'indignation and vengeance'? To the Hindu, Rama is a historical figure as much as a deity, and his life and deeds are as deserving of respect as the lives of Christ or the Prophet Mohammed. 'Historians should not, therefore,' warns Chatterjee, 'step beyond what can be described as their jurisdiction by seeking to test the Hindu's faith by the yardsticks of historical evidence.'[47]

There is no denying that the faith of Hindus, not to mention Muslims and secularists, has most severely been tested by the particular concatenation of circumstances associated with Ayodhya, but Chatterjee's strictures against 'Marxist historians', as they have been billed by proponents of the temple theory,[48] deliberately obscure the limited design that has guided them in their research and public pronouncements. The suggestion that their endeavours constitute a travesty of the beliefs of Hindus, or that they are determined to deny that Rama was a historical personage (a matter that Chatterjee deems as being quite 'irrelevant' in any case), or that they would deny to Hindus what they would allow adherents of other faiths, namely the privilege of indulging them in their beliefs, is scarcely borne out by the writings and pronouncements of these 'Marxist historians'. If these historians are 'Marxist', we can be assured that they have no motivation in elevating one faith over any other, and no particular inclination towards disparaging Islam rather than Hinduism. Their intent, which is by no means unproblematic, as I shall argue shortly, is to unmask the attempt by the proponents of the temple theory to camouflage what are mere 'myths' as 'history'; as is quite clear to them, the instrumental use of history to gain political power and render 'Muslims' into 'others' for Hindus must be unequivocally deplored.

The proponents of the temple theory, in any case, cannot be accused of irony or self-reflexivity. Having castigated the historian for meddling in matters of faith, Chatterjee proceeds to furnish historical evidence that would establish, beyond any reasonable doubt, 'that Babar's mosque was constructed by demolishing the Janmabhoomi temple, which stood at the site, and using its debris'. Chatterjee belongs to that school of thought which is only too pleased to discount European accounts of India as generally unreliable, a not unreasonable position to adopt if we take into account the Orientalism thesis, but which greedily devours these accounts when it appears to suit their purpose to do so. Thus Chatterjee's authorities for the view that a Rama temple existed on the spot where the mosque was subsequently built are all—with the exception of the 'Ayodhya-Mahatmya', a text that as we have seen can scarcely be invoked in support of the temple thesis—European travellers and scholars. As Chatterjee says, 'For at least two and a half centuries, all travellers (Tiffenthaler 1766–71), surveyors (Martin 1838, Carnegie 1870, Neville 1905), archaeologists (Cunningham 1862–4, Fuhrer 1891), historians (Beveridge 1922) and scholars (Hans Bakker 1984) find the available evidence to leave no doubt that Babar's mosque was constructed by demolishing the Janmabhoomi temple, which stood at the site, and using its debris.'[49]

Had Chatterjee taken care to read these aforementioned texts, instead of relying upon some second-hand accounts, many of them unquestionably in a garbled form, he might have understood the difficulties in appropriating them to his ends. Hans Bakker, for example, has come to the tentative conclusion that Rama as a figure of divinity had no substantial following in India until the eleventh-twelfth centuries,[50] and if that is so, it is hardly possible that the worship of Rama has been a central tenet of Hindu belief since time immemorial as has been claimed, or that a temple stood at the Rama Janmasthan, the existence of which is supposed to be mentioned in the *Skanda Purana*, 'composed centuries before', as Chatterjee maintains, 'the invasion of Babur'. Perhaps Chatterjee may have had some awareness of the incongruities in his argument, for elsewhere in his piece the 'conclusive' evidence is offered in a somewhat tamer fashion. Thus, he insists on the fact that there is 'conclusive proof that material obtained by destroying a Hindu temple, or palace, had been used in building the mosque',[51] but the unexplained substitution of a 'palace' for the 'temple' is achieved in so nonchalant a manner as though to suggest that it made no material difference what sort of structure, if any, existed before the mosque came up in 1528–9. One thought, after all, that what has been in question is whether a particular temple dedicated to Rama, and marking the very spot where he is said to have been born, was demolished to pave way for the mosque.

The attraction to history among the advocates of the temple theory has not gone unnoticed by scholars. One historian who interviewed kar sevaks in Ayodhya drawn from western Uttar Pradesh has noted that they displayed a 'preoccupation with history': 'many of them specifically mentioned historical dates, notably the birth of Ram (nine lakh years ago), Babur's invasion (1528), the installation of the deity (1949).'[52] Yet this invocation of purported historical 'facts' has not precluded, among the ideologues of the movement, a disavowal of history when it has appeared to them as an insubstantial mode of defending their position. 'The facts of history', we find stated in one issue of the *Organiser*, the organ of the RSS, 'appear fiction only to a person suffering from Historologia [sic!] and not to a balanced mind who is not afraid of any unpalatable fact whether it is for or against'; and yet in the same journal it is averred, in another article on the dispute over Ayodhya, that

The belief of millions in such matters is enough to bestow upon them the sanctity more than History can .... The very fact that Ram is worshipped from far east to Arabian sea, from Himalayas to Kanyakumari, and tradition passing from father to son believes him to be a living person of a prehistoric era is proof enough that a person of that name existed and was born in a city called Ayodhya.[53]

Neeladri Bhattacharya has put together these and numerous other citations from the writings emanating from the VHP/RSS camp to point to both the appeal that the rhetoric of history has among the advocates of the temple theory and their inability to have a command over this rhetoric. He has characterized the approach of VHP ideologues as the 'mythification of history'. Several narratives of the story of Rama Janmabhoomi are possible; the particular narrative chosen by the proponents of the temple theory includes a certain modicum of verifiable general historical facts, because on the basis of this 'concretization' it is rather easier to induce in people the belief that the entire narrative has a certain credibility. 'Once the reader is made to identify with such familiar facts', which have less to do with Ayodhya or the status of the Rama Janmabhoomi, but more with widely accepted circumstances pertaining to the reigns of Akbar, Aurangzeb, and others, 'he is persuaded to believe in the authenticity of the narrative'. Thus 'invented details' and the grossest distortions of history are, through this mode of familiarization, 'sought to be authenticated'. As Bhattacharya argues, the narrative of the proponents of the temple theory and their supporters transforms, or attempts to transform, various myths—'the myth of ancient Ayodhya, the myth of its loss and recovery, the myth of the destruction of the temple and the construction of the mosque', and so forth—into history. The Rama Janmabhoomi movement derives its very sustenance from this falsified or 'mythic history'.[54]

It is the manner in which the VHP's appeal to history has been contested that one begins to find how far the two parties to the dispute converge, rather than (as one had thought) diverge, in their

views; more significantly, we can begin to understand why the ideologues of the Rama Janmabhoomi movement can so readily abandon
the recourse to history, invoking in its place a whole set of beliefs that
are said to belong to the common tradition of the Hindus, while their
antagonists must perforce remain committed to history and the indubitable evidence that it claims to furnish; and perhaps we might then
perceive why this very commitment to history, and to the 'truth' that
we tease out of it, constitutes the precise grounds for the inability of
secularists and other antagonists of the temple theory to understand
why 'mythic history' has, and certainly ought to have, an attraction
for many even in the age of modernity.[55] To begin with, and this is a
point well worth reiteration, history—that is to say, historical facts,
the resort and appeal to historical evidence, the historical sensibility,
and historicization—remains the terrain on which the battle is sought
to be fought and, it would not be too much to say, brought to a
decisive finish. As we have seen, the enterprise on both sides has
revolved around a series of questions, to wit: was there or was there
not a temple at the site on which the mosque was built in 1528? If so,
was the temple brought down at the orders of Babur? What does
archaeology have to say in this matter? What, if any, kind of concrete
testimony do the pillars in the now-demolished mosque offer to the
student of history and archaeology? These questions could, as long as
we are confined to questions of 'fact', easily be multiplied.

What is equally arresting is the easy separation between myth and
history, and the almost naive invocation of positivism, that we find in
the critiques which secular and left historians have offered of the
Rama Janmabhoomi movement. Bhattacharya writes as though there
could be a 'true' history of Ayodhya, as though this history could, by
the mere sifting of evidence at the hands of a skilled, detached, and
dedicated historian, be made available to us. He writes as if history
and myth, or even history and historiography, could be separated, as
though the historian could be like the proverbial swan, the
Paramhansa, that can separate the water from the milk in the tumbler.
Thus we hear the constant reprimand: stories circulated by VHP
ideologues and historians 'have no support in any historical evidence', and 'it is easy to demonstrate that many of the records referred to do not exist': myths and history become indistinguishable.[56]
As far as the Babri Masjid-Rama Janmabhoomi affair is in question,
secular historians have shown themselves to be uneasy with what
might be called category confusions and with the ambiguities that
arise not merely from discarding conventional disciplinary pieties

but from a supreme indifference to fundamental distinctions that modern historians take for granted. Though no one can doubt that secular historians have by far the better 'evidence' than their proponents, they fail to recognize that the writers of the pamphlets and books emanating from the Hindu right conform to a very old tradition which makes no distinction between history and myth.

Nor is Bhattacharya alone, let us be certain, in attempting to demarcate myths from history. In the special 'Black Sunday' issue of their newsletter *Manas*, the Sampradayikta Virodhi Andolan [Movement Against Communalism], a small organization comprised mainly of left-wing activists, historians, and other scholars, enumerates various myths propagated by the Bharatiya Janata Party, and then goes on to provide a contradiction of each of these myths.[57] To counter the myth that 'the Muslim majority state of Kashmir has special privileges through Article 370', the reader is informed that 'all the provisions which gave it a greater degree of autonomy than other states ceased to operate in 1954', and thus Kashmir, far from enjoying any special privileges, has been in the unfortunate position of being under the rule of the central government. Again, it is suggested that the myth of a rapid increase in the population of Muslims, owing to the provision in Islamic law whereby a man is permitted to have four wives, is a brazen lie that is 'easily disproved by census figures'.[58]

Clearly what the authors of 'Black Sunday' present is, on the whole, not merely well-intentioned but also a good deal more sensible and accurate than anything that their antagonists may have to say. Yet certain insuperable problems persist in the manner in which they have joined the debate. They are absolutely right to point out that, even if it were established that a temple was torn down to make way for the Babri Masjid, the destruction of the mosque would not thereby be justified. A historical wrong which can be laid at the foot of a conqueror is scarcely corrected by demolishing, some 500 years later, a religious edifice at which prayers were still offered by members of the community. 'The destruction of places of worship in medieval and ancient times', note the authors of 'Black Sunday', was 'an integral part of political power'; those who wielded temporal power also exercised religious control, and had a temple been destroyed to make way for the mosque (a proposition in itself difficult to substantiate), one is to infer from it nothing more than the fact that in 'medieval' times the destruction of religious edifices signified not necessarily the animosity between adherents of different faiths but rather an essential aspect of political authority and the whims of conquerors.

The authors of 'Black Sunday' are entirely right in insisting that the actions of warriors, leaders, and invaders in the pre-modern period might be better understood within a framework of the politics of conquest, and that is also the productive path pursued by Romila Thapar in her interpretation of Mahmud of Ghazni's raid in 1026 on the fabled Hindu temple at Somnath, about which I have written in the previous chapter.[59] We may well wish to commend the authors of 'Black Sunday' for their efforts to secure communal harmony and peace through the articulation, in a tone of moderation, of generally acceptable views, but their analysis brings forth fresh problems. If their suggestion that in 'medieval' times the separation between religion and politics was inconceivable is to be pursued to its logical conclusion, then naturally Hindu rulers were just as likely to be implicated in that unholy marriage of religion and politics as Babur or any other Muslim ruler. Not surprisingly, then, the reader is informed that destruction of 'places of worship was not done exclusively by Muslim rulers.' A number of instances of Hindu kings engaging in the plunder and destruction of religious edifices are then furnished, and at least one example is offered of a temple built at the site of a Buddhist vihara. While it is unquestionably an imperative to establish that the adherents of no one faith have a monopoly on evil and barbarism, the pamphlet gives the inescapable feeling that the argument stems from the logic of *quid pro quo*: if, that is, it is conceded that the Rama temple was demolished to make way for the Babri Masjid, then let us concede, on the basis of historical evidence, that the Hindus themselves were guilty of similarly heinous acts many times over. The veracity of such an argument apart, its morality, whereby equivalencies of evil are established, is exceedingly questionable, and even more uncertain must be the socio-cultural and political effects of this mode of historicization and recall of historical memory. By way of analogy, no one expects that abuse of a person within her or his own family makes abuse by an outsider any more tolerable.

Secondly, one cannot object too strongly to the unqualified valorization of modernity in 'Black Sunday' and indeed other like-minded literature. The attack on the mosque, argue the authors of 'Black Sunday', 'is an act which utilises the destruction of religious places for political power. Therefore, it is reminiscent of the barbaric politics of ancient and medieval rulers that defies all modern, democratic, and civilised institutions of our society.'[60] Likewise, to Neeladri Bhattacharya's way of thinking, it is a 'medieval logic' that is 'at work behind the struggle for the Ramajanmabhumi', while Amartya Sen is of the view that the Hindu communalists are guided partly by 'militant obscurantism', which he describes as the 'political use of people's credulity in *unreasoned and archaic* beliefs in order to generate fierce extremism' (italics added).[61] One could begin with asking how, considering India's recent admission to the community of 'modern' nations, the Babri Masjid was able to stand for nearly five hundred years, and why it had to be knocked down at the very moment when India has been eager to demonstrate to the world its renunciation of tradition, archaic customs, and other vestiges of 'backwardness'.

One could also point to the most peculiar and embarrassing circumstance that not only has the twentieth century been particularly violent, but that it has enlisted the aid of science and technology to refine and perfect barbaric methods of inflicting pain and suffering on victims and exterminating entire populations chosen for no other reason than they constituted, or appeared to constitute, distinct identities that were deemed to be undesirable.[62] If anything, it is the modern world which has had an acute difficulty in living with multiple identities, and its mode of dealing with this difficulty has been to freeze, demarcate, and isolate identities. It is the 'modern' rather than 'medieval' Hinduism of the proponents of the Rama Janmabhoomi movement that has insisted on stripping the Hindu faith of the numerous, often contradictory, strands of belief, devotion, and practice with which it has been fed for three millennia. It was the so-called non-modern world that lived comfortably with multiple and often conflicting traditions of the Ramayana story; and it is unmistakably the modern movement associated with the agitation over the alleged Rama Janmabhoomi temple at Ayodhya that has sought to narrow our interpretations of the Ramayana and elevate the *Ramacaritmanas* of Tulsidas over other Ramayanas as the authoritative version of the story of Rama.[63] Is the homogenization of Hinduism, a project that the 'liberators' of the Rama Janmabhoomi temple are sworn to uphold, characteristic of the 'medieval' period, over a long duration of which India was swept by the bhakti movement and renditions of the Ramayana appeared in the 'vernacular' Indian languages, or is it not rather a sign of the modern?[64]

IV

In my representation of secular historians and their communalist opponents, I may have, it is possible to argue, inadvisably eschewed the larger and social and political context, and may not have been sufficiently attentive to the respective strengths of the two camps, or to facts of political patronage. But I make no pretence of offering a comprehensive account of the events leading to the destruction of the Babri Masjid, its extraordinary aftermath as violence engulfed many urban centres, or the role of the principal political actors; and I have, in keeping with my interests in this book, remained resolutely fixed on how, and in what manner, history came to be so ascendant in the affair of the Babri Masjid. Some readers may object that even within the limited scope of my enterprise, it should have been incumbent on me to recognize that the secularist and communalist interpreters were not evenly matched, and that the very terrain of history was scarcely a level playing field. The proponents of the temple theory belong to an intricate web of networks—the VHP and RSS among them—and though the BJP and its allies did not form the government at that juncture in Indian history, communalist scholars must have been emboldened by the political patronage extended to them. Senior members of the present Vajpayee government, including Vajpayee himself and the Home Minister, L. K. Advani, have been long-time members of the RSS, and the construction of a Hindu temple at Ayodhya remains very much on the agenda of the RSS. The VHP has grown immensely since its inception in the 1960s, and had already, by the late 1980s, become not merely a worldwide organization but a conduit for funnelling money from the affluent Indian diaspora in the industrialized democracies in the West, and especially the US and the UK, to organizations committed to the rejuvenation of political Hinduism. Though the paper trail from VHP-America to Ayodhya—and in the twenty-first century to Gujarat—is not always easily deciphered, it is widely known that both institutional and personal contributions from diasporic Indians and their organizations have come into the hands of the VHP and related organizations in India.

As one anonymous reader of this manuscript put it, 'a handful of professional historians' was matched against a wide network of organizations.[65] However, the supposition that the antagonists of Hindutva should be viewed as 'a handful of professional historians' struggling against immense odds and powerful political interests needs to be treated with considerable scepticism. There were twenty signatories alone to a single document produced by S. Gopal and fellow historians at a single university; but perhaps this is reading 'handful' too literally. Consider, then, that almost no historian could be found either at Jawaharlal Nehru University or Delhi University, both of which have large and easily the most renowned history faculties in the country, to support the temple theory; nor is it inconsequential that the historians at these two universities, and a handful of others at various other institutions, are the ones who have gained the most recognition among colleagues overseas. To speak of these historians and other secular intellectuals who had immersed themselves in the debate as a very small group that found itself besieged by much larger communalist organizations is to overlook the institutional associations of the country's leading secular historians, their leadership of institutions such as the Indian Council for Historical Research and the Nehru Memorial Library, their access to privileges and sinecures, and the patronage they themselves received under more hospitable regimes. It is also to ignore the fact that though these secular historians were at a great ideological remove from the Jamaat-i Islami, the Jamiyat al-ulama, the Muslim Personal Law Board, and even the Babri Masjid Action Committee, they were nonetheless in agreement with these organizations that the Babri Masjid deserved the protection of the state. So to represent the secular historian as some kind of lone ranger is to obscure the complex if provisional alliances that the crisis of the Babri Masjid produced in the Indian polity.[66]

If, as seems indubitably to be the case, the proponents of the temple theory are among the same people who in the last couple of years have succeeded in placing astrology in the national curriculum, then one might well be inclined to marvel at the access to power which communalist scholars and the organizations on whose behalf they speak evidently have. But, conversely, the commentary in English-language newspapers on the attempt to introduce astrology into educational curriculums has so unequivocally signalled opposition to the proposed changes that no one can possibly mistake the secular consensus on this question for a mere aberration or think that secular intellectuals and their supporters constitute, to appropriate Lord Dufferin's characterization of the Congress in its early years, a 'minuscule minority'. The sheer scorn with which 'Vedic astrology' and other ancient and medieval 'superstitions' have been received point, I would submit, to the fundamental issues at stake in the dispute between secular and communalist scholars. In the characterization of the Rama Janmabhoomi movement as a relic of barbarism, as an example of 'medieval' logic and unrepentant primitivism, we arrive at the crux of the matter.

The antagonists (and proponents too) of the temple theory have a great deal invested in modernity, but as I have previously suggested, it is not a commitment to modernity—and thus to 'correct' history, backed by the force of evidence, not disgraced or disfigured by 'myth'—that will render India less susceptible to communal conflagrations and hatred in the future, but rather the very abandonment of the discourse of history. I have furnished an argument about the perils of the historical enterprise in Chapter I, but a number of points can bear reiteration in order to bring my perspective into sharper focus. Hindu India became known to Europeans for the absence of historical records and, more significantly, the lack of an historical sensibility. Hegel, in his 1830–1 lectures on the philosophy of history, was to pronounce emphatically upon the absence of historical compositions in India. He went so far as to say that in India, 'History, is not to be looked for; and here the distinction between China and India is most clearly and strongly manifest'.[67] On the one hand, given that the Hindus had acquired, from the time of remote antiquity, a formidable reputation in 'Geometry, Astronomy and Algebra', and had displayed 'great advances in Philosophy', besides producing the most complex works of Grammar, the neglect of the 'department of *History*' appeared to be all the more anomalous. Yet it was completely understandable that the 'Hindoos have no History in the form of annals (historia) [and] no History in the form of transactions (*res gestae*)'. India presented, in Hegel's view, the most remarkable example of a polity without a State, for the only proper basis of a 'State, the principle of freedom', was 'altogether absent' in India. In that ancient land of the Hindus, subjective freedom was an impossibility. Hegel had no doubt that 'the contradictory processes of a dissolution of fixed rational and definite conceptions in their Ideality, and on the other side, a degradation of this ideality to a multiformity of sensuous objects', made the Hindus 'incapable of writing History'.[68] Here Hegel anticipates the argument, frequently encountered in recent critiques of history, that history has been called too often to service the nation-state, though Hegel obviously did not view the nation-state as an encumbrance upon emancipatory histories.

We scarcely need to pursue Hegel's argument in all its ramifications; and as for its place within Orientalism, that is all too evident. But indignation and consternation at the preposterousness of the philosophical argument should not obscure the critical detail, namely Hegel's observation that historical compositions were not to be found in Hindu India. What Hegel could not conceive was that perhaps Hindu India did not care much for such compositions, but this was to be understood nonetheless as a presumed 'incapacity'. The notion that Hindus were without much of a sense of the past had been a commonplace since at least the time of the Arab geographer Alberuni, who visited India around AD 1,000. As Alberuni put it, 'Unfortunately the Hindus do not pay much attention to the historical order of things, they are very careless in relating the chronological succession of their kings ... .'[69] Hegel and his generation, however, were to render this argument into an episteme, and in the early part of the nineteenth century, as delineated in Chapter I, James Mill, Thomas Macaulay, and numerous other British scholar-administrators of India took up this question in a concerted fashion;[70] subsequently, Indians themselves were to adopt this argument. As for Hegel, so for Mill nothing attested better to the backwardness of Hindus than their lack of histories; lack of historical compositions pointed to the intellectual immaturity of a civilization, and to the low place of such a civilization in an evolutionary and evaluative scale. 'All rude nations', Mill averred, 'neglect history, and are gratified with the productions of the mythologists and poets.'[71] The conclusion, quite inescapably so, was that as Hindus had failed to produce historical works, they were still a medieval and, in the language of the day, 'rude' people.

History had then to be enshrined as the pre-eminent discourse of emancipation, a discourse that would awaken the Hindu consciousness, bring the greatness of the past before the eyes of Hindus, and evoke the collective memory of a people who had fallen from the state of grace into decadent if not evil ways. And so Hindus fell captive to the historical mode, as the writings of educators, philosophers, nationalists, and other civic-minded people so amply testify. The works of Bankimchandra Chatterjee and Vivekananda, to name only two legendary figures for whom Hindu India's acceptance of the historical enterprise marked the beginning of India's engagement with modernity, are well known in this regard, but hundreds of lesser-known figures were all too ready to commence the study of history. In Bengal, the first 'three books of narrative prose' intended for use by 'young officials of the Company learning the local vernacular were books of history', while the immensely popular *History of India* by Tarinicharan Chattopadhyay, which had gone through eighteen editions between 1858 and 1878, unequivocally created a niche for itself with the argument that 'All Sanskrit sources that are now available are full of legends and fabulous tales; apart from the *Rajatarangini* there is not a single true historical account'.[72] In Indian schools, historical studies were henceforth to occupy a prominent place in the curriculum, and the histories of Mill, James Marshman, and

Mountstuart Elphinstone were to reinforce, 'with remarkable consistency', the argument that 'as long as Indian youth were without a historical consciousness, they would remain shackled to the tyranny of forms'.[73]

The study of history enjoyed the patronage of a much wider circle of admirers in England itself, being the favoured mode of knowledge for the modernizing middle classes. This interest in history can be traced back to the Elizabethan period, and owes something to the expansion of English trade overseas as it does to the creation of a new middle class. As Britain's empire grew, so did the interest in history. Sir Thomas Munro (1761–1827), who was to spend the greater part of his adult life in India, the last eight years as Governor of Madras, was echoing more than his own view when he wrote:

It is distressing that we should persevere in the absurd practice of stifling the young ideas of boys of fourteen or fifteen with logic. A few pages of history give more insight into the human mind, in a more agreeable manner, than all the metaphysical volumes that ever were published.[74]

Eventually historical studies were to have a programmatic place in Utilitarian theories and designs for the 'Improvement' of India, and indeed Indians were overfed with history on the supposition that their proclivity towards superstitions, abstractions, and fanciful exaggerations could not be checked otherwise.

If the study and valorization of history continue to occupy an important place in school curricula across India today, as demonstrated by the bitter disputes over the teaching of history in schools in states under the control of the BJP or its ideological allies, the particular association of history with the middle classes has not diminished either. As I have argued, the controversy over the now-demolished Babri Masjid marked the first occasion in the history of independent India that the historian was brought to the forefront of national politics, and that the discourse of history was seen as having a unique place in settling a dispute of national proportions; and perhaps it would not be too much to aver that blood was shed over competing versions of history. It would be rather trivial (though nonetheless true) to remark that the profession of the historian is eminently within the domain of the middle classes. More pointedly, we must recall that the membership of the BJP and the RSS is drawn largely from the middle classes,[75] and it is precisely these people for whom history appears as the most reliable guide as an indisputable chronicle of Muslim misdeeds. In states where BJP governments have held power, history textbooks have been significantly altered.[76] There is nothing unexceptionable in this, for history textbooks have always, across cultures,[77] been the first casualty in disputes of this sort; what is notable is the attraction that history has for the middle classes on the one hand, and the compelling place of communalism in middle-class ideology on the other hand. It is precisely this connection which has been missed by most of the commentators, who on the contrary assume, as I have discussed at considerable length, that 'communal-ism' is most effectively to be contested by writing histories which are not 'contaminated by a flood of "theories", some mythical, some invented, but all masquerading as historical facts'.[78]

This new-found faith in history among India's middle classes, which will one day yield a Santoshi Ma of Itihasa, is exemplified in numerous other ways. The eminent Hindi writer, Nirmal Verma, has in a long essay deplored the lack of a historical sensibility among Indians, their indifference to the past. He points out that in Britain, nearly 500,000 monuments have been entrusted to the care of the National Trust for Historic Places, thus ensuring not merely their preservation but their passage into the hands of the coming genera-tions; in India, by comparison, only 30,000 monuments have been designated as 'historic' landmarks worthy of the attention of the Archaeological Survey of India, notwithstanding the fact that India is much larger than Britain and can boast of an even longer past.[79] This is also the tone of two pieces by the late Arvind Das, one of India's most respected editorialists, that appeared in a national daily less than a decade ago. The burden of these pieces is that 'the method Indians appear to have found to deal with their past is to mythologise it. Fact is at a discount. ... Thus, while myths move millions, the actual and complex historical reality is often ignored.'[80] The panacea evi-dently lies in transforming a 'passive' citizenry, submerged under a 'dark cloud of a-historicity', into active denizens of the historical faith.[81] It is this very mentality that would have entrusted the 'dis-puted structure' of Ayodhya to the Archaeological Survey of India, and that would entrust similarly 'ambivalent' structures at Benares, Mathura, and other places for safekeeping to the state.

Under the secularist dispensation, living monuments, where forms of religious practice are critical to the constitution of a community, are to be transformed into dead ones, on the false supposition that the state is a better custodian of monuments, when in fact the state has everywhere been as much responsible for their decimation as any other force. Nor is it the case that monuments classified as 'protected' are necessarily beyond dispute or even immune from destruction.[82]

One might well say, considering what happened to the Babri Masjid, better 'dead' than destroyed, but that would be to obfuscate a number of critical questions. If England today is parasitic on tourism, living on the consumerism of millions besot by the changing of the guard at Buckingham Palace and other inane thrills, is that what is to become of India also? Must we, like the advanced post-industrial countries of the West, force our culture into museums, giant amusement parks, historic homes, and other bracketed spaces? Or consider another set of questions: if we believe that politics and public life are both contaminated by 'communalism', how are we to ensure what we assume, namely the neutrality and 'objectivity' of the Archaeological Survey? By turning over 'disputed structures' to the Archaeological Survey, do we not commit the much greater error of substituting, for modes of cultural accommodation and lived practices of pluralism, the impersonal authority of purportedly transcendent institutions?

There is no compelling reason why the language of history should be of interest to Indians, and rather than berating them for their indifference to the discourses of history and neglect of the past, the secularists and modernizers would do well to reflect on the shortcomings in their own intellectual practices and their unfortunate surrender to the historical mode. Their respective claims have become possible only with the emergence of the discipline of history and modern forms of historiography. Far more than chiding the Hindu 'fundamentalists' for their deployment of an 'unscientific' and politicized history, and for contaminating history with myths, which is about the most substantive critique of Hindutva historians that has so far emerged, the secular historians need to make better use of Indian myths. Though, to take one striking instance, the secular historians have been sensitive to the manner in which Rama, and the notion of Ramarajya, have been masculinized, they have made almost nothing of Sita-ki-Rasoi,[83] a building which constituted part of the Babri Masjid complex. Sita has disappeared from both Hindutva and secular discourses, and it is not inapposite to suggest that this congruence has some relation to the privileging of history by both camps. Sita (meaning 'furrow') came from the earth, is of the earth, and returns to the earth: thus the preferred ending of the Ramayana among many devotees where Sita charts her own life after the return to Ayodhya and eventually descends into the earth. She is the one who nourishes, and her repudiation by the Hindutvavadis is a telling fact not only of their narrow reading of the Ramayana but of the cultural traditions of Hinduism, which stress the fertility principle and the importance of the kitchen as a sacred space.[84]

That myth-making, and particularly a judicious use of the vast terrain of Indian myths, should be left to the 'fundamentalists' is not merely incomprehensible but indefencible. If the secular intellectuals and modernizers have nothing else to resort to but brute 'facts', and the unappetizing language of history, that is only an admission of how far removed they are from Indian civilization, and how far they must travel before they can enter the arena of Indian public life, an arena that at this point must necessarily appear to them as little more than a den of demagoguery, obscurantism, archaic beliefs, and repository of medieval ills. Ironically, while some of these very historians and intellectuals have celebrated the subaltern, endowed him or her with agency, the language of the subaltern continues to escape them, and the subaltern must appear in the present scenario as little more than an illiterate lumpen proletariat easily duped by masters of deception. Thus, for example, we have it on the authority of no less a person than Amartya Sen, who acquired renown for his writings on economics and philosophy, but lately has taken to pontification on virtually every subject, that the Ayodhya movement owes a great deal to the illiteracy of the Indian masses.[85] The 'low level of elementary education in that part of India [the "cow belt"] surely contributes to this gullibility' of Indian people, Sen wrote recently, adding for good measure that 'it was here that the Rama agitation assumed such force, and in fact, most of the Ayodhya agitators came from three states in the Hindi belt'.[86] The offensive suggestion that the lower classes are more prone to 'communalism' ignores, as I have argued above, the attraction of the ideology of communalism for the middle classes.[87] Sen admits that 'Hindu middle classes in some parts of India have suddenly become more aware of alleged misdeeds of Muslim rulers in the past', but feels no need to reconcile this statement with the avowed declaration of the communalism of the lower classes; to the contrary, we are merely furnished with the banal explanation that 'the Hindu political activists have been trying to recreate a mythical past, mixing fact with fantasy'.[88]

Perhaps, as the resuscitation of historical memories suggests, we always need an 'Other'. When a people have not had a conception of the 'Other', they have paid for their humanity, for their acceptance of pluralism, with their lives. Todorov put on offer the plausible argument that the defeat of the Aztecs by a few hundred Spaniards cannot be accounted for other than by the circumstance that the Aztecs, having no conception of the Other, no vocabulary by means of which they could speak of the 'Other', could only comprehend the Spaniards as 'Gods'.[89] Before 'Gods', men must crumble; and when the 'Gods' were as rapacious, bloodthirsty, and merciless as the Spaniards, the elimination of the Aztecs was writ large. Yet, if we are to have an 'Other' as the condition of our survival, must the 'Other' necessarily be conceptualized in human terms? Plato banished the poets from his republic, and though we can scarcely banish historians, we must endeavour to render history itself into the 'Other'. The ahistoricism of the Indian, and Indian civilization's profound indifference to history, has been the source of sanity in that ancient civilization. Can it be hoped that from the sorrow of Ayodhya we will learn the folly of indulging in the fond belief that the language of history can ever be a force of emancipation? Perhaps we might then recognize, true to the genius of Indian civilization, that in banishing the discourse of history, we will not be rendering it into an unredeemable, absolute 'Other', for even from banishment, as the Indian epics have reminded us, there is always the return.

ENDNOTES

1. One way to normalize 'disturbances' in India is to speak of them in the abstract, with a certain kind of imprecision that, apropos a 'developed' country, would never be tolerated. Whenever a calamity takes place, 'thousands' are killed, and 'tens of thousands' appear affected, and no doubt that has happened on more than one unfortunate occasion. The killings following Indira Gandhi's assassination, and the calamitous gas leak at the Union Carbide factory in Bhopal, readily come to mind. In the wake of Ayodhya, such rhetorical flourishes, sad to say, have not been without justification. Between 6 December 1992 and 31 January 1993, if we are to rely on (disputed) official figures alone, 1,801 people were killed, and 226 places were affected by the 'disturbances'. All over the country, 119 million people were placed under curfew: 'thousands' and 'millions' take on legitimate meanings in such circumstances. See People's Union for Democratic Rights, *Cry the Beloved Country: Ayodhya, 6 December 1992* (Delhi: PUDR, February 1993).

2. Whatever similarities there may be between the BJP and the Shiv Sena, the differences are no less significant: see Thomas Blan Hansen, *Wages of Violence: Naming and Identity in Postcolonial Bombay* (Princeton: Princeton University Press, 2001).

3. See Shashi Tharoor, 'The Revenge of History', *New York Times* (11 December 1992), sec. A, p. 39; on the fear of symbols, see also Amitav Ghosh, *In an Antique Land* (Delhi: Ravi Dayal, 1992), pp. 204–10.

4. Tabish Khair, 'Stripped of my Indian identity', *Sunday Times of India* (10 January 1993), p. 24.

5. Sushil Srivastava, in *The Disputed Mosque*, has argued with some degree of persuasion that Babur never built a mosque at Ayodhya. According to Srivastava, the closest that Babur came to Ayodhya was a place at the junction of the rivers Sirda and Ghagra (Sarayu), some 72 miles from Ayodhya. Babur's whereabouts between 29 March and 18 September 1528 cannot be ascertained, for the pages of his memoirs for those days are missing. With respect to the more difficult question of the tablet with the inscription inside the mosque, Srivastava does not contest that the inscription records the construction of a mosque, or at least the renovation of a mosque that already stood at that spot; what he does doubt is that the mosque was built at the *order* of Babur, for the Persian quite possibly can be read as suggesting that the mosque was built at the initiative of the nobleman Mir Baqi in the anticipation that it would give Babur considerable pleasure (see Chap. 5, esp. pp. 72–6, 85–9).

6. See *Anatomy of a Confrontation* ed. Sarvepalli Gopal. Rama Janmabhoomi, which is the spelling that I shall be employing, is literally the 'ground' or 'earth' on which Rama was born; Janmasthan is the 'place' of birth.

7. See Justice Deoki Nandan, *Sri Ramjanmabhumi: Itihasik evam Vidik Samiksha* [*Ramjanmabhumi: Historical and Legal Review*] (Allahabad: Suruchi Printers, n.d.), and Sri Ramjanmabhumi Mukti Yagya Samiti, *Sri Ramjanmabhumi ke Bare me Tathya, Ham Mandir Wahin Banayenge* [*The Truth about Ramjanmabhumi: We Shall Build the Temple There*] (New Delhi: Suruchi Prakashan, 1989). The pamphlet literature on Ayodhya by the Hindu right dates back to an earlier period: see, for instance, Ram Gopal 'Sarad' Pandey, *Sri Ram janmabhumi ka romanckari itihas* [*The Wonder-Filled History of Sri Ramjanmabhumi*] (Ayodhya: Pandit Dvarikaprasad Sivgovind Pustakalay, 1976).

8. Statement by P. Parameswaran, Director, Bharatiya Vichar Kendra (Trivandrum), as recorded in the *Organiser*, 15 February 1987, quoted in Gopal, *Anatomy of a Confrontation*, p. 138.

9. See *Sri Ramajanmabhumi ke Bare me Tathya*, p. 17, quoted in Gopal, p. 138.

10. S. Gopal, Romila Thapar, et al., *The Political Abuse of History: Babri Masjid–Rama Janmabhumi Dispute* (New Delhi: Centre for Historical Studies, Jawaharlal Nehru University, 1989), reprinted in *Social Scientist* 18, nos 1–2 (January–February 1990):76–81, and in the *South Asia Bulletin* 9, 2 (1989):65–7; citations will be to the reprint in the *Social Scientist*.

11. R. S. Sharma et al., *Ramjanmabhumi–Baburi Masjid: A Historians' Report to the Nation*. We have encountered some of these scholars in the preceding chapter. Sharma is well-known as a historian of ancient India; Jha, a widely published authority on ancient Indian history, and General Secretary of the Indian History Congress from 1985–8, is a member of the history faculty at Delhi University. M. Athar Ali is one of the principal figures in the study of medieval Indian history; Suraj Bhan, an archaeologist, was then Dean, Faculty

of Indic Studies, Kurukshetra University. This work will be cited henceforth as *Historians' Report to the Nation*.

12. Ibid., p. 3.

13. For the use of the *Skanda Purana* and the 'Ayodhya-mahatmya' by VHP/RSS sympathizers, see for example Abhas Kumar Chatterjee, 'Ram Janmabhoomi: More Evidence', *Indian Express* (26 March 1990), p. 8: 'That a janmasthan temple existed in Ramkot is equally well proved by the ancient Sanskrit text of Ayodhya Mahatmya, which is part of the *Skanda Purana* composed centuries before the invasion of Babar. It eulogises the glory of the Janmasthan as the holiest of holy spots in Ayodhya and describes the virtues of worshipping at this shrine, specially on Ram Navami day.' As we shall see, none of this has been 'proved'. Hans Bakker, in his voluminous study, *Ayodhya* (Groningen: Egbert Forsten, 1986), has suggested a time span of the thirteenth to the seventeenth centuries for the composition of the 'Ayodhya-mahatmya'.

14. In his informed and well-known (if somewhat dated) study, *Hindu Places of Pilgrimage in India: A Study in Cultural Geography* (Berkeley: University of California Press, 1973), Surinder Mohan Bhardwaj makes virtually no mention of Ayodhya. A 'Grand Pilgrimage of India according to the Mahabharata' did not include Ayodhya; in the *Garuda*, *Matsya*, and *Agni Puranas* Ayodhya appears as a pilgrimage site (*tirtha*), albeit far less important than Prayag, Gaya, Varanasi, and numerous other places. The most compelling evidence about the status of Ayodhya may come from the *Krtyakalpatru* of Bhatta Laksmidhara, a compendious nine-volume digest dated to about AD 1110, a work that Bhardwaj describes as uniquely reliable 'in the religious literature of medieval India'. Bhardwaj notes that on sacred places in South India it is less authoritative, as Laksmidhara was an inhabitant of North India, but if anything that would have made Ayodhya's inclusion as a great pilgrimage spot more understandable. The eighth part of the work, entitled *Tirthavivecana Kandam*, celebrates the glories of Varanasi, Prayag, Kurukshetra, Pushkar, Ujjain, Kedarnath, and a few other tirthas, as well as of sacred rivers such as the Ganga and Narmada, but Ayodhya does not figure in that list. Modern sources yield a similar consensus: twenty-eight sites, a list in which Ayodhya does not find a place, are recognized by six or seven scholarly works as the holiest places in India; another twenty-six places, including Ayodhya, are recognized by four to five sources as belonging to the next order of significant pilgrimage spots (see pp. 44, 62, 66, 69, 72–4, and 80–3). This is not inconsistent with the argument that Ayodhya only came to acquire an importance after the sixteenth century, certainly long after a temple is supposed to have been established in Ayodhya to celebrate the glory of Rama and mark his birthplace. One of the very few texts from the pre-modern period asserting the claims of Ayodhya as a great place of Hindu pilgrimage is the *Ain-i-Akbari* of Abu'l Fazl, who characterized Ayodhya as 'one of the holiest places of antiquity', the 'residence of Ramacandra who in the Treta age combined in his own person both the spiritual supremacy and

the kingly office' (cited by Bakker, *Ayodhya*, 1:137). One wonders what the advocates of the temple theory would think of using a 'Muslim source' to substantiate their claims?

15. Cf. also S. Gopal, Romila Thapar, et al., 'In the Name of History', *The Indian Express* [Sunday Magazine] (1 April 1990), p. 8, where it is argued that Rama Janmabhoomi was not recognized in the ancient and medieval texts as an important pilgrimage spot. Rama Janmabhoomi is not mentioned in an eleventh-century inscription of a Gahadvala ruler who took a pilgrimage to Ayodhya and recorded the sites where he performed worship. 'As is well known to scholars of early medieval history', continue the authors in their rejoinder to A. R. Khan's article in *Indian Express* on 25 February 1990, 'there is no mention of the Ramajanmabhumi as a place of pilgrimage in a large number of texts of this period such as those of Lakshmidhara, Mitra, Mishra, Jinaprabhasuri, or the Bhushundi *Ramayana* and the *Purana*s, which refer to major places of pilgrimage including Ayodhya.'

16. See the discussion in Bakker, *Ayodhya*, 1:4–11, as well as in van der Veer, *Religious Nationalism*, pp. 157–8.

17. Gopal et al., 'The Political Abuse of History', p. 77.

18. The importance of Tiffenthaler's account to proponents of the Rama Janmabhoomi movement can be gauged by the fact that a great deal of the literature in support of the movement cites the relevant fragments from Tiffenthaler's travel narrative. See, for example, M. B. Chande, *Shree Ram Janma Bhoomi* (Nagpur: M. B. Chande, 1992), pp. 61–2. This book appeared on 26 December 1992, twenty days after the destruction of the mosque, and is accompanied by an acknowledgement to one Anand Govindrao Puranik, the printer, for 'processing this book within a fortnight'. The haste with which this work was produced brings to mind a story (howsoever apocryphal) about the famous poet Saadi. Upon being told by Saadi that it took him several days to produce a few good lines of poetry, a fellow poet of his said, 'Why, I spin out a ghazal every time I take a shit', whereupon Saadi is reported to have said, 'No wonder your ghazals smell of shit too.' As a work of scholarship, Chande's work is pathetic, and even as a work of propaganda it is shoddy in the extreme; it is typical that the 'Trefiethaler [sic] Account' is reproduced without the slightest indication of where the original and the translation were published. A couple of other 'original' accounts by Europeans are offered as evidence, but again one is left without a clue as to the author, title, and publisher of the works in question. The question of Hindutva's relationship to the social sciences as a whole is deserving of scholarly treatment, marked as this relationship is by a profound ambivalence and sentiments of unease, admiration, contempt, and downright manipulation.

19. All citations from Abhas Kumar Chatterjee, 'Ram Janmabhoomi: More Evidence'.

20. Srivastava, *The Disputed Mosque*, p. 87.

21. This point is also made by S. Gopal, Romila Thapar, et al., 'In the Name of History'. Rajeev Saxena, 'Tulsidas' Silence on Ram Mandir at Ayodhya',

Mainstream (9 January 1993), pp. 3–4, notes that Tulsidas wrote about the attack on lower-caste Hindus such as himself by Brahmins, his problems with arthritis, and a number of other issues, but not about the supposed destruction of the Babri mosque. I have some reservations, however, about this line of argumentation. A recent book on Marco Polo, which makes a similar kind of argument, suggests that he never visited China, since Marco Polo's account makes no mention of the Great Wall or of the custom of foot-binding, and it is inconceivable that an European visitor to China would not have noticed these 'peculiarities' of Chinese history and culture. See Frances Wood, *Did Marco Polo Go to China?* (Boulder, Colorado: Westview Press, 1998 [1995]). Recent interpretive work on European travel narratives has drawn attention to the politics of representation and the specious strategies by means of which accounts were constructed and furnished of other societies, but nonetheless every interpretive move is not, as a consequence, licensed.

22. See Tulsidas, *Sri Ramacaritmanas* (Gorakhpur: Gita Press, 2000 [large print edition, in Hindi], p. 378; the gloss states that 'wherever Rama resides, there is Ayodhya'.

23. D. Mandal, *Ayodhya: Archaeology after Demolition*, Tracts for the Times, no. 5 (New Delhi: Orient Longman, 1993).

24. Romila Thapar, Editorial Preface', in ibid., p. xi.

25. See, for example, S. P. Gupta, 'Ram Janmabhoomi-Babri Masjid: Archaeological Evidence', *Indian Express* (2 December 1990), p. 3; Dr Murlidhar H. Pahoja, 'Archaeological Data on Temple', *Indian Express* (14 May 1990), p. 8; and the pamphlet *Ramajanma Bhumi, Ayodhya: New Archaeological Discoveries* (New Delhi: Historians' Forum, 1992), p. 16. Note that the pamphlet was issued by a group calling itself the 'Historians' Forum', an association of scholars with links to the VHP/RSS/BJP combine.

26. See, for example, the introduction by Shereen Ratnagar to Mandal, *Ayodhya: Archaeology after Demolition*, p. 3. A more modest appraisal of the 'evidence' offered by the VHP is to be found in the comment by Professor R. Champakalakshmi of the Centre for Historical Studies at Jawaharlal Nehru University: 'Thus the evidence', she says, 'for the existence of a Hindu temple and more particularly a Vaishnava temple dedicated to Rama at the very same site as the present mosque is *far from conclusive*. Any attempt to use the available evidence as conclusive is questionable' (italics in original). See Gopal, *Anatomy of a Confrontation*, p. 232.

27. Mandal, *Ayodhya: Archaeology after Demolition*, p. 1.

28. Gopal et al., 'The Political Abuse of History', p. 77.

29. *Indian Archaeology 1976–77—A Review*, p. 53, cited by Sharma, *Historians' Report to the Nation*, p. 11, and quoted also in Gopal et al., *Anatomy of a Confrontation*, p. 225.

30. See Note by Professor R. Champakalakshmi in Gopal, *Anatomy of a Confrontation*, pp. 228–32, and Sharma et al., *Historians' Report to the Nation*, pp. 8–9.

31. Sharma, *Historians' Report to the Nation*, p. 10. This opinion is shared by

the contributors to Gopal, *Anatomy of a Confrontation*, for whom the issue of the acceptability of the evidence 'also raises a question of archaeological method and procedure which archaeologists feel has been violated in the publicity sought by the claims' (p. 223).

32. This is the claim of Murlidhar H. Pahoja, 'Archaeological Data on Temple', *Indian Express* (14 May 1990), p. 8; likewise, see Chande, *Shree Ram Janma Bhoomi*, pp. 24–5, although this is barely readable.

33. Mandal, *Ayodhya: Archaeology after Demolition*, pp. 39–40, and Sharma, *Historians' Report to the Nation*, pp. 9–10.

34. *Ramajanma Bhumi, Ayodhya: New Archaeological Discoveries* (New Delhi: Historians' Forum, 1992), p. 16, cited by Mandal, *Ayodhya: Archaeology after Demolition*, p. 17. As one might expect, Chande makes a great deal of these 'findings', and a small section of his 'book', entitled 'Archaeological Evidence on Ayodhya', puts forth the claim that as 'pillars inscribed with vedic verses or figurignes [sic] of Hindu gods' cannot be found in mosques, churches, 'or any place of worship other than of Hindus', 'the only incontravertible [sic] conclusion, that can be drawn, is that the Shree Ram temple existed at the present site' (p. 25).

35. Mandal, *Ayodhya: Archaeology after Demolition*, pp. 22, 41.

36. Ibid., pp. 42–3.

37. Thapar, 'Editorial Preface', in Mandal, *Ayodhya: Archaeology after Demolition*, p. xii.

38. Comment by Dr. Suraj Bhan, in Gopal, *Anatomy of a Confrontation*, pp. 225–6. Bhan's critique tallies with the observations of Sharma, Champakalakshmi, Mandal, and others; for an opposite view, see Dr. S. P. Gupta, 'Ram Janmabhoomi-Babri Masjid: Archaeological evidence', whose article seeks to establish that a temple was demolished and its debris utilized in the construction of the Babri Masjid.

39. Gupta, 'Ram Janmabhoomi-Babri Masjid', *Indian Express* (2 December 1990), p. 3; see also Mandal, *Ayodhya: Archaeology after Demolition*, p. 27, and comment by Dr. Suraj Bhan, in Gopal, *Anatomy of a Confrontation*, pp. 225–7.

40. Sharma, *Historians' Report to the Nation*, p. 13.

41. Mandal, *Ayodhya: Archaeology after Demolition*, p. 65.

42. Ibid., p. xiv, preface by Thapar.

43. See 'PM urged to use "Gandhi formula"', *Times of India* (3 December 1990), p. 1, and Anupam Goswami and V. Venkatesan, '"Formula" not Gandhiji's', *Times of India* (4 December 1990), p. 1.

44. This problem, with respect to nationalist thought, has been discussed by Partha Chatterjee, *Nationalist Thought and the Colonial World*, especially Chapter 1.

45. Chatterjee, 'Ram Janmabhoomi'.

46. Gopal et al., 'The Political Abuse of History', p. 76.

47. Chatterjee, 'Ram Janmabhoomi', p. 8. To follow Chatterji's train of thought, if 'mere suggestion' could have incited Muslims to go on a rampage,

and that too in a matter where a work of fiction [*The Satanic Verses*] was in question, is it at all surprising that Hindus should have been moved to action confronted by the historical memory of bondage to an alien faith and of a deeply felt injury to their religion and culture to which the Babri Masjid stood witness? In this narrative, the Muslim is always more easily swayed by faith, a creature prone to impulsiveness (as the rapidity with which the worldwide community of Islam was able to stir up a campaign against Rushdie showed), and though the Hindu's faith is no less ardently felt, it is a testimony to the Hindu's restraint that a monument that spoke loudly and clearly of his enslavement should have been allowed to stand so long. It is also worth noting Chatterjee's attraction for arguments showing the affinity of religion and science: the mathematician Kurt Godel is invoked to the effect that 'in every axiomatic system, there is always a proposition which can neither be proved nor disproved'. Similarly, certain religious beliefs can neither be proved nor disproved, and we should treat them in the manner in which we accord sanctity to mathematical axioms.

48. See *Ramajanma Bhumi and the Marxist Historians* (New Delhi: Historians' Forum, 1992).

49. Chatterjee, 'Ram Janmabhoomi'.

50. Hans Bakker, 'Reflections on the Evolution of Rama Devotion in the Light of Textual and Archaeological Evidence', *Wiener Zeitschrift fur die Kunde Sudasiens* 31 (1986), pp. 21–2; idem, *Ayodhya*, 1:67 ff. Bakker's argument is dubious, if not unacceptable, for other reasons. If we ask why the Rama cult assumed an importance no earlier than the eleventh–twelfth centuries, on Bakker's view we have only to think of that time as the period of Muslim invasions of India and the beginnings of Muslim rule. Here was an absolute 'other'; and in the Ramayana Hindus found a text for demonizing the other. A polemical use had to be found for the Ramayana before the worship of Rama acquired many adherents; and though Bakker suggests that a similar development took place in the time of the later Guptas, the twelfth century assumes heightened importance in his work. It is around this time that Sanskrit manuals which furnished guidelines for the private and public modes of worshipping Rama were first composed.

The effect of Bakker's argument is to push back the history of communalism into the twelfth century. The argument ignores numerous other considerations, such as the increasing importance of bhakti movements from the ninth–tenth centuries onwards, and besides the evidence on which Bakker rests his argument is so slim as to be scarcely worthy of consideration. But the critical point for us is that this part of Bakker's argument should, logically speaking, offer no satisfaction to Chatterjee and other advocates of the Rama Janmabhoomi movement, for its effect is to suggest that the Ramayana as a text can be, and has been, mobilized to foment hatred of the Muslim, and secondly that Rama was not a figure of divinity, worthy of veneration as a God (as opposed to a hero), until the eleventh–twelfth centuries, an exceedingly late time in history given that Rama is supposed to have been born several thousand years ago.

Bakker's argument is extended by Sheldon Pollock, 'Ramayana and Political Imagination in India', *The Journal of Asian Studies* 53, no. 2 (1993), pp. 261–97; for a searching critique of Bakker and Pollock, see Brajadulal Chattopadhyaya, *Representing the Other? Sanskrit Sources and the Muslims* (Delhi: Manohar, 1998), pp. 98–115.

51. Chatterjee, 'Ram Janmabhoomi'.

52. Pradip K. Datta, 'VHP's Ram at Ayodhya: Reincarnation through Ideology and Organisation', *Economic and Political Weekly* 26, no. 44 (2 November 1991), p. 2519. See also Gyanendra Pandey, 'The Culture of History', in Nicholas Dirks, ed., *In Near Ruins: Cultural Theory at the End of the Century* (Minneapolis: University of Minnesota Press, 1998), pp. 19–37 esp. pp. 24–6.

53. *Organiser*, issues of 20 July 1986 and 5 April 1987, cited by Neeladri Bhattacharya, 'Myth, History and the Politics of Ramjanmabhumi', in Gopal, *Anatomy of a Confrontation*, p. 138, notes 3 and 9.

54. Bhattacharya, 'Myth, History and the Politics of Ramjanmabhumi', esp. pp. 137 and 132.

55. Needless to say, the arguments of the antagonists of Hindu 'fundamentalists' are rather more complex than what I have perhaps suggested. There is, for example, the recognition that VHP ideologues have sought to render Hinduism into a 'masculine' religion; if Rama was before a 'soft', even faintly 'feminine' God, full of warmth and tenderness, now he is 'an aggressive, masculine, warrior God' (ibid., p. 129). But it is not clear what appeal such an argument would have with the Hindu public, and whether this kind of reading is at all of interest to most people. Just as intellectually persuasive (though scarcely unproblematic) has been the argument that the VHP ideologues have, while criticizing other religions for their monolithic unity, themselves aspired to render Hinduism into a monolithic or 'Semitic' religion, but again it is far from being certain that most Hindus see the traditional pluralism of their religion, evident for example in the multiplicity of deities and in the multiplicity of diverging traditions of the Ramayana story, as being incompatible with the attempts to provide Hinduism with, as it were, a centre. These points are, in any case, quite incidental to my thesis that it is really to the question of how history has been deployed by both parties to the dispute, and the consequences of those invocations to history, that we must turn to gain some comprehension of the Rama Janmabhoomi movement and the possibilities of constructing a future for us that would be less encumbered by historical discourses that seek to arbiter the destinies and contours of a civilization.

56. Ibid., pp. 124, 133.

57. 'Black Sunday', issue of *Manas* (Delhi: Sampradayikta Virodhi Andolan, December 1992), pp. 2–3. More recently this little four-page pamphlet has been reprinted in Mushirul Hasan, *Legacy of a Divided Nation: India's Muslims since Independence* (Boulder, Colorado: Westview Press, 1997), pp. 348–51.

58. 'Black Sunday', p. 4; Hasan, *Legacy of a Divided Nation*, p. 351. The myth is 'disproved by census figures', state the authors, and they go on to state: 'The Report on the Status of Women in India (1975) shows that the number of polygamous marriages was greater among Hindus than among Muslims, 5.05% of Hindu marriages were polygamous and 4.31% of Muslim marriages (9 out of 25) were polygamous.' However, there is some amount of evasion, if not prevarication, here: census figures on the Muslim population are not actually cited, which may convey to some readers the impression that claims about the accelerated growth of the Muslim population in India are not without foundation. The first census taken after the partition, in 1951, is not compared with the 1991 census; nor is the possible rejoinder that Hindu men are more likely to take two wives rather than four wives anticipated. The incidence of polygamy is less significant than the quantum of polygamy in each polygamous marriage. My point here is not that the rate of population growth among Muslims necessarily exceeds that of Hindus, but rather that the question is seldom handled with absolute conviction and probity. The 'myth' has two discrete elements: one is a claim about the disproportionate increase of Muslims in the last five decades, the other is a claim about polygamous marriages as the supposed norm among Muslims. Repudiation of the second claim, which is more frequently encountered in the literature, does not settle allegations contained in the first claim. The real rejoinder to the communalists, moreover, must lie in the emphatic declaration that the increased demographic growth of any one community cannot constitute the grounds for their oppression by others.

59. Romila Thapar, 'Somanatha: Narratives of a History', *Seminar*, no. 475 (March 1999), pp. 15–23.

60. 'Black Sunday', p. 2.

61. Bhattacharya, 'Myth, History and the Politics of Ramjanmabhumi', p. 129; Amartya Sen, 'The Threats to Secular India', *New York Review of Books* (8 April 1993), p. 30. By Sen's standard, Gandhi must stand convicted as well; to a liberal, secular humanist descended from a distinguished line of Bengali modernists, Gandhi has always appeared as someone who held 'unreasoned and archaic beliefs'. Even Tagore, a much more nuanced, sensitive, and ecumenical thinker than Amartya Sen, had perforce, on more than one occasion, to charge Gandhi with holding unreasoned beliefs and superstitions. See the recent collection by Sabyasachi Bhattacharya, ed., *The Mahatma and the Poet: Letters and Debates Between Gandhi and Tagore 1915–1941* (Delhi: National Book Trust, 1997).

62. For a lengthier consideration of these issues see Vinay Lal, *Empire of Knowledge: Culture and Plurality in the Global Economy* (London: Pluto Press, 2002).

63. See Paula Richman, ed., *Many Ramayanas: The Diversity of a Narrative Tradition in South Asia* (Berkeley, California: University of California Press, 1991).

64. The argument for the ideological modernity of the movement behind the attempt to destroy the Babri Masjid is best made by Ashis Nandy et al., *Creating a Nationality*.

65. A similar sentiment was conveyed to me by Romila Thapar, personal conversation at Smith College, Northampton, The Kahn Institute Colloquium on Religious Tolerance and Intolerance, 3 October 2001.

66. The experience of SAHMAT, a cultural organization set up to honour the memory of Safdar Hashmi, a prominent theatre activist with pronounced communist sympathies who was murdered in broad daylight by Congress Party thugs on 2 January 1989, might seem to corroborate the view that secular intellectuals operate, most particularly since the Congress suffered a precipitous decline in the mid-1970s, amidst immense hostility and the far-reaching influence of the Hindutva advocates. The SAHMAT exhibition, *Hum Sab Ayodhya* ('We Are All Ayodhya'), which aimed to present an ecumenical narrative of Ayodhya's past, and to show the immense divergences in Ramayana traditions around the country, was severely disrupted by activists of the Bajrang Dal in August 1993 and became the subject of parliamentary recriminations. One panel which depicted a Jain version of the Ramayana according to which Rama and Sita were siblings became the pretext for initiating an open assault upon SAHMAT as an organization which had dared to suggest that Rama and Sita were engaged in incestuous behaviour. However, as one critic who is sympathetic to SAHMAT is constrained to admit, the defence of SAHMAT—as indeed there should have been one—almost always overlooks a number of difficulties in SAHMAT's own outlook and the political economy of the organization. SAHMAT's interventions on the question of the Babri Masjid have been possible only with state funding, and its music festival, *Muktnaad*, was held in war-torn Ayodhya, so to speak, with the evident patronage of the state at the highest level. But commentators who are accustomed to thinking of Hindutva organizations as the only beneficiaries of the state have nothing to say on this matter. SAHMAT's own membership and support is derived largely from the elites, and the *Muktnaad* festival, for all its posturing as a statement of people's art and an eloquent testimony to the composite culture of Ayodhya, was apparently staged without any consultation with the people of Ayodhya. The discussion in Rustom Bharucha, *In the Name of the Secular: Contemporary Cultural Activism in India* (New Delhi: Oxford University Press, 1998), pp. 52–74, is useful.

67. Georg Wilhelm Friedrich Hegel, *The Philosophy of History*, trans. J. Sibree (New York: Dover Publications, 1956), p. 161.

68. Ibid., pp. 161–3.

69. Edward C. Sachau, trans. and ed., *Alberuni's India*, Vol. II, pp. 10–11.

70. The close connection between colonialism and the emergence and teaching of history in India is recognized by Ranajit Guha, *An Indian Historiography of India*. Guha, however, shows a singular incapacity to step outside the paradigm of history; and, indeed, as his contributions to the numerous

volumes of *Subaltern Studies* suggest, he thinks it is only a matter of substituting—no easy matter, as he concedes—subaltern history for elite history, whether of the colonialist or nationalist variety. See, in particular, the programmatic note by Guha, 'On Some Aspects of the Historiography of Colonial India', in Ranajit Guha, ed., *Subaltern Studies I*, 1982, pp. 1–8, and 'The Prose of Counter-Insurgency', in Ranajit Guha, ed., *Subaltern Studies II*, 1983, pp. 1–42. Both these pieces are also collected together in Ranajit Guha and Gayatri Chakravorty Spivak, eds, *Selected Subaltern Studies* (New York: Oxford University Press, 1988), and are discussed below, in Chapter IV.

71. James Mill, *History of British India*, ed. with notes by Horace Hayman Wilson, 10 vols (5th edn, London: James Madden, 1858), Vol. 2, p. 47; Vol. 1, pp. 114–15; Vol. 2, pp. 46–7. The first edition of this work appeared in 1817. More recently, one scholar has stressed that Mill's *History* is the 'oldest hegemonic account of India within the Anglo-French imperial formation', a work that throughout the nineteenth century was to provide the model for textbook histories of India. See Ronald Inden, *Imagining India*, p. 45.

72. Cited by Partha Chatterjee, 'History and the Nationalization of Hinduism', *Social Research* 59, 1 (Spring 1992), pp. 113, 131.

73. Gauri Viswanathan, *Masks of Conquest: Literary Study and British Rule in India* (New York: Columbia University Press, 1989), p. 125. The examination questions given to students of history are preserved for us in numerous British records. One such question, apparently put to students in the 1840s, was: 'What are the earliest Historical Records among uncivilized nations? And what are the changes which they usually undergo before we arrive at the period of true History? Illustrate this by instances from the Histories of Greece and Rome, of India, and of Europe.' See W. H. Sykes, 'Statistics of the Educational Institutions of the East India Company in India', *Journal of the Statistical Society of London* 8 (September 1845), p. 236.

74. Letter to his sister, 15 September 1795, cited by Eric Stokes, *The English Utilitarians and India*, p. 12.

75. The composition of the BJP and RSS is discussed in Tapan Basu et al., *Khaki Shorts and Saffron Flags: A Critique of the Hindu Right*, Tracts for the Times, No. 1 (Delhi: Orient Longman, 1993). Far more detailed, but unfortunately inadequate on the class composition of Hindutva organizations, is Christophe Jaffrelot, *The Hindu Nationalist Movement and Indian Politics, 1920s to the 1990s*, 2nd edn with a new afterword (New Delhi: Penguin, 1999).

76. Parvarthi Menon and T. K. Rajalakshmi, 'Hindu Fascists Doctoring textbooks for hate', and T. K. Rajalakshmi, 'A master's version', both in *Frontline* 15, no. 23 (7–20 November 1998). The report (1993) of the National Steering Committee on Textbook Evaluation noted that BJP governments in Madhya Pradesh, Rajasthan, and Uttar Pradesh in the early 1990s had amended textbooks with the intention of furnishing a 'communal view of Indian history'. In these textbooks, according to one expert reviewer, India was at its most developed in the ancient period, and the struggle for Indian

independence can be said to commence with the opposition over Alexander's invasion of India in the fourth century BC. See Aditya Sinha, 'RSS targets history textbooks', *Hindustan Times* (17 June 1998). As I write these lines, news is emerging of ferociously communal arguments encountered in Gujarati textbooks, some of which describe all non-Hindus in India as 'foreigners', while others suggest that Hitler 'lent prestige and dignity' to Germany. See Monobina Gupta, 'In Gujarat, Adolf Catches 'Em in Schools', *Telegraph* (29 April 2002), and 'Gujarat School Text Teaches Hate', *Asian Age* (8 May 2002). The South Asia Citizens Wire web site, run by Harsh Kapoor, has a great deal of material on this subject: see <*http://www.mnet.fr/aiindex*>.

77. The 'doctoring' of textbooks in Pakistan has been at least just as remarkable, and has been taking place for longer than it has in India: see K. K. Aziz, *The Murder of History in Pakistan: A Critique of History Textbooks Used in Pakistan* (Lahore: Vanguard, 1993); Pervez Amirali Hoodbhoy and Abdul Hameed Nayyar, 'Rewriting the History of Pakistan', in *Islam, Politics and the State: The Pakistan Experience*, pp. 164–77 (London: Zed Books, 1985); Suroosh Irfani, 'Murderers of History', *Jang* (6 October 1999), online at: <*http:// www.jang.com.pk/thenews/oct99-daily/06–10–99/oped/o5.htm*>; and K. Hasanain and A. H. Nayyar, 'Conflict and Violence in the Educational Process', in *Making Enemies, Creating Conflict: Pakistan's Crises of State and Society*, eds Zia Mian and Iftikhar Ahmad (Lahore: Mashal Press, 1997). A search of <*http:// www.mnet.fr/aiindex*> would be quite productive.

78. Parvathi Menon, 'Ayodhya and all that: Communalism and the discipline of history', *Frontline* (11–24 May 1991), p. 47. The author of this piece takes the view that we have heard from the vast majority of the proponents of science: history is neither 'good' nor 'bad'; it can service the cause of 'communalism' as much as the cause of liberty.

79. Nirmal Verma, *Word and Memory* (Bikaner: Vagdevi Prakashan, 1988).

80. Arvind Das, 'The past is present. And absent', *Sunday Times of India* (11 July 1993), p. 17.

81. Arvind Das et al., 'When history causes ennui', *Sunday Times of India* (11 July 1993), p. 17.

82. I might note parenthetically that the Taj Mahal, India's most famous monument and largest foreign exchange earner, was closed to visitors in the evening hours for several years, and thus could not be viewed in moonlight. The Government of India pointed in the late 1980s and early 1990s to threats issued by Sikh terrorists to blow up the Taj Mahal; in the aftermath of the destruction of the Babri Masjid, Hindu 'communalists' are said to have threatened the destruction of the Taj, and in 2001 Bajrang Dal activists stormed it and vandalized the monument. But threats to blow up the Taj emanated not only from Sikh terrorists and Hindu extremists. Following orders issued by the Supreme Court to forcibly close a large number of refineries and other industries in the vicinity of the Taj, on the grounds that the smoke belching from these factories was causing permanent damage to

the monument, a number of Hindu merchants again spoke of destroying the Taj if these orders were not revoked. These Hindus were undoubtedly unaware that even the Taj Mahal has been claimed as a 'Hindu' monument, by no less than a historian. The claims of P. N. Oak were discussed in the previous chapter.

83. It is no surprise that the most sensible interpretation of the conflict around Ayodhya also shows the most imaginative use of Indian myths and of the rich stock of stories originating from the great epics and the lives of Indian philosophers and religious leaders. See Ramchandra Gandhi's *Sita's Kitchen*, and my review, entitled 'Advaita's Waterloo', *Social Scientist* (New Delhi), Vol. 21, nos 5–6 (May–June 1993), pp. 82–9. Gandhi's book was clearly inspirational for one of the very few scholarly treatments of Sita-ki-Rasoi found in the literature: see Phyllis Herman, 'Relocating Ramarajya: Perspectives on Sita's Kitchen in Ayodhya', *International Journal of Hindu Studies* 2, no. 2 (August 1998), pp. 157–84.

84. No inference can be drawn about Sita herself being in the kitchen; indeed, in Valmiki's Ramayana, Sita is nowhere near a kitchen, though she is everywhere else.

85. No one, to the best of my knowledge, has ever argued that the holocaust perpetrated by the Nazis upon Jews, gypsies, homosexuals, and other 'undesirables' owed anything to the illiteracy of the German masses. But such arguments are easily available when it comes to India and obviate the necessity of serious interrogation of all that is taken for granted in any body of knowledge.

86. Sen, 'The Threats to Secular India', p. 30. The Bengali intellectual, I think it not unfair to say, is often prone to think of the Hindu from the Hindi-speaking heartland, the 'cow belt', as a village bumpkin, even perhaps as 'dirty' and 'uncouth'. The historians of the subaltern school have made some sorely needed amends in this regard.

87. A large number of studies have shown that education, far from constituting the solution to 'communalism', contributes to it in a great measure. People who are more highly educated are likely to be more communalized: besides the intense competition for lucrative positions and government dispensations, their sense of history is more acute. In a study conducted in the schools of Bombay in the aftermath of the 1992–3 communal conflagration, it was found that children attending private schools, who come mainly from the Hindu middle classes, had more pejorative views of Muslims than children at municipal schools. See 'The darker side of riots', *Times of India* (5 December 1993), Bombay edition.

88. Sen, 'The Threats to Secular India', p. 30.

89. Tzvetan Todorov, *The Conquest of America: The Question of the Other* [1982], trans. Richard Howard (New York: Harper Perennial Book, 1992), pp. 76, 95, 117.

4

Subalterns in the Academy
The Hegemony of History

It is a rare moment indeed when a school of thought, whether in history or in any other discipline, from a formerly colonized nation that is still resoundingly a part of the Third World (whatever its pretensions to nuclear or great power status), receives in the Western academy the critical attention that has been bestowed upon the subaltern school of historians whose work revolves largely around the colonial period of Indian history. Historians might ruminate on the fact that even the *American Historical Review*, which—notwithstanding its reputation as the flagship of the profession in the United States—is seldom a journal at the cutting edge of theory, or otherwise prone to the bacchanalia of postmodern excesses or flights of postcolonial theory, devoted the greater part of the pages of one of its issues to Subaltern Studies and its rather wide impact across not only historical studies in the Anglo-American academy, but beyond as well.[1] A Latin American Subaltern Studies Group, citing the inspirational work of the Indian historians, ten years ago declared its intent to install the subaltern at the centre of Latin American studies, though it is revealing that their programmatic statement appears in a cultural studies journal.[2] There is, in the warm reception given to Subaltern Studies in some circles in the Anglo-American world, more than just a whiff of avuncular affection: trained almost entirely in British universities, the original group of subaltern historians stand forth, or so it is sometimes fondly imagined, as living testimony to the continuing power of the 'mother' country to influence its peripheries.[3]

However, if I may mix metaphors, the return of the prodigal son is not an unmixed blessing. A few years after the publication of the first volume of *Subaltern Studies*, the rumblings of discontent about the ascendancy of subaltern history, which have since greatly increased, began to appear. Social historians, for instance, argued that in substance there was little to distinguish subaltern history, stripped of its veneer of post-structuralism and Gramscian thought, from 'the history from below' associated with E. P. Thompson, Eric Hobsbawm, and many others belonging to the venerable tradition of British Marxist history. Others are inclined to attribute the success of the subaltern historians to the fact that Indians, in comparison with say Japanese, Chinese, and Latin American historians, could with relative ease take advantage of the English language's inescapable hegemony in the global marketplace of scholarship, though incipient in this criticism are numerous unsavoury suggestions about the manner in which colonialism's deep structures continue to inform the political economy and political sociology of scholarship in the formerly colonized world. When, a mere few years into the emergence of *Subaltern Studies*, Edward Said and Gayatri Chakravorty Spivak lent their formidable voices to the enterprise, its short-term future was certainly assured. Thus, argue the critics, subaltern history was propelled into fame not as a mode of writing history, but as another form of postcolonial criticism. This impression is reinforced by the rather bizarre recommendation with which the new *Subaltern Studies Reader* (1997), whose contributors are described as being 'instrumental in establishing' postcolonial studies, is brought to the reader's attention.[4] There is, indeed, a rather widespread impression, at least outside India, that subaltern studies is a mode of doing postcolonial practice, and that expertise in postcolonial 'classics', with a modicum of knowledge of some European masters, fully equips the reader to understand subaltern history.

I will again advert to some of these criticisms later in the chapter, but suffice to note that just as India is represented as having sought to gate-crash its way into the estate of the nuclear powers, only to be rebuffed by the zealous guardians at its doorway, so subaltern scholarship is sometimes seen as an intruder into domains whose inhabitants are scarcely accustomed to seeing themselves in need of interpretive and analytical lessons from the East. It is one thing to turn to India for its wisdom, and indeed what would India be (for the West) without its mystics, sages, yogis, gurus, and half-naked fakirs, but no one is prepared to countenance the view that in the realm of history and reason, these being construed as one and the same, Western social scientists and historians could turn with profit to the work of Indian historians. I would like to remind the reader of James Mill's observation in the early part of the nineteenth century that the Hindus, being 'perfectly destitute of historical records', displayed every signs of being an irrational people: 'all rude nations neglect history, and are gratified with the productions of the mythologists and poets.'[5] If one should dismiss this cavalier assessment with the trite observation that Mill was merely a creature of his times, a captive of a European age unabashedly fond of its imperialist credentials, it behooves us to listen to the words, not so far removed from our times, of that 'friend' and historian of India, Edward Thompson, the father of E. P. Thompson: 'Indians are not historians, and they rarely show any critical ability. Even their most useful books, books full of research and information, exasperate with their repetitions and diffuseness, and lose effect by their uncritical enthusiasms. ... So they are not likely to displace our account of our connection with India.'[6]

Nearly twenty years after the emergence of subaltern history, no one doubts that the old colonial histories have been displaced, or that the interpretation of Indian history is presently, to a very substantial extent, an affair of the Indians themselves, even though Delhi and Calcutta may not entirely rule the roost. The likes of Edward Thompson have almost been confined to oblivion, and the old British accounts of their connections with India lie largely in tatters, worthy only of the dustbin of history. But it is also equally the case that no one can say with complete confidence what subaltern history stands for, with what voices the subaltern historians speak, and to what purposes. Eleven volumes of *Subaltern Studies* have appeared so far, and the fifty or sixty scholars (by no means all historians) associated with the enterprise, a few of them since its very inception, have between them produced hundreds of articles and a few dozen monographs. A certain coherence seemed to mark the work of the collective in the first decade of its existence, when Ranajit Guha, then based at the Australian National University, presided over its deliberations and saw the first six volumes of *Subaltern Studies* into print. However, the imperatives to diversify the membership of the collective, and bring subaltern history into a more palpable relationship with literary narratives, the discourses of political economy, the intellectual practices of the other social sciences, and the contemporary realities of India, must have been present even then, and were only to become accelerated in the 1990s. Volume IV, which appeared in 1986, featured a critical intervention by Gayatri Spivak, and so marked subaltern history's first engagement with feminism, and indeed the first explicit attempt to locate it in relation to deconstructionism. It also established the pattern whereby one or more contributions in most of the subsequent volumes of *Subaltern Studies* were to offer a critical perspective on the enterprise as a whole, and in Volume V this was attempted by placing *Subaltern Studies* under the scrutiny of historical materialism and Marxist economics,[7] just as the following volume featured an anthropological perspective on the enterprise, accompanied by a debate on the representations of women in Indian feminist histories.[8]

Still, it is a striking feature of the first six volumes of *Subaltern Studies* that, with the exception of a solitary piece by Tanika Sarkar,[9] the work of no women practitioners of Indian history was on display. This may not be entirely surprising, since the impulse towards feminist critiques in India had emanated from largely literary circles, where the disposition to engage in what was considered 'theory' was also more clearly visible.[10] Though the debate on feminism's relation to subaltern history had commenced in *Subaltern Studies*, feminist readings of history were nowhere to be seen, except somewhat tangentially in Gayatri Spivak's translation of, and commentary on, a short story by Mahasweta Devi,[11] one of India's leading women writers and an activist who has worked extensively alongside women and tribals in Bengal. Spivak had forged a unique but nonetheless ambivalent and curiously disjunctive intellectual relationship with Mahasweta, but the history of this collaborative work forms a chapter in the sociology of Indian intellectual life, rather than a chapter in subaltern historiography.

There were doubtless other sources of discomfort for certain members of the collective. In his opening salvo on elite historiography, Ranajit Guha had condemned it for neglecting and obscuring the 'politics of the people',[12] but it was not until 1996, when Volume IX of *Subaltern Studies* was published, that the politics of the Dalits, historically the most disempowered segment of India's population, and now at least 150 million in number, received its first explicit articulation.[13] Despite the grandiose celebrations of subalternity, and the promise to furnish complex and compelling narratives of how far the 'people *on their own*, that is, *independently of the elite*', had contributed to the nationalist movement and the making of Indian society, Subaltern Studies seemed far too interested in the activities of the middle classes. This disenchantment with Subaltern Studies's alleged abandonment of its originary ambitions, namely to understand *how far* the activity of the people constituted an 'autonomous domain', and what their modes of resistance were to both imperialist and elite nationalist politics, can be witnessed in the caustic assessment by Ramachandra Guha, who himself had once been a contributor, of Volume VIII of *Subaltern Studies* (1994). Guha gave it as his considered opinion that the essays comprising the volume, though unquestionably constituting 'intellectual history, reframed as "discourse analysis"', were 'emphatically not Subaltern Studies'. Guha described it as a shift towards 'bhadralok studies', fully aware that no greater insult was possible. The word 'bhadralok', made common in the 1960s by American scholars working on India, who have specialized in taking the politics out of knowledge (a characteristically American trait),[14] refers to the 'gentle folk', or the gentry, but its far more pejorative connotations call to mind a class of people who, being the progeny of Macaulay, were imitative of their colonial masters, and even professed to be more English than the English themselves. Solidly middle-class, and unfailingly enslaved to the grand narratives of science, reason, constitutional politics, and progress, the 'bhadralok' disassociated themselves equally from Gandhian politics, which smelled too much of disloyalty, and the politics of the masses, which smelled too much of the gutter.

To say that Subaltern Studies had transformed itself into bhadralok studies, in a curious return of the repressed, was to aver that the subaltern historians, for the most part, had moved from studies of popular consciousness to unravelling the mentalities of nationalist leaders and the world of middle-class Bengali domesticity, 'from documenting subaltern dissent to dissecting elite discourse, from writing with (socialist) passion to following the postmodernist fashion'.[15] Similarly Sumit Sarkar, himself one of India's most distinguished historians and a founding member of the Subaltern Collective, in tracing the post-modernist turn in Subaltern Studies to what he alleges is the wholesale and unreflective deployment of the Saidian framework among a section of the subaltern historians, has not only disavowed any further association with his former colleagues, but is unremitting in his critique of Subaltern Studies for those very sins of essentialism, teleology, and fetishization which were associated with elite historiography.[16] Sarkar's apostasy has not gone unnoticed: thus Ranajit Guha's introduction to his *Subaltern Studies Reader* (1997) was to excise all trace of Sarkar and his important role in the collective.[17] Having built an entire school of historical interpretation around the silenced voices of the past, Guha sought to silence Sarkar and push him into oblivion.

Thus, as the Subaltern Studies collective enters into the third decade of its existence, the enterprise of subaltern history means many different things to different people. Over the course of time, people drift into different sets of habits, take up new ideas, and form new associations. However, Subaltern Studies's sharpest critics are some former members of the collective, and it is trifle too gentle to speak of the fragmentation of the collective as though one were describing the tendency of rivers to form tributaries. The 'high-priest' of the collective, Ranajit Guha, is no longer formally associated with his own creation, and the group of historians he gathered around him rendered him an intellectual tribute by designating Volume VIII of *Subaltern Studies* as a collection of essays in his honour. If some members of the collective had wandered into postmodernism, or were more seriously engaged with Western philosophy or feminist theory, Volume IX of *Subaltern Studies* was to show that the collective had the capacity to re-invent itself in yet more diverse ways, by embracing voices more generally associated with postcolonial theory and cultural studies, as well as with the study of contemporary Indian society. Indeed, in the American academy especially, Subaltern Studies is seen, as I have previously suggested, as the form in which 'cultural studies' has taken root in India, while others recognize it as constituting the particular Indian inflection of postcolonial theory.

In all this, Subaltern Studies is beginning to look like the banyan tree, whose magisterial presence pervades the Indian landscape, and under its enormous canvas social and cultural historians, postmodernists, postcolonialists, feminists, poststructuralists, and post-Marxists have alike found some sustenance. A banyan tree, I might add, is not the same thing as a tropical jungle, whatever the temptation to let those luxuriant metaphors which the study of India invites inform our understanding of the particular relationship of Indian intellectual endeavours to Indian history and society. One does not tackle a banyan tree as a whole; and, in like fashion, I can only lop away at some of its branches, and merely hint at some of the trajectories that a critique of Subaltern Studies, around which a formidable mass of critical literature has developed, should take. What gives shade also blocks sunlight; and so, perforce, one must also wonder whether the capaciousness of Subaltern Studies might not breed its own forms of sterility.

BACKDROP TO A HISTORY

In the words of one of the relatively newer members of the subaltern collective, 'subalternist analysis has become a recognizable mode of critical scholarship in history, literature, and anthropology.'[18] Yet very few people outside the field of Indian history understand its particular place in Indian historiography, and fewer still are able to assess the precise departures signified by subaltern history. Subaltern Studies has certainly thrived on the impression, which it did everything to encourage, that all previous histories of India represented the collusion of imperialist and nationalist forces, just as they were singularly lacking in any theoretical impulse. It is noteworthy that, despite the avowedly Marxist orientation of some of the subaltern historians, and certainly their repudiation of neo-Hindu histories, their work offers no engagement with an entire generation or two of Indian Marxist historians (and sometimes sociologists) who preceded them, such as Rajne Palme Dutt, D. D. Kosambi, and A. R. Desai, or even with their older and still active contemporaries such as Romila Thapar, R. S. Sharma, D. N. Jha, Satish Chandra, and Irfan Habib. Doubtless, the greater majority of India's most distinguished historians before the advent of subaltern history worked on the pre-colonial period, just as subaltern historians have worked exclusively on the colonial and post-independence periods: this may, in part, explain why earlier Marxist histories have received little attention, though it cannot help resolve the question why the pre-colonial period has not fallen under the purview of subaltern historians. Certainly one might well think, on reading the subaltern historians, that nothing in the tradition of Indian historiography speaks to their interests, and that insofar as one might wish to evoke any worthwhile lineages, the past is a *tabula rasa*. Here subaltern history echoes, ironically, the early nineteenth-century British histories of India, which were predicated on the assumption that, the Indians being supremely indifferent to their past, the British were faced with the onerous task of starting entirely afresh, dependent only on their own resources.

The advent of subaltern history is better appreciated against the backdrop of other trajectories of twentieth-century Indian history, which are delineated in an earlier chapter. As we have seen, the first generation of Indian historians such as R. C. Dutt (1848–1909) and R. G. Bhandarkar (1837–1925) had expended its labours largely on the study of ancient India, which was envisioned as the high point of Indian civilization. The tomes of the Bengali historian Jadunath Sarkar

(1870–1958) on the Mughals and Aurangzeb were based on a representation of political Islam as tyrannical and iniquitous, an impression equally conveyed by his celebratory biography of the Maratha leader Shivaji, who was elevated as the founding father of Indian nationalism. With the attainment of independence in 1947, the creation of an Indian history, for and by Indians, became something of a national imperative, and it was never doubted that the 'freedom struggle', waged under the leadership of Mohandas Gandhi and the Congress party, would constitute one of the more glorious chapters of Indian history. As mentioned in Chapter II, a number of state-sponsored histories of the struggle for independence were published. In the gargantuan 11-volume *History and Culture of the Indian People* (1951–69), under the general editorship of R. C. Majumdar, whose own contributions to the volumes were formidable, the nationalist devotion to the Hindu past saw its most sustained expression, and history was to be yoked to a particular vision of nation-building.

From the point of view of locating subaltern history, however, it is other trajectories, associated with Marxist or materialist historians such as Saumyendranath Tagore, D. D. Kosambi, Romila Thapar, R. C. Sharma, Irfan Habib, and Bipan Chandra, or with Calcutta-based historians and scholars—Sushil Kumar De, Barun De, and Asok Sen, among others—of the Bengal Renaissance, that demand our attention. The latter group, in revisiting the hagiographic accounts of the Bengal Renaissance, had come to the realization that Rammohun Roy, Iswar Chandra Vidyasagar, Keshub Sen, and other nineteenth-century social reformers were constrained by the colonial context and unable to enter into anything but an uncritical engagement with Western modernity.[19] Rammohun Roy, in particular, would be brought down to size, and it now became possible to speak of Roy's casteism, polygamy, financial greed (to the point that he sued his own mother), and philandering.[20] The insights of these revisionist histories, though shorn of any theoretical apparatus, would clearly inform the work of subaltern historians. Among the Marxist historians, a number of other considerations, stemming from the immense political and social dislocations of the 1970s, predominated. Under Jawaharlal Nehru, the country had seemed committed to secularism, but this consensus began to show signs of strain under Indira Gandhi. The war with Pakistan in 1971, leading to the creation of Bangladesh, brought to the fore questions of ethnicity, language, and nation-formation, just as the massacre of Bengali intellectuals by the retreating Pakistani army brought an awareness of the precariousness of intellectual life in

South Asia. Yet four years later Indira Gandhi was to impose an internal emergency, and political calculations impelled her, as well as various other politicians, to court religious bodies and organizations. Henceforth the 'religious vote bank' would be an invariable factor in Indian politics.

At the same time, 'communalism', or the supposition that identity in India was constituted preeminently through membership in religious communities, broadly defined as 'Hindu', 'Muslim', 'Sikh', and so on, was assuming a heightened importance in historical narratives. The effect, from the Marxist standpoint, was to introduce manifold distortions in the understanding of Indian history: not only were Hindu-Muslim relations being cast as drenched in blood, but conflicts among the ruling elite were being construed as conflicts at the broader social level. Marxist historians who dared to challenge conventional orthodoxies found themselves ostracized or ridiculed, as the debate centring on beef-eating in ancient India was to show. But the Marxist historians were by no means an undifferentiated lot: while Bipan Chandra veered towards the view that the nationalist movement could not be dismissed as a bourgeois endeavour, other historians were hostile to the received view and pointed to the Congress party's unwillingness to stand for radical economic and land reform, or its inability to draw workers, peasants, minorities, women, and other disenfranchised into the nationalist movement or into the mainstream of public life in the period after independence.

In the delineation of the circumstances under which the Subaltern Studies collective was formed, it becomes important to dwell at length on what was then the dominant strand in Indian historiography, namely the so-called Cambridge School. The work of historians identified with this school of historical thought is well-known to historians of India, and would scarcely have required any explication, but for the fact that among the advocates of postcolonial theory who have so readily embraced subaltern history, Indian historiography as a whole remains an entirely unknown domain. Earlier generations of imperialist historians had sought to make a decisive link between education and politics: in their view, it was the largely English-educated Indian middle-class, nourished on the writings of Mill, Locke, and Milton, and brought to an awareness of the place that institutions, organized along rational and scientific lines, could play in the life of a society, which had first raised the demand for some form of political representation. Cognizant of the principles of liberty, democracy, the separation of powers, constitutional agitation, and freedom of speech enshrined in Western political practices, these Indians were construed as the main, and only rightful, actors in the drama of nationalism that began to unfold in overtly political ways in the late nineteenth century. They recognized, or so it was argued, that political action must be within the framework of the law, and nothing should violate the 'rule of law'. The British themselves might well be despotic, as the wise and the just must often be, but among a people such as the Indians who before the blessings of Western civilization were brought to their doorstep had never experienced anything but despotism, the adherence to the 'rule of law' served as the indispensable condition of their acceptance in the political domain. All other political activity must perforce be 'criminal'. The British could well be proud of these middle-class or bhadralok Indians, as they provided unimpeachable evidence of the bountiful effects of the civilizing mission, the judiciousness of British policies, and the universal truth of the great narratives of science and reason. The only Indian politics was the politics of the English-educated bhadralok, and as it is they who stoked the fires of nationalism, Indians were bound to recognize that even their nationalism was the very gift of a magnanimous people endowed with enlightened traditions.

Trite and comical as this narrative might now sound, it appears in a refurbished and seemingly more subtle form in the writings of the Cambridge School of historians. Many commentators have been fixated on Anil Seal's *The Emergence of Indian Nationalism* (1968), where it is argued that education was 'one of the chief determinants' of the politics of Indian nationalism, the genesis of which 'is clearly linked with those Indians who had been schooled by Western methods',[21] as the originary point of the Cambridge School's explorations in Indian history, but in point of fact the framework for this school of thought is derived from a broader swathe of work on the partition of Africa and the economic history of the British empire. Rejecting the view of both Marxist theoreticians and late Victorian historians that the essence of imperialism consisted in the scramble for colonies, in the extension of Western political control over territories in the non-Western world, John Gallagher and Ronald Robinson argued in an article published in 1953 that the emphasis on formal empire had blinded scholars to the continuity between formal and informal empires, as well as to the history of continued expansion of British trade and investment. Gallagher and Robinson posited a *reluctant* imperialism; their Empire, moreover, had nothing to do with power. The 'distinctive feature' of British imperialism, they boldly argued, resided in the 'willingness to

limit the use of paramount power to establishing security for trade';
and power was only deployed when native collaborators could not
be found to preserve British interests.[22]

The thesis for the 'Non-European Foundations of European Imperialism' emerges more clearly in Robinson's article by the same name,
significantly subtitled 'Sketch for a Theory of Collaboration'.[23] The
use of the word 'theory' implies something lofty, but Robinson had no
more prosaic observation than that 'imperialism was as much a
function of its victims' collaboration or non-collaboration—of their
indigenous politics, as it was of European expansion'. If imperialism
had perforce to be rescued (though why that should be necessary—at
a time when Britain had already been divested of India, Burma, and
Ceylon, and was facing insurgencies elsewhere in its empire, at a time
that is when the writing was on the wall and Britain could choose to
leave with grace—is another question), it only remained to demonstrate that the natives, or the class of natives that alone mattered, were
enthusiastic in their embrace of colonial rule: as Robinson puts it, 'the
choice of indigenous collaborators, more than anything else, determined the organisation of colonial rule'. Imperial takeovers in Afric?
and Asia were actuated less by the expansion of European capitalism
than 'by the breakdown of collaborative mechanisms in extra-Euro-
pean politics which hitherto had provided them with adequate opportunity and protection'.

Moreover, if imperialism is only another name for collaboration,
then it is even possible to say that the natives were imperialists in
their own right. Robinson can, thus, quite brazenly even speak, apropos the Tswana tribe of Bechuanaland, of the natives 'exploit[ing] the
European'. European imperialism is moved to the margins, rendered
into an epiphenomenon: 'imperialism in the form of colonial rule was
a major function not of European society, but a major function of
indigenous politics.' Imperialism was consequently not the cause but
the consequence of the partition of Africa; to adopt the formulation of
Eric Stokes, more well-known for his work on India, 'the powers were
scrambling in Africa and not for Africa'.[24] Writing on India a few
years later, David Washbrook, one of the more sophisticated of the
Cambridge historians, used remarkably similar language, adverting
to 'the indigenous logic of military fiscalism and commercial expansion' to situate British colonialism. 'In a certain sense,' Washbrook
argued, 'colonialism was the logical outcome of South Asia's own
history of capitalist development.'[25] The word 'indigenous' surfaces
so frequently in Cambridge School writings in relation to the origins

of colonialism that one begins to suspect that the European powers had no role to play in the colonies except to furnish the indigenous elites with some assistance as they gravitated towards exploiting their own people.

Seal's work on Indian nationalism, to which I have alluded, points to the ways in which this purportedly 'new' view of imperialism found its way into the study of late British India. The subtitle of his work, 'Competition and Collaboration in the Late Nineteenth Century', gives the game away. In accounting for the origins of Indian nationalism, Seal constructs an entire narrative around the lives and activities of a handful of English-educated men in the Presidencies, who competed for those jobs and opportunities that the British had provided through educational and administrative reform. A new class of people had also emerged as a consequence of the disruption of the village economy and the increasing penetration into the town and countryside of trading companies which employed educated Indians in increasing numbers as middlemen, brokers, and agents. However, the growth of this middle-class soon outpaced the availability of jobs, leading to increasing disaffection among the educated youth. In the altered conditions brought forth by British rule, characterized by new opportunities for advancement, social change, and institutional reform, the existing rivalries that divided one caste from another, the Muslim from the Hindu, community from community, became even more accentuated. Now the educated, whether Brahmins or Muslims, tradition-bound or modernizers, Bengali or Tamil, forged their own horizontal alliances—a natural enough response, but one that Indians, among whom the idea of the 'individual' has no salience in the colonial sociology of knowledge, were bound to adopt in a predictable surrender to primordial community instinct. Seal stops short of describing all these beneficiaries of English education as a 'new social class', for in his view the changes introduced in the economy were not so substantial as to 'give India social classes based on economic categories'. Seal could not argue otherwise, for to impute a form of social stratification based on social classes would be to obscure the differences between a colonized people and the more advanced society of the 'mother' country.[26]

In a later paper on 'Imperialism and Nationalism in India', Seal professes to have abandoned the theory so elaborately constructed in his earlier work, on the grounds that the 'graduates and professional men in the presidencies [Bombay, Calcutta, and Madras]' were 'not quite as important as they once appeared'.[27] But in fact the 'horizontal alliances' that had once seemed so paramount to Seal now turn into 'vertical alliances' of 'bigwigs and followers', 'factions' with patrons and clients.[28] Accordingly the nodal point of the analysis is shifted from the presidencies to the localities, where 'the race for influence, status and resources', which alone 'decided political choices', is better observed. In the localities 'the unabashed scramblers for advantage at the bottom' become more visible; and it is not incidental that this scrambling is all done by Indians, not Englishmen. Driven by self-aggrandizement, by the lust for economic gain and political power, 'Hindus worked with Muslims, [and] Brahmins were hand in glove with non-Brahmins';[29] and the religious taboos and social constraints of centuries were cast aside. Money will make untouchables even of Brahmins; so much for the incorruptible purity of the sacerdotal caste. In the words of one of Seal's colleagues at Cambridge, 'the most obvious characteristic of every Indian politician was that each acted for many interests at all levels of Indian society and in so doing cut across horizontal ties of class, caste, region and religion.'[30] Indians jockeyed with each other for position and power in this wild scenario of collaboration and competition.

In the view of Indian history propounded by the Cambridge School, there is no room for ideology.[31] Indian nationalists, animated only by self-interest, relentlessly pursued rationally calculated ends, and their pious declarations must not be allowed to obscure the nature of 'Indian nationalism' as 'animal politics'.[32] Annie Besant, an Irishwoman who came to occupy an important place in Indian politics, is described as joining the Congress 'undoubtedly ... to bring her increased public attention', and militancy in the Krishna-Godavri deltas during the Civil Disobedience movement is attributed to the inability of some people to 'find a satisfactory niche in local government'.[33] When Indians fail to become clerks, they opt for rebellion: such are the doings of a highly impulsive people. Writing about politics in the South, Washbrook avers that 'the provincial political struggle was not about the nature of interests which were to be represented to the British; it was about who was to earn the money and achieve the prestige which came from carrying out the representation.'[34]

Political activity at the provincial level, in the Cambridge School view, is thus seen to revolve around the institutions of government. Here, again, Seal had set the tone for the argument: as he wrote, 'It is our hypothesis that the structure of imperial government can provide a clue to the way Indian politics developed.'[35] Where before the 'genesis' of Indian politics was said to lie in the actions of the English-educated elite in the presidencies, now the motor of political behaviour was described as the government, which itself showed Indians the way to political activity. The argument is rendered more explicit in Gordon Johnson's monograph on Bombay, where Indian politicians are generally described as being consumed by local politics, and compelled to take interest in national politics only when prompted by the government at the national level: in Johnson's words, 'nationalist activity boons and slumps in phase with the national activity of the government.'[36] Indians had to be pushed towards nationalism; they could not think beyond their village or town, nor was their gaze set on anything nobler than short-term tactics, local grievances, and petty gains. Imperialist stimulus, nationalist response: the scientist in the laboratory, the rat in the cage: here is the story of Indian nationalism, that sordid tale of every man desperately seeking to find his place under this sun.

THE MOMENT OF ARRIVAL: THE BIRTH OF THE SUBALTERN IN NEGATION

It is against the immediate backdrop of the Cambridge School that subaltern history emerged, though this is scarcely to say that there was anything in a history of 'vertical' or 'horizontal' alliances to warrant the claim that it represented a novel reading of Indian nationalism or political history. But in the writings of the historians belonging to the Cambridge School was to be found a template which pointed, in the most tangible way, to what Ranajit Guha has described as the 'bad faith of historiography', to everything that a historiography which is responsible to its subjects, politically emancipatory, sensitive in its treatment of the evidence, and theoretically astute must avoid.[37] (I may here note, and shall adumbrate on the point later, that subaltern history knows itself principally as negation, as the opposite of what it does not desire.) Since the emphasis in earlier imperialist writings on the activities of a small segment of the English-educated elite now appeared as a gross caricature of Indian political activity, the Cambridge School historians, let us recall, were to shift the locus of their attention to the government, whose actions were eagerly watched by the nationalists. Seal attempted to seal this argument with a cryptic formulation: 'The British built this framework; the Indians fitted into it.'[38] Agency never belongs with the Indians; they are condemned to be reactive. Moreover,

whether the chief 'determinant' of Indian political activity is construed as the activities of the educated elite, or the actions of the
government, the Cambridge School history of India is a history of
native *collaboration*. As is quite transparent, the effect of this argument
is to make *resistance* invisible, to write it out of the political history of
nationalism altogether; collaboration also renders Indians into willing partakers of their own submission. This is the house-cleaning and
refurbishing of the Cambridge School variety: since Indians must be
conceived as agents in their own right, they were to be endowed with
a greater share in the institutional mechanisms that kept them suppressed and bid them to look to the *state* as the principal locus of
political agency.

No one reading Ranajit Guha's programmatic note in the first
volume of Subaltern Studies would have missed the implicit references to the Cambridge School, or to the older liberal-imperialist
histories from which its arguments are derived. But Guha was to be
equally unsparing of nationalist histories, which in some respect,
since they invited and even demanded allegiance from loyal-minded
Indians, were more insidious in their effect. 'The historiography of
Indian nationalism has for a long time been dominated by elitism',
Guha wrote in the opening sentence, and added in elaboration that
elitism contained both 'colonialist' and 'bourgeois-nationalist elitism', the former defining Indian nationalism 'primarily as a function
of stimulus and response'.[39] 'The general orientation' of nationalist
historiography, on the other hand, 'is to represent Indian nationalism
as primarily an idealist venture in which the indigenous elite led the
people from subjugation to freedom'.

Elsewhere, in a later work, Guha represented this congruence
between two seemingly opposed strands in other terms: both
colonialist and nationalist regimes were represented as embodying
'domination without hegemony', and the authoritarian idiom of colonialism was seen as matched by the nationalist's resort to the
indigenous notion of *danda* [literally, stick].[40] In either case, to return
to Guha's earliest formulation, elitist historiography failed to 'acknowledge, far less interpret, the contribution made by the people *on
their own*, that is, *independently of the elite* to the making and development of this nation'. Nationalist historiography understood the 'mass'
articulation of nationalism mainly 'negatively', that is as a problem of
'law and order', and positively, if at all, 'as a response to the charisma
of certain elite leaders or in the currently more fashionable terms of
vertical mobilization by the manipulation of factions.' Colluding

with the imperatives of imperialist histories, nationalist historiography had no space for 'the politics of the people'. Consequently, the task of a non-elitist, or subaltern, historiography is to interpret the politics of the people as 'an autonomous domain' that 'neither originated from elite politics nor did its existence depend on the latter'.

In the inelegant, albeit passionate, formulations of Guha's agenda-setting document lie the seeds of Subaltern Studies's peculiarities and failures; and the novel readings of familiar phenomena encountered in some of the papers in the ten volumes, and in other related scholarly works, occur in spite of the extraordinarily clumsy attempt to theorize the grounds for a new historiography.[41] The peculiarities can be said to begin with Guha's deployment of the words 'elite' and 'subaltern', and the particular manner in which they stand in relation to each other. In a note appended to his programmatic statement, Guha states that the term 'elite' signifies 'dominant groups, foreign as well as indigenous'. Though even his use of the term elite, where a crude distinction is drawn between 'foreign' and 'Indian'—as though 'Indian' were a given category, not one that is constantly put into question in India itself—hearkens back to the equally crude notion of *false consciousness*, as when he describes dominant indigenous groups at the 'regional and local levels' as those which 'acted in the interest' of the dominant groups at the national level 'and not in conformity to interests corresponding truly to their own social being', it is his deployment of the word 'subaltern' which beggars belief.

In his preface to the opening volume of the series, Guha describes the word 'subaltern' as meaning a person 'of inferior rank', for which his authority is the *Concise Oxford Dictionary*. 'It will be used in these pages', Guha writes, 'as a name for the general attribute of subordination in South Asian Society whether this is expressed in terms of class, caste, age, gender and office or in any other way'. As is quite likely, the inspiration for this usage came to him from a reading of Gramsci's 'Notes on Italian History', which is mentioned as offering a six-point programme of subaltern history and resistance. But as Guha is undoubtedly aware, the word 'subaltern', which can hardly be described as having general currency in the English language, properly belongs to the realm of the military, to designate a non-commissioned officer of very inferior rank, or even an orderly. Indeed, the *Oxford English Dictionary* concedes, in its 1989 edition, that the word 'subaltern', to designate a person or body of person of 'inferior status, quality, or importance', is 'rare', and the last quotation from any text that is furnished as an instance of the word's usage is from 1893. This, too, is the colonized Bengali's mentality: an archaic, or nearly archaic, word from the English language is resuscitated, the writings of an esoteric Italian Marxist theoretician are evoked, and all this in the cause of delineating the *autonomous* realm of a people in a colonized country who are stated as having acted under their own impulse. Beckett could have done no better, if the intention was to furnish a preliminary sketch of the theatre of the absurd. Guha has sense, but clearly lacks sensibility.

Doubtless, one could argue that the use of the word 'subaltern' was a strategic choice which, so it was thought, would enable Guha and other subaltern historians to remain within a broad Marxist framework while bypassing the Marxist analysis of the relationship between classes and the emphasis on the means of production. 'Subaltern' in 'Subaltern Studies' stands for something resembling the subordinate 'classes' that are not quite 'classes', for much the same reasons that E. P. Thompson once hinted at an eighteenth-century English history as a history of 'class struggle without class'.[42] If even apropos England, where the industrial revolution was born, there was some risk of speaking of classes as reified and bounded identities, how much more difficult is it to speak of classes in colonial India, where social relations were in a state of very considerable flux and class formation, in conditions resembling 'feudalism', existed in the most rudimentary form?[43] Since 'subaltern' sufficiently points to relations of subordination and domination without the entrapment of the more familiar but rigid categories of class derived from orthodox Marxism,[44] categories that moreover are most meaningful when the language of 'citizen-politics' prevails (as it mostly does not in India), is not much gained by the deployment of subalternity as an analytical notion and as a locus for the location of consciousness?[45] But does not this argument then return us to the formulations of Anil Seal and his Cambridge brethren, to the contention indeed that India did not quite have social classes based on economic categories? Must India be condemned, in subaltern history as much as in the Cambridge School monographs, to remain an inchoate mess—something that, in a typical demonstration of Indian recalcitrance, remains resistant to the categories of social science discourse?

If the notion of the 'subaltern' is lifted from Gramsci to explicate the social relations prevalent in Indian history, it is well to recall also that Gramsci's discussion of subalternity is framed alongside his deployment of the idea of 'hegemony'. Suffice to note that Guha has throughout been insistent on characterizing the British Raj as an exemplification of 'domination without hegemony', yet he does not reflect on whether the deployment of the notion of subalternity is not contingent upon the deployment of the idea of hegemony. Though I do not here propose to offer a more substantive critique of Guha's notion of 'domination without hegemony', it is evidently the case that he does not consider whether the British *failure* to achieve hegemony (if indeed there is merit in the claim), or to universalize its socio-cultural values, may not in fact have been as much a 'failure' as part of a deliberate strategy to adapt themselves to the conditions of Indian political life and history.

As a further explication of Guha's usage of the word 'subaltern' shows, the entire edifice of Subaltern Studies is fraught with the most hazardous philosophical and political conundrums. Whether by his very usage of 'subaltern' Guha sought to impart a militancy to rebel consciousness, or to suggest that the realm of everyday life is inherently suffused with the spirit of insurgency, the suppression of which is a task to which dominant forces set themselves, is a question brought to the fore by his *Elementary Aspects of Insurgency in Colonial India* (1983),[46] the book with which Subaltern Studies is sometimes seen to have been inaugurated. Ranging widely and oftentimes indiscriminately across materials on rebellions, jacqueries, and insurgencies in India, Guha gave the distinct impression, howsoever subtly conveyed, that the consciousness of the subaltern is the consciousness of militancy. Peasants somehow appear not as persons who spend the greater part of their lives toiling on the fields, but as figures of resistance: that is to say, if I may invert Victor Turner, peasants are not only immersed in communitas, but also spend a good part of their life serving the structure.[47] Admittedly, their lives are not so easily pieced together, but peasant consciousness outside the mode of resistance is implicitly construed as uninteresting, unattractive, and unreflective.

Other, more obvious, objections have been raised to Guha's notion of the 'subaltern'. There are hierarchies among both elites and subalterns, and at what point one shades into another is not clear. As colonial rule was indubitably to establish, local elites were merely subalterns to the British, and even in the ranks of the indigenous elites, subalternity was a matter of negotiation. Guha is evidently sensitive to these questions, for instance in his recognition that local indigenous elites were sometimes subservient to indigenous elites at the national level, but nonetheless the contrast between elites and subalterns is too sharply drawn. Consequently, as one critic has

argued, those groups which 'occupy an uneasy marginal role between the elite and the subaltern, crossing and re-crossing the con-
ceptual boundary according to the precise historical circumstances
under discussion', receive 'short shrift' in subaltern history.[48] In
Elementary Aspects, moreover, Guha appears to be unable to distinguish between tribals and peasants, and often his discussion of peasant insurgency, such as in the chapter on 'modalities' of insurgency,
draws mainly upon materials pertaining to tribal insurrections. This
is no small problem, because this confusion obscures the fundamentally different manner in which colonialism affected tribal communities and peasant societies. Colonialism knew of no other way to profit
from tribal economies than by destroying them altogether, to pave the
way for plantations or for extraction of forest and mineral wealth; in
peasant communities, on the other hand, the colonial expropriation
of surplus took the form of rent or taxes.[49] This meant, as well, that
disaffection in tribal areas was more widespread, and given the
relatively egalitarian basis of most tribal societies, the resistance to
colonial rule was more thorough, integrated, and uniform.

If all this seems problematic enough, Guha yet moves from one
distinctly odd formulation to another. In the supplementary note to
his programmatic statement, he ventures to say of the 'people' and
the 'subaltern classes', used synonymously in his statement, that
'they represent the demographic difference between the total Indian
population and all those whom we have described as the elite'.[50] If we
recall his ambition to understand subaltern politics as an 'autonomous domain', it is extraordinary that his definition of the subaltern
is made contingent upon the definition of the elite, and the elite is
given ontological priority.[51] Having 'described' the elite, Guha thought
that the subalterns could be construed as the mere difference, the
remainder, the supplement. That the elite constitute a minuscule
portion of the Indian population only exacerbates the problem. Guha
could well have said that the elite represent the demographic difference between the entire Indian population and all those who are
described as subaltern, but the priority given to 'elite' clearly suggests that he considers it a less ambiguous category. It betrays as well
his own tendency to slip into those habits of elite thinking which he
otherwise deplores: when all is said and done, Guha's habits of
thinking are firmly Brahminical, and consequently he appears not to
recognize that at least some 'subalterns' may have welcomed British
'elites' as carriers of norms that promised them legal, social, and
political equality.

Having set apart, then, the elites and the subalterns, Guha admits that the subaltern classes could not originate initiatives 'powerful enough to develop the nationalist movement into a full-fledged struggle for national liberation'. The working-class did not have consciousness as a 'class-for-itself', and was unable to forge alliances with the peasantry; and so the numerous peasant uprisings eventually fizzled out, having 'waited in vain for a leadership to raise them above localism and generalize them into a nationwide anti-imperialist campaign.' If the subaltern classes 'waited in vain', to stress Guha's own words, one can only conclude that Guha does not consider their autonomy to be a fully desirable feature of their politics, which is hardly consistent with the very project of Subaltern Studies. If they 'waited in vain', the subalterns were betrayed by the bourgeoisie, who failed to exercise the requisite leadership required of them under the circumstances; and so we come to Guha's explication of the principal task of subaltern historiography:

It is the study of this *historic failure of the nation to come to its own*, a failure due to the inadequacy of the bourgeoisie as well as of the working class to lead it into a decisive victory over colonialism and a bourgeois-democratic revolution of either the classic nineteenth-century type under the hegemony of the bourgeoisie or a modern type under the hegemony of workers and peasants, that is, a 'new democracy'—*it is the study of this failure which constitutes the central problematic of the historiography of colonial India.*[52]

Subaltern history, if we are to follow Guha's argument, commences with a recognition of 'failure', and its provenance is the study of 'failure', that is the realm of what did not transpire. Somehow that 'failure' seems all but natural, since the native seldom arrives at the destination: either he is still averse to clock-time, or has overstepped his destination, or failed to keep his appointment; and when, after much expenditure of energy, the destination is in sight, and the threshold is eventually reached, the native finds that everyone else is departed. When India arrives at the doorstep of modernity, it is to find that the West is already living in the era of post-modernity; when the great industrial targets set by the five-year plans are eventually met, the part of the world that the Indian nation-state seeks to emulate is already post-industrial, living in the mad throes of the information superhighway; when the great dams, those 'temples' of the modern age as Nehru saw them, are finished to the cheering of the leaders of the nation-state, the news arrives that such mega-projects of the state are demeaning to the human spirit, productive only of waste, pollution, and ruined lives. The history of India is always 'incomplete', and here is Sumit Sarkar, one of the founding members of the subaltern collective, to remind us of the modernity which we in India still await: 'The sixty years or so that lie between the foundation of the Indian National Congress in 1885 and the achievement of independence in August 1947 witnessed perhaps the greatest transition in our country's long history. A transition, however, which in many ways remains grievously incomplete, and it is with this central ambiguity that it seems most convenient to begin our survey.'[53] What would it mean for the history of India to be less incomplete or near completion? To speak of 'completion' is to raise the spectre of the 'end of history', and as we are aware, the tribe of Francis Fukuyama, Paul Johnson, Bernard Lewis, and many other Western commentators have already stated that the destiny of the developing world is to follow in the footsteps of Western democracies.

Thus the 'history' of India, a land of immense fertility and embarrassing fecundity, is itself conceptualized as a 'lack', a 'want' for something better—call it the bourgeoisie that could have, to quote Guha again, led the nation to a 'decisive victory' over colonialism, or call it a revolution of the 'classic nineteenth-century type'. If only India had been like France, we might have been a fulfilled nation; indeed, we wouldn't need a history, since someone else's history would have served us better.

THE JOURNEY:
THE PRACTICE OF SUBALTERN HISTORY

From a reading of Guha's programmatic note, as well as of other subaltern histories which bemoan the incompleteness of modernity in India, one would be entitled to draw the conclusion that subaltern history itself exists in a position of subalternity to Europe. This is an argument that can be developed at several levels. The *Subaltern Studies* volumes, as well as the other works of the scholars associated with the project, suggest that India still furnishes the raw data, while the theory emanates from Europe. India is the terrain on which the investigations are carried out, and the analytical tools are derived from the West: this is hardly a departure from the older models of indological scholarship. The subaltern historians are comfortable with Marx, Hegel, Heidegger, Jakobson, Habermas, Foucault, Barthes, and Derrida, as well as with French, American, and British traditions of social history, but the interpretive strategies of the Indian epics or Puranas, the political thinking of a Kautilya,[54] the hermeneutics of devotional poetry, the philosophical exegesis of Nagarjuna, and the narrative frameworks of the *Panchatantra* or the *Kathasaritsagara*, are of little use to them; and even the little literature of the countless number of little traditions, such as proverbs, ballads, and folk-tales, *seldom* enters into their consciousness.

Still, perhaps this is not so substantive a criticism of subaltern history as one might imagine. The origins of the modern social sciences lie in Western intellectual practices, and it is not unreasonable that the interpretive models should also be derived from these practices, though that does not obviate the path of inquiry that some scholars have taken, which is to ask whether one can speak of an 'Indian sociology', 'Indian anthropology', and so on. There is also the argument, which subaltern historians and their friends would doubtless advance, that India is at least as much heir, for example, to Marxist thought as any other place, and in some respects India has made more of Marx than have the Western democracies. In the United States, for instance, Marxism has little place outside small (and generally inconsequential) pockets of the academy and the arts world, but in India it has generated a vibrant political, artistic, and intellectual culture, not to mention the dominant ruling party in a few states. Consequently, the objection that is frequently encountered, namely that Guha and his colleagues show an inconsistency in denouncing Western historiography at the same time that they draw upon the work of Gramsci, would strike the subaltern historians as having little merit. The precise uses to which Gramsci is put is certainly, as I have suggested, an open question. But what is quite certain is that in intellectual matters, there is still no reciprocity, and one wonders what reception, if any, subaltern history would have received in the West had it not so obviously been the carrier of theoretical trajectories that were simultaneously finding a resonance in the Western academy. That this is not an idle question is clearly demonstrated by the fact that the work of many fine Indian historians—Majid Siddiqi, Neeladri Bhattacharya, Sabyasachi Bhattacharya, D. N. Jha, and Muzaffar Alam, to name a few—whose work is less indebted to streams of poststructuralist thinking or postcolonial theory, remains relatively little known outside the Indian academy and certainly the field of Indian history.

The more critical point is that Europe is still, in two fundamental respects, the site of all histories. The present of India is the past of Europe, and India's future is only Europe's present. In fact, if the recipe furnished by the developmentalists and the modernists were followed, one suspects that India's future will merely yield a poor version of Europe's present. If history already happened somewhere else, India has no history to speak of, a proposition to which Hegel would give his joyous assent. Secondly, subaltern historians, except occasionally,[55] have fundamentally stopped short of asking how it is that history came to be so decisive a terrain for establishing the autonomy and agency of a subject people or understanding the modality of resistance, and what the consequences are for locating agency, subjecthood, and resistance in the discourse of history, tethered as it is to the narratives of modernity, the nation-state, and bourgeois rationality. It is history, more than any other discourse, which has enshrined the narrative of the nation-state as the reference point for all agency, and which has made it difficult to derive other arrangements for the organization of human affairs. This is not a point I wish to belabour here, as I have addressed it in the first three chapters of this book and a number of other papers,[56] but it bears reiteration that history as a universalizing discourse, which is less tolerant of dissent than even the master narratives of science, is not merely a novel phenomenon, but has immeasurably narrowed the possibilities for conceptualizing alternative modernities, political identities, and different forms of community. History is not the only mode of accessing the past; it may not even be the most desirable one, at least for certain communities, but I shall return to this point later.

Poor theorizing does not always yield poor histories, and so it is with very considerable surprise, given the rather ill-conceived programmatic agenda as set out by Ranajit Guha, that one finds the practice of subaltern history to have far outpaced its theoretical ambitions or philosophical posturing, and to have often yielded some remarkable insights into the study of colonial India. In *Elementary Aspects of Peasant Insurgency*, Guha provided a reading of peasant insurgency through the texts of counter-insurgency, a strategy with particular salience for the study of subaltern agency in colonial India, given that the rebels and insurrectionists rarely if ever left behind any texts. This point is similar to Dipesh Chakrabarty's observation, apropos his study of the jute workers of Calcutta, that unlike E. P. Thompson's study of the working class in England, which could make use of the diaries, journals, and pamphlets left behind by his subjects, he was constrained in having to use only the documents of the ruling class, which would then have to be 'read both for what they say and for their "silences"'.[57] It is the reading of these silences, of the insurgent consciousness, that leads Guha, in his essay 'The Prose of

Counter-Insurgency', to develop, with the aid of semiotic analysis, a typology of the discourses of counter-insurgency, which he describes as constituting three layers, primary, secondary, and tertiary.

The primary discourse, which is constituted by the immediate accounts of insurgency produced by colonial officials or what were fondly called the men-on-the-spot, furnishes the first instance of what Guha calls the 'counter-insurgent code'; at a further remove in time and place, this account is processed and transformed into official reports, memoirs, and administrative gazetteers, but even this secondary discourse is unable 'to extricate itself from the code of counter-insurgency'. The secondary discourse shares in the primary discourse's commitment to the 'code of pacification', which entails turning the language of insurgency upside down: thus peasants become insurgents, 'Islamic puritans' become 'fanatics', the resistance to oppression is written as 'daring and wanton atrocities on the inhabitants', the self-rule desired by the peasants is turned into treason, a slogan-chanting but peaceful crowd is turned into an howling mob, and 'the struggle for a better order' is reduced to the 'disturbance of public tranquility'. The 'rebel has no place', writes Guha, 'in this history as the subject of rebellion', and whatever the sympathies for the peasants, the 'official turned historian' opts to come down on the side of what he thinks of as law and order. At the final or tertiary level of historiography, the 'code of pacification' encountered in the primary and secondary levels is redistributed, regurgitated, and replicated, since this discourse is read without the acknowledgment of the occluded other, that is the insurgent. Indeed, tertiary discourse is in some respects more nefarious, emboldened and fattened with the authority of the historian and the purported impartiality produced by the passage of time: and so the 'discourse of history, hardly distinguished from policy, ends up by absorbing the concerns and objectives of the latter'. If, for instance, the primary and secondary discourse of colonial officials pinned the responsibility for a peasant rebellion on the local elites for their exploitative behaviour towards the peasants, in the tertiary discourse of nationalist historiography this blame is shifted onto British rule, which is said to have aggravated the sufferings of the peasants. In either case, the peasant is not seen as a rightful subject, as an agent possessing a will of his own, as the maker of his own destiny.[58]

Not only 'canonical' texts, but the revered figures of the nationalist movement, none more so than Mohandas Karamchand Gandhi, become the proper subjects of inquiry for subaltern historians. How

Mohandas became transformed into the Mahatma is a long story, but what his deification might have meant to the subaltern masses, and how they read the message of the Mahatma, is the theme of Shahid Amin's brilliantly original study of 'Gandhi as Mahatma'.[59] In the received version of Gandhi's life that predominates in nationalist historiography, Gandhi captured the Indian National Congress a few years after his return from South Africa, moved the masses with his principled attachment to truth and commitment to non-violence, and led the country to independence after waging several movements of civil disobedience and non-cooperation with the British. All this may very well be true, but nationalist historiography has had no place for Gandhi except as the example par excellence of the 'great man', and contrariwise no place for the masses, who are seen as the flock that humbly followed the great master, though on occasion they may have been led astray by trouble-mongers, the advocates of violence, or those other elements in society which refused to act in the national interest. We know of the impression that Gandhi left on Nehru, Patel, Maulana Azad, and others who were to rise to the helm of political affairs in the nationalist movement, but how did Gandhi's charisma register with the masses? The burden of Amin's essay is to establish that there was no single authorized version of the Mahatma, and the masses made of the Mahatma what they could; indeed, they stepped outside the role which nationalist historiography habitually assigns to them. This historiography also seeks to marginalize competing or varying accounts of the Mahatma. For all their religious beliefs and alleged superstitions, the subaltern masses appear to have been more worldly-wise than the elite as they attempted to grapple with the mystique of the Mahatma.

Amin's narrative of the subaltern engagement with the Mahatma commences with an account of Gandhi's visit, at the height of the non-cooperation movement in 1921, to the district of Gorakhpur in the then eastern United Provinces. Here Gandhi addressed numerous 'monster' meetings at which immense crowds gathered to have a *darshan* of their Mahatma. Ordinarily, in Hindu religious practices, the worshipper seeks a darshan, or sight of the deity; this sighting is said to confer blessings upon the worshipper.[60] Gandhi's hagiographers were to summon this as an instance of the reverence in which the Mahatma was held, but they seem to have been less alert to the fact that, as Amin suggests, the worshipper does not, as did many of Gandhi's followers, demand darshan. The crowds nearly heckled him, and after a long day of travelling and speech-making, the

Mahatma might have had nothing more to look forward to than a long stream of visitors who desired to have his darshan, and who forced themselves upon him. At one point in his travels the crowds had become so obstinate that Mahadev Desai, Gandhi's secretary, stepped forth when the crowd started shouting Gandhi's name, and presented himself as the 'Mahatma'; whereupon the people bowed to him, and then left the train.[61] Their fervour was quite possibly increased by the rumours that circulated about the Mahatma's capacity to cause 'miracles', and certainly the local press was fulsome in its description of the 'magic' that the Mahatma had wrought on the villagers. 'The very simple people in the east and south of the United Provinces', adjudged the editorialist of the *Pioneer* newspaper shortly after Gandhi's visit to Gorakhpur, 'afford a fertile soil in which a belief in the powers of the "Mahatmaji", who is after all little more than a name of power to them, may grow.' The editorialist saw in the various accounts of the miracles purported to have been performed by Gandhi 'the mythopoeic imagination of the childlike peasant at work', and expressed concern that though the events in question all admitted of an 'obvious explanation', one saw rather signs 'of an unhealthy nervous excitement such as often passed through the peasant classes of Europe in the Middle Ages, and to which the Indian villager is particularly prone'.[62]

It was, however, far more than the 'mythopoeic imagination of the childlike peasant at work' in the circulation of the rumours. Gandhi's teachings—among others, the stress on Muslim-Hindu unity; the injunction to give up bad habits, such as gambling, drinking, and whoring; the renunciation of violence; and the daily practice of spinning or weaving—were doubtless distilled in these rumours, but an entire moral and political economy was also transacted in their exchange. One set of rumours and stories referred to the power of the Mahatma; another enumerated the consequences of opposing him, or particular aspects of his creed; and yet another referred to the boons conferred on those who paid heed to Gandhi's teachings. In one story, a domestic servant declared that he was only prepared to accept the Mahatma's authenticity if the thatched roof of his house was raised; the roof lifted ten cubits above the wall, and was restored to its position only when he cried and folded his hands in submission. A man who abused Gandhi found his eyelids stuck; another man who slandered him began to stink; more dramatically, a lawyer of some standing in the local area discovered shit all over his house, and no one doubted that this was because he opposed the non-cooperation movement which Gandhi had initiated. Gandhi was said to punish the arrogance of those who considered themselves exempt from his teachings, or, much worse, boldly defied his creed of non-violence, vegetarianism, and abstention from intoxicants. One pandit who was told to give up eating fish is reported to have said in anger, 'I shall eat fish, let's see what the Mahatmaji can do.' When he sat down to eat, it is said, the fish was found to be crawling with worms.[63]

In the name of the Mahatma, an entire nation could be swung into action. That much is clear, and the 'elite' histories have belaboured that point; but as Amin's study shows, at the local level another set of meanings was imparted to the Mahatma's name. Gandhi's name could be used to enforce order in the village, establish new hierarchies, expunge violators of caste norms, drive the butcher out of the village, settle old scores, compel the wearing of khadi, or restore communitas. In Gorakhpur, faulting debtors were threatened that Gandhi's wrath would come down on them if they failed to meet their obligations; likewise, the Cow Protection League, eager to halt the killing of cattle, impressed upon recalcitrant Muslims the consequences of ignoring the Mahatma's message. Utilizing the name of the Mahatma, money-lenders and Hindu zealots sought to refurbish their image; contrariwise, peasants heavily in debt and burdened by enormous tax burdens invoked the name of the Mahatma, who had warned moneylenders that they should not bleed their poor brethren, and suggested that unimaginable blessings would fall upon those moneylenders who saw fit to offer them financial relief. The Mahatma's name, Amin argues, could lend itself to all kinds of purposes, and as he argues towards the conclusion of his study, even the violence that was committed at Chauri Chaura in February 1922, when a score of policemen were killed by a crowd provoked to extreme anger, was done in Gandhi's name.[64] The very understanding of Gandhi's teachings to which the masses held often conflicted with the tenets of Gandhi's creed; he could be shouted down by his own disciples or by a crowd gathered to hear him. No nationalist historiography has had room for those masses who, turning the Mahatma into a floating signifier, thought that they could justifiably, for the higher end of Swaraj or self-rule, commit violence in the name of the very prophet of non-violence.

In Amin's use of local literatures, vernacular newspapers, rumours, and village proverbs, all in the service of a reading which establishes the extraordinarily polysemic nature of the name of the 'Mahatma', we have a demonstrably good instantiation of subaltern studies at work.[65] But if his concern is with the silences effected by nationalist historiography, in Gyanendra Pandey's work we are furnished with a powerful reading of the overt posturing and palpable presences of colonial historiography—a historiography that, in this case, offers a seamless account of Hindu-Muslim conflict, as if it were the eternal condition of Indian existence.[66] In reviewing British writings on Banaras in the nineteenth century, Pandey found, with respect to a Hindu-Muslim conflict that took place in October 1809, widely divergent colonial accounts of the events that are said to have transpired at that time. The colonial government records of that time described the 'outbreak' as having occurred at the 'Lat Bhairava' [site of an image] between 20 and 24 October 1809, and placed the number of casualties at 28 or 29 people killed, and another 70 wounded; the cause of the conflict is described as a dispute over attempts by Hindus to render a Hanuman shrine built of mud into a more permanent structure of stone, and the subsequent Hindu outrage over the alleged pollution of the 'Lat Bhairava'. Writing some twenty years later, James Prinsep was inclined to attribute the cause of the conflict to the 'frenzy excited by Muharram lamentations'; and writing still another 20 years later, in 1848, the colonial official W. Buyers considered the conflict as having emanated from the clash between Muslims celebrating Muharram and Hindu revelers playing Holi. But all agreed at least that the initial outbreak had taken place at the 'Lat Bhairava'. How, then, asks Pandey, did the District Gazetteer of 1907 transpose the site of the initial rioting to the Aurangzeb mosque, and even more significantly, how did the 28 or 29 people who were killed become transformed into 'several hundreds killed'? Is this the much celebrated colonial respect for 'facts', the supreme indifference to which was described by colonial officials as a marker of the Indians' poor rational faculties?[67]

It is the particular features of the colonial construction of 'communalism', that is the narrative of a Hindu-Muslim conflict that is said to be timeless, beyond resolution, and the eternal condition of Indian society, which Pandey illuminates in his study of British discourses. Many of his interpretive strategies are familiar to students of colonial discourse, for instance his analysis of the 'type-casting' commonly found in Orientalist writings, such that the Muslims become 'fanatics' or given to 'frenzy', or the brahmins are viewed as 'crafty'. He notes the tendency in colonial texts to describe the reaction of the Hindus as a 'conspiracy' instigated by the 'wily' Brahmins, and the depiction of the rioting as a 'convulsion' that shook Banaras:

'convulsion' seeking to indicate the spontaneous, primordial, pre-political, nearly cataclysmic nature of the 'outbreak'. Hindu and Muslim practices—the lamentations of the Muslims at Muharram, the excitability of the Hindus over their images, the fanatic attachment to places of worship—become the predictable sites of representations of an exotic, bizarre, and primitive Other. But Pandey takes us much further along in his understanding of how the 'communal riot narrative', purporting to describe the event, itself creates the object of its discourse. The 1907 Gazetteer, which had described the dead as numbering in the 'several hundreds', when previous sources placed them at less than thirty, introduced the 1809 riots with the observation that 'the city experienced one of those convulsions which had so frequently occurred in the past owing to the religious antagonism of the Hindu and Musalman sections of the population.'[68] A *history* of *Muslim-Hindu conflict* did not have to be established; it could be presumed: as another colonial writer put it much later in his book *Dawn in India*, 'the animosities of centuries are always smouldering beneath the surface.'[69] If Banaras had Hindus and Muslims, they had perforce to be in conflict; and perforce they had to be in conflict over religion, that being the preeminent marker of Indian identity. More remarkably still, the observations of the 1907 Gazetteer appear, virtually verbatim, in the report of the Indian Statutory Commission of 1928, drawn up to consider the constitutional condition of India and the arrangements to be devised for granting Indians a greater degree of self-rule. Only now, the 'grave Banaras riots' of 1809 are furnished not as an instance of Hindu-Muslim antagonism in Banaras, but as an indicator of the state of Muslim-Hindu relations all over India: it was one of those 'convulsions which had frequently occurred in the past owing to the religious antagonism of the Hindu and Moslem sections of the population'.[70]

The 'communal riot narrative' ranges widely over time and space, a scant respecter of history or geography; events can be transposed, the locale of disturbances can be shifted, one riot can stand in place for another,[71] an analogue to what I have elsewhere described as the *principle of infinite substitutability*, whereby any one native was construed as capable of standing in place for any other.[72] No history ever transpired in India: so, writing apropos Hindu-Muslim conflict in Mubarakpur, the district gazetteer described the Muslims as made up mainly of 'fanatical and clannish Julahas [weavers], and the fire of religious animosity between them and the Hindus of the town and neighbourhood is always smouldering. Serious conflicts have occurred between the two from time to time, notably in 1813, 1842 and 1904. The features of all these disturbances are similar, so that a description of what took place on the first occasion will suffice to indicate their character.'[73] Even the future can be read from this history: the colonial official as futurist, prophet, forecaster. Like animals, Indians have no past or future: they live only in the present, for the present, but this is not the present of the enlightened who have gained *satori*. In this colonialist form of knowledge, '"violence" always belonged to a pre-colonial condition',[74] and the Hindu-Muslim conflict becomes the very justification for the intervention by a transcendent power, namely the British.

If Hindu-Muslim strife did not exist, it would have to be invented—and invented, too, so that the colonial state, the mender of fences, can become the locus of all history.[75] Earlier, but not the twentieth-century, accounts of the 1809 Banaras riots had invariably also noted that the conflict was accompanied by a fast commenced at the riverside by Brahmins and other upper-caste Hindus, but this form of political action, which was deemed to be only an instance of native eccentricity and mendacity, had to be excised out of history. The following year, the Hindus and the Muslims joined together in Banaras in a great movement to resist the imposition of house tax: a rather unhappy circumstance for the British, who by the early twentieth century, as resistance to their rule became more marked, had further political compulsions for sketching the Hindu-Muslim past as a bloody affair. But because these histories of independent political action, resistance, and political pluralism could not be reconciled with the history of the colonial state, which refuses to grant the people any legitimate agency or will of their own, they had to be rendered invisible. Another history, which it was the task of the state to create and nourish, all the better that it should become the handmaiden to policy, would stand in for the Indian past. In the twentieth century, Pandey observes, a name had to be found for this history: that name was 'communalism'. We are still living with that history.

ACCESSING THE PAST, AND THE SUBALTERNITY OF HISTORY

Of the dozens of papers that have been published in *Subaltern Studies* and associated works, the papers of Guha, Amin, and Pandey, which I have discussed at some length, and which are among some of the more well-known contributions to the enterprise, appear to be subtle demonstrations of the power and promise of Subaltern Studies. I have, at the same time, already pointed the way to a partial critique of subaltern history, but its limitations need to be addressed at greater length, particularly in view of the consideration that subaltern history has a very substantial following outside India, just as historians in India have themselves become something of public figures, however inconsequential their part in the formulation of policy. The ascendancy of historians is all the more remarkable in a country where historical knowledge had, until recently, an altogether subaltern status in relation to other forms of knowledge and other modes of accessing the past, and even today it is not particularly clear that history enjoys wide legitimacy among the common people. (There is no equivalent to the History Book Club yet, and the day when we might have a Military History Book Club is, I suspect, quite remote. No doubt the scholarly advocates of Hindutva, such as they are, are busily collecting whatever sparse notes exist on the great military battles, real and alleged, fought by Prithviraj Chauhan, Shivaji, Holkar, Tantia Topi, and other martial heroes, so that the canard about the effeminacy of the Hindus should forever be removed from the history books and Indians should be emboldened to think of themselves as endowed with a great military past.) As we have seen in a previous chapter, historians became prominent in the public controversy surrounding the Babri Masjid.[76] Ironically, questions of faith were largely dispensed with, as both the proponents of the temple theory, that is those Hindus alleging that the mosque was built after a temple on the same site was razed to the ground in a brazen display of Muslim prowess, and the defenders of the mosque, which included not only Muslims but the avowedly secular elements of the Hindu intelligentsia, decided to wage the battle on the field of history.

Doubtless the secular historians had by far the 'better' evidence in support of their views, but this seems to have left hardly any impression upon the militants and their scholarly supporters, or even the general public. The principal shared area of agreement among the 'secularists' and the 'fundamentalists' is seen to be their readiness to deploy historical evidence,[77] though the secular historians added the necessary caveat that irrespective of the historical evidence, the destruction of the mosque could not conceivably be justified. From the standpoint of secular historians, moreover, the eventual destruction of the mosque signalled the (evil) triumph of myth over history, blind faith over principled reason, religious fundamentalism over secularism. Not many of these historians, however, asked whether the language of secularism spoke to the condition of those Hindus who, without supporting Hindu militancy, nevertheless felt themselves to be devout Hindus. What did the secular historians have to say about belief, except to acknowledge, most likely with a tinge of embarrassment, its presence in the life of most Indians? Few paused to ask why the 'hard' evidence of historical 'facts' had little attraction for most Indians, and not only the upwardly mobile Hindus who were held to be responsible for creating a climate of opinion hospitable to the resurgence of Hindu militancy. Fewer still reflected on the adequacy or even soundness of their proposed solution to the dispute, which was to turn the mosque over to the Archaeological Survey of India, which would in effect transform it from a place of religious worship claimed by both Hindus and Muslims into a dead monument existing in 'museum time', of interest to no one except archaeologists, antiquarians, scholars, and Western tourists.[78] Nor is it at all axiomatic, if the evidence from the carnage in Gujarat—where the desecration and destruction of protected cultural and religious properties has been widespread—may be construed as indicative, that protection of a monument by the Archaeological Survey ensures its survival. None of the historians or secularists showed themselves capable of a creative response to one of the most pressing crises to face India in the post-independent period, and it devolved upon the philosopher and cultural critic, Ramachandra Gandhi, to transcend the parameters of historical discourse within which the discussion over the Babri Masjid had been trapped, and furnish a radical and emancipatory reading of the events that transpired in Ayodhya. As Gandhi showed, historians had been grossly negligent in failing to take serious notice of a building, Sita-ki-Rasoi ('Sita's Kitchen'), adjoining the mosque; and from this proximity Gandhi spins a tale, and moral fable, which allows us to consider the conflict at Ayodhya as part of the violent ecological disruption of the world.[79]

It is particularly noteworthy that the subaltern historians, who (insofar as they are in India) are concentrated at Delhi University (rather than Jawaharlal Nehru University) and the Centre for Studies in Social Sciences, Calcutta, had almost no part to play in the debate. An eloquent plea or two appeared from the pen of Gyanendra Pandey, as mentioned earlier, but the subaltern historians appeared stunned and paralysed: subaltern history seemed unable to speak to the present. Though subaltern historians are able to theorize communalism, they are still unable to speak with ease about religion or the supernatural.

In common with social scientists, quite unlike the physicists or biologists who have shown themselves perfectly capable of distinguishing their own religious beliefs from the epistemological assumptions of the sciences which they practice in their professional lives, the subaltern historians, for all their sophisticated strategies of reading texts, are still captive to positivism and its disdain for anything which cannot be encompassed within the circle of reason. Thus, willy-nilly, subaltern histories, on closer inspection, appear to echo those familiar juxtapositions of 'faith' and 'reason', 'Enlightenment' and 'superstition'; and at every instance of religious belief, the subaltern historian falters, slips, and excuses himself.

How else can one explain Guha's constant slippage into the language of that very elite historiography which he so unequivocally condemns? He writes of the peasants that their 'understanding of the relations, institutions and processes of power were identified with or at least over determined by religion', but adds in the same breadth that they were possessed of a 'false consciousness' on account of their 'backward ... material and spiritual conditions'.[80] Though the subaltern historian is inclined to concede autonomy and agency to the subaltern, how does the historian negotiate the problem that arises when the subaltern, disavowing any agency, declares—as happened often—that he or she was instigated to act by the command of God, or the local deity? Speaking of a Santal rebellion, Guha concedes that 'religiosity was, by all accounts, central to the *hool*'; and he relapses then into the idioms familiar to him from Marx, and so this 'religious consciousness' becomes 'a massive demonstration of self-estrangement ... which made the rebels look upon the project as predicated on a will other than their own'.[81] The voices of the subalterns do not always, or even seldom, speak to us, and yet it is the ambition of subaltern history that it desires to make these voices, by transforming them into the language of modernity, scholarship, or narratives organized along other principles of 'rational' ordering, touch us. Is it only Gandhi's resort to the 'Idiom of Obedience', or his intolerance for indiscipline, that makes Gandhi so unattractive a figure to Guha, or is there something of disdain that a Bengali modernizing elite wedded to 'bourgeois' notions of liberalism and secularism—this language being very much Guha's own—has for a man who resorted to the inner ᵥₒᵢce, declared himself zero without God, and endeavoured to create a Ramarajya?[82]

That the subaltern historians did not so much as lift their voices while the debate over the Babri Masjid raged across north India may

be indicative of a wide and disturbing disjunction between the espousal of radical politics and history in the academy and, on the other
hand, the nearly complete surrender in the public domain. I am by no
means suggesting that historians should become policy-makers, and
the historian may have no particular or special responsibility to bear
the burden of that famous query, 'What Is To Be Done?' I am rather
adverting to the failure of historical discourses to transplant themselves into the public consciousness, and the abject failure of those
who describe themselves as opponents of 'elite' histories to speak in
the voices of public intellectuals. This brings me to a more commonly
expressed general criticism, which I would argue should be treated
with considerable caution, that subaltern history has thrived on the
fetishism of exile encountered in the American academy.[83] Of the core
members of the collective, the greater majority of them are now
placed in some of the leading universities in the United States and
Britain, and of those who are settled in India, they have sinecures and
arrangements for leave that are the envy of Indian academics. Some
among the former sometimes represent themselves, usually infor-
mally, as unwilling exiles, as receiving a more sympathetic hearing in
the Western academy than in Indian universities, as speaking in a
language that places them at odds with their Indian colleagues. There
are other ambivalent narratives woven into this tale as well, since
educated Indians, who are sworn to the motto that 'there is no honour
in one's own country', like to believe that recognition in the West is a
precondition of success in India.

The criticism that seems to deserve a more sympathetic hearing,
and which is a corollary to the suggestion that the subaltern historians have rendered themselves into exiles, pertains to the manner in
which subaltern historiography has itself been rendered into exilic
history. The argument, encountered in the eloquently written essays
of Gyan Prakash, who through his debates and interventions had by
the early 1990s become something of a spokesperson for the subaltern
historians in the West, that subaltern historiography can content itself
with deconstructing master narratives, with—in his words—not un-
masking 'dominant discourses' but rather exploring their 'fault lines
in order to provide different accounts, to describe histories revealed
in the cracks of the colonial archaeology of knowledge', justifiably
lends itself to the multiple charges that subaltern history, in something of a mockery of its name, is committed, if only negatively, to the
printed text, to elite discourses, and to a revived form of colonial
textualism. The supreme reliance on the text may be one reason,

among many others, why subaltern history has virtually nothing to say about pre-modern Indian history, where one is constrained to deploy archaeological evidence, numismatics, epigraphy, and material artifacts. According to Prakash, 'subalterns and subalternity do not disappear into discourse but appear in its interstices, subordinated by structures over which they exert pressure', and there is the insistent reminder that 'critical work seeks its basis not without but within the fissures of dominant structures'.[84] If the fissures and gaps in dominant, almost invariably printed, discourses are enough to furnish us clues and even histories of subalternity, why go outside the realm of elite texts at all? Indeed, Prakash admits as much, and calls for a 'complex and deep engagement with elite and canonical texts',[85] which is what the 'elitist historiography' that Guha and the collective so roundly condemned has been doing since the inception of historical work.

And what of the voices of the subalterns? What of the experiences, so celebrated in the abstract, of peasants, workers, the slum dwellers, the Dalits, rural and urban women, and countless others? If one can repair from time to time to 'elite and canonical texts', and repeatedly deploy those interpretive strategies that teach us how to read between the lines, which show us the precise moments at which these texts unwittingly betray themselves, then why bother even with the archive—not to mention oral histories, urban legends, folktales, ballads, and numerous minor literatures? What, other than political and ideological disposition, makes the subaltern historian so radically different from James Mill, who authored an eight-volume history of British India without having ever visited the country about whose destiny he pontificated, or from Max Müller, the revered father of late nineteenth-century Indology, who absolutely forbid his students from visiting India, lest the contemporary India of colonial rule should irretrievably suffer in comparison with the Aryan India of the sages and philosophers which he had instilled into their imagination?[86] If subaltern history is to become another species of postcolonial criticism, as the very title of Prakash's essay bids us to understand, why call it 'subaltern history' at all? Moreover, though this point is deserving of far greater elaboration, nowhere does Prakash show any real awareness that postcolonial criticism arose in the societies of the West where the forces of homogenization had historically operated with such power as to create a desperate need for plural structures, while India is a society where the ground reality, so to speak, has always been plural, whatever the attempts of militant Hindus in recent years to transform India in the image of the West. To speak, then, of 'subaltern history' as 'postcolonial criticism' is to lose sight of the fact that the task of criticism and intellectual inquiry is substantively of a different order in India and the West.

Subaltern India, one suspects, will prove itself rather more recalcitrant to subaltern history than Prakash and some of his cohorts in the collective imagine. Until very recently, subaltern history showed itself as entirely impervious to contemporary urban India, as if the slum-dwellers, urban proletariat, small-town tricksters, the countless number of street vendors, and even the millions of lower middle-class Indians suffocating in dingy office buildings do not constitute the class of clearly subordinate people that Guha designated as the 'subalterns'. The subaltern collective has doubtless been moving towards a more expansive conception of its mandate, even while Gyan Prakash has been announcing that 'elite and canonical texts' furnish subaltern historians with their most effective material, and in Volume IX one finds the first explicit attempts to engage with subalternity in the contemporary urban context.[87] The later volumes of *Subaltern Studies* seem to warrant some optimism that subaltern history is extricating itself from the legacy of anthropology, with its conception of 'Village India', or from the stress on rural India with which post-independent anthropology and sociology have been preoccupied.[88] Still, one wonders whether subaltern history does not secretly hold to the view that the India of villages and peasants, that realm of rebellion and insurrectionary activity, is somehow the authentic India, the India where the 'autonomous' realm of the people is more clearly discerned.

Though Indian subalterns have been making their history in myriad ways in post-independent India, and have moved from one form of subalternity to another, and often to other destinations, it is transparent that subaltern historians have not kept up with the subjects of their study. Even their understanding of village India, to advert to one instance, seems curiously predictable, though this limitation may well have to do with the limitations of historical thinking than with their own shortcomings. India characteristically transforms its urban areas into villages, and ruralizes its urban landscapes: in India the village is everywhere, and there is the village outside the village. There may well be the villager in most urban Indians, though increasingly urban Indians are getting disconnected from the village. Many of the subaltern historians—Shahid Amin, Partha Chatterjee, Sumit Sarkar, and Ranajit Guha—have tackled Gandhi, but it seems that they are yet to understand the village within Gandhi. This may seem like an unlikely proposition, considering that Gandhi spent a very considerable part of his life in urban settings, whether London, Durban, or Ahmedabad. Notwithstanding his very long spells in Britain and South Africa, Gandhi never left the village; he inhabited its structures, its modes of thought, and its imagination. That is no discredit to him at all, and Amin's reading of the polysemic nature of the Mahatma myths, which as I have suggested is accomplished with extraordinary verve and imagination, could have been richer still had he had understood not only how the peasants worked on Gandhi, but how the village served as a symbiotic link between the Mahatma and the masses.

The subaltern historians, to put the matter bluntly, have been riding along with the academy, but they must now walk with the subalterns. There is great merit in walking, and the subaltern historians may take a lesson or two from Gandhi, who walked as many as ten kilometres most days, and often a great deal more. It is with the walk to the sea that a revolution was launched, but Gandhi would have said that walking puts us in touch with our body in different ways, as well as in touch with India. Walking introduces a different conception of time, working with (not only within) the boundaries set by clock-time: it formulates, to evoke Raymond Williams's phrase, 'structures of feeling' that cannot be encapsulated by the body put in mechanical motion. The subaltern historians have mastered the analytical models derived from European philosophy and the social sciences; they are placed in conversation with some of the other academic trajectories of thought that have become inspirational for our times; their work offers a trenchant critique of colonial, neo-colonial, and nationalist historiographies; and, though this consideration will be of more interest to Indians, and perhaps to those in the Southern hemisphere of the world, they have succeeded—a mixed blessing, this one—in placing Indian history on the world map. Yet the subalterns on whose behalf they speak are not very responsive to the historical mode of inquiry, or even to the historical mode of living in the body. Their language has more in common with the epics, Puranas, bhajans, folk tales, proverbs, songs, and poems than it does with the language of history. The subaltern historian, reliant on modern knowledge systems, theorizes the subaltern and works on the village; the subaltern, who inhabits the village within and without, has not entirely abandoned the indigenous knowledge systems. There is something fundamentally out of joint with subaltern studies, and a recognition of that disjointedness may yet lead to a more enriched conception of this historical enterprise. Meanwhile, as the following chapter suggests, some of the debates have now moved on to another domain, and strikingly here, too, the subaltern historians have had no role to play.

ENDNOTES

1. See Gyan Prakash, 'Subaltern Studies as Postcolonial Criticism'; Florenica E. Mallon, 'The Promise and Dilemma of Subaltern Studies: Perspectives from Latin American History'; and Frederick Cooper, 'Conflict and Connection: Rethinking Colonial African History', all in 'AHR Forum', *American Historical Review* 99, no. 5 (December 1994), pp. 1475–90, 1491–1515, and 1516–45.

2. Latin American Subaltern Studies Group, 'Founding Statement', *boundary 2* 20, no. 3 (1993), pp. 110–21. See also John Beverley, *Subalternity and Representation: Arguments in Cultural Theory* (Durham, North Carolina: Duke University Press, 1999), which focuses on Latin America.

3. Some readers may recognize that I am rendering far more ambivalent the characterization, made popular by Edward Said among others, of subaltern history as 'the empire striking back', or 'writing back to the centre'. See his foreword to Ranajit Guha and Gayatri Chakravorty Spivak, eds, *Selected Subaltern Studies* (New York: Oxford University Press, 1988); idem, 'Third World Intellectuals and Metropolitan Culture', *Raritan* 9, no. 3 (Winter 1990):27–50; and idem, *Culture and Imperialism* (New York: Viking, 1993).

4. Ranajit Guha, ed., *A Subaltern Studies Reader, 1986–1995* (Minneapolis: University of Minnesota Press, 1997), back cover.

5. James Mill, *History of British India*, 2:46–8; 1:114–15.

6. Edward Thompson, *The Other Side of the Medal* (London: Hogarth Press, 1925), pp. 27–8.

7. See Asok Sen, '*Subaltern Studies*: Capital, Class and Community', and Ajit K. Chaudhury, 'In Search of a Subaltern Lenin', both in *Subaltern Studies V: Writings on South Asian History and Society*, ed. Ranajit Guha (Delhi: Oxford University Press, 1987), pp. 203–35 and 236–51, respectively. The first ten volumes of *Subaltern Studies*, hereafter cited as *SS*, have been published by Oxford University Press, Delhi. Volumes I–VI (1982, 1983, 1984, 1986, 1987, and 1989), were edited by Ranajit Guha. Volume VII (1992) is edited by Partha Chatterjee and Gyanendra Pandey; Volume VIII (1994) by David Arnold and David Hardiman; Volume IX (1996) by Shahid Amin and Dipesh Chakrabarty; and Volume X (1999) by Gautam Bhadra, Gyan Prakash, and Susie Tharu. This chapter was written largely before the appearance of Volume X.

8. Veena Das, 'Subaltern as Perspective', *SS* VI:310–14; and for the debate

on feminist readings of Indian women, see Julie Stephens, 'Feminist Fictions: A Critique of the Category "Non-Western Woman" in Feminist Writings on India', and Susie Tharu, 'Response to Julie Stephens', both in *SS* VI:92–125 and 126–31, respectively. Vol. IV also offered, in Dipesh Chakrabarty's 'Invitation to a Dialogue' (pp. 364–76), a defence of Subaltern Studies against its critics.

9. Tanika Sarkar, 'Jitu Santal's Movement in Malda 1924–1932: A Study in Tribal Protest', *SS* IV:136–44.

10. I have discussed some of these issues in the introduction to my book, *South Asian Cultural Studies: A Bibliography* (Delhi: Manohar, 1996).

11. Mahasweta Devi, 'Breast-Giver', Appendix A to *SS* V:252–76, and Gayatri Chakravorty Spivak, 'A Literary Representation of the Subaltern: Mahasweta Devi's "Stanadayini"', ibid., pp. 91–134.

12. Ranajit Guha, 'On Some Aspects of the Historiography of Colonial India', SS I:4.

13. Kancha Ilaih, 'Productive Labour, Consciousness and History: The Dalitbahujan Alternative', SS IX:165–200.

14. I refer here to the work, among others, of John Broomfield, Leonard Gordon, and David Kopf.

15. Ramachandra Guha, 'Subaltern and Bhadralok Studies', *Economic and Political Weekly* 30 (19 August 1995), p. 2057.

16. Sumit Sarkar, 'Orientalism Revisited: Saidian Frameworks in the Writing of Modern Indian History', *Oxford Literary Review* 16, nos 1–2 (1994):205–24, especially pp. 205–7. I have taken up Sarkar's criticisms at much greater length in my review essay, 'Subaltern Studies and Its Critics: Debates over Indian History', *History and Theory* 40 (February 2001), pp. 135–48, and do not propose to traverse much of that ground in this chapter.

17. See Guha, ed., *A Subaltern Studies Reader*, pp. ix–xxii, and my review of the volume in *Emergences* 9, no. 2 (November 1999), pp. 397–9.

18. Gyan Prakash, 'Subaltern Studies as Postcolonial Criticism', p. 1476.

19. V. C. Joshi, ed., *Rammohun Roy and the Process of Modernization in India* (Delhi: Vikas, 1975) and Asok Sen, *Iswarchandra Vidyasagar and His Elusive Milestones* (Calcutta: Riddhi-India, 1977).

20. See the discussion in Schwarz, *Writing Cultural History*, pp. 86–7, 178 n.15.

21. Anil Seal, *The Emergence of Indian Nationalism: Competition and Collaboration in the Late Nineteenth Century* (Cambridge: Cambridge University Press, 1968), p. 16.

22. John Gallagher and Ronald Robinson, 'The Imperialism of Free Trade', *Economic History Review* (2nd Series) 6, no. 1 (1953), reprinted in *Imperialism: The Robinson and Gallagher Controversy*, ed. William Roger Louis (New York: New Viewpoints, 1976), p. 60; cf. also Gallagher and Robinson, 'The Partition of Africa', in *The Decline, Revival and Fall of the British Empire*, ed. Anil Seal (Cambridge: Cambridge University Press, 1982), p. 71.

23. Ronald Robinson, 'Non-European Foundations of European Imperialism: Sketch for a Theory of Collaboration', in Louis, ed., *Imperialism*, esp. pp. 130, 133–4, 141, 144, 146–7, from where the quotations in this paragraph are drawn.

24. Eric Stokes, 'Imperialism and the Scramble for Africa: The New View', reprinted in Louis, ed., *Imperialism*, p. 183. Cf. Ronald Robinson, John Gallagher, and Alice Denny, *Africa and the Victorians: The Climax of Imperialism* (London: St. Martin's Press, 1961; paperback ed., New York: Anchor Books, 1968).

25. David Washbrook, 'Progress and Problems: South Asian Economic and Social History, c. 1720–1860', *Modern Asian Studies* 22, no. 1 (1988), pp. 74–6.

26. Seal, *The Emergence of Indian Nationalism*, p. 34.

27. Seal, 'Imperialism and Nationalism in India', in John Gallagher, Gordon Johnson, and Anil Seal, *Locality, Province and the Nation: Essays on Indian Politics 1870 to 1940* (Cambridge: Cambridge University Press, 1973), p. 2.

28. Many historians and political scientists of India have been complicit in this kind of analysis: see the piercing critique by David Hardiman, 'The Indian "Faction": A Political Theory Examined', SS I:198–231.

29. Ibid., p. 3.

30. Gordon Johnson, *Provincial Politics and Indian Nationalism: Bombay and the Indian National Congress 1880 to 1915* (Cambridge: Cambridge University Press, 1973), p. 10.

31. In a different context, it is worth recalling Louis Dumont's lamentation that studies of Indian society and specifically the caste system had been wholly insensitive to questions of ideology, and that empirical studies could not substitute for the understanding of the caste system as an ideology. This is not to say that his work is free of other problems, or that it is not totalizing in its own fashion, but these problems have been addressed in the critical literature surrounding his book. See *Homo Hierarchicus: The Caste System and Its Implications*, trans. Mark Sainsbury (Chicago: University of Chicago Press, 1970); and for a 'subaltern' reading of Dumont, Partha Chatterjee, 'Caste and Subaltern Consciousness', *SS* VI:169–209.

32. See the scathing review of Cambridge School history by Tapan Raychaudhuri, 'Indian Nationalism as Animal Politics', *Historical Journal* 22 (1979):747–63.

33. Ibid., p. 750.

34. D. A. Washbrook, *The Emergence of Provincial Politics—The Madras Presidency, 1870–1920* (Cambridge: Cambridge University Press, 1976), p. 255.

35. Seal, 'Imperialism and Nationalism in India', p. 6.

36. Gordon Johnson, *Provincial Politics and Indian Nationalism*, p. 193.

37. Guha, 'Dominance without Hegemony and Its Historiography', *SS* VI:210–309, esp. p. 290.

38. Seal, 'Imperialism and Nationalism in India', p. 8. The modern variant of this argument has been expressed all too often by V. S. Naipaul, who

opines that the Third World knows how to use the telephone, but is incapable of having invented it.

39. Guha, 'On Some Aspects of the Historiography of Colonial India', *SS* I:1–7, esp. p. 1.

40. Ranajit Guha, 'Dominance without Hegemony', SS VI:210–309, esp. pp. 229–39, 270.

41. This is less heretical than it might sound to an informed outsider, who, cognizant of the acute differences that have sometimes arisen among the original and present members of the collective, would have noticed the near deference that they accord to Guha's writings. Though members of the collective will doubtless signal their profound unease with 'essentialisms', they have handled their differences with Guha, whose role in bringing them together and nurturing a new generation of teachers and scholars of Indian history is readily acknowledged, in characteristically *Indian* fashion. His formulations have not been explicitly contested, or critiqued; but the most viable of the exercises in 'subaltern' history have, it seems to me, bypassed Guha's naked sociological equations.

42. E. P. Thompson, 'Eighteenth-Century English Society: Class Struggle Without Class?', *Social History* 3, no. 2 (May 1978).

43 I use the word 'feudal' advisedly, as there is considerable debate, to which I do not propose to speak, as to whether one can reasonably transfer an understanding of feudalism derived from the history of Western societies to the study of Indian history.

44. 'Elite' and 'subaltern' is not the only operative dichotomy in Guha's work; not less important is 'domination' (D) and 'subordination' (S). Guha says of the latter two terms that they 'imply each other: it is not possible to think of D without S and vice versa. As such, they permit us to conceptualize the historical articulation of power in colonial India in all of its institutional, modal and discursive aspects as the interaction of these two terms—as D/S in short.' See 'Dominance without Hegemony and Its Historiography', *SS* VI:229. Though the relationship of dominance and subordination enables some understanding of power relations, this abstract relation is configured in Guha as the Hegelian Subject and stands forth as a general history of power in colonial India.

45. This is the argument of Dipesh Chakrabarty, 'Invitation to a Dialogue', *SS* IV:375–6.

46. Ranajit Guha, *Elementary Aspects of Insurgency in Colonial India* (Delhi: Oxford University Press, 1983). A glowing assessment of this work, and of Guha's entire corpus, is to be found in T. V. Sathyamurthy, 'Indian Peasant Historiography: A Critical Perspective on Ranajit Guha's Work', *The Journal of Peasant Studies* 18, no. (October 1990):92–141.

47. See Victor Turner, *Dramas, Fields and Metaphors: Symbolic Action in Human Society* (Ithaca, New York: Cornell University Press, 1974).

48. C. A. Bayly, review article on Volumes I–IV of *Subaltern Studies*, 'Rallying Around the Subaltern', *Journal of Peasant Studies* 16, no. 1 (1988), p. 116.

49. That large body of administrative and scholarly literature which deals with patterns of land settlement and revenue management in colonial India speaks entirely of peasant, rather than tribal, communities.

50. Guha, 'On Some Aspects of the Historiography of Colonial India', p. 8; see also p. 4.

51. As an analogue, it is useful to recall that for St. Augustine, evil is the deprivation of good, but good is not defined as the absence of evil; the existence of good is not contingent upon the existence of evil, but evil has no ontological existence of its own.

52. Ibid., pp. 6–7; emphasis in original.

53. Sumit Sarkar, *Modern India, 1885–1947* (Delhi: Macmillan, 1985), p. 1.

54. My invocation of Kautilya, the author of the famed *Arthasastra*, is perhaps clichéd; one is habituated to hearing of him as the Machiavelli of the East, and there is a widespread impression that the *Arthasastra* is just about the only political and social treatise ever written in pre-colonial India. But if the political thinking of Kautilya offers no insights to the subaltern historians, much less would one expect them to have any engagement with, or use for, the substantial literature on statecraft generated in India for 1,000 years before the advent of British rule.

55. See, in particular, the following series of papers by Chakrabarty: 'History as Critique and Critique(s) of History', *Economic and Political Weekly* 26, no. 37 (14 September 1991):2162–6; 'Postcoloniality and the Artifice of History: Who Speaks for "Indian" Pasts?', *Representations* 37 (Winter 1992):1–26; and 'Minority Histories, Subaltern Pasts', *Postcolonial Studies* 1, no. 1 (1998):15–29.

56. Vinay Lal, 'Discipline and Authority'; and idem, 'Gandhi, the Civilizational Crucible, and the Future of Dissent', *Futures* 31 (March 1999):205–19.

57. Dipesh Chakrabarty, 'Conditions for Knowledge of Working-Class Conditions: Employers, Government and the Jute Workers of Calcutta, 1890–1940', *SS* II:259–310; see p. 259.

58. Ranajit Guha, 'The Prose of Counter-Insurgency', *SS* II:1–41; quotations are from pages 15, 26–7.

59. Shahid Amin, 'Gandhi as Mahatma: Gorakhpur District, Eastern UP, 1921–2', *SS* III:1–61.

60. The idea of 'darshan' is not as distinctly 'Hindu' as is represented in the literature, for instance in Diana Eck's book by the same name. [See *Darsan: Seeing the Divine Image in India*, 2nd edn (Pennsylvania: Anima Books, 1985).] What is lacking from Amin's account is the notion of darshan as it came to be seen with reference to the Mughal Emperors. Akbar's trusted aide and biographer, Abu Fazl, was to write in the *Ain-i-Akbari* that Akbar would come out on to the balcony of his palace and confer darshan on the crowds, and so provide his subjects with an assurance that he was well and capable of discharging his duties. In an era when palace rivalries could lead to the

dethronement of kings, and the Emperor himself commanded the armies on the field at risk to his life, it was perforce necessary to demonstrate with a vivid display of sovereignty that the ship of the state was afloat.

61. Amin, 'Gandhi as Mahatma', pp. 1–3, 18–20.

62. Ibid., p. 5, citing the *Pioneer* (Allahabad), 23 April 1921, p. 1.

63. Ibid., pp. 22–45.

64. Ibid., pp. 51–5.

65. One of the other pieces which offers a similarly complex, detailed, and nuanced reading of local sources is Sumit Sarkar's 'The Kalki-Avatar of Bikrampur: A Village Scandal in Early Twentieth-Century Bengal', *SS* VI:1–53.

66. Gyanendra Pandey, 'The Colonial Construction of "Communalism": British Writings on Banaras in the Nineteenth Century', *SS* VI:132–68.

67. Ibid., pp. 135–40.

68. Ibid., p. 135, citing H. R. Nevill, *Benares: A Gazetteer, being Vol. XXVI of the District Gazetteers of the United Provinces of Agra and Oudh* (Lucknow, 1921; Preface dated December 1907), pp. 207–09.

69. Ibid., p. 151, citing Francis Younghusband, *Dawn in India*, p. 144.

70. Ibid., p. 136.

71. Ibid., pp. 166–7.

72. Vinay Lal, 'Committees of Inquiry and Discourses of "Law and Order" in Twentieth-Century British India', unpublished Ph.D. dissertation, Department of South Asian Languages and Civilizations, The University of Chicago, 2 vols (1992), Vol. 2, ch. 8.

73. D. L. Drake-Brockman, *Azamgarh: A Gazetteer, being Vol. XXXIII of the District Gazetteers of the United Provinces of Agra and Oudh* (Allahabad, 1911), pp. 260–1, cited by Pandey, 'The Colonial Construction of "Communalism"', p. 165.

74. Pandey, 'The Colonial Construction of "Communalism"', p. 151.

75. My sympathetic reading of Pandey's article should not be construed to mean that I have adopted the view, of which there are fewer adherents to begin with than commonly supposed by such disparate individuals as V. S. Naipaul and Achin Vanaik, that the pre-modern past of India was characterized by the absence of conflict and violence. Both Naipaul (a rabid Muslim-hater, a self-professed expert on Islamic civilizations who postures as a breaker of myths) and Vanaik (a staunch secularist, equally dismissive of myths and eager to restore reason to its apparently rightful place), who otherwise belong to the opposite ends of the political spectrum, are united in their contempt for those 'romantics' (a real term of abuse from the standpoint of hard-nosed realists and Marxists alike) who tend to view the pre-modern Indian past as shorn of violence. The substantive question is what kind of violence took place in pre-modern India, what its relationship was to the state, and whether it can be described as communal, indeed whether it is even meaningful to speak of Hindus and Muslims as monolithic, corporate entities.

76. Sushil Srivastava's *The Disputed Mosque* provides a balanced historical account, and finds it probable that a Buddhist stupa stood at the original site of the mosque (pp. 113–24).

77. I have discussed this question in detail in Chapter III and sections V–VI of Chapter II.

78. I am aware, of course, that there are temples and mosques under the care of the Archaelogical Survey (ASI) where worship is still permitted, or where worship persists despite regulations to the contrary. This is, however, not true of the vast bulk of religious edifices under the care of the ASI, and in principle a monument acquires a different life, if 'life' is what one might call such cultural evisceration, once it is placed under the care of the ASI. It is one kind of consideration that the very institution championed, if only as a last resort, by the secularists should itself have stood accused by them on more than one occasion of having been communalized. On a more substantive point, if secularists wish to insist upon the separation of 'church' and 'state', it is curious that they should have thought of investing their hopes in the ASI, another state institution. A similar response is encountered in the outrage over Roop Kanwar's sati that took place in Deorala in 1987: there the secularists demanded that the state, once it became known that a sati was being planned, should at once have rushed in police and armed forces to prevent the violent abrogation of women's rights and legal protections, and that at the very least an armed contingent of police or troops should have prevented the deification of Roop Kanwar and the transformation of the sacrificial site into a pilgrimage spot once it became impossible to forestall the performance of sati. Yet the advocates of these measures are also inclined to the view that the Indian state is the most flagrant violator of human rights, and in general their prescription consists in strengthening the institutions of civil society and working towards the erosion of the state's power. My point here is not that there is any necessary contradiction in the advocacy of such views, but rather that there has been inadequate reflection on the ethical probity and efficaciousness of the proposed solutions to India's social problems that one encounters in the secularist lexicon.

79. Ramachandra Gandhi, *Sita's Kitchen*.

80. Guha, *Elementary Aspects*, pp. 265–8.

81. Guha, 'The Prose of Counter-Insurgency', *SS* II:34.

82. Ranajit Guha, 'Discipline and Mobilize', *SS* VII:69–120, and idem, 'Dominance without Hegemony', *SS* VI:210–309, esp. pp. 244–56. For an incisive critique of Guha's mechanical model of dominance and subordination, or his dualist ontology, see Frederique Apffel-Marglin, 'Gender and the Unitary Self: Looking for the Subaltern in Coastal Orissa', *South Asia Research* 15, no. 1 (Spring 1995), pp. 78–130, esp. pp. 84–7.

83. I would associate this argument with the likes of Aijaz Ahmad, whose voice is mistakenly seen to carry greater moral authority as he is himself a US-returned Indian academic.

84. Gyan Prakash, 'Subaltern Studies as Postcolonial Criticism', p. 1482, 1486–7. Prakash's writings are shot through with Homi Bhabha's language, nowhere more so than in *Another Reason: Science and the Imagination of Modern India* (Delhi: Oxford University Press, 1999).

85. C. A. Bayly, 'Rallying Around the Subaltern', quite rightly anticipates Prakash in his observation that in contrast to those American historians who had used 'indigenous sources (including popular ballads)', the 'subalterns' forte has generally lain in rereading, and mounting an internal critique, of the police reports, administrative memoranda, newspapers and accounts by colonial officials and the literate', in other words 'elite texts', 'which earlier historians had used for different purposes' (p. 111).

86. Müller himself never visited India: the discussion in Nirad Chaudhuri, *Scholar Extraordinary: The Life of Professor the Rt. Hon. Max Müller, P.C.* (New York: Oxford University Press, 1974), pp. 287–8, is of some interest.

87. See Vivek Dhareshwar and R. Srivatsan, '"Rowdy-sheeters": An Essay on Subalternity and Politics'; and, to a much lesser extent, Susie Tharu and Tejaswini Niranjana, 'Problems for a Contemporary Theory of Gender', both in *SS* IX:201–231 and 232–60, respectively. It is a telling comment that of these four authors, only Vivek Dhareshwar, who earned his Ph.D. from the History of Consciousness Program at the University of California, Santa Cruz, has any training in history. Professional historians have been relatively slower to embrace the ambitions of subaltern history.

88. This problem is encountered in other domains of Indian life and intellectual work. I am reminded of the poignant observations of one of India's most famous environmentalists, the late Anil Agarwal, founder and director of the Centre for Science and Environment. In one of the recent issues of the magazine that he founded, *Down To Earth* (31 January 1999), Agarwal relates how, when he was asked in 1986 by the then Prime Minister Rajiv Gandhi to address his council of ministers on the 'environmental challenges' facing the country, he spoke forth with confidence that 'rural environmental problems are more important than urban environmental problems'. He admits that he did not anticipate the extraordinary speed with which industrial pollution would become a nightmare for virtually the entire country, and so provided the country with 'poor environmental leadership' (p. 6). The historical, sociological, and anthropological literature on modern India seems largely oblivious of the fact that there is an urban India, where nearly 25 per cent of the country's one billion people live, and an ethnography of urban India, particularly the urban population outside the cities of Delhi, Calcutta, and Mumbai, has barely emerged. The observations of small-town India by one young writer, Pankaj Mishra, make for better subaltern history than most of the laborious post-colonial ruminations of Indian academics. See his *Butter Chicken in Ludhiana* (Delhi: Penguin, 1995).

5

Aryavarta and Silicon Valley
Indian History on the Net in the Age of Cyber Hinduism

DEMOCRACY AND AUTHORITARIANISM IN CYBERSPACE

Nothing has been as much celebrated in our times as the information superhighway. Everyone is agreed that never before has information proliferated so profusely, diminishing (as is commonly thought) the boundaries and barriers that have held people apart, though many voices have sought to distinguish between 'knowledge' and 'information', while others have railed at how the overwhelming surfeit of information has made some people incapable of thinking beyond trivia and the 'factoid'. We speak with unreflective ease of the 'information revolution', and in this cliched expression there is the most unambiguous assertion of confidence in the benign telos of history. Some commentators, alluding to more recent developments such as e-commerce, speak even of going 'beyond the information revolution', but there is something of a consensus that the 'information revolution' has been to our age what the 'industrial revolution' was to the eighteenth century.[1]

The advocates of the information superhighway have been prolific in voicing the view that cyberspace embodies immense revolutionary possibilities for creating democratic polities and enfranchising those communities that have so far existed only at the margins of the tremendous information explosion of recent years. The Internet, so argue its unabashed votaries, creates a polyphony of voices, allows the hitherto silenced to speak,[2] offers forums for dissenting views, destroys the monopoly of old elites, disperses the sources of information and knowledge, empowers the dispossessed, and assists in the formation of new identities—constituted not only by such obvious markers as race, gender, and ethnicity, but also by religious and sexual preferences, linguistic affiliation, political ideologies, intellectual interests, customs, shared traditions and histories, and hobbies. The 'imagined communities' of which Benedict Anderson spoke flower in unprecedented ways on the Internet; the shackles that chained the working classes, 150 years after Marx invoked the cry of revolution and urged them to take destiny into their own hands, now seem broken. In the hip voice of *Mondo 2000*, to quote from the inaugural issue in 1989, 'The cybernet is in place .... The old information elites are crumbling. The kids are at the controls. This magazine is about what to do until the *millennium* comes. We're talking about Total Possibilities. Radical assaults on the limits of biology, gravity and time. The end of artificial Scarcity. The dawn of a new humanism. High-jacking technology for personal empowerment, fun and games.'[3] Just when boredom appeared to be the most pressing problem for the affluent West, and the usual sources of entertainment seemed to have exhausted their potential to amuse, the Internet arose to offer a jaded people a new source of enchantment. Cyberspace, some fondly imagine, has restored to the West that ludic element which was once so essential an element of its being, to vanish when confronted with the unrelenting demands, whether upon the family, the workplace, or social institutions, of modernity. Meanwhile, boredom, a disease that is inextricably linked to Western notions of time, is now poised to find its newest victims in the developing world.

The enthusiastic advocates of cyberspace have stretched the case for its allegedly democratic properties much further. The futurist Alvin Toffler and his associates speak of the post-scarcity information civilization as a Third Wave of humankind. If in the First Wave civilization was predominantly agricultural, and the Second Wave ushered in the age of industrial production, so in the Third Wave 'the central resource—a single phrase broadly encompassing data, information, images, symbols, culture, ideology and values—is actionable knowledge'. Cyberspace is universal, it is its own ecosystem: it is 'inhabited by knowledge, including incorrect ideas, existing in electronic form'. As one might expect, that perennial American language of the *frontier* is incurably a part of the language of cyberspace enthusiasts: thus Toffler and his cohorts speak of the 'bioelectronic frontier', which has emerged just as the American dream of the limitless, yet again contracting, frontier seemed doomed to extinction. The bioelectronic frontier points to the death of that fundamental embodiment of centralized values, namely the bureaucratic organization of which the government is the supreme instantiation; and consequently cyberspace is the space of unregulated freedom, the logical culmination of the human hunger for liberty from constraints and access to limitless markets. 'Cyberspace is the land of knowledge', write Toffler and his associates, 'and the exploration of that land can be a civilization's truest, highest calling.' Here, at the frontier of knowledge, one can create one's own basket of the fruits of wisdom: 'Demassification, customization, individuality, freedom—these are the keys to success for Third Wave civilization.' In cyberspace is writ large the continuing story of America's espousal of the values of individuality over conformity, achievement over consensus, and the celebration of difference—all typified, if only as an instance of the occasional negative excess of American democracy, in the figure of the hacker,[4] a near impossibility in 'the more formalized and regulated democracies of Europe and Japan'. If the destiny of the world is to follow the example and leadership of the United States, as Francis Fukuyama and other exponents of the end of history have repeatedly reminded us,[5] then the values of cyberspace, which are none other than expressions of the American ethos, become the values of the world. Cyberspace confers on humankind a 'Magna Carta for the Knowledge Age'.[6]

If the conquest of the Americas furnished the Spaniards with a charter for conquest and colonization, the enthusiasts of cyberspace point—500 years after the conquistadors first began to leave behind a trail of charred ruins, shattered lives, and decapitated Indians—to the Americas as the site for new forms of resistance to global capitalism, as the originary point from where a truly new world order can be envisioned at the cusp of the millennium. The laboratories and universities of the United States may have seeded the script for the cyberspace revolution, but it was enacted in the relatively remoter areas of Mexico, when the Ejército Zapatista de Liberación Nacional (EZLN) led the people of Chiapas in an insurrection on New Year's Day 1994. Occupying San Cristobal de las Casas and five smaller towns, the Zapatistas declared war against the Mexican government, issued a manifesto of demands, invited foreign observers, monitors, and sympathizers to Chiapas, and initiated an international media campaign to gain support for their cause. Vastly outnumbered by army and security forces, which were rushed to Chiapas within a couple of days of the insurrection, the Zapatistas nonetheless not only held out, forcing the government to the negotiation table, but they also introduced a new element in revolutionary warfare. Writing in April 1995, the Mexican Foreign Minister, Jose Angel Gurria, doubtless bewildered at the developments of the previous year, noted that 'Chiapas ... is a place where there has not been a shot fired in the last fifteen months. ... The shots lasted ten days, and ever since the war has been a war of ink, of written word, a war on the Internet.'[7]

Subcommandante Marcos, the energetic and mystery-shrouded leader of the Zapatistas, himself remarked that 'one space ... so new that no one thought a guerilla could turn to it, is the information superhighway, the Internet. It was territory not occupied by anybody ... the problem that distresses Gurria is that he has to fight against an image that he cannot control from Mexico, because the information is simultaneously on all sides.'[8] It is this phenomenon, of a war inspired by the battle tactics of Genghiz Khan but made possible by the 'information revolution', which the RAND researcher David Ronfeldt has variously described as 'cyberwar', when the conflict takes on a military aspect, and 'netwar', to describe conflict at the 'societal' level.[9] Though from his standpoint the advent of netwar is scarcely to be welcomed, as it poses new threats to American national security, 'digital Zapatismo' has gained many voluble adherents,[10] who construe the rhizomatic characteristics of the Internet as the most likely fount of new forms of insurrectionary activity.[11]

The advocates of cyberspace do not, however, have the field to themselves. Their critics have constructed a less elaborate, but by no means insignificant, account of the deleterious consequences of the new computer-based information and communication technologies. Most obviously, the use of the Internet and the world wide web by terrorists and outlawed organizations raises alarming prospects, though terrorists have left fewer trails in cyberspace than their overt exploitation of the web might suggest.[12] But the critics have something more substantive at mind than the mere abuse of cyberspace: they are inclined to describe the information superhighway as a charter for the disenfranchisement of those who are already underprivileged, authorizing the further polarization of the rich and the poor. The grave inequities between the post-industrial nations and the rest of the world will be further aggravated, and cyberspace, argue its detractors, can only sharpen the boundaries between the haves and the have-nots in the industrializing nations. In even as large a country as India, typically characterized as the largest democracy in the world, much fewer than two million people have

Internet connections, and they are the ones who already have at their disposal fax, telephone, and other means of communication, just as they are the ones who are privileged to take overseas trips: the surfers and the tourists are two classes of people who largely coincide. It is their views, which are wedded to transforming India in the image of the West, and making India into a strong modern nation-state, which predominate among Indian policy-makers, and which are critical in shaping the view of India in the West.

It is the agenda of the 'Internet elites', if they may be so termed, which dictates the modernization and liberalization of the Indian economy, and recent congratulatory pronouncements, such as those of Clinton when he visited India in his capacity as President of the United States, are only calculated to convey the impression that India can look forward to a bright future if it continues to furnish cyber coolies to the West. It is the interests and ambitions of these Internet elites and their soul-mates in the worlds of management, banking, and consultancy that have led to the emergence of a cellular phone culture, while the greater part of the country remains without reliable ordinary telephone service. The emergence of an internationally re-nowned software industry even while nearly 50 per cent of the Indian population remains mired in poverty is yet another one of the anoma-lies engendered by the culture of the Internet elites. Their mobility in cyberspace furnishes them with those opportunities that allow them to work within the world of international finance and business; like the elites of the first world, they are beginning to live in time, and space poses no barriers for them.[13] The time-space compression that cyberspace typifies only works to the advantage of these elites. Cyberspace, then, is yet another mode of self-aggrandizement, and it is calculated, certainly in India and the rest of the 'developing' world, to narrow a franchise which was achieved with great struggle.[14]

Questions of political economy aside, it has been argued that cyberspace represents a more ominous phase of Western colonialism, the homogenization of knowledge and, in tandem, the elimination of local knowledge systems. Cyberspace stands for the renewed tri-umph of all those categories of thought by means of which the West has been able to establish its dominance over other parts of the globe. 'Western civilization has always been obsessed with new territories to conquer', writes Ziauddin Sardar on cyberspace as the 'Darker Side of the West', and cyberspace is the newest domain that it seeks to colonize.[15] Where the long arm of the colonial state and fascist organizations could not reach, there cyberspace has made inroads;

those remote spots which were inaccessible to missionaries and colonial administrators, where the Coke bottle could not be dropped from the air, now enter the stream of globalization. Where before the notion of 'place' was displaced by 'space' to render local histories indistinct and so pave the way for colonialism,[16] now 'space' is regurgitated back into 'place', the place from where the browser is guided into unknown domains. Radical dissent, which is only possible with incommensurability, and profits from inassimilation into dominant strands of thought, is brought into the marketplace; and so dissent itself becomes homogenized, and those very modalities of thought which held out the possibility of 'interrogating' received notions arrive in packaged forms. Cyberspace renders complete that colonization which sheer force and military might could not achieve; indeed, while cyberspace may not entirely obviate the necessity of a military-industrial complex, as the immensely technologically-driven NATO assault upon Serbia and America's war on terrorism have visibly demonstrated, it enlists more hegemonic and insidious categories to eliminate dissent and create new hierarchies. Some critics of cyberspace, even while agreeing with Carlos Fuentes that the Zapatista insurrection was no 'Sandinista-Castroite-Marxist-Leninist' rebellion, but rather the first 'post-communist' and 'postmodern' insurgency,[17] have profound misgivings that anything 'postmodern', most eminently cyberspace, can be anything other than a sign of imperialism.[18]

Though the activists who staged a marvellously disruptive demonstration against the World Trade Organization (WTO) on the occasion of its ministerial meetings in late November 1999 were summoned to Seattle by messages widely dispersed on the Internet,[19] it is doubtful that these activists, buoyed by their Internet successes, have reflected sufficiently on the ironical fact that the Internet is avowedly the most expressive realization of that very idea of 'globalization' against which they militate. To make the point more sharply, though scattered intellectuals and activists might, say, militate against 'development', as one of the most unfortunate ideas to afflict humankind, cyberspace is itself intrinsically disposed towards the idea of 'development', effortlessly hospitable to the idea of limitless growth. Similarly, though proponents of cyberspace speak of its role in creating communities, particularly in societies where the family is presumed to have broken down, and where other traditional institutions have been unable to offer the succour that people require in the course of daily life, the critics argue that cyberspace trivializes the notion of 'community'. It is the particular feature of real, or shall we say, grounded communities that they are born amidst conflict, and must thrive amidst conflicting interests: they must perforce accommodate the fat and the slim, the healthy and the diseased, women and men, white and coloured, the aged and the young; cyber communities, contrariwise, are founded on the principle of exclusion, and inclusion in the community is only a mode of signaling someone else's marginalization. Cyber communitarians, who have no appetite for pluralism, recognize no community that does not exist to do their own bidding, or which would ask of its members the fulfilment of responsibilities. With the click of a mouse, the community can be shut out: but 'real' communities, as these have been ordinarily understood, require immense labour to maintain. As for the notion that cyberspace heralds the arrival of a post-scarcity civilization, the detractors can only mock at the presumptuousness and hubris of the affluent. True, there is no 'scarcity' of information, but it is foolish to confuse information with knowledge, and far more depraved to imagine that knowledge can substitute for wisdom. Put rather plainly, the so-called information revolution, whose votaries trumpet inane cliches—'information wants to be free' and 'information belongs to us all', to name two—seems to be little better than what one writer has described as 'data smog'.[20] There is yet the cruel irony that while the advocates of cyberspace work to create the rules governing the post-scarcity information civilization that they inhabit, in many parts of the world a new scarcity has emerged as the grinding reality for the masses. Surprisingly, even when the realization has dawned that starvation, famines, and the shortages of food are political problems, the supposed surfeit of information has done nothing to diminish the supposed scarcity of food.[21]

One of the iron rules of cyberspace, suggests the author of *Data Smog*, is that it is intrinsically Republican, or inegalitarian; its most keen enthusiasts are white, upper-class males.[22] There is the obvious consideration that if cyberspace can be deployed to enfranchise marginalized people and communities, it also services the ambitions and designs of racist ideologues, misogynists, anti-Semites, and other white male supremacists. As the Simon Wiesenthal Center's recent, ominously massive, CD-ROM compilation of over 500 web sites devoted to white supremacy indubitably suggests,[23] in this matter as in most others, the supporters of racism, fascism, and Nazism have been more diligent in turning to new technologies than those people committed to more democratic and egalitarian forms of politics.

Against this, the proponents of cyberspace can point to the mobilization of tribal peoples throughout the world, and the effectiveness of
the Internet in yielding a possibly emancipatory Fourth World politics, a worldwide coalition of aboriginal people. Or they can advert to
the deployment of the Internet in garnering worldwide support for
the International Campaign to Ban Landmines and alerting the world
to suppressed Palestinian histories.[24] But if cyberspace is what its
enthusiasts admit, namely a deregulated and decentralized zone
with minimal rules for engagement, those are the very conditions
that laissez-faire advocates describe as optimal for the attainment of
free markets. In this paradise of deregulation, in the name of freedom,
all dissenting histories are absorbed, commemorated only as relics of
a previous age. Could these be the conditions under which certain
histories will predominate, while other histories are erased; and
could these be the conditions under which a cyberdiasporic politics
of Hinduism, whose most ardent defenders in and outside India have
recently discovered their religion's compatibility with liberalization
and nuclear testing, has found comfortable refuge and a refurbished
home? To ponder how the politics of Hinduism has played itself out
in cyberspace, and Hinduism itself gradually merged, partly through
the vehicle of new Hindu histories, into what is very nearly its
opposite, namely Hindutva politics, it is well to consider first the
Indian diasporic presence in the United States.

THE POST-INDUSTRIAL VEDIC DIASPORA: HINDUS IN THE UNITED STATES

Nearly 1.7 million Indians reside in the United States, and of these the
preponderant number are Hindus. Indian-Americans are the fastest
growing community in the United States, according to the 2000 census, and the community more than doubled in ten years.[25] The dramatic increase in the size of the community may well have some
relation to the rapid ascendancy, also over the last ten years, of Hindu
militants to the helm of power in India, but this relationship, on
which I shall have recourse to comment later, has not explicitly been
observed, much less theorized, by any commentator. Most Indians
have done exceedingly well for themselves in, to appropriate the
Biblical metaphor of a people who are the very embodiment of a
diasporic sensibility, the land 'flowing with milk and honey' (cf.
Exodus 3.8). Numerous studies have established that their per capita
income is among the highest of any racial or ethnic group in the

United States, and for some years they were the most affluent community.[26] Almost everywhere in the professions Indians are well represented, and in some they have created an enviable niche for themselves. Though they make up 0.7 per cent of the American population, as far back as the early 1990s they comprised 5 per cent of the investment bankers and financial consultants on Wall Street. According to the 1990 census, 58.1 per cent of Indians in the US had at least a bachelor's degree, by far the highest of any ethnic group, and far more than the 21 per cent of white Americans with the same credentials. Their contribution to the sciences and engineering is even more formidable, perhaps even overwhelming; and it has become something of a cliché, at least among Indians, to speak of Silicon Valley as though it were a part of an Indian landscape. One major American newspaper recently carried on its front page a story entitled, 'Asian Indians Remake Silicon Valley': the Indians here are termed 'Silicon desis'.[27]

In middle-class homes in India, particularly where English is routinely spoken, it is not uncommon to find parents anticipating and even planning a future for their children not merely in 'Silicon Plateau', the new name for the 'Garden City' of Bangalore, where the software explosion in India took place a few years ago, but in Silicon Valley.[28] It may not even be long before Indians, like a previous generation of first-time visitors from Bombay and Calcutta to London who saw in the metropole a copy of their home town, might start thinking of Silicon Valley as the Bangalore (or Hyderabad, if future trends may be predicted) of the West Coast. In the crucible of this culture of Silicon Valley-Plateau, Indians have even generated their own postmodern and cyberdiasporic jokes: thus, the Hindi film villain Ajit, around whom an entire industry of jokes has developed, commands his henchman Robert to render extinct the life of the hero by placing him in a 'microprocessor', so that he can die 'bit by bit'.[29] From these manifold computer companies a sizable number of Indians have moved into venture capital, in a spirit that is perhaps reminiscent of the entrepreneurship, trading acumen, and financial ambitions of earlier generations of Gujarati and other Indian traders and businessmen who once dominated the Indian Ocean trading networks. Finally, in the domain of medicine, where over 4 per cent of the doctors are estimated to be of Indian origin (though much higher numbers have been furnished by some researchers), a similar tale of Indian success is easily told, and the strength of an organization such as the American Association of Physicians of Indian Origin can be gauged by the fact that its 1995 annual meeting was addressed by no less a luminary than a sitting President of the United States.[30]

Along with some other Asian-Americans, Indian-Americans are often characterized as a model minority; and yet they construe themselves as 'invisible'. In the United States, the Sinic element has always predominated over the Indic in the understanding of what was meant by 'Asian', and the presence of the Chinese and the Japanese antedates the presence of Indians by one generation. The Asian-American, in the imagination of the white American, is an Oriental figure of Mongoloid features; and Asian-Americans themselves, viewed as a whole, appear to have been largely indifferent, except very recently, to claims that Indian-Americans should be accommodated under that rubric. Nor is 'Indian' very useful as a marker of identity, since that is liable to render the Indian into a specimen of a Native American tribe. It is only a very slight exaggeration to suggest that from 'India' one easily moves onto 'Indiana', a rather more familiar terrain to Americans, though no one, if optimism be allowed, ought to think of India as similarly nondescript as its near namesake. Nor, in the matter of colour, is the Indian easily positioned. In the early part of the century, Indians (or 'Hindoos' as they were then called, regardless of their religious faith) endeavoured to be treated as whites;[31] in more recent years, when affirmative action was more warmly received than it is in the present political climate, Indians strove to be considered non-white, a minority people.[32] In Britain, they are lumped with 'black' people; in South Africa under apartheid, Indians were distinguished from white, black, and coloured people.

This apprehension of 'invisibility' is compounded by other psychological and cultural factors, far too numerous for any detailed consideration at present. Suffice it to note that since India has for some time been 'the largest most unimportant country in the world',[33] Indians in the United States fear that this stigma is attached to their own persons; and since South Asia has historically been the only home of Hindus, with the exception of Hindu communities that as far back as a millennium ago came to be established in Bali, Java, and some other parts of Southeast Asia, Indians do not doubt that India is condemned to oblivion, unless of course Hinduism can somehow be construed as a threat to the Stars and Stripes. I suspect that at times devout Hindus, whose piety is in no way incompatible with a barely concealed aspiration to see the emergence of a powerful Indian nation-state, have wanted nothing more than that India should turn staunchly communist, or into a hotbed of 'Islamic fundamentalism':

their anxieties about invisibility would certainly disappear. India might then even be the beneficiary of the kind of monumental aid that was pumped into Pakistan when neighbouring Afghanistan came under Soviet influence and when, two decades later, America declared war on al-Qaeda and the Taliban. Such is the Hinduism of some Hindus that even communism can be construed as a form of Hinduism: not only are Hindu deities multi-armed, but Hinduism can be fruitfully and ecumenically multi-pronged. At least communism was international; Hinduism, if its most zealous proponents in India and the US have their way, will similarly head that way.

However acute the problems Indian-Americans appear to have in nominating themselves and in allowing themselves to be named, they indubitably belong as well, or so one might think, to a post-industrial civilization. In several respects, the Cold War climate was propitious for Indians desirous of settling in the United States. As the principal political and economic power, the United States was bound to spend increased amounts on research and development to retain its edge in military technology, aerospace engineering, telecommunications, medical research, and 'big science'. The American military, notwithstanding the conclusion of the Cold War, has continued to display a monstrous and insatiable appetite for new and ever more sophisticated hardware, and with the exponential growth of the computer industry and computer applications over the last decade, the need for professionals with backgrounds in science, engineering, computer, and medicine has persisted. In Indians, American universities, industries, scientific organizations, and other public and private enterprises found a people who, while proficient in English, also had the requisite skills and professional training. Thus, unlike Indians in many parts of the globe whose presence arose from circumstances of indentured servitude, or the labour shortages in the aftermath of World War II, Indians in the US are predominantly professionals, playing a critical role in shaping a post-scarcity, post-industrial, information civilization. It is only very recently that they have thought their professional services, which have earned them considerable affluence, also entitled them to some measure of political influence and thereby to lessen that 'invisibility' the fear of which shadows every successful Indian-American. Indeed, it rankled endlessly with these successful Indian-American professionals that Pakistan and Pakistani-Americans were, as they perceived, more successful lobbyists on Capitol Hill; and the reverse suffered by Pakistan in mid-1999, when the United States unequivocally condemned Pakistani adventurism in the Himalayan heights of Kargil, was assessed by professional Indians, who waged a tremendous and ultimately successful campaign to have Congress pass a resolution condemning Pakistan's abrogation of the Line of Control, as the first sign of the political influence that they feel they can rightfully exercise among American lawmakers.[34] It is these same professional Indian Hindus who, now mindful of the strength of their numbers, their professional standing in society, and the power of the Internet, orchestrated with success a campaign to have Warner Brothers, producers of Stanley Kubrick's *Eyes Wide Shut*, delete from the film verses from the Hindu scripture Bhagavad Gita that had been inserted in the midst of an orgy scene.[35]

The post-industrial civilization of North American Hindus is also, if a paradox may be entertained, a Vedic civilization. Its conception of India, as I argue later, is largely derived from the texts and practices of remote antiquity, which supposedly furnish us with a vision of Hinduism in its pristine state. There are indubitably those Hindus who, without the least trace of humour or irony, fervently argue that there is virtually no scientific advancement which was not already anticipated in the Vedas or other ancient Hindu texts, and that in the visions of Indian seers are to be found the blueprints for rocket science, satellites, and the supersonic jet fighters of our times. That very term, 'Stealth Fighters', seems to evoke subliminal memories, among the unamused Hindus, of awe-inspiring and magical weapons wielded—often treacherously, as if with stealth—by Brahma, Vishnu, or Shiva, usually with incalculable and devastating effect. These Hindus are dedicated to the proposition that the highest truths of Hinduism are easily reconciled with the highest truths of science, and that the ancient seers and nuclear physicists have intuited the same ultimate reality. These Hindus point to Robert Oppenheimer's famous invocation, at the precise moment of the first nuclear test, of a passage from the Bhagavad Gita ('I have become death, the destroyer of Worlds'), or to the interest that the most eminent physicists, such as Einstein and Chandrasekhar, have taken in Indian philosophical thought.

However, this is scarcely the most substantive sense in which the Hindu diaspora in the United States is a harbinger of Vedic civilization. Though in Uttar Pradesh a dalit woman,[36] who not long ago would have been resigned to having herself viewed as part of a collective of 'untouchables', rose some years ago to become the Chief Minister of the state, a position only second to that of the Prime

Minister in any traditional reckoning of Indian political fortunes in the electoral age, in the Vedic diaspora of Hindus such an outcome is considered to be well beyond the ken of contemplation. It defies their sense of Hindu hierarchies that a lower caste person, and a woman at that, could be elevated to such eminence. To gain an inkling of what this Vedic civilization of diasporic Hindus looks like, one has only to consider the activities of the Saiva Siddhanta Church in the northern California town of Concord. A few years ago, the *pujari* or priest of this temple placed a rope about ten feet away from the deity, and strung a sign on it that loudly proclaimed, 'Vegetarians only beyond this point'. At a slightly greater distance, another rope was strung across the room, and the sign on this advised the worshippers, 'Hindu clothing only beyond this point'.[37] Numerous devotees suddenly found themselves out in the cold, denied darshan (that is, the gaze, and thus the blessing) of their deity, condemned to be pariahs. While it is true that this particular Hindu institution is headed by an American swami who is based in Hawaii, where a magnificent Hindu temple is being constructed according to the stipulations of the ancient *shilpasastras*, or Hindu temple-architecture manuals, its following consists largely of Indian Hindus.[38] Though Marxist scholarship has, with reasonable certainty, established that the ancient Aryans were beef-eaters,[39] and at the very least this continues—as suggested in my introduction and Chapter II—to be a matter of debate in India, among Hindus in the US it is an article of faith to suppose that vegetarianism has been critical to Vedic civilization from the outset. On 'Hindu clothing', the innovation here is a reversion to the practice, common among the most orthodox Hindu temples in South India, whereby men must shed themselves of leather products and stitched clothes before entering the temple and drape a *dhoti* around them. It is well to argue that one must come before God unstitched and untethered, but the Hindus in the United States show every tendency to adopt the literalism that is so characteristically an American trait.

To suggest that the Hindu diaspora in the United States aspires to be Vedic is to point to the manner in which Hindu devotees have developed an ossified conception of their faith, frozen in time. Though 'homeland' Hinduism continues to evolve, and deities are born and die, and the faith acquires new resonances while shedding some of its older emphases, the Hinduism of its Indian-American devotees, one can reasonably maintain, displays the most retrograde features. Certainly, as far as I am aware, there is nothing to suggest that Hinduism in the United States has jettisoned some of the rituals that accompany the faith in India; quite to the contrary, as even a cursory examination of *India-West*, a California-based 150-page weekly with a circulation in excess of 20,000, suggests, the Hindus here have embraced forms of worship pursued by only the most dedicated Hindus in India. The religion pages of the weekly newspaper are full of announcements about various obscure *pujas*, many conducted to celebrate rites, or in honour of one or more deity, that are scarcely celebrated by any but the most orthodox Hindus in India itself. Whether in the political, cultural, or psycho-social domain, the Hinduism of North American Hindus can in no manner be viewed as a 'lighter' form of the faith.

Indeed, it would be no exaggeration to argue that Hinduism in the United States has been transformed, to a degree that is not merely unhealthy but politically undesirable, into what is known as Hindutva, a Hinduism stripped to its imagined essences, and purportedly reinvigorated by arming it with attributes commonly thought to belong to the more masculine faiths of Christianity, Islam, and Judaism. It is no accident, I might note parenthetically, that relations between India and Israel, which is seen by admiring proponents of militant Hinduism as a no-nonsense masculine state that knows how to deal with terrorists, secessionists, and disgruntled rebels, have improved vastly over the last few years that the Bharatiya Janata Party, which of course openly advocates Hindu rule in India, has been in political power. Though Israel's feared state security apparatus could not prevent the assassination of Prime Minister Rabin, nor the suicide bombings that have been so critical to the Second Intifada, Hindu leaders and middle-class elites admire Israel for its repudiation of 'appeasement', its refusal to negotiate with 'terrorists' (this being the preferred designation for all Palestinian patriots), and its disdain for the Arab states: they see in Israel's conduct an exemplary model of how India should deal with Pakistan and Pakistani-backed terrorists in Kashmir. Many retired Israeli army officers and security personnel have found lucrative appointments as consultants to the Indian state.

While the rise of militant Hinduism in India is a phenomenon too well-known and documented to require any elaborate mention, it merits mention that the consolidation of identity around the notion of highly differentiated religious communities, a process that was first set in motion by the colonial state in the nineteenth century, began to acquire ominous overtones around the mid-1980s. With the increasing turn to history—among a people typically characterized in colonial discourses as devoid of the historical sensibility—as a mode of living with the present and acquitting oneself for the tasks of citizenship, Hindus began to think of the wrongs, as they thought, committed against them by Muslim invaders. The burden of a cruel past, in which they had been reduced to subjection and their faith trampled upon by those 'foreigners' who had acquired political power, began to weigh heavily upon them; and the colonial argument, that the Hindus were a supine people incapable of defending their own interests, left its impress upon them.

The sense of grievance among Hindus began to crystallize further when the government was seen as pandering to the economic and cultural demands of minority communities, particularly Muslims, from the grossest political calculations. Militant Hindus speak disparagingly of Indian secularism, and proclaim that the Indian state is wedded to 'pseudo-secularism'; the minorities are said to be the beneficiaries of government largesse, and certain Hindus, belonging to a community that accounts for about 78 per cent of India's population, complain of how they have been reduced to a minority in their own country. Diasporic Hindus in North America, who are evidently minorities in the US but have seldom expressed anguish at any disabilities that may have arisen from that position, are even more easily prevailed upon to think of Hindus in India as a minority, and a recent course at Stanford, arranged by students affiliated with the Hindu Students Council, devoted an entire week to 'Hindus as a Minority'—and this in a course on 'Hinduism'.

Drawing upon the writings of Savarkar, Golwalkar, and other Hindu ideologues, who defined India as the eternal land of the Hindus, and insisted that the 'blood of Hindus' streamed through everyone born in the motherland (*janmabhoomi*), the advocates of a renewed Hindu militancy have endeavoured to turn India, to deploy Islamic terminology, into the land of the pure and the faithful. Muslims and exponents of other faiths are asked to reflect on the 'fact' that in their origins they are Hindus,[40] and they are enjoined to return to the bosom; and as for those who unremittingly cling to their faith, they must perforce understand, so argue militant Hindus, that they live in India at the pleasure of the Hindus.[41] Following the recent pogrom against Muslims in Gujarat, the RSS has again affirmed that Muslims must earn the goodwill of Hindus if they seek to live in freedom from fear of persecution.[42] While loudly declaring themselves to be tolerant of other faiths, in keeping with the idea that Hinduism has been an intrinsically pluralistic religion, these Hindutvavadis or militant exponents of Hinduism have sought to shape their faith in the image of those very other faiths which they decry. Consequently, both Islam and Christianity are seen as displaying an admirable unity and rationality, not stricken by the effeminacy, devotional excess, or the needless multiplicity—whether in the arena of deities, or sources of doctrinal authority—that are construed as having crippled Hinduism. The militant Hindus have no greater desire than to turn Hinduism into a more masculine faith, more vigorous and uncompromising in the defence of its devotees; and, as I have already argued in Chapter III, the destruction of the Babri Masjid in December 1992 was the most visible sign of that ferocious intent. Thus has Hinduism, in their hands, become Hindutva ideology.

Among Hindus in the United States, the Hindutvavadis appear to have gained ascendancy. Though Hindus in the US are just as fragmented and dispersed as anywhere else, their organizations torn apart by common rifts over ethnic and linguistic affiliations, leadership struggles, or other anxieties about their 'identity', over the last few years they have shown signs of being able to cohere together, carried forth by pride in those features of Indian civilization that are seen as specially emblematic of Hindu tradition and culture. Indeed, they have collapsed the distinction between 'Indian' and 'Hindu', and some might also be inclined to altogether jettison the category 'Indian'. One of the most prominent of the Hindutva ideologues, Ashok Singhal, General-Secretary of the Vishwa Hindu Parishad (VHP), an organization set up to perform the cultural work of Hinduism and make it into a religion with a worldwide presence, has written that 'the Hindu Rashtra can only be a state where there must be Hindu churches and Hindu mosques, for Hinduism is not a religion. It is the collective experience of thousands of individuals unlike Christianity and Islam which are experiences of single individuals. In Hindu India, every one has to call himself a Hindu.'[43] The Rama Janmabhoomi Movement, leading to the destruction of the Babri Masjid, received considerable support from Hindus settled overseas, and the funding of Hindu institutions, temples, and other purportedly 'charitable' enterprises by non-resident Indian (NRI) Hindus, particularly those from the United States, can be established beyond doubt.[44] Strikingly, though in the aftermath of the destruction of the mosque nearly 2,000 Indians were killed in Hindu-Muslim riots, the Hindus in Southern California, describing themselves as 'Concerned NRIs ', could think of no more reasoned intervention than to take out an advertisement in the *Indian Express*, one of the largest English-language daily newspapers in India, deploring the government's [alleged] ban of 'nationalistic [Hindutva] organizations', and urging their 'brothers and sisters in India' to aim at the 'restoration of common sets of values and laws based on the 6,000 year heritage'. As if in anticipation of questions about their entitlement to intervene in the politics of the homeland, they argued that 'of the one million NRIs living in the United States, over 900,000 call Bharat [India] as [sic] their Mother. Hindus have only one place (other than Nepal) to call home. Their roots are in Bharat.'[45]

If in India the clarion call of militant Hindus is that 'another Pakistan' must at all costs be avoided, in the US they insist that their children be spared the evils and excesses of American culture (which Indians seldom consider to be 'culture'), and be exposed to the incontestable virtues of Hindu civilization. In the US, where proximity to the Muslim can be avoided, and views about the fanaticism of Islam are seen as receiving the endorsement of the wider culture, Vedic India appears in illumined glory as the opposite of all that is evil. An extraordinary, but by no means atypical, illustration of the besieged Indian-American Hindu mentality at work can be seen in a book published recently by the Federation of Hindu Associations (FHA), a Los-Angeles based organization, of which over 10,000 copies were distributed free at the November 1999 Diwali *mela* or celebrations in the part-Indian neighbourhoods of Cerritos and Artesia. Entitled *Bhagwan's Call for Dharma Raksha*, or God's appeal for the protection of the (Hindu) faith, this book purports to set out the facts about the truly destructive nature of Islam and the unique innocence of Hinduism. Over the course of 'The Last (1000) Dreadful Years', the Hindu readers are reminded, 'we have lost more than half of our Vedic land'; 'Crores [Tens of millions] of Hindus were converted to Islam and other religions'; 'Thousands of our temples were demolished'; 'Temples of Hindus, some of whom [sic] like Mathura and Kashi, are half temple-half mosque, indicating destruction by the invaders and establishment of their mosques', stand forth as signs of the humiliation of Hindus; and 'The % of non-Hindus in India increased dramatically whereas Hindus continued family planning'. Hindus are reminded that merely because their forefathers survived the genocidal onslaught of Muslims and other invaders, they should not be complaisant, thinking that Hinduism 'will anyhow survive'; and they are asked to reflect on the ominous fact that, 'by all calculations', given the Muslim's alarming propensity to breed hordes of children, 'Hindus could become [a] minority in [the] very near future'.

Consequently, Hindus are enjoined to engage in 'Dharma Raksha', the protection of the faith, so that:

- Rigid religions may not harm this flexible way of Hindus.
- Revelations may not harm this philosophical religion of Hindus.
- Fanatics may not destroy the compassionate Hindus.
- Narrow-minded may not spoil the broad-minded Hindus.
- Theocracies may not destroy the secular & democratic Hindus.
- There is at least one Vedic land.
- Cultural experience, known as Hindutva, may not go waste.[46]

The alarming susceptibility of NRI Hindus in the US to resurgent Hinduism is nowhere more clearly exemplified than in their admiration for the most intolerant Hindus to have gained public eminence in India over the last fifteen years. In 1994 the FHA, the publisher of *Dharma Raksha*, took it upon itself to institute a new award, called the 'Hindu of the Year Award', which was then promptly conferred upon Bal Thackeray and Sadhvi Rithambara. The citation accompanying the award commended Thackeray, an avid admirer of Hitler who has acquired immense notoriety for his part in instituting pogroms against Muslims in Maharashtra, and Rithambara, whose shrill rantings against the *yavanas* [foreigners] have left many wounded and trembling, for their role in, of all things, 'the creation and preservation of Hinduism'.[47] The FHA could well have pondered on the longevity of an ancient faith, and wondered how such a faith has fared so well in the absence of such defenders in the past; rather, in the following year, the award was bestowed upon Uma Bharati, who summons Hindu men to arms with the observation that Hindus want no cut-up (partitioned) nation any more than they want cut-up (circumcised) men in their midst.[48] The speeches of Uma Bharati and Sadhavi Rithambara, whom Hindutvavadis doubtless see as modern-day Durgas, wielders of that immense feminine energy which in Hindu theology is seen as generating the universe and undoing the wrongs that even the Hindu male gods are incapable of arresting, are so incendiary that they have been subjected to repeated bans in India.

What, then, is this post-industrial civilization of diasporic Hindus, particularly those settled in the United States and the 'advanced' West? Hindu communities in the US appear to know the contours and meaning of Hinduism better than do Hindus in India, and these diasporic Hindus can routinely invoke Indian civilization with a self-assurance that, in an Indian in India, would at once provoke mockery and consternation. Far removed as these Hindus are from the lived practices of the faith, their Hinduism is ossified; equally distanced in their adopted country from the cultural life and political aspirations of black people, Hispanics, and other racial or ethnic minorities, and often xenophobically proud of the allegedly unique spiritual qualities of their own Hindu traditions, might their sense of the moral community not be inadequate? Most trenchantly, Indian-American Hindus have taken to cyberspace to press forth their own claims about the nature of Hindu civilization, and they have been unrelenting in their attempt to give shape to a new Hindu history. This history, which aggressively sets itself against the long trajectory of colonial histories, the 'pseudo-secular' agenda of the Indian state, the secularism of the Indian left, the nefarious designs of the Pakistani state, the Western contempt for Hindu culture, and the intellectual pusillanimity and moral cowardice of the Indian academy, furnishes a point of entry into debates about the political uses of cyberspace, just as it suggests that the battle for contending versions of history, which had appeared to reach its acme in the debate surrounding the Babri Masjid, will surely intensify as it is played upon new turfs in the homeland and the diaspora alike.

CYBER-DIASPORIC HINDU MILITANCY AND REVISIONIST INDIAN HISTORIES

It is perhaps apposite that the North American proponents of Hindutva, as well as revisionist Hindu historians, should have found the Internet an agreeable avenue for the propagation of their worldview. More than any other organized religion, Hinduism is a decentred and deregulated faith, and in this it appears akin to cyberspace. It has no one prophet or saviour, nor are Hindus agreed upon the authority of a single text. Only in the older Indian diaspora created by indentured labour, such as in Fiji and Trinidad, did a single text, namely Tulsidas's *Ramacaritmanas*, become supremely authoritative—and here too for reasons that had to do with the cultural, political, and economic characteristics of the migration, its point of origin mainly in the Gangetic plains where Tulsidas's devotional book was deeply revered, and so on. Moreover, if Trinidad or Fiji Hindus even for a moment thought they had become the people of the book, their distinctly second-class status in these societies was enough to disabuse them of that far-fetched notion. Hinduism not only has multiple sources of doctrinal authority, it is polycentric. Varanasi [Benares] is not to Hinduism what Mecca and Medina are to Islam, and the pilgrimage sites of Hindus are almost as numerous as their deities. While for Muslims the pilgrimage to Mecca can be nothing other than a literal visit to Mecca, for Hindus the sacred river Ganga can be fully recreated by mixing Ganga *jal* in almost any body of water.[49] The circumambulation around any number of temples or sacred lakes could, for a Hindu, stand in place of the circumambulation around the Kaaba: even Hinduism's most sacred sites are largely places of myth rather than history.

In the language of the cybernetic postmodernists, one could say that Hinduism is rhizomatic, with multiple points of origin, intersection, and dispersal. If the modular form for netwar conforms to what one early analyst described as 'a segmented, polycentric, ideologically integrated network' (SPIN), where by 'segmented' is meant 'cellular, composed of many different groups', and by 'polycentric' many 'different leaders or centers of direction',[50] then Hinduism most certainly inhabits those very properties that characterize cybernetworks. In a manner of speaking, Hinduism even makes the head *spin*; and if 'electronic civil disobedience' consists in 'swarming' and 'flooding' the web sites of the foe, popular Hinduism displays a similar tendency to create an immense sensory overload and swarm one's sensibilities. Hinduism and the Internet, one might conclude, were happily made for each other; even the millions of web sites evoke the '330 millions gods and goddesses' of Hinduism.[51]

The Internet, it could also be argued, is a particularly happy medium for those who construe themselves as members of a diaspora, or who have what might be termed diasporic sensibilities. Though the Indian diaspora is much smaller than the Chinese or African diasporas, it has perhaps a greater geographic reach, and is represented in virtually every country of the world: in the cliched saying, the two things that are found everywhere in the world are a potato and a Sikh. Through cyberspace, Hindus have found a new awareness of themselves as part of what they now imagine is a global religion, and nothing could be more calculated to augment Hindu pride than the perception that Hinduism is on the verge of arriving as a 'world religion', so to take its place alongside Islam, Christianity, and even Buddhism. Though the adherents of Hinduism are still overwhelmingly confined to the subcontinent, what Arjun Appadurai has called 'the globalization of Hinduism'[52] was evidently on witness in 1995 when the news spread that *murtis* or images of Ganesh, the elephant-headed God, had been seen drinking prodigious amounts of milk in Hindu temples; and so from Delhi and Bombay this news was rapidly flashed to Leeds, London, Leicester, Chicago, New York, Los Angeles, and elsewhere. Reflecting on the 'milk miracle' of September 1995, one long-time scholar of the Hindu overseas population observed that a 'South Asian religious diaspora was now linked through advanced global telecommunications'.[53]

Moving to more mundane considerations, it is an empirical observation that in the United States, many professional Indians, and particularly Hindus, earn their living in the computer and software industries, and they take readily to the culture of the Internet. It is not in the least coincidental that a preponderant number of the people associated with what may be termed Hindutva web sites owe their livelihood to computer industries or are drawn from the hard sciences, and that their Hinduism is without those soft and porous edges which gave the religion its historically amorphous and ecumenical form. Significantly, very few professional historians, if any, contribute to these web sites, which is scarcely to say that the expertise of professional historians is necessarily reliable. Judging from recent events in India, such as the endeavour, alluded to in a previous chapter, to reduce professional historical associations—the Indian Council for Historical Research being a case in point—to mouthpieces of the VHP and the BJP, one might feel relieved that Hindutva web sites are largely amateurish undertakings, however much scientific credibility their creators might attach to such enterprises. While no complete sociological profile of the people who labour on such web sites, whether in a technical capacity or by way of providing substantive content, is available, typically they are male graduate students from middle-class backgrounds, drawn evidently to revisionist histories of India; they are also the ones who have contributed most frequently in the past to various list servers and bulletin boards, such as *alt.hindu* and *soc.culture.indian*.

Although the subjects on which the most substantial contributions to the web sites are made vary considerably, the web masters and their associates are united in their resolve to offer radically altered accounts of even the most common verities of Indian history. Thus, while it is generally agreed that the Mughal Emperor Akbar (reigned 1556–1605) was, especially for his times, a just ruler, that his policies of tolerance were conducive to the expansion of his empire and the good of his subjects, and that he is said to have introduced elements of Hinduism into his own practices of worship and even the culture of the court, in Hindutva web sites he appears as a 'tyrannical monarch'; not unexpectedly, then, Aurangzeb (reigned 1658–1707), who has always been disliked by Hindu historians as a sworn enemy of the Hindus and breaker of idols, is viewed as entirely beyond the pale. The Taj Mahal, which no serious historian doubts was built at the orders of Shah Jahan (reigned 1628–58), is transformed into a Hindu monument by the name of Tejomahalay, as though its history as one of the finest examples of Mughal architecture was wholly inconsequential, a malicious invention of Muslim-loving Hindus. Lest these revisionisms be considered merely arbitrary and anomalous, the systematic patterning behind these re-writings is also evidenced by the attempt to argue, for example, that the Aryans, far from having migrated to India, originated there.[54]

As I have already indicated the tenor of the discussions about Aurangzeb in an earlier chapter, I turn to a lengthier consideration of the other claims encountered on these web sites and their design. They weave their own intricate web of links, conspiracies, and nodal points: at one moment one is in one web site, and at another moment in another. Even Krishna, who by his *leela* or divine magical play could be among several *gopis* (lovers) simultaneously, might have found his match in the world wide web; he might have gazed with awe at rhizomatic Hindutvaness at its propagandistic best. Among the most remarkable and most comprehensive of the sites are those created by the VHP and students who have constituted themselves into the Global Hindu Electronic Network (GHEN). Links take the surfer to such sites as *hindunet*, the Hindu Vivek Kendra, and the various articles culled from the archives of *Hinduism Today*, a glossy magazine published by a white sadhu (mendicant) who is constructing a lavish temple amidst the rich tropical green of Hawaii's Kaui island. There are links to other spiritual matters of interest to non-resident Hindus, such as the teachings of Swami Chinmayananda,[55] whose associations with the VHP have been explored by scholars at some length, and to comparatively more esoteric sites on Indian philosophy, devotional literature, the legends of gods and goddesses, and the like. The importance attached to cyberspace communication and politics and the Non-Resident Hindu Factor is, incidentally, nowhere better illustrated than in the fact that the BJP, which used to shout itself hoarse over *swadeshi* (self-reliance) and is nauseatingly jingoistic, locates its web site in the United States, as does the paramilitary organization, the Rashtriya Swayamsevak Sangh (RSS).[56]

GHEN is sponsored by the Hindu Students Council, and the astuteness of its creators, no less than their zeal and ardour, can be gauged by the fact that it had developed into the most comprehensive site on Hindutva philosophy and aggressive Hindu nationalism at least eight years ago, when such work in cyberspace was in its infancy. GHEN was the recipient in 1996 of an award from IWAY, then one of the leading Internet magazines, for the 'Best Web Page Award' in the religious category, and one of GHEN's members described himself as pleased that the world was finally 'taking cognizance of the most important movement in this century, "The Hindutva Movement"'.[57] The home page takes one into predictable categories, namely 'Introductions', 'Scriptures', 'Temples', 'Organizations', 'Latest News', and the bulletin board *alt.hindu*; another link opens onto what is called the 'Hindu Universe' and is graced by the sign of AUM, which believing Hindus describe as the primal sound that stands for the Supreme Godhead, and this in turn leads to pages on five categories, enumerated as follows: 'Latest News from Bharat (India)', 'Kashmir', 'Terrorism in Bharat (India)', 'Hindutva: Nationalist Ideology', and 'Shri Ramjanmabhoomi Movement'. Each page, in turn, furnishes links to a dozen or more related articles: the aspiration to be comprehensive, and to leave the surfer with an impression that neutrality is being maintained, is suggested by the characterization of each page as a 'Reference Center'.

Though the page on Kashmir offers a Hindu perspective on the rebellion that has been taking place in the Valley over the last decade, highlights the suffering of Kashmiri Pandits (Brahmins), and reiterates the role of Pakistan in aiding and abetting the rebellion, it is the manner in which Kashmir is assimilated into the 'Hindu Universe' that is deserving of comment.[58] The assumption is that one can ignore the largely Muslim population of the state, and presumably the Buddhists of the Ladakh region of Kashmir are construed as belonging to the Hindu fold; moreover, the creators of the site show little awareness of the plural histories of Islam, since the argument that would have best served their own interests, namely that the Islam of Kashmir historically shares little with the orthodox Sunni culture of the ulama and the jihadis in Pakistan, receives no mention at all. Whatever awareness there is about the complex histories of what now passes for 'Hinduism', and there is precious little of that in GHEN and other ideologically similar sites, Islam is always rendered as monolithic. While there is undoubtedly a Saivite substratum in Kashmir's religious history as well, the positioning of Kashmir within a 'Hindu universe' betrays an acute anxiety about the reality of Kashmir as a composite culture, the claims of 'Kashmiriyat', and the eventual disposition of what is generally termed the 'Kashmir problem'.

Though Kashmir is recognized in GHEN as a matter of jurisdiction for the Indian nation-state, its transposition into a Hindu universe signifies the ease with which 'India' can effortlessly be elided into 'Hindu', a manoeuvre that is repeatedly encountered in Hindutva web sites.[59] Other similar sleights of hand are visible throughout the GHEN site. Thus, in the 'Shree Ramjanmabhoomi Reference Center' page, which like much of GHEN offers an array of articles culled from Indian newspapers, in this case about the dispute over the Babri Masjid, it is quite baldly stated that the 'Ramjanmabhoomi movement is carried out by hundreds of millions of Hindus in Bharat (India)'.[60] Far too many studies have already established that the movement leading to the destruction of the mosque drew its membership from precisely those elements of society from which the BJP, RSS, and VHP draw their support, namely the trading castes, the petite-bourgeoisie, and small town dwellers.[61] The destruction of the Babri Masjid itself was an affair orchestrated to the extreme, and as with many riots that require careful engineering, volunteers had to be drawn upon from the outside.[62] It is also an indubitable fact that there are millions of Hindus in Bharat, and that Rama is one of the principal deities, particularly in the so-called cow belt in north India; yet this does not inescapably lead to the logic that the preponderant number of Hindus put their weight behind the movement, or that the millions of Rama bhaktas can be safely described as adherents of the movement.

If GHEN shares something ominous in common with Hindutva web sites, it is the deliberate attempt to obfuscate the distinction between Hinduism and Hindutva. Swami Vivekananda, to take one instance, becomes in their histories an exponent of Hindutva ideology, not an advocate of a mere Hinduism; and this idea is perhaps lent some credence by the circumstances surrounding the life of Vivekananda, who, as the sole representative of Hinduism at the World Parliament of Religions in Chicago in 1893, can be described as playing a not inconsiderable role in furnishing Hinduism something of a place on the world stage.[63] Though Hindutvavadis do not care much for Gandhi, finding it fit even to abuse him as something of a *hijra* (eunuch) and father of Pakistan, or even for Vivekananda's own spiritual master Ramakrishna, whose spirituality they admire but whose androgyny poses something of a problem to their own sense of masculinity, they have ferociously struggled to claim Vivekananda as one of their own. For some years now, even within the Ramakrishna Mission, it has been apparent that Vivekananda has been gaining more prominence, and when he began to be championed in Rajiv Gandhi's India as a model for Indian youth, it became imperative for the VHP and its friends to declare themselves the true inheritors of Vivekananda's legacy. In Hindu communities, from Port of Spain to Chicago, it is the image of Vivekananda which looms large over the landscapes that Hindus inhabit.[64] He is seen, in the first instance, as the prophet who energized the Indian nation, urged his brethren to social action, critiqued the devotional excess of the faith (what he would have made of his master, one cannot say), and strove to make Hinduism into a more rational and masculine religion. Vivekananda, it is believed, won Hinduism its first devotees in the West. It is his stridency and proselytizing that, doubtless, make him an attractive feature to Hindutva advocates, who are prone to take the view that Hindus have, for too long of their history, remained a pacific and tolerant people upon whom others trod not too gently. 'The message has reached far and wide throughout the world', states Ashok Singhal, the general-secretary of the VHP, 'that the Hindu will no more be subdued. Eventually the world at large will come to the conclusion that after all now they have to deal with a Hindu India.'[65]

Judging from GHEN's 'Swami Vivekananda Study Center', which presents the RSS as the fulfilment of Vivekananda's ideas, the Swami was a militant Hindutvavadi who desired 'the conquest of the whole world by the Hindu race'.[66] If Argentina is nothing other than 'Arjuna town', where Arjuna—one of the five Pandava heroes who in the Mahabharata are condemned to spend thirteen years in exile—went for the year that he was enjoined to remain incognito; if Denmark, rich in dairy products, is none other than 'Dhenu Marg', the abode of cows (which the cowherd Krishna would have recognized as his own home); if the 'Red Indians' are the signposts for the advance of an Indian civilization in remote antiquity; and if Vivekananda's own name, 'Vive!Canada', is a ringing testimony to his reach over the world, even demonstrable proof of intrepid Indian explorers having used the scientific advances of the ancient Hindus to reach Canada centuries before the European Age of Exploration commenced, then surely it is not too far-fetched to imagine that Vivekananda desired the worldwide supremacy of the Hindu race.[67] His militancy is high-lighted with his observation that the Bhagavad Gita, which Gandhi would interpret as a text counseling non-violent resistance, would be better understood with the 'biceps', by 'strong men with muscles of steel and nerves of iron inside of which dwells a mind of the same material as that of which the thunderbolt is made'.[68] Yet, in their haste to turn Vivekananda into the apostle of Hindutva, the defender of the faith, the VHP and its allies appear to have forgotten his admonition to others who would dare to be the guardians of Hinduism. Once, on a visit to Kashmir, Vivekananda felt pained at seeing the ruins of temples and the idols of Hindu deities scattered around the country. Approaching the goddess with anger and trepidation, Vivekananda bowed before her, and asked in an anguished tone, 'Mother, why did you permit this desecration?' Vivekananda reports that Kali whispered to him: 'What is it to you if the invaders broke my images? Why do you trouble yourself over it? Do you protect me, or do I protect you?'[69]

Evidently, if one is to consider the rather gargantuan web site of the VHP-America, the Hindutva advocates, quite oblivious to Vivekananda's teachings, dwell on the ruins of temples and the Muslim hatred of idolaters. No one who has looked at the VHP site can fail to be impressed by the fact that its home page, which takes surfers to GHEN's 'Hindu Universe', to a list of temples in the United States, and other activities of interest to Hindus, also takes readers to the 'History of Hindu Temples', which in turn features a section on 'Temple Destruction'. Though readers can rejoice in the presence of monumental temple complexes as varied as Angkor Wat and Hampi, the engagement with the history of *destroyed* temples appears to be more intense; the destruction of Somnath evokes greater passion than the dancing stones of Belur, Halebid, Konarak, and other temples. Here, again, the cue may have come from Vivekananda, who reminded his countrymen and women that their 'forefathers underwent everything boldly, even death itself, but preserved their religion. Temple after temple was broken down by foreign conquerors, but no sooner had the wave passed than the spire of the temple rose again'.[70] If the valiant Hindu woman, by the very act of choosing self-immolation (*jauhar*) and immortality rather than the ignominy of sexual violation by the Muslim invader, bore in negation the mark of the Muslim upon her body, so the Hindu temple carried the history of regenerative violations: 'Mark how the temples bear the marks of a hundred attacks and a hundred regenerations, continually destroyed and continually springing out of the ruins, rejuvenated and as strong as ever! That is the national life current.'[71]

Vivekananda had, however, asked the Hindu to look to his own resources, and to consider what weaknesses in Indian society, and in particular in the Hindu social structure, made the country vulnerable to invasion and attack. For the Hindutvavadi in the diaspora, the alterity of the Muslim—the 'Indian Muslim' is something of an anomaly from that perspective, because the Muslim in India is never sufficiently Indian, and as a Muslim he is seen as having promised his loyalty to the *qaum*, the worldwide community of Muslims—is paradoxically the *sine qua non* of Hindu identity and history. Sometimes the expression of Hindu identity is manifested by waging a virulent attack on Islam, as in the web site, located in the United States, that takes its name from the Sanskrit phrase 'Satyameva Jayate', 'The Truth Alone Triumphs', which is the national motto of sovereign India.[72] Though viewers are invited to send e-mail to a person carrying a Muslim name, 'Zulfikar', the web site is almost certainly operated by a Hindu. The site is linked to the home page of a 'Vedic astrologer',[73] and the remarks about Islam and its Prophet are so slanderous that it is nearly inconceivable that any Muslim, howsoever much an unbeliever, would have dared to be so foolishly offensive. Four of the twenty articles, all unsigned, available on this web site purport to establish that Muhammad was the 'Prophet of Terror', two document Islam's supposed worldwide network of terrorism, and some others venture into descriptions of Islam as a religion of lust, murder, rape, and genocide. Attempting to unmask the 'sadistic cruel nature of Prophet Mohammed', the author argues that 'Mohammed was in fact a terrorist, criminal and murderer whose entire life was based on victimizing innocents and indulging in mindless violence, carnage and massacre.'[74] The author alleges that the Prophet, whose own sexual appetite for young boys and beautiful virgins could never be satiated, promised the Arabs sex slaves and booty, and 'to please the homosexuals among his followers he promised them pre-pubescent boys in Paradise'.[75]

More often, the Hindutva notion of history comes wrapped around a tale of Hindu innocence, and more precisely the tale of the destruction of Hindu temples. This is quite transparent in the 'Satyameva Jayate' web site, where another four of the twenty articles are devoted to an enumeration of the 'Destruction of Hindu Temples by Muslims'. The very sense of history, by no means unique to Hindutvavadis, is marked by violence, wars, and technological achievements: historians have become habituated to speaking of World War I, World War II, the Vietnam war, and the Indo-Pakistan war of 1971 as 'watersheds',[76] and it is this language that is absorbed into Hindutva web sites, where the 'watersheds' are those periodic invasions of India that led to the destruction of Hindu temples. What remains—the ordinary passage of time, men and women at work in the fields, raising families, engaged in the arts and crafts, and the thousands of other activities that make up life—evokes no sense of history; the present is always transcendental, and is less easily hitched to the anguished sense of a past where one was wronged. And all this is not in keeping with the VHP's ideological interests, which, as I have on more than one occasion in this book remarked, are to transform Hinduism—viewed by Hindutvavadis as having been wrongly condemned as a form of myth-making—into a religion of history. No Hindutvavadi is prepared to countenance the observation that the particular genius of Hinduism may lie in none other than its mythicity, and the ire expressed at the recent web site, 'www.hindumythology. com', inaugurated by the *Indian Express*, suggests how far militant Hinduism remains captive to the mode of historical thinking.[77]

Let us recall that the historical sensibility has, fortunately from a civilizational standpoint, never been a marked feature of Indian thinking; indeed, it is a commonplace to argue that the historical sense was severely underdeveloped in ancient India, and the view of Jawaharlal Nehru, not only India's first Prime Minister, but a man with a distinctly historical sensibility whose *Discovery of India* still serves as one of the better introductions to Indian history, may be taken as representative:

Unlike the Greeks, and unlike the Chinese and the Arabs, Indians in the past were not historians. This was very unfortunate and it has made it difficult for us now to fix dates or make up an accurate chronology. Events run into each other, overlap and produce an enormous confusion. ... the ignoring of history had evil consequences which we pursue still. It produced a vagueness of outlook, a divorce from life as it is, a credulity, a woolliness of the mind where fact was concerned.[78]

A number of scholars have attempted, in an overdetermined reaction to save India from the Orientalist structures of thought,[79] to provide a more complex scenario of India's engagement with historical thinking, but they have been less attentive to Nehru's observation that 'this lack of historical sense did not affect the masses ... they built up their view of the past from the traditional accounts and myth and story that were handed to them from generation to generation. This imagined history and mixture of fact and legend became widely known and gave to the people a strong and abiding cultural background.'[80] But the attack on the *Indian Express* web site, by those who purport to speak for Hindu civilization, displays precisely this profound anxiety that Hinduism should in no manner be construed as a religion of myth, an unscientific and unhistorical enterprise; and even the slight nuances of Nehru's view are lost in the Hindutvavadi's unabashed celebration of the historical mode. Notably, it is only the destruction of temples that, in the VHP's mistaken view, serves to distinguish Hinduism from other faiths: it is what renders the Hindus singularly into victims, and gives them a history they otherwise are said to lack.

GHEN's home page on Hindu temples disavows any interest in 'the politicization of temples and the[ir] history', but nonetheless avers that 'those who do not learn from history are condemned to relive it'.[81] Should there be any doubt as to what history might be in store for those obdurate Hindus who do not comprehend the evil genius and mental psyche of the Muslim, a page reminds readers of 'what happened' to Hindu temples. The 'Moslem behavior pattern as recorded by Moslem historians of medieval India', we are told, furnishes a decisive account of the murderous activities of 'Islamized invaders'. Why these 'invaders' are represented as 'Islamized' rather than 'Islamic' is not certain, but it is surely not for the charitable reason that they were not true Muslims, who had merely the veneer of Islam around them. One Islamic chronicle after another, it is maintained, documents the hatred of the invaders for the faith of the infidels, their contempt for idols, and their destruction of the idolater's temples. (This is doubtless the case, though the author of the web page scarcely understands that these chronicles betray a characteristic tendency of the oppressors to leave behind an archive, even an exaggerated one, of their own ill-doings.) The invading Muslims, in brief, engaged in 'mass slaughter of people not only during war' but after they had 'emerged victorious'; they captured non-combatants and sold them throughout the Islamic world, so rendering a free people into slavery and violating the convention whereby civilians are spared the retributions due to soldiers; they engaged in 'forcible conversion to Islam of people who were in no position to resist', and stripped those who could not be so converted of their citizenship, turning them into 'zimmis' or non-citizens; and on these 'zimmis' they imposed 'inhuman disabilities', appropriating their wealth and 'holding in contempt all their institutions and expressions', cultural, religious, and social.[82] In this narrative, which seeks to etch in bold the 'magnitude of Muslim Atrocities', a web page derived from yet another site which calls itself the 'Library of Hindu History',[83] it becomes wholly unnecessary to consider the politics of conquest, and a vocabulary inherited from modern institutional practices and political theories is introduced as the benchmark by which the conduct of Muslim invaders is to be judged. What, for instance, was the theory of 'citizenship' in pre-Muslim India, and was there any notion of 'rights', a term that everywhere is of relatively recent vintage? In that paradise called Aryavarta, the land of the Aryas or Hindus before Islam rudely entered into the scene, who conferred 'citizenship' on whom, by what criteria, and with what consequences?

Not unexpectedly, the destruction of Hindu temples by Aurangzeb, who for Hindus has been iconic of Muslim barbarity since the colonial histories of the eighteenth century began enumerating the despotic tendencies of Islam, is enumerated at great length, but far more significant is the clustering together, on this home page, of tales of the destruction or appropriation of Hindu temples throughout the subcontinent and into the far-flung parts of the Indian diaspora. If one were to ask what makes the Indian diaspora Indian, if not the ubiquitousness of the commercial Hindi film, the enthroning of 'Bharat Natyam' as the quintessential dance form of India which every young Indian woman must embrace, or the emergence of tandoori chicken as a metonym for Indian cuisine,[84] then to the VHP it is the poignant desecration of Hindu temples in varied landscapes throughout the world. A ruined or discarded temple is the sure sign of a Hindu presence, it is the only living evidence of a diaspora extending to antiquity: it is the reminder that everywhere the Hindus, who (in the Hindutvavadi view) knew nothing of the ways of the world and the evil intent of monotheistic religions, have suffered the same fate. '600 Hindu Temples Destroyed/Damaged in Pakistan and Bangladesh!', screams one headline on Hindunet, and from there we jump to another headline drawn from the archives of *Hinduism Today*: 'Fiji Temple Burned'. For the one mosque destroyed by Hindus in Ayodhya—a destruction that is never fully conceded, since the Hindus chose to repossess what in truth had always been theirs—there were a dozen temples that the Muslims swiftly desecrated in Britain by way of revenge. Who else, the Hindutvavadi asks, writes that history?[85]

Etymology—the science of comparative linguistics, so to speak, itself born in the crucible of eighteenth-century theories of race and human origins—and destroyed temples *together* give the Hindutvavadis the universal history they have always desired. 'Hindu Kush means Hindu Slaughter', Shrinandan Vyas reminds us in an article on the Internet, for it is in the mountain ranges of Eastern Afghanistan that goes by the name of 'Hindu Kush' that the first, and still unacknowledged, 'genocide' of Hindus took place.[86] 'Genocide' strikes Hindutvavadis as the apposite term, especially on web sites, where the visceral effect is critical, to describe the cruel fate suffered by peaceful Hindus at the hands of Muslim barbarians. There is always the hope that the world will look upon the Hindu as it does upon the Jew, as a specimen of a race that must continually stave off the threat of extinction, and that has more than once been dealt a terrible death. Hindutvavadis deplore the 'fact' that the world does not know of the many holocausts perpetrated by the Muslims, and the 'Kashmir Information Network' on the web accords a prominent place on its site to the 'AUSCHWITZ IN KASHMIR', highlighting with pictures the 'atrocities on Kashmiris by Pakistan-trained terrorists'.[87]

I have given a mere inkling of the Hindu histories that dominate on the Internet, and in conclusion it merits reiteration that the very proclivity to argue in the language of the historian shows how far the proponents of Hindutva have abandoned the language of Hinduism for the epistemological imperatives of modernity and the nation-state. Nothing resonates as strongly as their desire to strip Hinduism of myth, of its ahistoricist sensibilities, and to impose on the under-standing of Hinduism and the Indian past alike the structures of a purportedly scientific history. The Hindutva historians have, in all these matters, embraced the methods of their adversaries: thus nearly every lengthy article *pretends* to carry with it the paraphernalia of scholarship, and many are prefaced with a summary of the 'sources' marshalled to construct the argument. 'All the Encyclopaedias and *National Geographic* agree', writes Vyas at the outset of his aforemen-tioned piece on the Hindu holocaust, 'that the Hindu Kush is a place of Hindu genocide (similar to Dakau [sic] and Auschwitz). All the references are given. Please feel free to verify them.' Of course, only the uninitiated would think of *National Geographic* as an unimpeach-able source of scholarly authority, but all this is well beyond the comprehension of Vyas and his like-minded associates.

Typically, as in the article on 'The Destruction of the Hindu Temples by Muslims, Part IV', found on the 'Satyameva Jayate' web site, no page numbers are ever furnished, nor are titles of works enumerated; nonetheless, a tone of authority is sought and injected by the note placed at the end: 'Works of Arun Shourie, Harsh Narain, Jay Dubashi, and Sita Ram Goel have been used in this article.'[88] The mention of 'references' imparts a scholarly note to the piece, and the invitation to employ the verifiability hypothesis suggests the detachment of the scientist, the objectivity of the social scientist who has no ambition but the discernment of truth, and the scrupulousness of the investigator. I hasten to add that this is keeping well within the norm of Hindutva history: the unattributed article, 'The Real Akbar, The (not) so Great', is likewise based on a number of sources, though their worthiness as specimens of authoritative scholarship can be construed from the great affection that Hindutva historians have developed for Will Durant. 'The world famous historian, Will Durant has written in his Story of Civilisation', writes Rajiv Varma in his Internet article on Muslim atrocities, that '"the Mohammedan conquest of India was probably the bloodiest story in history."'[89] The West be damned, but when the occasion demands, the authority of even its mediocre historians is construed as incontestable.

From their concerted endeavours to impart a precise historical specificity to the Mahabharata and the Ramayana, as evidenced by the laborious efforts at reconstructing the chronology of the events depicted in the epics and turning the principal characters into live historical figures who were the Moses, Abraham, Isaac, and Christ of Hinduism,[90] to the onslaught on the generally accepted theory of an Aryan migration to India—an onslaught at first headed, it is no accident, by an Indian aerospace engineer, N. S. Rajaram, who is described as valiantly having temporarily set aside his career in the interest of exposing the largest 'hoax' in human history[91]—the Hindutvavadis have signified their attachment to historical discourses. The critics of Hindutva who dwell on it as a form of religious fanaticism and fundamentalism, doubtless with political ambitions, may be obfuscating a great deal more than they reveal in their analyses. That is not only because the Hindutvavadis are the least of the Hindus that one is likely to encounter; even their religiosity has something in it of mercantilism and the secular ethos of the marketplace.

Historical discourses are preeminently the discourses of the nation, and the Internet, which has something in common with the historical archive, making it intrinsically hospitable to the modernist sensibility of the historian, is poised to become the ground on which the advocates of Hindutva will stage their revisionist histories. Whether cyberspace is 'Republican' is a matter on which we can defer judgment; but it is poised, alarmingly, to become a Hindutva domain, considering that there are scarcely any web sites which offer competing narratives.[92] Dharmakshetre, kurukshetre [on the field of dharma, righteousness; on the field of the Kurus, the clan that is said to have given birth to Bharat or India], says the Bhagavad Gita in its opening line, but today this might well be: *dharmakshetre, cyberkshetre*. If the computer scientist-historian types who inhabit Silicon Valley, and their diasporic brethren, have it their way, Hinduism will become that very 'world historical religion' they have craved to see, and Hindutva history will be the most tangible product of the wave of globalization over which they preside from their diasporic vantagepoint.

ENDNOTES

1. Peter F. Drucker, 'Beyond the Information Revolution', *Atlantic Monthly* (October 1999), pp. 47–57.

2. As an instance, one might adduce the report of how the homeless in the greater Los Angeles area have taken to the Internet, nursing not only e-commerce ambitions, but creating a new home for themselves. Apparently, according to this report, librarians in Los Angeles and elsewhere report that on some days, as many as 75 per cent of the free Internet terminals in public libraries are being used by the homeless. See Greg Miller, 'Cyberspace Comes to Skid Row', *Los Angeles Times* (18 November 1999), pp. A1, 20–1.

3. *Mondo 2000*, no. 1 (1989), p. 11.

4. Even a cursory reading of the literature leaves one with the inescapable feeling that though the hacker is viewed as a dangerous figure, who is liable to crack open the computer files of the Pentagon and compromise the national security of the United States, he is simultaneously a widely admired figure. The daredevil in him taunts not only bureaucrats at the Pentagon, the sleuths of the Justice Department, and the managers of complex financial and banking systems, but even computer scientists and the software specialists of Silicon Valley. He is the Jesse James and Billy the Kid of the late twentieth century: however regrettable his violation of, and disrespect for, the law he is that maverick, entrepreneur, and lone ranger who stands forth as an American icon. For a preliminary consideration of 'hacktivism', see Amy Harmon, '"Hacktivists" of All Persuasions Take Their Struggle to the Web', *New York Times* (31 October 1998); more scholarly is Dorothy E. Denning, 'Activism, Hacktivism, and Cyberterrorism: The Internet as a Tool for Influencing Foreign Policy', Nautilus Institute, San Francisco, online at: *<http://www. terrorism.com/documents/denning-infoterrorism.html>* though more insightful is G. Meyer and J. Thomas, 'The Baudy World of the Byte Bandit: A Postmodernist Interpretation of the Computer Underground', Department of Sociology, Northern Illinois University (1990), online at: *<http://ei.cs.vt.edu/ ~cs704/papers/meyer.txt>*. There is a burgeoning literature on the hacker, but his political biography still remains to be written.

5. Francis Fukuyama, 'Capitalism and Democracy: The Missing Link', *Journal of Democracy* 3 (1992), pp. 100–10; idem, *The End of History and the Last Man* (New York: Free Press, 1992).

6. Esther Dyson, George Gilder, Jay Keyworth and Alvin Toffler, 'A Magna Carta for the Knowledge Age', *New Perspectives Quarterly* 11, no. 4 (Fall 1994), pp. 26–8, 31–2.

7. From a speech reported by Rodolfo Montes, 'Chiapas is a War of Ink and Internet', *Reforma* (26 April 1995), and quoted in David Ronfeldt, John Arquilla, Graham E. Fuller, and Melissa Fuller, *The Zapatista Social Netwar in Mexico* (Santa Monica: RAND, for the United States Army, 1998), p. 4. Even the mainstream American media, which is notorious for its insularity, could scarcely ignore the Zapatistas' deployment of the net as the insurrection continued over time: see, for example, Tod Robberson, 'Mexican Rebels Using a High-Tech Weapon: Internet Helps Rally Support', *Washington Post* (20 February 1995), p. A1; and Russell Watson et al., 'When Words are the Best Weapon ... How Rebels use the Internet and satellite TV', *Newsweek* (27 February 1995), pp. 36–40.

8. Cited by Ronfeldt et al., *The Zapatista Social Netwar*, p. 70.

9. Ibid., p. 8; see also John Arquilla and David Ronfeldt, *Cyberwar is Coming!* (Santa Monica: RAND, 1996), reprinted from *Comparative Strategy* 12 (1993):141–65. For the earliest articulation of Internet warfare, see David Ronfeldt, *Cyberocracy, Cyberspace, and Cyberology: Political Effects of the Information Revolution* (Santa Monica: RAND, 1991). The same ideas are recycled in more recent publications by Arquilla and Ronfeldt.

10. See Ricardo Dominguez, 'Digital Zapatismo', 1998, <*http://www.nyu.edu/projects/wary/DigZap.html*>.

11. As is now well-known, the term 'rhizomes' made its first appearance in Gilles Deleuze and Felix Guattari, *A Thousand Plateaus: Capitalism and Schizophrenia*, trans. Brian Massumi (Minneapolis: The University of Minnesota Press, 1987). 'Rhizomatic' thinking—non-linear, anarchic, nomadic, deterritorialized, multiplicitous, and so on—is differentiated from the 'arbolic' thinking—linear, hierarchic, sedentary, territorialized, binary, and homogeneous—which has characterized the scientific thought of the modern West. It is a commonplace in left Internet circles to celebrate the work of Deleuze and Guattari as the theoretical platform for a radical Internet-based insurrectionary democracy: for the most extended Internet expression of these sentiments, see Stephen Wray, 'Rhizomes, Nomads, and Resistant Internet Use', July 7, 1998, at: <*http://www.ny.edu/projects/wray/RhizNom.html*>.

12. For a lengthier discussion, see Michael Whine, 'Cyberspace: A New Medium for Communication, Command and Control by Extremists' (April 1999), online at: <*http://www.ict.org.il/articles/cyberspace.htm*> (accessed 25 March 2002), and Vinay Lal, 'Terror and Its Networks: Disappearing Trails in Cyberspace', unpublished Working Paper for the Nautilus Institute, April 2002; an inventory of websites by terrorists and proscribed organizations can be found (last modified on 19 April 2002) at: <*http://www.cromwell-intl.com/security/netusers.html*>.

13. Cf. Zygmunt Bauman, *Globalization: The Human Consequences* (New

York: Columbia University Press, 1998), p. 88. To speak of Indian elites as finally learning to 'live in time' is not to echo the cliched Orientalist expressions of Indians (especially Hindus) as outside time, or the supposed Indian propensity to conceive of time as 'cyclical' rather than 'linear', but rather to point to the manner in which clock-time has begun to impose its tyranny on a people who have lived with pluralistic conceptions of time. In India, as elsewhere, the American idiom of 'time is money' has begun to alter the frameworks of social relations. For a brief consideration of the cultural histories of time, see Vinay Lal, 'The Politics of Time at the Cusp of the Millennium', *Humanscape* 6, no. 12 (December 1999): 5–12.

14. For an unraveling of the term 'franchise', see Vivian Sobchack, 'Democratic Franchise and the Electronic Frontier', in Ziauddin Sardar and Jerome R. Ravetz, eds, *Cyberfutures: Culture and Politics on the Information Superhighway* (London: Pluto Press, 1996), pp. 77–89.

15. Ziauddin Sardar, 'alt.civilizations.faq: Cyberspace as the Darker Side of the West', in Sardar and Ravetz, eds, *Cyberfutures*, p. 15.

16. On the distinction between 'place' and 'space', see Anthony Giddens, *The Consequences of Modernity* (Stanford: Stanford University Press, 1990).

17. Carlos Fuentes, 'Chiapas: Latin America's First Post-Communist Rebellion', *New Perspectives Quarterly* 11, no. 2 (Spring 1994), p. 56.

18. For a withering critique of postmodernism's pretensions, see Ziauddin Sardar, *Postmodernism and the Other: The New Imperialism of Western Culture* (London: Pluto Press, 1998).

19. Greg Miller, 'Internet Fueled Global Interest in Disruptions', *Los Angeles Times* (2 December 1999), p. A24. Mike Dolan, field director for Public Citizens' Global Trade Watch, one of the principal groups which orchestrated the demonstrations against WTO, is reported as saying: 'The Internet has become the latest greatest arrow in our quiver of social activism. ... The Internet benefits us more than the corporate and government elites we're fighting.' The anti-globalization activists had planned the protests months ago, and the Internet was conceived as the principal mode of resistance at the very outset; cognizant of the fact that the mainstream media was unlikely to give them much support or coverage, they formed the Independent Media Center, and registered a website for their activities, <*www.indymedia.org*>. The scholarly journal on the Internet, *First Monday*, has carried several analyses of Indymedia: see, for example, Gene Hyde, 'Independent Media Centers: Cyber-Subversion and the Alternative Press', online (accessed 8 April 2002) at: <*http://www.firstmonday.org/issues/issue7_4/hyde/index.html*>; a shorter piece is Hillary Rosner, 'A Very Different View of Genoa', *Independent* (30 July 2001). Among the many web sites then launched to combat the WTO were <*www.seattle99.org*>, <*www.agitprop.org*>, <*www.globalizethis.org*>, and <*www.gatt.org*>.

20. David Shenk, *Data Smog: Surviving the Information Glut* (New York: HarperCollins, 1997).

21. Amartya Sen has more than once made the empirical observation that no modern democracy has ever been afflicted by famine. In the course of the last fifty years, the people who have had to face famine have all been victims of authoritarian or despotic regimes, as the examples of the Soviet Union under Stalin, China under Mao, or contemporary Somalia unequivocally suggest. See his *Poverty and Famines* (Oxford: Clarendon Press, 1981); and Jean Dreze and Amartya Sen, eds, *Hunger and Public Action*, 3 vols (Oxford: Clarendon Press, 1989). It must be added that Sen's work on famines is, for all its purported advances, resoundingly within a Malthusian framework, as is brought out in the recent work of Jenny Edkins, *Whose Hunger? Concepts of Famine, Practices of Aid* (Minneapolis: University of Minnesota Press, 2000).

22. No doubt, as with colonization of untamed territories and what were termed 'wastelands', the women will—to put it provocatively—follow men. It can be argued that the Internet might possibly furnish women with a way of bypassing patriarchal institutions and social practices, and enable them to forge their own democratic communities, but as of the moment this is an open question. Rates of Internet use among women in India are rising rapidly, and the website <*www.sitagita.com*>, which caters to women and was launched in late 2000 at a cost of Rs 2 crores, was reporting an astronomical 90,000 hits per day in mid-2001. But all this is no evident demonstration of the democratization of cyberspace, since such web sites perform on the Internet the same function that do women's printed magazines, which generally tend to reinforce women's roles and notions of authentic femininity.

23. Simon Wiesenthal Center, *Digital Hate 2000* (Los Angeles: Simon Wiesenthal Center, 1999).

24. See <*www.icbl.org*> as well as <*www.landminesurvivors.org*>; among the most interesting of the sites dedicated to the Intifada is <*http://electronicintifada.net/introduction.html*>.

25. K. Connie Kang and Robin Fields, 'Asian Population in U.S. Surges, but Unevenly', *Los Angeles Times* (15 May 2001), p. A16; Richard Springer, 'Calif. Has Most U.S. Indians', *India-West* (25 May 2001), p. A1.

26. The 1990 census placed the average household income of Indian-Americans at $60,903, above that of Japanese-Americans and Chinese-Americans. I have seen them described as the most affluent ethnic community in the United States; other studies place them below whites and Jews; and yet others describe them as the community with the largest household income. This problem is commonly encountered, since researchers draw upon different data bases; but what is transparent is that Indian-Americans are well-placed in American society.

27. See *Los Angeles Times* (6 July 2001), p. A1; the article is by Bettina Boxall.

28. On the development of the software industry in Bangalore, see Salim Lakha, 'Growth of Computer Software Industry in India', *Economic and Political Weekly* 25, no. 1 (6 January 1990); John Stremlau, 'Bangalore: India's Silicon City', *Monthly Review* (November 1996); Richard Heeks, *India's Software Industry: State Policy, Liberalisation, and Industrial Development* (New Delhi:

Sage Publications, 1996); and Monica Prasad, 'International Capital on "Silicon Plateau": Work and Control in India's Computer Industry', *Social Forces* 77, no. 2 (December 1998):429–52, especially pp. 434–7. A less scholarly, but engaging, account is offered by Richard Rapaport, 'Bangalore: Western Technology Giants?' *Wired* 4, no. 2 (February 1996), pp. 109–14, 164–70.

29. In the Hindi version of the joke, Ajit asks Robert to place the hero in 'liquid oxygen': liquid won't let him live, and oxygen won't let him die.

30. For a recent profile of the Indian-American community , see Karen Leonard, *The South Asian Americans* (Westport, CT: Greenwood Press, 1997).

31. Ronald Takaki, *Strangers from a Different Shore: A History of Asian Americans* (New York: Penguin Books, 1989), pp. 294–314.

32. The best treatment of these issues is to be found in Susan Koshy, 'Category Crisis: South Asian Americans and Questions of Race and Ethnicity', *Diaspora* 7, no. 3 (1998).

33. I owe this humorous, incisive, and not inaccurate formulation to my ethnomusicologist friend, Daniel Neuman.

34. John Lancaster, 'Activism Boosts India's Fortunes: Politically Vocal Immigrants Help Tilt Policy in Washington', *Washington Post* (9 October 1999), p. A1.

35. A message demanding that Warner Brothers issue an apology to Hindus and the film be altered was circulated on the Internet by American Hindus Against Defamation (AHAD), a group convened by the Vishwa Hindu Parishad-America, whose activities are discussed below at greater length. AHAD's letter to Warner Brothers on 3 August 1999 stated that 'We, American Hindus Against Defamation are baffled, disgusted and annoyed by the use of the *shloka* [verse], and fail to understand your intent and the relevance of its usage.' On a subsequent occasion, AHAD warned Warner Brothers that the 'billion strong Hindu community around the world' would not remain a 'silent spectator to the humiliation of its religious beliefs and scriptures'. See the message of 21 August 1999 circulated by Devant [devant@tstt.net.tt]

36. The dalits were formerly referred to as 'untouchables'; they are the outcastes of the Indian society, the 'wretched of the earth' who make their living as scavengers, sweepers, tanners, landless laborers, or pursuing other jobs which most caste Hindus consider polluting.

37. Viji Sundaram, 'Diet, Dress Code Enrage Hindu Worshippers', *India-West* (31 March 1995), p. A1, 12.

38. It is important to mention this, as some people may argue that American or white Hindus are more likely to adopt the orthodox versions of the faith than Indian Hindus in the United States. White Sikhs, for instance, are known to be more rigidly observant of the symbols and practices of their faith than Indian Sikhs.

39. R. S. Sharma, *In Defence of 'Ancient India'*, pp. 20–1.

40. The most obvious sense in which Muslims are claimed as Hindus rests

upon the acceptance of various strands of the argument. One has to accept that the bulk of the Muslims in South Asia were converts, which would appear to be true, as well as the further implication, of considerable importance to the Hindutvavadi claim, that conversion was largely forcible—and is, therefore, justifiably reversible. Hindutva ideologues do not engage with the problem that people can choose to convert, since this is a problem, in their view, for philosophers rather than for those attuned to 'real' histories. They assume as well that identity is framed by ancestral 'origins', and that a certain kind of false consciousness prevents South Asian Muslims from seeing themselves as Hindus. The fetishization of 'origins', and the zealous attack on the zealotry of converts, are indispensable elements of the Hindutvavadi claim about the 'true' identity of South Asian Muslims. But there is another argument, far subtler, to which recourse is sometimes taken, and it runs as follows: Since it is the genius of Hinduism that it is particularly tolerant and ecumenical, the true Hindu encompasses within himself the cardinal elements of the religious beliefs associated with Muslims, Christians, and practitioners of other faiths. The good Hindu is perforce a good Muslim and a good Christian, but the reverse is unquestionably false: the opposition is of the inclusive whole to the exclusive part. Logically, then, the good Muslim can only be good by forsaking Islam.

41. Madhav Sadashiv Golwalkar's *We or Our Nationhood Defined* (1939), one of the foundational texts of Hindu militancy, had this to say about Muslims and other 'foreigners' in India: 'The foreign races in Hindusthan must either adopt the Hindu culture and language, must learn to respect and hold in reverence Hindu religion, must entertain no idea but those of the glorification of the Hindu race and culture, i.e., of the Hindu nation and must lose their separate existence to merge in the Hindu race, or may stay in the country, wholly subordinated to the Hindu Nation, claiming nothing, deserving no privileges, far less any preferential treatment—not even citizen's rights.' Cited by A. G. Noorani, *The RSS and the BJP: A Division of Labour*, 2nd edn (New Delhi: LeftWord Books, 2001), p. 20.

42. For a critical commentary, see Asghar Ali Engineer, 'Minorities Cannot Be at the Mercy of RSS', *Secular Perspective* (1–15 April 2002).

43. Quoted in Vishwa Hindu Parishad of Chicago, *Seventeenth Annual Calendar*, 1995 (Chicago: Vishwa Hindu Parishad, 1995).

44. One could point to the financial activities of the World Hindu Council, or Vishwa Hindu Parishad (VHP), or the support lavished upon the Hawaii-based newspaper *Hinduism Today*, which is devoted to diasporic Hinduism, by the Hindu Heritage Endowment. VHP-America became a registered non-profit organization in the 1970s; its IRS code is 051–0156325, and its donors— American Cancer Society, the Salvation Army, United Way (Alexandria, Virginia), India Culture Society, Chinmaya Mission, and many more—include corporations, universities, other non-profit organizations, and numerous wealthy individuals. The financial dealings of the VHP are discussed by

Biju Mathew, 'Byte-Sized Nationalism: Mapping the Hindu Right in the United States', *Rethinking Marxism* 12, no. 3 (Fall 2000), pp. 121–5. See also Ajit Jha, 'Saffron Sees Red; Secular groups pose a challenge to the Hindutva brigade', *India Today* (15 August 1993), p. 56g, and A. Rogers, 'India Seeks Financial Help from Overseas Indians', *Traces World News Digest 3* (July–September 1998), available online at: <*http://www.transcomm.ox.ac.uk*>.

45. *Indian Express* (16 January 1993), various city editions; the ad was reprinted in *India-West* (12 February 1993). It is heartening to note that a group of people describing themselves as 'Indian Citizens in India' placed an ad in the same newspapers (*Indian Express*, 26 January 1993; *India-West*, 12 February 1993) questioning the political and ethical propriety of nonresident Hindus: 'Is it not presumptuous of the Indians who left 'mother Bharat' and caused a severe brain drain to dictate how we Indians, who remained behind should run our country?' There was no ban on Hindutva organizations, but the rumour took on a life of its own—as indeed rumours do.

46. Federation of Hindus-Associations, *Bhagwan's Call for Dharma Raksha* [including the publication *Hinduism Simplified*] (Diamond Bar, California: FHA, [1999?]).

47. See the letter, protesting the award, by Vinay Lal et al. in *India-West* (23 June 1995), p. 5.

48. See Sudhir Kakar, *The Colours of Violence* (Delhi: Viking, 1995), pp. 197–214, for the analysis of a similar speech by Sadhvi Rithambara.

49. Among observing Hindus, it is widely believed that the water (*jal*) of the Ganga is sacred, and dying persons are often given a sip of this water to provide them solace and ease their passage into the next life. This Ganga jal is sometimes stored in a bottle at home.

50. See Luther P. Gerlach and Virginia Hine, *People, Power, Change: Movements of Social Transformation* (New York: The Bobbs-Merrill Co., 1970), and Luther P. Gerlach, 'Protest Movements and the Construction of Risk', in B. B. Johnson and V. T. Covello (eds), *The Social Construction of Risk* (Boston: D. Reidel, 1987), p. 115, as cited by Ronfeldt et al., *The Zapatista Social Netwar*, p. 114.

51. On 'swarming' and 'flooding', see Ronfeldt et al., *The Zapatista Social Netwar*, but also: Stefan Wray, 'Transforming Luddite Resistance into Virtual Luddite Resistance: Weaving a World Wide Web of Electronic Civil Disobedience', April 7, 1998, at: <*http://www.nyu.edu/projects/wray/luddite.html*>.

Needless to say, '330 million' is merely a conventional number, but the anxiety experienced by diasporic Hindus that this subjects Hinduism to mockery is once again amply witnessed in *Bhagwan's Call for Dharma Raksha* and scores of other like publications. In a section under 'Hinduism Simplified', this 'problem' of 'millions Gods' [sic] is described as 'lots of misunderstandings', and later, in a portion entitled 'What Hinduism Is Not?', it is averred that 'Hinduism is not a religion of 330 million Gods. In fact, it is monotheistic polytheism' (unpaginated).

52. Arjun Appadurai, 'Global Ethnoscapes: Notes and Queries for a Transnational Anthropology', in Richard G. Fox (ed.), *Recapturing Anthropology: Working in the Present* (Santa Fe: School of American Research Publications, 1991), p. 202.

53. Steven Vertovec, 'Three Meanings of 'Diaspora', Exemplified among South Asian Religions', *Diaspora* 6, no. 3 (1997), p. 281.

54. All these instances are drawn from the 'Library of Hindu History', which can be found at: *<http://www.vhp.org/hindu_history>*.

55. *<http://www.tezcat.com/~bnaik/chinmaya.html>*.

56. See *<http://www.bjp.org>* and *<http://www.rss.org>*.

57. 'Award Recipient', *India-West* (15 March 1996), p. C20.

58. *<http://rbhatnagar.csm.uc.edu:8080/kashmir/html>*. Over four dozen articles are linked to the page.

59. See *<http://hindunet.org/srh_home/1997_12/0040.html>* for an article, reproduced from the *Times of India* (22 December 1997), by Srichand P. Hinduja entitled 'All Indians are Hindus'.

60. *<http://rbhatnagar.csm.uc.edu:8080/ramjanmabhoomi.html>*.

61. A partial profile of the membership of the RSS and the supporters of Hindutva can be found in Tapan Basu et al., *Khaki Shorts and Saffron Flags*.

62. See Ashis Nandy et al., *Creating a Nationality*.

63. Narendra Nath Datta (1863–1902), better known as Swami Vivekananda, was the chief disciple of Sri Ramakrishna, a renowned Bengali mystic who is often seen as one of the supreme embodiments of Indian spirituality. Vivekananda established the Ramakrishna Mission, and so introduced not only a new monastic order, but also a set of charitable institutions, such as schools and hospitals, which are still active in India today. He took the teachings of Hinduism to the West, propagated a more integral version of the faith, and urged the youth to work towards a 'new India'. Though his master, Sri Ramakrishna, could become delirious with devotion to Kali, Vivekananda is said to have attached more importance to social work and intellectual discrimination as modes of apprehending the divine.

64. Large statues of Vivekananda have been installed recently in both Trinidad and Chicago.

65. *<http://rbhatnagar.csm.uc.edu:8080/vivekananda/as_interview>*.

66. *<http://rbhatnagar.csm.uc.edu:8080/vivekananda/as_interview>*.

67 The Vishwa Hindu Parishad of the United States has embraced an expansionist program for the Indian nation-state. One of its recent publications cites, with evident approval, the cherished hope of the R.S.S. that the 'next century will surely [be] the Hindu century', and should this sound implausible, readers are reminded that after the 'Mahabharatha War, our culture spread to China, Japan and [the] Americas. The Red Indians of America are the descendants of Hindus who went there some 4000 years ago.' These are the words of K. S. Sudharshan, 'Sat Sarkaryavah' (Joint General Secretary) of the R.S.S. (Rashtriya Swayamsevak Sangh), quoted in *V.H.P.'s 14th Anniversary 1992 Calendar* (Chicago: V.H.P., 1992), p. 1.

68. <*http://rbhatnagar.csm.uc.edu:8080/vivekananda/gv_2000_talks/ sr_rss_fulfills*>.

69. The episode is discussed in Ramachandra Gandhi, *Sita's Kitchen*, p. 10. The discussion by Rajni Bakshi, *The Dispute over Swami Vivekananda's Legacy: A Warning and an Opportunity* (Mapusa, Goa: The Other India Press, 1994), is of some use.

70. Swami Vivekananda, 'The Future of India', in *Complete Works of Swami Vivekananda*, 8 vols (Mayavati, India: Advaita Ashram, 1964), 3:289.

71. Ibid.

72. See <*http://www.flex.com/~jai/satyamevajayate*>.

73. <*http://members.aol.com/_ht_a/Jyotishi/index.html*>.

74. 'Prophet of Terror and the Religion of Peace—Part I', at: <*http://www. flex.com~jai/satyamevajayate/mohwar1.html*>. Part III is available at 'mohwar3'.

75. 'The X-Rated Paradise of Islam', at: <*http://www.flex.com/~jai/satyame vajayate/heaven.html*>.

76. An impressive web site, designed from the standpoint of Indian nationalism, is devoted to the 1971 war of 'Liberation' that led to the decimation of Pakistan and the creation of the new sovereign state of Bangladesh: see <*http://freeindia.org/1971war*>.

77. See the e-mail message, 17 October 1999 [available from <*devant@ tstt.net.tt*>] by Aditi Chaturvedi, entitled 'Undermining Hinduism by Labeling it as Mythology', which begins thus: 'Last month *Indian Express* inaugurated their new site on Hinduism and contemptuously titled it "www.hindumythology.com". The title of course is a not so subtle reflection of the regard that *Indian Express* has for Hindu beliefs. The implicit suggestion is clearly motivated by a negative approach towards Hinduism. *Obviously many Hindus on the net are not very happy at having their spiritual beliefs termed as "mythology"* (emphasis added)'. I by no means wish to convey the impression that myths do not on occasion create their own oppressions, but it has been one of the main burdens of this book to suggest that secularists and their 'fundamentalist' foes are united in their aversion for myth, and it is the consensus behind history as a form of knowledge that has barely been investigated or critiqued.

78. Jawaharlal Nehru, *The Discovery of India*, p. 102.

79. Among the more naïve of such attempts to furnish Indians with a historical sensibility is Peter van der Veer's *Religious Nationalism*; among the more complex efforts to contest the colonial charge that Indians were insensitive to historical thinking is the influential work by Nicholas Dirks, *The Hollow Crown*. It is possible to agree with the Orientalist reading that Indians did not produce a historical literature; but that cannot be taken as signifying one's consent with the proposition that this was a 'lack' as such. The ahistoricity of the Indian sensibility remains one of the most attractive features of Indian civilization. See the discussion in Chapter 1, above.

80. Ibid., p. 102.

81. <http://www.vhp.org> 'History of Hindu Temples'.

82. <http://www.hindunet.org/alt_hindu/1994/msg00658.html>.

83. Rajiv Varma, 'The Magnitude of Muslim Atrocities' and 'Destruction of Hindu Temples by Aurangzeb': <http://www.hindunet.org/hindu_history>.

84. Though there are many Indian cuisines, they have been reduced to north Indian tandoori food in the diaspora; similarly, though there are several dance forms—Kathak, Odissi, Bharat Natyam, Manipuri, among others—Bharat Natyam, literally 'the dance of India', reigns supreme among diasporic Indian women, or rather their parents. Ironically, as much recent scholarship has established, Bharat Natyam, seen in the diaspora as an embodiment of the timeless cultural traditions of an ancient civilization, is not unreasonably described as an 'invented tradition', and in its present form it was essentially revived in the early twentieth century. [See, for example, Avanthi Meduri, 'Bharatha Natyam—What Are You?' Asian Theatre Journal 5, 1 (Spring 1988), pp. 1–23.] Scholars of the Indian diaspora have not been sufficiently attentive to these kinds of considerations, just as they have studiously ignored the place of the commercial Hindi cinema in the diaspora. Far too much attention has been lavished on Gurinder Chadha, Hanif Kureishi, Mira Nair, and Deepa Mehta, though Indian families show comparatively little interest in these films. Indeed, these films point to an emerging history of the Indian diaspora as consumption for advocates of multiculturalism; meanwhile, in Indonesia, Fiji, Mauritius, Canada, Guyana, the US, and elsewhere the popular Hindi film continues to provide the Indian population, and often the 'locals', with some clues about the mythic structuring of their civilization.

85. <http://www.hindunet.org/alt.hindu/1994/msg00365.html> and <http://www.spiritweb.org/HinduismToday/94-08-Fiji_Temple_Burned.html>.

86. <http://hindunet.org/hindu_history/modern/hindu_kush.html>.

87. See <http://jammu-kashmir.org/KIN/Atrocities/index.html>.

88. <http://www.flex.com/~jai/satyamevajayate/temples4.html>.

89. <http://hindunet.org/hindu_history>.

90. The following articles, by Dr. P. V. Vartak and others, in the 'Library of Hindu History' are useful: 'Mahabharata: A Myth of Reality'; 'The Mahabharat Chronology'; 'Mahabharat: An Astronomical Proof from the Bhagavat Purana'; 'The Scientific Dating of the Mahabharat War'; and 'Astronomical Dating of the Ramayan', all to be found at: <http://www.hindunet.org/hindu_history>. The attempt in each case, wholly unsuccessful, is to provide a firm date for events described in the Ramayana and the Mahabharata. Why this might be important for Hindutvavadis can be understood, as I have argued in Chapter I, from the fact that the earliest firm (or nearly firm) dates that can be furnished for ancient Indian history relate to the lives of the Buddha (founder of Buddhism) and Mahavira (founder of Jainism), both of whom signaled their dissent from Hinduism in the sixth century BCE. The mythicity of Hinduism was never much of an embarrassment to Hindus until the nineteenth

century, and the ascendancy of history, alongside the emergence of the nation-state, has greatly accelerated the process in the period after independence. An engaging perspective on these questions, focusing on the Tamils and Sinhalese in Sri Lanka, is to be found in E. Valentine Daniel, *Charred Lullabies: Chapters in an Anthropology of Violence* (Princeton: Princeton University Press, 1996).

91. Aryan Invasion Theory Links can be found at: <*http://www.vhp.org/hindu_history*>.

See also the lengthy article by David Frawley, 'The Myth of the Aryan Invasion of India', which claims that the Aryans dispersed from India to the rest of the world: <*http://www.spiritweb.org/Spirit/myth-of-invasion.html*>.

Frawley and Keonraad Elst, whose support of Hindutva history and politics is unequivocal, are widely cited in Hindutva histories. For all their nationalism, Hindutvavadis still crave recognition by the white man.

92. One small exception is the Forum of the Indian Left, a New York-based organization, which hosts four or five articles on Indian history on its web site. See <*http://www.foil.org/history*>.

Postscript

Since this book was completed in the autumn of 2002, the most significant development in Indian politics is doubtless the electoral defeat of the Bharatiya Janata Party (BJP) and its allies in the election of 2004. That was, I am inclined to believe, a—what else—shining moment in Indian democracy. Indeed, it was India's moment in the world, notwithstanding the fact that the Indian elections received only a fraction of the coverage extended to the American elections, with its predictably calamitous results, later in the year.[1] It is, of course, possible and even reasonable to aver that such shifts in political power are precisely the kind of rearrangements that modern democracies permit to prevent more radical alterations in the socio-economic and political life of the nation. Some commentators have been merely inclined to attribute the defeat of the BJP to what they call the 'anti-incumbency' factor, though this appears to be more of a magical incantation than anything that might pass for reasoned analysis. Apparently, on this view, in 'mature' democracies the electorate is guided by issues, but a democracy of the developing world operates more on the instinct and whimsy of its subjects. The proverbial capriciousness of the Oriental despot is now replaced by the arbitrariness of the masses, one kind of effeminacy paves way for another form of feebleness. Moreover, while it is transparent that the BJP's pompous advertising blitzkrieg, most conspicuously captured in the slogan 'India Shining', did not go down well with a considerable segment of the Indian population, it is far from certain, at this juncture, that the victors will be more sensitive to the growing disparities between the elites and the subalterns and initiate policies designed to ameliorate the growing distress of farmers, ordinary wage labourers, and others who clearly have not profited from what is described as a booming economy. No one should view the results as a triumph, much less an unequivocal victory, for the Congress and its allies, and even those who rejoice that the central government under whose watch the Gujarat pogrom of 2002 took place now stands evicted from power should perhaps be reminded that the perpetrators of the massacres of 1984, openly aided and abetted by the Congress party in the nation's capital, have yet to be brought to justice.[2]

Still, the elections of 2004 were a supreme moment in India's modern history, and the reasons for that are less removed from the subject matter of this book than one might imagine. Since the late 1980s, sternly secular commentators have been issuing ominous warnings about India's decline into 'fascism'. These warnings were greatly accelerated after the Babri Masjid was brought down in 1992, and are invariably revived at pivotal moments—the nuclear tests of 1998, the rapid passage of the draconian piece of legislation known as the Prevention of Terrorism Act (POTA), and the brutal killings of Muslims in Gujarat easily come to mind as greatly troubling moments in recent years—or when the intellectual and cultural institutions of the country seem to be placed under immense threat. The word 'fascism' has been routinely encountered in the debates over history textbooks and in the numerous allegations against scholars, whether Indian or foreign, who are viewed by advocates of Hindutva as having inflicted unjust blows upon Hinduism, the cultural heritage of India, or the history of India's supposed martial heroes. Institutions as diverse as the Indian Council of Historical Research (ICHR) and the Bhandarkar Oriental Research Institute (BORI) are said to have been savaged by fascists, and the brutal vandalization of the latter institution, which led to the destruction of priceless manuscripts, certainly stands out as dire testimony to the fact that the goons who now view themselves as the arbiters of India's cultural heritage cannot be summarily dismissed as mere irritants. The hullabaloo, on the one hand, over M. F. Husain's paintings of an Hindu goddess in the nude, or Deepa Mehta's proposed film on Hindu widows in Varanasi, and attempts, on the other hand, to resuscitate the political reputations of Vinayak Damodar Savarkar, one of the principal architects of Hindutva ideology, and Nathuram Godse, the assassin of Mohandas Gandhi, have been put forth as ominous examples of fascism's creeping influence in India.[3] If these appear to be palpably true illustrations both of fascism's intolerance for what it takes to be degenerate art and its embrace of the killers of Gandhi, then it is worth considering that even the popular Indian film *Roja* (1992), which most viewers will remember as something of a political thriller with haunting songs, became to many of its dissenters an example of an insidious fascism.[4]

Historians were among the academics and intellectuals who were most insistent in using the word fascism to describe 'the cultures of cruelty' spawned by right-wing politics.[5] Though the cultural historian M. S. S. Pandian was among the first to highlight fascism in the political career of the famous star of Tamil cinema,[6] M. G. Ramachandran, the opening salvo in the historians' war on Indian fascism was fired by Sumit Sarkar, the deservedly famous historian of the Swadeshi movement. Sarkar identified many features common to European fascism and what he called 'the fascism of the Sangh Parivar', from their careful orchestration of street violence to the 'deep infiltration' of fascist elements into the bureaucracy, the police, and the army. Sarkar noted that fascist regimes are unabashed violators of the law even as they profess deference and respect for the law.[7] Of course, any such definition would make a fascist of many contemporary politicians, the pack being led by the leader of the 'free world', George W. Bush. We need not, however, be detained by this consideration, nor by the objection that the classic fascist state was 'not just a very authoritarian form of rightwing reactionary nationalism in power but a very special kind of authoritarian state representing the most *extreme form of political centralization* ... necessitated by the exceptional severity of the crisis faced by capitalism in the country concerned.'[8] Sumit Sarkar was by no means the first commentator to point to fascist tendencies inherent in certain strands of Indian politics, and it is remarkable that in December 1947, more than a month before the assassination of Gandhi and the subsequent ban on the RSS, Jawaharlal Nehru, in one of his weekly letters to Chief Ministers of Indian provinces, warned that 'we have a great deal of evidence to show that the Rashtriya Swayamsevak Sangh is an organization which is in the nature of a private army and which is definitely proceeding on the strictest Nazi lines, even following the technique of organization.'[9] It is, consequently, not the originality of Sarkar's observations, but rather the respect that he has earned as a professional historian, which has given his writings on contemporary politics wide circulation. Sarkar has insisted on deploying the term 'fascism', and has been followed by many other historians, social scientists, and political commentators. Thus K. N. Panikkar, associated until recently with the Center for Historical Studies at Jawaharlal Nehru University, has unequivocally described the character of Hindutva's politics as incorporating 'the familiar fascist traits of irrationality and coercion, as evidenced, among others, by the movement culminating in the demolition of the Babri Masjid.'[10]

The debate on how far militant Hindu nationalism can be assimilated to the phenomenon of fascism has, then, persisted for a long time in Indian left circles. There is much in this debate to fascinate nominalists, but it is clear that apparently opposed parties to this debate were agreed, at least before the elections of mid-2004, that much of India was falling into the vice-like grip of forces representing an extreme and violent form of chauvinist Hinduism. 'Those who believe that fascism has arrived may not be very much off the mark,' wrote Panikkar sometime after the Gujarat killings, 'as it is only waiting to cross the doorsteps when the state and society finally succumb to Hindutva.'[11] The triumph of the BJP in the Assembly elections of late 2003 across a number of states in north India further appeared to convey the impression that Hindutva had made deep, and possibly irreversible, gains among ordinary people. Few liberal or left commentators unabashedly condemned what they were at least privately inclined to view as the mainstay of the BJP and its allies, namely the unwashed and superstitious masses of the much derided 'cow belt', but BJP's electoral gains in 2003, and the confidence exuded by the party's leaders and their supporters, did not fill them with much hope that fascism's forces could be defeated in the general elections. Several dozen Delhi-based academics, writers, and other public figures constituted themselves into the 'BJP Harao Manch' [Defeat BJP Forum] in March 2004, a month before the elections were to commence, and their manifesto enjoined upon the people to understand that 'this is the most crucial election since Independence.[12] At stake is the survival of India's republican constitution and the plural, democratic conception of society on which it is based and which it defends.' Yet the singular fact remains that virtually no commentator, however bold or strident the appeals to defeat the BJP and the wider National Democratic Alliance (NDA), thought the circumstances warranted an optimistic reading.

Fascists may call for elections and indeed are very likely to do so. They find it pleasing to think that they are loved by the people whom they oppress. 'Fascism sees its salvation in giving these masses not their right,' wrote Walter Benjamin, whose own run from the fascists might have been successful but for the bureaucratic traps that all modern nation-states have set for 'aliens', 'but instead a chance to express themselves.'[13] We have all heard of fascists and despots—Saddam Hussein in Iraq, Houphouet-Boigny in the Ivory Coast,

Mobutu Sese Soko in Zaire—who have won 99 percent of the popular vote. But fascists who surrender power after an electoral defeat have seldom before been encountered, and the electoral results of 2004, while they by no means led to a resounding victory for the Congress and its allies, dealt a crushing blow to the BJP and its allies. (This was followed, later in 2004, by a humiliating defeat for the Shiv Sena, an intensely xenophobic political party which prizes itself on its open and violent intimidation of Muslims and certain ethnic communities, in its own backyard of the state of Maharashtra.) If fascism was already at the doorsteps, only waiting to be invited in, or ready to make a bid for power at the slightest opportunity, one must explain not merely the normal transfer of power of the kind that one encounters in democracies that was effected after the BJP's defeat, but, even more significantly, the clear repudiation by the electorate of the BJP and the ruling alliance. The BJP had, stepping into the elections, grounds to be complacent—or so it seemed to large segments of the population, if the opinion polls are an even remotely reliable barometer. The BJP's victories in the assembly elections apart, the Indian cricketing team had done rather well. The Italian-born Sonia Gandhi was trumpeted as the sure sign of Congress's desperation, indeed of the reversals of fortune of the party that wrought India's independence and was now, it was insinuated, shamelessly compromising India's integrity. The monsoon rains had once again been good, and food stocks stood at a record high; the economy was described as 'booming', and whatever the cynics might have said, India's foreign exchange reserves had skyrocketed to levels all but inconceivable a few years ago. Though the BJP's advocacy of realpolitik, its open advocacy of the interests of Hindus and withering contempt for what it described as pseudo-secularists, and undiminished zeal in promoting the territorial integrity of India appeared to offer conclusive proof of its resolve to yield nothing to Pakistan, the BJP had nonetheless entered into peace negotiations with its traditional foe. Many experienced in this circumstance alone an element of surprise somewhat akin to the surprise with which many seasoned observers received Ronald Reagan's overtures to Mikhail Gorbachev, chief representative of what the American President had characterized as the 'evil empire'. The BJP's supporters and detractors alike had, apparently, every reason to think that its victory was a foregone conclusion.

Whatever the shortcomings of electoral democracy in India, the untutored Indian voter still retains the capacity to surprise and inflict punishment. The BJP had sought to make light of the killings of 2000 or more people, predominantly Muslims, in Gujarat. Narendra Modi, far from being chastised, had even been rewarded as senior BJP leaders campaigned by his side. That there should have been no adverse consequences for the BJP was perhaps one thought that did not go down well with some voters, or, to put this in another vein, the vote in 2004 sought to provide affirmation of forms of pluralism that the perpetrators of the killings and their patrons were determined to reject. Political commentators scrambled to find other explanations for the electoral defeat of the BJP as well as of its supposedly unimpeachable allies, such as the Telugu Desam party led by the self-styled CEO of Andhra Pradesh, Chandrababu Naidu. In seeking to turn Hyderabad into a hub for information technology, a modern city of corporate parks and sleek glass towers, Naidu had earned the plaudits of India's elite. The foreign investment pouring into the city was construed as an unmistakable sign of the approbation with which the actions of this progressive, broad-minded, and ambitious Chief Minister were received by overseas investors and venture capitalists. But, in opting for the information superhighway, Naidu had clearly overlooked the needs of those who, not to speak of highways, are content with ordinary paved roads. The plight of Andhra's farmers, some 200 of whom were committing suicide every month, was making news around India. The 'predatory commercialization of the countryside', as Professor K. Nagaraj of the Madras Institute of Development Studies puts it, had gone much further under Naidu's watch.[14] Whatever the achievements of specialists in virtual reality, they appeared incapable of meeting the needs of those in the real world. The government boasted of immense stocks of grain, but nearly half the country's own population suffered from malnutrition. All over the country, the ordinary infrastructure fell under disrepair as the elites, constituting no more than a minuscule portion of the population, opted for private (and generally more expensive) services, turning to cell phones in place of land lines, resorting to courier services rather than to the government-owned India Post, and embracing the automobile in lieu of public transportation. Certainly not many in the BJP appeared to have noticed that the claim of 'India Shining' did not speak to the condition of the majority.

The 2004 elections in India point, as others besides myself have observed, to the disconnect between two (and some will say many more) Indias. This disconnect is often represented as the gulf between urban and rural populations, the city and the countryside, the educated and the illiterate, and the modernizing middle classes (many with at least one relative settled in the affluent portion of the Indian diaspora) and those larger segments of the population still entwined in traditional lifestyles. These distinctions are not, in general, without their salience, though one must obviously question the approbation with which the first term of each pair is viewed by most modern commentators. Ever the champion of the urban proletariat, Marx could still speak casually of the 'idiocy of the rural countryside'. If at least a few forms of dissent emanate from among those who have been the beneficiaries of higher education, it is also the educated who have enthusiastically championed the emergence of Hindutva politics and see resurgent Hindu pride in the nation and its history as the *sine qua non* of India's imagined ascent to world power status.[15]

The Indian elections furnish very good reasons for the extreme suspicion with which we should view the tendency, common among the educated middle-classes, to decry the rural, substantially illiterate, and allegedly custom-bound population as a force that has kept India from flourishing and realizing its full potential. Students of Indian politics have doubtless much to explain about the circumstances that led the BJP and its allies to an electoral defeat, and there is, obviously, also reason to aver to the immense disjunctions between the everyday Hinduisms of common practitioners of the faith and the rigorous championing of militant Hinduism by Ashok Singhal, Uma Bharati, and the goons of the Bajrang Dal and the Shiv Sena. Though Indian leftists have been staunchly committed to secularism and have every reason to feel satisfied by the outcome of their principled opposition to religious extremism, their worldview cannot be reconciled so easily with the worldview of India's rural masses. Admirable, again, as has been the role of secular and progressive organizations, such as SAHMAT and ANHAD, as well as various Ekta committees in various cities,[16] in combating communalism, it would be an immense stretch to suppose that their activities were instrumental in swaying the electorate to reject the BJP and its allies at the polls. A strong predisposition towards technology, the regime of science, and the ideology of development have long characterized the Indian left,[17] and the dream that India should become a proper and modern nation-state is one that the Indian left, notwithstanding the critique of Indian nationalism encountered among some of its adherents, shares with the Hindu right. The non-modern sectors of the population—the much-derided and allegedly backward people of what is jeeringly called the 'cow belt' or 'saffron belt' of north India—also played their part in dealing an uneven hand to the twin constituencies of Hindu nationalists and technocrats. Whatever the enlightened commentators might tell us about 'tolerance' being a supremely Enlightenment virtue, or the lessons that India should allegedly derive from the multicultural societies of the modern West, the people of India showed themselves capable of exercising judgments that the more educated sectors of the population have seldom displayed. These ordinary Indians derive their values not from the world of modern science, but from what might be described as 'customs in common', lifeforms shared between adherents of different languages, religions, and even castes.

It is my submission that the disconnect between the two Indias can also be read as the gulf between those Indians who are comfortably attuned to discourses of history and have embraced the historical sensibility, if only as one of the indispensable accoutrements of modern citizenship, and those Indians who still dwell largely in the house of myth. In one of its forms, more pertinent to the narratives that inform this book, this disconnect can also be described as a divide, certainly in India, between the professional historian and the wider public, but let me turn to the question of historians and their audiences shortly. This divide might have appeared to some readers of this book as far too sharply etched, as some kind of naked opposition between history and myth, and to other readers, who are entirely predisposed towards viewing Hindutva as the skillful manipulation of histories to manufacture myths, as a divide which I endorse, considering that I have been at pains to show Hindutva's attachment to scientific history and its palpable addiction to facticity, by embracing it from the wrong side. Neither view should be allowed to occlude the fact that my book is centrally about history-making, and those who have closely followed the arguments of this book will come to the recognition that, in my view, communalists and secularists alike are deeply committed to the enterprise of history. Some might be tempted to affiliate my position to the view voiced by K. R. Malkani, a Hindutva ideologue: 'The fact is that there is often more history in myths and more myth in history.'[18] Whatever the merits of this position, I would assert that in the debates which have transpired between communalists and secularists there has been far too little invested by either side in Indian myths and the cultural worlds to which myth-making gives shape. How else can one fathom the irony that communalists, who otherwise pose as ardent and profound defenders of the unique worldview said to inform Hinduism, object to secular histories on the grounds that they are not sufficiently attentive to facts and not sufficiently respectful of history's scientificity?

A dramatic illustration of the immense distance between those who are enamored of the protocols of history, enamoured enough—in the case of communalists—to create new protocols as well, and those who have watched the ascendancy of history and now given voice to their disquiet, is furnished by the long career and work of Romila Thapar. Her recent, somewhat voluminous, study of Somnath (or, in its Sanskritized form, Somanatha) will, in due course, suffice more than adequately as a brief case study of the Indian historians' supreme indifference to reading publics.[19] She might seem, in the first instance, as a poor candidate for the views I wish to advance here, if indeed the object of my views were to summon her as an instance of a professional historian who does not deign to address anyone outside the fraternity of historians. Quite to the contrary, Thapar is perhaps exemplary as the historian who has made a serious endeavour, at least in the recent years of her lengthy academic career, to (in the jargon of the day) 'reach out' to wider audiences. Her pieces are frequently encountered in the opinion-editorial pages of English-language newspapers, she appears on the lecture circuits in India and the Unites States more frequently than any other historian of India (and certainly pre-modern India), and interviews with her have proliferated over the course of the last decade.[20] Thapar's appointment to the Kluge Chair at the Library of Congress generated a firewall of controversy, or more accurately a sustained campaign by her critics, drawn from the ranks of the professional Indian communities in the United States rather than from academia, to have her appointment aborted. One can be quite certain that, notwithstanding any intellectual objections that her critics were able to muster, the ire directed at her was in proportion to the immense public stature that she has occupied in the arena of Indian history. What seemed intolerable to her critics was that Thapar should have become the public face of Indian history.

What is the interface between professional historians and the wider public? Writing in a recent issue of the respected Delhi journal, *Seminar*, an issue significantly devoted to 'Rewriting History', Partha Chatterjee makes the useful point that 'high' academic history in India is an enterprise confined to an extraordinarily small group of scholars and publishers. The Indian historians who are published by prestigious publishing houses and whose articles appear in some leading journals come from 'no more than half a dozen institutions in

India,' and the bulk of them, as a recent survey showed, are from a single city, Delhi. The products of academic history, Chatterjee argues, have made their way into fiction, cinema, and theatre, but he suggests that academic historians have seldom displayed any interest in understanding how other forms of recounting the past come to occupy a place in the public sphere.[21] Historians might not recognize anything of their work in the numerous TV serials on historical subjects, in the growing genre of Bollywood films devoted to nationalist figures and the anti-colonial struggle, or in the new Hindu temples with their dioramic representations of famous patriots alongside Hindu gods and goddesses, and they might even be repulsed by mutilations, manglings, and incongruent adaptations of their work. Yes, as Chatterjee warns, 'by looking aghast and turning away from what people have done to our carefully researched histories, we [historians] only reinforce our insularity.' This insularity is heightened, argues Chatterjee, by the fact that professional history in India is practiced very largely in English.[22]

What kind of publics does, then, Romila Thapar address? No Indian historian has been more insistent publicly about the observation of protocols of historical scholarship, and advocates of Hindutva who have ventured into academic history have repeatedly been chastised by Thapar for their failure to respect the procedures of the discipline, their cavalier dismissal of facts, their ignorance of elementary rules of citation, their attempt to furnish myths with respectability, and their wilful manipulation of histories in the service of an ideological politics. Many of those she admonishes inhabit decidedly provincial worlds of scholarship, and to them English, the only language in which Thapar writes,[23] is almost certainly a second language. Surprisingly, for someone who works principally in ancient Indian history, and whose work can be expected to show familiarity with the Ramayana and the voluminous puranic literature, Thapar treats the puranic and mythic literature purely as material to be worked on, rather than as a corpus of literature that might yield an aesthetics and epistemology which might be deployed to question a modern aesthetics of time, memory, history, narrative, and chronology, or modern notions of event, occurrence, and repetition.

Thapar's recent book on Somnath suggests that she works with an expansive conception of sources. In 1026, as is well-known, Mahmud of Ghazni raided the temple of Somnath; he plundered it of its wealth and broke the idol. Thapar disavows any ambition of attempting to discern just what happened during that raid, or provide a reconstruction of the events, and she justly states that it is rather more productive to understand how the varying sources provide different perspectives on the events at Somnath, and how these events came to be remembered over time. She draws upon contemporary or near contemporary chronicles written in Persian and Arabic, Sanskrit inscriptions from Somnath and the area around it, Jaina chronicles, the Rajput epic tradition, the writings of Muslim historians such as Ferishta, British narratives, and the writings of Indian nationalists and some contemporary commentators. Why should Thapar have had to write a book on Somnath? The reasons are obvious, and as I have discussed the enduring topicality of Somnath elsewhere in the book, they need not now be delineated at length. Hindu nationalist forces were rallying around Somnath even before independence, and the reconstruction of Somnath after the attainment of independence has been pointed to as an example of what can be achieved if Hindu nationalists remain uncompromising.[24] The Rath Yatra of 1990 commenced at Somnath, and the ideologues of the BJP and VHP were keen that the history of Ayodhya should, in popular consciousness, be linked to the history of Somnath. But perhaps the most pressing reason for writing such a history is that no one's name is more calculated to send the Indian middle-class into a seething fury than Mahmud of Ghazni, and nothing has appeared to them to stand for the victimization of Hindu India as much as the desecration of Somnath. In the middle-class communities around which I grew up, Somnath was a keyword well before Advani's jaunt through Bharat. Yet, for all her interest in seeing how the events at Somnath have been understood through the ages by diverse Indian communities, and what traces of this history reside in the present, Thapar does not enter into middle-class drawing rooms. An ethnography of the present might, perhaps, have told her more about Somnath's traces than the meticulous devotion to her source material.

Historians, thankfully, are not missionaries, and no one is asking Thapar, who is, I suspect, not altogether bereft of that missionary spirit which lurks behind history's most enthusiastic proponents, to convert the obdurate advocates of Hindutva to an acceptance of more reasonable histories. Yet Thapar stands in a more ambiguous relationship to these communities than their indifference to her historical scholarship, or her occlusion of their worldviews, suggests. History is, in these educated middle-class communities, one of the currencies in which ideas are traded, and Hindutva's ideologues are applauded by many educated Hindus for not surrendering the domain of history entirely to secular or professional historians. The precise contours of Thapar's arguments might be somewhat obscure to this emerging class of educated Indians, but they are increasingly comfortable with discourses of history even as they might be little conversant with the protocols of historical scholarship. To some extent, they even embody a healthy disdain for expert knowledge, though almost nothing has irked Thapar as much as the supposition that history is anyone's territory for asking. The journalist who remembered her lectures at the University of California, Berkeley in November 2002 with the newspaper heading, 'Historian Says Hindutwa Threat to Scientific Inquiry', appears to have grasped Thapar's disdain for those who treat history with anything less than the respect due to a demanding discipline with scientific standing.[25] If Thapar's disconnect with these new and fellow votaries of history is so considerable, what of the disconnect with those for whom Somnath is not history—not even a name? Luckily for India, its future does not reside, not yet in any case, with those who think that history is the only game in town.

VINAY LAL
Los Angeles, 30 January 2005

ENDNOTES

1. I have discussed both elections at greater length in 'India's Moment', *Humanscape* 11, no. 6 (June 2004), 8–9 and 'US Elections: What the Electorate Voted For', *Economic and Political Weekly* 39, nos. 46–47 (20 November 2004), pp. 4986–87.

2. The recent interim report (January 2005) of retired Supreme Court justice U. C. Banerjee on the fire aboard a train near Godhra station, which became the pretext for launching a wholesale attack on Muslims, describes the fire as an accident rather than, as was held to be the case by militant Hindus and their supporters, the handiwork of Muslim mobs.

3. A. G. Noorani, *Savarkar and Hindutva: The Godse Connection* (New Delhi: Leftword, 2002), is the most recent detailed exposition of Savarkar's ideological and personal impact on Godse. The lengthy review by Pradip Kumar Datta, 'Savarkar Re-examined', *Frontline* (12–25 April 2003), is useful. The installation in early 2003 of Savarkar's portrait in the Central Hall of the Indian parliament occasioned, as indeed it should have, much public commentary. The BJP availed itself of two different positions, adverting on the one hand to the legal view that Savarkar was acquitted by the court of the charge of partaking in the conspiracy to assassinate Gandhi, and invoking, on the other hand, the public memory of him as an intrepid freedom fighter

who paved the way for Indian independence. See the discussions in A. G. Noorani, 'Every Picture Tells a Story', *Hindustan Times* (4 March 2003) and 'Savarkar Cannot be a Role Model', interview with Bipan Chandra, http:www.rediff.com/cms/print.jsp?docpath=/news/2003/mar/ 03inter.htm. Certain letters written by Godse to Savarkar between 1938 and 1946 have recently come to light — see Jyotirmaya Sharma, 'Please Don't Get Angry With your Shisya''', *The Hindu* (20 September 2004). A piece, 'Gandhi and His Killers', by Nalini Taneja appearing in *People's Democracy* (10 October 2004) is perhaps the most poignant commentary on how far the memory of Savarkar has been revived in middle-class India. The author commenced her piece with this observation: 'It tells something about the crisis of our nationhood that even on Gandhi Jayanti, this year, one saw more references to Savarkar than Gandhi in the national and regional newspapers. In the days preceding Gandhi's birthday, Gandhi's killers occupied more space in newspapers and popular magazines than Gandhi was given, if one discounts the routine advertisements.'

4. See the discussion in Rustom Bharucha, *In the Name of the Secular: Contemporary Cultural Activism in India* (Delhi: Oxford University Press, 1999), pp. 115–139.

5. The phrase, 'culture of cruelty', is drawn from Aijaz Ahmad, 'Right-Wing Politics, and the Cultures of Cruelty', *Social Scientist* 26, nos. 9–10 (September–October 1998), pp. 3–22. The editorial note accompanying the article, delivered as a memorial lecture, describes it as 'remarkable *inter alia* for its uninhibited use of the term "fascist" to describe the Hindutva brand of ideology and politics' (p. 1).

6. M. S. S. Pandian, *The Image Trap: M. G. Ramachandran in Film and Politics* (New Delhi: Sage, 1992).

7. Sumit Sarkar, 'The Fascism of the Sangh Parivar', *Economic and Political Weekly* 28 (30 January 1993), pp. 163–67.

8. Achin Vanaik, *The Furies of Indian Communalism: Religion, Modernity and Secularization* (London: Verso, 1997), p. 19; see also idem, 'Situating the Threat of Hindu Communalism: Problems with the Fascist Paradigm', *Economic and Political Weekly* 29, no. 28 (1994).

9. Cited by Bipan Chandra, *Communalism: A Primer* (Delhi: Anamika Publishers, 2004), p. 73.

10. K. N. Panikkar, 'Introduction' to K. N. Panikkar, ed., *The Concerned Indian's Guide to Communalism* (Delhi: Viking, 1999), p. xxxi.

11. K. N. Panikkar, *Before the Night Falls: Forebodings of Fascism in India* (2nd ed., Delhi: Books for Change, 2003), p. 142.

12. The same assertion, namely that the election of 2004 was the most critical one in the living memory of most people, was frequently voiced during the US election. The Japanese-American survivors of incarceration camps and those old enough to remember the witchhunts of the McCarthy

period were just as likely as those who have 'witnessed' no war other than the 'war on terror' to voice such sentiments. One rejoinder, to which I am sympathetic, is that the Republican and Democratic parties are both captive to corporate culture, influential lobbyists, and the compulsions of the militarist state, and there is something to be said for the view that these two parties, notwithstanding some genuine differences with respect to questions of welfare and ameliorative social policy, are practically indistinguishable. Democratic presidents have embraced retrograde social positions and what used to be called 'gunboat diplomacy' just as readily as the purportedly more hawkish Republicans. However, considering that the outcome of the American election has consequences for people around the world, one can well understand why the election results should have been eagerly watched all over the world by people who, while agonizing over their inability to vote, were nonetheless united in their open loathing for George W. Bush. This is one American election that the rest of the world, rightly or wrongly, was inclined to view as 'crucial'.

My point in adverting to the relation between elections and history is two-fold. If the vast bulk of histories are national histories, elections are even more so foregrounded in the idea of national boundaries. When certain Britishers, doubtless thinking of themselves as enlightened specimens of the world's oldest operative democracy, took it upon themselves to 'adopt' an American town in Ohio and advise its inhabitants to abandon Bush, little they did realize that Americans have reserved for themselves the prerogative of interfering in the elections of others while insisting upon their own electoral sovereignty to others. This calls to mind the recent revival of interest in 'world history', especially in the United States where courses and jobs in world history are proliferating and the field is rapidly acquiring all the paraphernalia of a recognized sub-discipline, from professional journals and associations to graduate programs. If it is claimed that this interest owes much to America's embrace of empire, and that the assumption of imperial duties is nowhere more pointedly on display than in the American sponsorship of 'free' elections around the world, the argument is certainly not without its attractions. The hawks who have shaped present American foreign policy have trumpeted the elections in Iraq and Afghanistan as the ultimate instantiation of genuine democracy at work, indeed of a country's admission into the ranks of nations that can now be viewed as commencing a new, more authentic, era in their history. 'Elections' and 'history' are, it is my submission, among the more fundamental elements of the business of creating charters for new nation-states. They make possible new forms of global history.

The other pointed consideration is that, in many nations, the commitments to history and to elections share a similar trajectory. The arrival of independence in India signified not only the universal extension of the franchise but the initiation of new national histories, and the same can well be said for many countries that were formerly under colonial rule. Decolonization means also the decolonization of the past, and elections, harbingers of the future, are always set against the implied background of despotism, authoritarianism, or other forms of unfree regimes. The past and future are attempted to be woven into a single narrative; as for the space of the present, it is amply filled by the act of consuming. The only thing that is fundamentally required of moderns is that they should have a sense of history, be willing consumers, and subscribe to 'free elections' as the most desirable form of political activity. It is perhaps no exaggeration to suggest that history comes to the fore in popular discourses on elections. If an election is characterized as the most 'crucial' for an electorate over a period of time, we must obviously ask: crucial in relation to what conception of the past? A study of the tapestry of history in discourses on elections remains to be attempted.

13. Walter Benjamin, *Illuminations*, ed. Hannah Arendt (New York: Schocken, 1969 [1955], p. 241. The structure of oppression is preserved, even as the masses are indulged in the belief that their rights are supremely important. Benjamin's walk to freedom across the Pyrenees, which ended catastrophically in his death, is explored in Rebecca Solnit, 'Hatred at One End, Rejection at the Other', *Los Angeles Times* (1 August 2004), p. M2.

14. See P. Sainath, 'A Gruelling Season: High-tech, Low Nutrition', *Hindu Magazine* (22 June 2003); idem, 'When Farmers Die', *The Hindu* (22 June 2004).

15. I have explored this at greater length in 'India in the World: Hinduism, the Diaspora and the Anxiety of Influence', *Australian Religion Studies Review* 16, no. 2 (Spring 2003), pp. 19–37.

16. The Ekta committee associated with Asghar Ali Engineer in Mumbai is a case in point.

17. This modernist utopia of science and technology is avidly embraced by Meera Nanda, *Prophets Facing Backward: Postmodern Critiques of Science and Hindu Nationalism in India* (New Brunswick, New Jersey: Rutgers University Press, 2003).

18. K. R. Malkani, 'History and Nationalism', *The Statesman* (23 December 2001).

19. Romila Thapar, *Somanatha: The Many Voices of a History* (Delhi: Viking, 2004).

20. For a sampling, see Romila Thapar, 'Sangh Parivar are Pseudo-Hindus', interview on Tehelka, 17 April 2001; idem, 'Hindutva and History', *Frontline* 17, no. 20 (30 September–13 October 2000), pp. 15–16; idem, 'History as Politics' [Professor Athar Ali Memorial Lecture, 8 February 2003], *Outlook* (1 May 2003); and idem, 'Do We Need Consensus on History?', *India–West* (21 December 2001), p. A4.

21. Partha Chatterjee, 'History and the Domain of the Popular', *Seminar*, no. 522 (February 2003), pp. 31–34.

22. Ibid., pp. 33–34.

23. A shortcoming to which I must plead guilty as well.

24. The same ground, in much more truncated form, is traversed in Richard H. Davis, *Lives of Indian Images* (Princeton: Princeton University Press, 1997; Delhi: Motilal Banarsidass, 1999), pp. 187–221.

25. See *India-West* (22 November 2002), p. B14. The author is Ashfaque Swapan.

Select Bibliography

The following abbreviation has been used:
SS *Subaltern Studies*

HISTORIOGRAPHY AND REFLECTIONS ON HISTORY

BOOKS, SCHOLARLY ARTICLES, AND PAMPHLETS

Aziz, K. K. *The Murder of History in Pakistan: A Critique of History Textbooks Used in Pakistan*. Lahore: Vanguard, 1993.

Banerjea, Krishna Mohun. 'Discourse on the Nature and Importance of Historical Studies', in *Selection of Discourses Delivered at the Meetings of the Society for the Acquisition of General Knowledge*, Vol. 1 (Calcutta, 1840), reprinted in Gautam Chattopadhyay, ed., *Awakening in Bengal in Early Nineteenth Century* (Selected Documents), Vol. I, pp. 1–29. Calcutta: Progressive Publishers, 1965.

Banerjea, S. N. 'The Study of Indian History', in *Speeches of S. N. Banerjea, 1876–1880* (n. p.; n.d.), pp. 2–3.

Bayly, C. A. 'Rallying Around the Subaltern', *Journal of Peasant Studies* 16, no. 1 (1988), pp. 110–20.

Behera, Navnita Chadha. 'Perpetuating the Divide: Political Abuse of History in South Asia', *Contemporary South Asia* 5, no. 2 (1996), pp. 191–205.

Carr, E. H. *What is History?* New York: Vintage Books, 1961.

Chakrabarty, Dipesh. 'History as Critique and Critique(s) of History', *Economic and Political Weekly* 26, no. 37 (14 September 1991), pp. 2162–6.

——. 'Postcoloniality and the Artifice of History: Who Speaks for "Indian" Pasts?', *Representations* 37 (Winter 1992), pp. 1–26.

——. 'Minority Histories, Subaltern Pasts', *Postcolonial Studies* 1, no. 1 (1998), pp. 15–29.

Chatterjee, Abhas Kumar. *Ram Janma Bhumi and Marxist Historians*. New Delhi: Historians' Forum, 1992.

Chatterjee, Partha. 'History and the Nationalization of Hinduism', *Social Research* 59, no. 1 (Spring 1992).

Chatterjee, Partha. 'Claims on the Past: The Genealogy of Modern Historiography in Bengal', in *Subaltern Studies VIII: Essays in Honour of Ranajit Guha*, pp. 1–49. Delhi: Oxford University Press, 1994.

Chaudhary, Vijay Chandra Prasad. *Secularism Versus Communalism: An Anatomy of the National Debate on Five Controversial History Books*. Patna: Navdhara Samiti, 1977.

Cohen, Sande. *Historical Culture: On the Recoding of an Academic Discipline.* Berkeley: University of California Press, 1986.

Cooper, Frederick. 'Conflict and Connection: Rethinking Colonial African History', *American Historical Review* 99, no. 5 (December 1994), pp. 1516–45.

Delhi Historians' Group. *The Communalisation of Education: The History Textbooks Controversy.* Delhi: Delhi Historians' Group, Jawaharlal Nehru University, 2001.

Deshpande, Madhav. 'History, Change and Permanence: A Classical Indian Perspective', in *Contributions to South Asian Studies* I, ed. Gopal Krishna. Delhi: Oxford University Press, 1979.

Gardiner, Juliet, ed. *What is History Today ... ?* London: Macmillan, 1988.

Gooch, George Peabody. *History and Historians of the Nineteenth Century.* London: Longmans, Green & Co., 1913.

Gopal, S. et al. 'The Political Abuse of History', as reprinted in *Social Scientist*, nos 200–01 (January–February 1990), pp. 76–81.

Gopalakrishnan, S. 'The South had a major role', *Madras Musings* (16–30 March 2002), pp. 4–5.

Grewal, J. S. *Muslim Rule in India: The Assessments of British Historians.* Calcutta: Oxford University Press, 1970.

Guha, Ramachandra. 'Subaltern and Bhadralok Studies', *Economic and Political Weekly* 30 (19 August 1995), p. 2057.

Guha, Ranajit. 'On Some Aspects of the Historiography of Colonial India', in Ranajit Guha, ed., *Subaltern Studies I: Writings on South Asian History and Society*, pp. 1–8. Delhi: Oxford University Press, 1982.

——. 'The Prose of Counter-Insurgency', in Ranajit Guha, ed., *Subaltern Studies II: Writings on South Asian History and Society*, pp. 1–42. Delhi: Oxford University Press, 1983.

——. *An Indian Historiography of India: A Nineteenth-Century Agenda and Its Implications.* Calcutta: K. P. Bagchi & Co., 1988.

——. 'Dominance without Hegemony and Its Historiography', *SS* VI:210–309.

Hardy, P. *Historians of Medieval India: Studies in Indo-Muslim Historical Writing.* London: Luzac & Co., 1960.

Herwadkar, R. V. *A Forgotten Literature: Foundations of Marathi Chronicles.* Bombay: Popular Prakashan, 1994.

Hoodbhoy, Pervez Amirali and Abdul Hameed Nayyar. 'Rewriting the History of Pakistan', in *Islam, Politics and the State: The Pakistan Experience*, pp. 164–77. London: Zed Books, 1985.

Inden, Ronald. *Imagining India*. Oxford: Basil Blackwell, 1990.

Institute for Rewriting Indian History. *Annual Report*. New Delhi: IRWI, 1976.

Jenkins, Keith. *Re-thinking History*. London: Routledge, 1992.

Jha, D. N. 'Against Communalising History', *Social Scientist* 26, nos 9–10 (September–October 1998), pp. 52–62.

Jha, Vishwa Mohan. *Investigative Journalism or Slander: Do You Have More Questions Mr. Shourie?* Delhi: SAHMAT, 1998.

Kumar, Krishna. 'Origins of India's "Textbook Culture"', *Comparative Education Review* 32, no. 4 (November 1998), pp. 452–64.

———. *Learning from Conflict*. Tracts for the Times, no. 10. Hyderabad: Orient Longman, 1996.

———. *Prejudice and Pride: School Histories of the Freedom Struggle in India and Pakistan*. New Delhi: Viking, 2001.

Lal, Vinay. 'Discipline and Authority: Some Notes on Future Histories and Epistemologies of India', *Futures* 29, no. 10 (December 1997), pp. 985–1000.

———. 'Gandhi, the Civilizational Crucible, and the Future of Dissent', *Futures* 31 (March 1999), pp. 205–19.

———. 'Subaltern Studies and Its Critics: Debates over Indian History', *History and Theory* 40 (February 2001), pp. 135–48.

Latin American Subaltern Studies Group. 'Founding Statement', *boundary 2* 20, no. 3 (1993), pp. 110–21.

Majumdar, R. C. 'Ideas of History in Sanskrit Literature', in C. H. Philips, ed., *Historians of India, Pakistan and Ceylon*. London: Oxford University Press, 1961.

———. *Historiography in Modern India*. London and Bombay: Asia Publishing House, 1970.

Mallon, Florenica E. 'The Promise and Dilemma of Subaltern Studies: Perspectives from Latin American History', *American Historical Review* 99, no. 5 (December 1994), pp. 1491–515.

Manuel, Frank E. *Shapes of Philosophical History*. Stanford: Stanford University Press, 1965.

Marx, Karl and Friedrich Engels. *The First Indian War of Independence 1857–1859*. Moscow: Foreign Languages Publishing House, n. d.

Megill, Allan. '"Grand Narrative" and the Discipline of History', in Frank Ankersmit and Hans Kellner, eds, *A New Philosophy of History*, pp. 151–73. Chicago: University of Chicago Press, 1995.

Menon, Parvathi. 'The Falsification of History', *Frontline* 17, no. 6 (18–31 March 2000).

——— and T. K. Rajalakshmi. 'Hindu fascists doctoring textbooks for hate', *Frontline* 15, no. 23 (7–20 November 1998).

Mittal, S. C. *India Distorted: A Study of British Historians of India*, Volume 1. New Delhi: M. D. Publications, 1995.

Mukherji, Subodhkumar. 'The Cultural History of India—An Apology', in *Proceedings of the Indian History Congress*, 3rd Session. Calcutta: Calcutta University Press, 1939.

Mukhopadhyay, Subodh Kumar. *Evolution of Historiography in Modern India: 1900–1960*. Calcutta: K. P. Bagchi & Co., 1981.

Nabokov, Peter. *A Forest of Time: American Indian Ways of History*. Cambridge: Cambridge University Press, 2002.

Nandy, Ashis. 'History's Forgotten Doubles', *History and Theory*, Theme Issue 34: World Historians and Their Critics (1995), pp. 44–66.

Nietzsche, Friedrich. *The Use and Abuse of History*, trans. Adrian Collins. 2nd rev. edn, Indianapolis: Bobbs-Merrill Company, 1957.

Novick, Peter. *That Noble Dream: The 'Objectivity Question' and the American Historical Profession*. Cambridge: Cambridge University Press, 1988.

Pandey, Gyanendra. 'The Colonial Construction of "Communalism": British Writings on Banaras in the Nineteenth Century', *SS* VI:132–68.

———. 'Modes of History Writing: New Hindu History of Ayodhya', *Economic and Political Weekly* 29, no. 25 (18 June 1994), pp. 1523–8.

———. 'The Culture of History', in Nicholas Dirks, ed., *In Near Ruins: Cultural Theory at the End of the Century*, pp. 19–37. Minneapolis: University of Minnesota Press, 1998.

Panikkar, K. N. 'Outsider as enemy: The politics of rewriting history in India', *Frontline* 18, no. 1 (6–19 January 2001).

Pargiter, F. E. *The Ancient Indian Historical Tradition*. London: Oxford University Press, H. Milford, 1922.

Pollock, Sheldon. 'Mimamsa and the Problem of History in Traditional India', *Journal of the American Oriental Society* 109, no. 4 (1989), pp. 603–10.

Prakash, Buddha. 'The Hindu Philosophy of History', *Journal of the History of Ideas* 16, no. 4 (October 1955).

Prakash, Gyan. 'Subaltern Studies as Postcolonial Criticism', *American Historical Review* 99, no. 5 (December 1994), pp. 1475–1490.

Prasad, Rajendra. 'The Role of History', in *Speeches of Rajendra Prasad 1952–1956*. New Delhi: Government of India, Ministry of Information and Broadcasting, Publications Division, 1958.

Rajalakshmi, T. K. 'Agendas and appointments', *Frontline* 16, no. 24 (13–26 November 1999).

———. 'Targeting history', *Frontline* 18, no. 9 (28 April–11 May 2001).

Raychaudhuri, Tapan. 'Indian Nationalism as Animal Politics', *Historical Journal* 22 (1979), pp. 747–63.

———. 'India, 1858 to the 1930s', in *The Oxford History of the British Empire, Volume V: Historiography*, ed. Robin W. Winks, pp. 214–30. Oxford & New York: Oxford University Press, 1999.

Rudolph, Lloyd I. and Susanne Hoeber Rudolph. 'Rethinking Secularism:

Genesis and Implications of the Textbook Controversy, 1977–79', *Pacific Affairs* 56, no. 1 (Spring 1983), pp. 15–37.

Sahlins, Marshall. 'Other Times, Other Customs: The Anthropology of History', *American Anthropologist* 85 (1983), pp. 517–43.

Said, Edward. Foreword to Ranajit Guha and Gayatri Chakravorty Spivak, eds, *Selected Subaltern Studies*. New York: Oxford University Press, 1988.

Sarkar, Sumit. 'Orientalism Revisited: Saidian Frameworks in the Writing of Modern Indian History', *Oxford Literary Review* 16, nos 1–2 (1994), pp. 205–24.

Sastri, K. A. Nilakanta, et al. 'Historiography: India and the West', *Bulletin of the Institute of Traditional Cultures* (Madras), Part 1 (1962).

Sathyamurthy, T. V. 'Indian Peasant Historiography: A Critical Perspective on Ranajit Guha's Work', *The Journal of Peasant Studies* 18, (October 1990), pp. 92–141.

Schwarz, Henry. *Writing Cultural History in Colonial and Postcolonial India*. Philadelphia: University of Pennsylvania Press, 1997.

Sen, Amartya. 'History and the enterprise of knowledge', *Frontline* 18, no. 2 (20 January–2 February 2001).

Shah, P. G. 'Munshi in the Field of Research', in Jayantkrishna H. Dave et al., eds, *Munshi Indological Felicitation Volume*. Bombay: Bharatiya Vidya Bhavan, 1963.

Sharma, R. C. *In Defence of 'Ancient India'*, New Delhi: People's Publishing House, 1978.

Shourie, Arun. *Eminent Historians: Their Technology, Their Line, Their Fraud*. New Delhi: ASA Publications, 1998.

Siddiqi, Majid H. 'Ramjanmabhoomi-Babri Masjid Dispute: The Question of History', *Economic and Political Weekly* 25, no. 2 (13 January 1990), pp. 97–8.

Stein, Burton. 'Early Indian Historiography: A Conspiracy Hypothesis', *Indian Economic and Social History Review* 6 (1969), pp. 41–60.

Stokes, E. T. 'The Administrators and Historical Writing on India', in *Historians of India, Pakistan and Ceylon*, ed. C. H. Philips. London: Oxford University Press, 1961.

Thapar, Romila. *The Past and Prejudice*. New Delhi: National Book Trust, 1975.

——. 'Society and Historical Consciousness: The *Itihasa-Purana* Tradition', in Romila Thapar and Sabyasachi Bhattacharya, eds, *Situating Indian History—for S. Gopal*, pp. 353–83. Delhi: Oxford University Press, 1986.

——. 'The Theory of Aryan Race and India: History and Politics', *Social Scientist* 24, nos 1–3 (January–March 1996), pp. 3–29.

——. [Conversation with Kumkum Roy and Rakesh Batabyal.] *Summerhill: IIAS Review* 4, no. 2 (December 1998), p. 3–8.

——. 'Hindutva and History', *Frontline* 17, no. 20 (30 September–13 October 2000), pp. 15–16.

——. 'Interpretations of Indian History: Colonial, Nationalist, Post-colonial', in Peter Ronald deSouza, ed., *Contemporary India–Transitions*, pp. 25–36. New Delhi: Sage Publications, 2000.

Thapar, Romila. 'Sangh Parivar are pseudo-Hindus', interview on Tehelka, 17 April 2001, online at <*www.tehelka.com*>.

——, Harbans Mukhia, and Bipan Chandra. *Communalism and the Writing of Indian History*. New Delhi: People's Publishing House, 1969.

Todorov, Tzvetan. *The Morals of History* [1991], trans. Alyson Waters. Minneapolis: University of Minnesota Press, 1995.

Trouillot, Michel-Rolph. *Silencing the Past: Power and the Production of History*. Boston: Beacon Press, 1995.

Wickramasinghe, Nira. 'History Outside the Nation', *Economic and Political Weekly* 30, no. 26 (1 July 1995), pp. 1570–72.

Witzel, Michael. 'Horseplay in Harappa', *Frontline* 17, no. 20 (30 September–13 October 2000).

NEWSPAPER ARTICLES

Chatterjee, Abhas Kumar. 'Ram Janmabhoomi: More evidence', *Indian Express* (26 March 1990), p. 8.

Das, Arvind. 'Cut-Price Culture: VHP Digs Up Myth, Buries History', *Times of India* (11 December 1990), p. 6.

——. 'When history causes ennui', *Times of India* (11 July 1993).

——. 'The past is present. And absent', *Sunday Times of India* (11 July 1993), p. 17.

——. 'Row Over BJP's Action of Politicizing Academics', *India-West* (24 July 1998), pp. A4, 6.

Engineer, Asghar Ali. 'Textbooks and communalism', *Hindu* (16 November 1999).

Goel, Sita Ram. 'Some historical questions', *Indian Express* (16 April 1989), p. 8.

Gopal, S., Romila Thapar, et al., 'In the name of history', *The Indian Express* [Sunday Magazine] (1 April 1990), p. 8.

Gupta, S. P. 'Ram Janmabhoomi-Babri Masjid: Archaeological evidence', *Indian Express* (2 December 1990), p. 3.

Irfani, Suroosh. 'Murderers of History', *Jang* (6 October 1999).

Khair, Tabish. 'Stripped of my Indian identity', *Sunday Times of India* (10 January 1993), p. 24.

Maloney, Clarence. 'Vedic-Indus debate: save Indian civilisation today', *Hindu* (4 February 2002), p. OB–1.

Mukhia, Harbans. 'Historical Wrongs', *Indian Express* (27 November 1998).

Pahoja, Murlidhar P. 'Archaeological data on Temple', *Indian Express* (14 May 1990), p. 8.

Rajaram, N. S. 'Historical divide: archaeology and literature', *Hindu* (22 January 2002).

——. 'Theory and evidence', *Hindu* (19 February 2002).

Tharoor, Shashi. 'The Revenge of History', *New York Times* (11 December 1992), p. A39.

Witzel, Michael. 'Indus Civilisation and Vedic society', *Hindu* (29 January 2002), p. OB–1.

—— and Steve Farmer. 'Harappan horse myths and the sciences', *Hindu* (5 March 2002).

NEWSPAPER ARTICLES ON THE TEXTBOOKS CONTROVERSY/
'SAFFRONISATION' OF HISTORY (2001–02)

Anon. 'What to Teach? Values yes, idiocy no', Editorial in *Statesman* (18 April 2001).

Bhargava, Rajeev. 'History and community sentiment', *Hindu* (2 January 2002), p. 10.

Chandra, Satish. 'Guru Tegh Bahadur's martyrdom', *Hindu* (16 October 2001), p. 10.

Gupta, Monobina. 'In Gujarat, Adolf Catches 'em in Schools', *Telegraph* (29 April 2002).

Khanna, Rajeev. 'Gujarat School Text Teaches Hate', *Asian Age* (8 May 2002).

Modi, Anjali. 'Supporters of Ram Janmabhoomi Rewriting History Texts', *Hindu* (14 October 2001).

——. 'Tailoring history', *Hindu* (21 October 2001).

——. 'Delete and control—the Parivar's mantra', *Hindu* (2 December 2001), p. 14.

Dev, Arjun. 'Corrugated curricula', *Hindustan Times* (22 October 2001).

Panikkar, K. N. 'Education for fundamentalism', *Hindu* (21 April 2001).

——. 'Manufacturing Myths', *Times of India* (30 April 2002).

Puniyani, Ram. 'Beef eating: strangulating history', *Hindu* (14 August 2001), p. OB–1.

Ranade, Sudhanshu. 'Sound, fury and significance', *Hindu* (4 December 2001).

Setalvad, Teesta. 'But whose values? NCERT's long overdue relook at the syllabus raises some disturbing questions', *Indian Express* (18 April 2001).

Sharma, R. S. 'The archaeology of faith', *Hindustan Times* (12 February 2002).

Sinha, Aditya. 'RSS Targets History Textbooks', *Hindustan Times* (17 June 1998).

Thapar, Romila. 'Do We Need Consensus on History?', *India-West* (21 December 2001), p. A4.

INDIAN HISTORY

BOOKS AND ARTICLES

Ahmad, Aijaz. 'Right-Wing Politics, and the Cultures of Cruelty', *Social Scientist* 26, nos 9–10 (September–October 1998), pp. 3–25.

Ali, M. Athar. *The Mughal Nobility Under Aurangzeb*. Bombay: Asia Publishing House, 1968.

Amin, Shahid. 'Gandhi as Mahatma: Gorakhpur District, Eastern UP, 1921–2', *SS* III:1–61.

Amin, Shahid and Dipesh Chakrabarty, eds, *Subaltern Studies IX: Writings on South Asian History and Society*. New Delhi: Oxford University Press, 1996.

Anon. *Ramajanma Bhumi and the Marxist Historians*. New Delhi: Historians' Forum, 1992.

——. *Ramajanma Bhumi, Ayodhya: New Archaeological Discoveries*. New Delhi: Historians' Forum, 1992.

Apffel-Marglin, Frederique. 'Gender and the Unitary Self: Looking for the Subaltern in Coastal Orissa', *South Asia Research* 15, no. 1 (Spring 1995), pp. 78–130

Apte, B. K., ed. *Chhatrapati Shivaji: Coronation Tercentenary Commemoration Volume*. Bombay: University of Bombay, 1974–75.

Arnold, David and David Hardiman, eds. *Subaltern Studies VIII: Writings on South Asian History and Society*. New Delhi: Oxford University Press, 1994.

Bakker, Hans. *Ayodhya*. 2 volumes. Groningen: Egbert Forsten, 1986.

——. 'Reflections on the Evolution of Rama Devotion in the Light of Textual and Archaeological Evidence', *Wiener Zeitschrift fur die Kunde Sudasiens* 31 (1986), pp. 21–22.

Bakshi, Rajni. *The Dispute Over Swami Vivekananda's Legacy: A Warning and an Opportunity*. Mapusa, Goa: The Other India Press, 1994.

Bardhan, A. B. *Sangh Parivar's Hindutva versus The Real Hindu Ethos*. New Delhi: Communist Party of India, 1992.

Basu, Tapan, et al. *Khaki Shorts and Saffron Flags: A Critique of the Hindu Right*. Tracts for the Times, no. 1. Delhi: Orient Longman, 1993.

Bhardwaj, Surinder Mohan. *Hindu Places of Pilgrimage in India: A Study in Cultural Geography*. Berkeley: University of California Press, 1973.

Bhattacharya, Sabyasachi, ed. *The Mahatma and the Poet: Letters and Debates Between Gandhi and Tagore 1915–1941*. Delhi: National Book Trust, 1997.

'Black Sunday', issue of *Manas* (Delhi: Sampradayikta Virodhi Andolan, December 1992).

Bose, Dilip. *Bhagavad-Gita and Our National Movement*. Delhi: People's Publishing House, 1981.

Cashman, Richard I. *The Myth of Lokmanya Tilak and Mass Politics in Maharashtra*. Berkeley: University of California Press, 1975.

Chakrabarti, Kunal. *Religious Process: The Puranas and the Making of a Regional Tradition*. Delhi: Oxford University Press, 2001.

Chakrabarty, Dipesh. 'Conditions for Knowledge of Working-Class Conditions: Employers, Government and the Jute Workers of Calcutta, 1890–1940', *SS* II:259–310.

Chakrabarty, Dipesh. 'Invitation to a Dialogue', *SS* IV:364–76.

———. *Provincializing Europe: Postcolonial Thought and Historical Difference.* Princeton: Princeton University Press, 2000.

Chand, Tara. *History of the Freedom Movement in India.* 4 volumes, with foreword by Humayun Kabir. New Delhi: Government of India, Ministry of Information and Broadcasting, Publications Division, 1961–72.

Chande, M. B. *Shree Ram Janma Bhoomi.* Nagpur: M. B. Chande, 1992.

Chandra, Bipan. *Modern India.* New Delhi: National Council for Educational Research and Teaching, 1971.

Chandra, Satish. 'Reassessing Aurangzeb', *Seminar*, no. 364: *Mythifying History* (December 1989).

Chatterjee, Bankim. *Durgesa Nandini* or *The Chieftain's Daughter* (1880), trans. Charu Chandra Mookerjee, 2nd edn. Calcutta: The Classic Press, 1903.

———. *Anandamath*, translated as *The Abbey of Bliss* by Nares Chandra Sengupta. Calcutta: Padmini Mohan Neogi, 1904.

———. *Bankim Racnabali*, ed. Yogesh Chandra Bagal. 2 vols. Calcutta: Sahitya Samsad, 1965.

———. *Krishna-charitra* [The Life of Krishna], trans. Pradip Bhattacharya. Calcutta: M. P. Birla Foundation, 1991.

Chatterjee, Partha. *Nationalist Thought and the Colonial World: A Derivative Discourse?* London: Zed Books, 1986.

———. 'Caste and Subaltern Consciousness', *SS* VI:169–209.

——— and Gyanendra Pandey, eds. *Subaltern Studies VII: Writings on South Asian History and Society.* New Delhi: Oxford University Press, 1992.

Chattopadhyaya, Brajulal. *Representing the Other? Sanskrit Sources and the Muslims.* Delhi: Manohar, 1998.

Chattopadhyay, Gautam, ed. *Awakening in Bengal in Early Nineteenth Century* (Selected Documents), Vol. 1. Calcutta: Progressive Publishers, 1965.

Choudhari, K. K. *Maharashtra and Indian Freedom Struggle.* Bombay: Government of Maharashtra, 1985.

Chowdhury, Indira. *The Frail Hero and Virile History: Gender and the Politics of Culture in Colonial Bengal.* Delhi: Oxford University Press, 1998.

Clark, T. W. 'Bengali Prose Fiction Up to Bankimcandra', in T. W. Clark, ed., *The Novel in India: Its Birth and Development.* Berkeley: University of California Press, 1970.

Cohn, Bernard S. 'The Command of Language and the Language of Command', *SS* IV: 276–329.

Das, Veena. 'Subaltern as Perspective', *SS* VI:310–14.

Datta, K. K., ed. *History of the Freedom Movement in Bihar.* 3 vols. Patna: Government of Bihar, 1957–58.

Datta, Pradip K. 'VHP's Ram at Ayodhya: Reincarnation through Ideology and Organisation', *Economic and Political Weekly* 26, no. 44 (2 November 1991).

De, Sushil Chandra. *Story of Freedom Struggle in Orissa*. Bhubaneswar: Orissa Sahitya Akademi, 1990.

Desai, Mahadev. *The Gita According to Gandhi*. Ahmedabad: Navajivan Publishing House, 1946.

Dhareshwar, Vivek and R. Srivatsan, '"Rowdy-sheeters": An Essay on Subalternity and Politics', *SS* IX:201–31.

Dirks, Nicholas. *The Hollow Crown: Ethnohistory of an Indian Kingdom*. Cambridge: Cambridge University Press, 1987; 2nd edn, paperback, Ann Arbor: University of Michigan Press, 1992.

Dumont, Louis. *Homo Hierarchicus: The Caste System and Its Implications*, trans. Mark Sainsbury. Chicago: University of Chicago Press, 1970.

Eaton, Richard M. *The Rise of Islam and the Bengal Frontier, 1204–1760*. Delhi: Oxford University Press, 1997.

Elliot, H. M. *The History of India as Told by Its Own Historians: The Muhammadan Period*, ed. (and continued) by John Dowson, 8 vols [1st edn, 1867–77]. Reprint edn, Allahabad: Kitab Mahal, [1963–4].

Forrest, George W., ed. *Selections from the Minutes and Other Official Writings of the Honourable Mountstuart Elphinstone, Governor of Bombay*. London: R. Bentley, 1884.

Gallagher, John and Ronald Robinson. 'The Imperialism of Free Trade', *Economic History Review* (2nd series) 6, no. 1 (1953), reprinted in William Roger Louis, ed., *Imperialism: The Robinson and Gallagher Controversy*. New York: New Viewpoints, 1976.

—— and ——. 'The Partition of Africa', in Anil Seal, ed., *The Decline, Revival and Fall of the British Empire*. Cambridge: Cambridge University Press, 1982.

Gandhi, M. K. *Hind Swaraj or Indian Home Rule*. Reprint edn, Ahmedabad: Navajivan Publishing House, 1962 [1909].

——. *Discourses on the Gita*. Ahmedabad: Navajivan Publishing House, 1960.

Gandhi, Ramchandra. *Sita's Kitchen: A Testimony of Faith and Inquiry*. New Delhi: Penguin Books, 1992.

Ghosh, Tapan. *The Gandhi Murder Trial*. New York: Asia Publishing House, 1976.

Gidwani, Bhagwan S. *Return of the Aryans*. Delhi: Penguin Books, 1994.

Godse, Gopal. *May It Please Your Honor: Statement of Nathuram Godse*. Poona: Vitasta Prakashan, 1977.

Gopal, Sarvepalli, ed. *Anatomy of a Confrontation: The Babri Masjid-Ram Janmabhumi Issue*. Delhi: Penguin Books, 1991.

Guha, Ranajit. *Elementary Aspects of Insurgency in Colonial India*. Delhi: Oxford University Press, 1983.

——. 'Discipline and Mobilize', *SS* VII:69–120

——, ed. *Subaltern Studies: Writings on South Asian History and Society*. 6 vols. New Delhi: Oxford University Press, 1982–9.

Guha, Ranajit, ed. *A Subaltern Studies Reader, 1986–1995*. Minneapolis: University of Minnesota Press, 1997.

Habib, Mohammad and Afsar Umar Salim Khan. *The Political Theory of the Delhi Sultanate*. Allahabad: Kitab Mahal, 1961.

Hallissey, Robert C. *The Rajput Rebellion Against Aurangzeb: A Study of the Mughal Empire in Seventeenth-Century India*. Columbia, Missouri: University of Missouri Press, 1977.

Hansen, Thomas Blan. *Wages of Violence: Naming and Identity in Postcolonial Bombay*. Princeton: Princeton University Press, 2001.

Hardiman, David. 'The Indian "Faction": A Political Theory Examined', *SS* I:198–231.

Hasan, Mushirul. *Legacy of a Divided Nation: India's Muslims since Independence*. Boulder, Colorado: Westview Press, 1997.

Herman, Phyllis. 'Relocating Ramarajya: Perspectives on Sita's Kitchen in Ayodhya', *International Journal of Hindu Studies* 2, no. 2 (August 1998), pp. 157–84.

Ilaiah, Kancha. *Why I Am Not a Hindu: A Sudra Critique of Hindutva Philosophy, Culture and Political Economy*. Calcutta: Samya, 1996.

———. 'Productive Labour, Consciousness and History: The Dalitbahujan Alternative', *SS* IX:165–200.

Jaffrelot, Christophe. *The Hindu Nationalist Movement and Indian Politics, 1920s to the 1990s*. 2nd edn, New Delhi: Penguin, 1999.

Jha, D. N. *Ancient India in Historical Outline*. Rev. and enlg. edn. New Delhi: Manohar, 2001 [1977].

Johnson, Gordon. *Provincial Politics and Indian Nationalism: Bombay and the Indian National Congress 1880 to 1915*. Cambridge: Cambridge University Press, 1973.

Joshi, V. C., ed. *Rammohun Roy and the Process of Modernization in India*. Delhi: Vikas, 1975.

Kakar, Sudhir. *The Colours of Violence*. Delhi: Viking, 1995.

Kalhana. *The Rajatarangini*, trans. R. S. Pandit. New Delhi: Sahitya Akademi, 1953; reprint edn, 1968.

Kane, P. V. *History of Dharmashastra*. 5 vols. 2nd rev. edn, Poona: Bhandarkar Oriental Research Institute, 1968–77 [1930].

Kautilya. *Arthasastra*, trans. R. Shamasastry. 8th edn, Mysore: Mysore Printing and Publishing House, 1967.

Kaviraj, Sudipta. *The Unhappy Consciousness*. Delhi: Oxford University Press, 1995.

Keay, John. *India: A History*. New York: Grove Press, 2000.

Khilnani, Sunil. *The Idea of India*. New York: Farrar, Straus and Giroux, 1997.

Kopf, David. *British Orientalism and the Bengal Renaissance: The Dynamics of Indian Modernization 1773–1835*. Berkeley: University of California Press, 1969.

Kulkarnee, Narayan H, ed. *Chhatrapati Shivaji: Architect of Freedom*. Delhi: Chhatrapati Shivaji Smarak Samiti, 1975.

Kulkarni, Chidambara. *Studies in Indian History*. Bombay: Shri Dvaipayana Trust, n.d.

Kumar, Krishna. 'Origins of India's "Textbook Culture"', *Comparative Education Review* 32, no. 4 (November 1998), pp. 452–64.

Lal, Vinay. 'Committees of Inquiry and Discourses of "Law and Order" in Twentieth-Century British India'. Unpublished Ph.D. Dissertation, Department of South Asian Languages and Civilizations, The University of Chicago, 2 vols (1992).

Macaulay, Thomas B. 'Minute on Indian Education', *Selected Writings*, ed. John Clive. Chicago: University of Chicago Press, 1980.

MacDonell, Arthur. *A History of Sanskrit Literature*. New York: Haskell, 1966 [1900].

Madhya Pradesh Government. *History of the Freedom Movement in Madhya Pradesh*. Nagpur: Government Printing, 1956.

Majumdar, R. C. *Glimpses of Bengal in the Nineteenth Century*. Calcutta: Firma K. L. Mukhopadhyay, 1960.

——. *History of the Freedom Movement in India*. 3 vols. 1st edn, 1962–3; 2nd rev. edn, Calcutta: Firma K. L. Mukhopadhyay, 1971–2.

—— ed. *The History and Culture of the Indian People*. 11 vols. Volume 1, London: George Allen & Unwin, 1951; Vols 2–11, Bombay: Bharatiya Vidya Bhavan, 1953–69.

Malcolm, John. *Political History of India*. 2 vols. London: J. Murray, 1826.

Mandal, D. *Ayodhya: Archaeology after Demolition*. Tracts for the Times, no. 5. New Delhi: Orient Longman, 1993.

Meister, Michael W. 'Mystifying monuments', *Seminar*, no. 364: *Mythifying History* (December 1989), pp. 24–7.

Menon, Parvathi. 'Ayodhya and all that: Communalism and the discipline of history', *Frontline* (11–24 May 1991), p. 47.

Menon, Parvathi and T. K. Rajalakshmi, 'Hindu Fascists Doctoring textbooks for hate', *Frontline* 15, no. 23 (7–20 November 1998).

Mill, James. *History of British India*. 1-volume abridged edn by John Clive. Chicago: University of Chicago Press, 1975.

——. *History of British India*, edn with notes by Horace Hayman Wilson. 10 vols. 5th edn, London: James Madden, 1858.

Minault, Gail. *The Khilafat Movement: Religious Symbolism and Political Mobilization in India*. New York: Columbia University Press, 1982.

Mishra, Amaresh. *Lucknow, Fire of Grace: The Story of the Renaissance, Revolution and the Aftermath*. New Delhi: HarperCollins, 1998.

Monier-Williams, Monier. [Address to the National Indian Association] *Journal of the National Indian Association* (January 1878).

Mookerji, Radha Kumud. *Local Government in Ancient India*. Oxford: Clarendon Press, 1919.

Mookerji, Radha Kumud. *Hindu Civilization*. 4th edn, Bombay: Bharatiya Vidya Bhavan, 1977 [1957].

——. *Harsha*. 3rd edn, Delhi: Motilal Banarsidass, 1965 [1925].

Munshi, K. M. *Somnath: The Shrine Eternal*. Bombay: Bharatiya Vidya Bhavan, 1953.

Nagaraj, D. R. *The Flaming Feet: A Study of the Dalit Movement in India*. Bangalore: South Forum Press, in association with Institute for Cultural Research and Action, 1993.

Nandan, Deoki. *Sri Ramjanmabhumi: Itihasik evam Vidik Samiksha* [*Ramjanmabhumi: Historical and Legal Review*]. Allahabad: Suruchi Printers, n.d.

Nandy, Ashis. 'The Final Encounter: The Politics of the Assassination of Gandhi', in *At the Edge of Psychology: Essays in Politics and Culture*. Delhi: Oxford University Press, 1980.

——. 'From Outside the Imperium: Gandhi's Cultural Critique of the "West"', *Alternatives* 3, no. 2 (June 1981); revised version in Ashis Nandy, *Traditions, Tyranny, and Utopias: Essays in the Politics of Awareness*, pp. 127–62. Delhi: Oxford University Press, 1987.

Nandy, Ashis, Shikha Trivedy, Shail Mayaram, and Achyut Yagnik. *Creating a Nationality: The Ramjanmabhumi Movement and Fear of the Self*. Delhi: Oxford University Press, 1995.

Nath, R. 'The Taj: A mausoleum', *Seminar*, no. 364: *Mythifying History* (December 1989), pp. 28–34.

Nehru, Jawaharlal. *The Discovery of India*. Calcutta: Signet Press, 1946; reprint edn, Delhi: Oxford University Press/Jawaharlal Nehru Memorial Fund, 1981.

——. *Toward Freedom: The Autobiography of Jawaharlal Nehru*. Boston: Beacon Press, 1958.

Noorani, A. G. *The RSS and the BJP: A Division of Labour*. New edn. New Delhi: Leftword, 2001.

Novikova, Vera. *Bankimchandra Chattopadhyay: His Life and Works*, trans. Nishitesh Banerjee. Calcutta: National Publishers, 1976.

O'Hanlon, Rosalind. 'Maratha History as Polemic: Law Caste Ideology and Political Debate in Late Nineteenth-Century Western India', *Modern Asian Studies* 17, no. 1 (1983).

Orme, Robert. 'Effeminacy of the Inhabitants of Indostan', *Historical Fragments of the Mogul Empire* ... London: F. Wingrave, 1805; reprint edn, New Delhi: Associated Publishing House, 1974.

Pandey, Ram Gopal. 'Sarad'. *Shri Ram janmabhumi ka romanckari itihas*. Ayodhya: Pandit Dvarikaprasad Sivgovind Pustakalay, 1976.

Pannikar, K. N., ed., *The Concerned Indian's Guide to Communalism*. New Delhi: Viking, 1999.

People's Union for Democratic Rights. *Cry the Beloved Country: Ayodhya, 6 December 1992*. Delhi: PUDR, February 1993.

Pollock, Sheldon. 'Ramayana and Political Imagination in India', *The Journal of Asian Studies* 53, no. 2 (1993), pp. 261–97.

Qureshi, I. H. *The Administration of the Sultanate of Delhi*. 4th rev. edn, Karachi: Pakistan Historical Society, 1958.

Raghavan, T. C. A. 'Origins and Development of Hindu Mahasabha Ideology: The Call of V. D. Savarkar and Bhai Parmanand', *Economic and Political Weekly* 18, no. 15 (9 April 1983), pp. 595–600.

Rajalakshmi, T. K. 'A master's version', *Frontline* 15, no. 23 (7–20 November 1998).

Rajaram, Navaratna S. *Aryan Invasion of India: The Myth and the Truth*. New Delhi: Voice of India, 1993.

——. *The Politics of History: Aryan Invasion Theory and the Subversion of Scholarship*. New Delhi: The Voice of India, 1995.

—— and Natwar Jha. *The Deciphered Indus Script: Methodology, Readings, Interpretations*. New Delhi: Aditya Prakashan, 2000.

Ratnabali, Chatterjee. 'The Rulers and the Ruled in Medieval India and VHP's Myth', in Madhusree Dutta, Flavia Agnes and Neera Adarkar, eds, *The Nation, the State and Indian Identity*. Delhi: Samya, 1996.

Ratnagar, Shereen. 'Revisionism at work: A chauvinistic inversion of the Aryan inversion theory', *Frontline* (9 February 1996), pp. 74–80.

Raychaudhuri, Tapan, 'The Mughal Empire', in Tapan Raychaudhuri and Irfan Habib, eds, *Cambridge Economic History of India*. Volume I. Cambridge: Cambridge University Press, 1982.

Richman, Paula, ed. *Many Ramayanas: The Diversity of a Narrative Tradition in South Asia*. Berkeley: University of California Press, 1991.

Rizvi, S. A. A., ed. *Freedom Struggle in Uttar Pradesh*. 6 vols with foreword by Jugal Kishore and preface by Kamalapati Tripathi. Lucknow: Government of Uttar Pradesh, Information Department, Publications Bureau, 1957–61.

Robinson, Ronald. 'Non-European Foundations of European Imperialism: Sketch for a Theory of Collaboration', in William Roger Louis, ed., *Imperialism: The Robinson and Gallagher Controversy*. New York: New Viewpoints, 1976.

——, John Gallagher, and Alice Denny. *Africa and the Victorians: The Climax of Imperialism*. London: St. Martin's Press, 1961; paperback edn, New York: Anchor Books, 1968.

Roy, Prodipto. 'Social Background', *Seminar* [Special Issue: 'The Cow'], no. 93 (May 1967), pp. 17–23.

Regani, Sarojini, ed. *Who's Who of Freedom Struggle in Andhra Pradesh*. Hyderabad: Ministry of Education and Cultural Affairs, Government of Andhra Pradesh, 1978.

Richard, John. *The Mughal Empire*, New Cambridge History of India, I:5. Cambridge: Cambridge University Press, 1993; Indian edn, Delhi: Foundation Books, 1995.

Sachau, Edward C., trans. and ed. *Alberuni's India*. London: Routledge & Kegan Paul, 1888; reprint edn, Delhi: S. Chand & Co., 1964, 2 vols in 1.

Sachau, Edward C. *Alberuni's India*. Abridged edn with introduction by Ainslie Embree. New York: W. W. Norton, 1971.

Sarkar, Jadunath. *Shivaji and His Times*. Calcutta: M. C. Sarkar and Sons, 1919.

——. *History of Aurangzib, Based on Original Sources*. 5 vols in 4. Calcutta: M. C. Sarkar, 1924–52.

Sarkar, Sumit. *Modern India, 1885–1947*. Delhi: Macmillan, 1985.

——. 'The Kalki-Avatar of Bikrampur: A Village Scandal in Early Twentieth Century Bengal', *SS* VI:1–53.

Sarkar, Tanika. 'Jitu Santal's Movement in Malda 1924–1932: A Study in Tribal Protest', *SS* IV:136–44.

——. 'Educating the Children of the Hindu Rashtra: Notes on RSS Schools', in Praful Bidwai, Harbans Mukhia, and Achin Vanaik, eds, *Religion, Religiosity and Communalism*, pp. 237–47. New Delhi: Manohar, 1996.

——. 'Imagining Hindurashtra: The Hindu and the Muslim in Bankim Chandra's Writings', in David Ludden, ed., *Making India Hindu* (Delhi: Oxford University Press, 1996), pp. 162–84.

Sastri, K. A. Nilakanta, ed. *A Comprehensive History of India, Volume 2: The Mauryas and Satavahanas, 325 BC–AD 300*. Bombay: Orient Longman, 1957.

Sathe, Shriram. *Search for the Year of Bharata War*. Hyderabad: Navabharati Publications, 1983.

Savarkar, Vinayak Damodar. *The Indian War of Independence, 1857*. Reprint edn, New Delhi: Rajdhani Granthnagar, 1970 [1910].

Saxena, Rajeev. 'Tulsidas' Silence on Ram Mandir at Ayodhya', *Mainstream* (9 January 1993), pp. 3–4.

Seal, Anil. *The Emergence of Indian Nationalism: Competition and Collaboration in the Late Nineteenth Century*. Cambridge: Cambridge University Press, 1968.

——. 'Imperialism and Nationalism in India', in John Gallagher, Gordon Johnson, and Anil Seal, *Locality, Province and the Nation: Essays on Indian Politics 1870 to 1940*. Cambridge: Cambridge University Press, 1973.

Sen, Amartya. 'The Threats to Secular India', *New York Review of Books* (8 April 1993).

——. 'India through Its Calendars', *The Little Magazine* 1, no. 1 (May 2000).

Sen, Asok. *Iswarchandra Vidyasagar and His Elusive Milestones*. Calcutta: Riddhi-India, 1977.

Sharma, R. S. *Communal History and Rama's Ayodhya*. New Delhi: People's Publishing House, 1990.

Sharma, R. S., M. Athar Ali, D. N. Jha, and Suraj Bhan. *Ramjanmabhumi-Baburi Masjid: A Historians' Report to the Nation*. New Delhi: People's Publishing House, 1991.

Shrimali, K. M. 'A Future for the Past?', *Social Scientist* 26, nos 9–10 (September–October 1998), pp. 26–51.

Spivak, Gayatri Chakravorty. 'A Literary Representation of the Subaltern: Mahasweta Devi's "Stanadayini"', *SS* V:91–134.

Spodek, Howard. 'On the Origins of Gandhi's Political Methodology: The Heritage of Kathiawad and Gujarat', *Journal of Asian Studies* 30, no. 2 (Feb. 1971), pp. 361–72.

Sri Ramjanmabhumi Mukti Yagya Samiti. *Sri Ramjanmabhumi ke Bare me Tathya, Ham Mandir Wahin Banayenge [The Truth about Ramjanmabhumi: We Shall Build the Temple There]*. New Delhi: Suruchi Prakashan, 1989.

Srivastava, Sushil. *The Disputed Mosque: A historical inquiry*. New Delhi: Vistaar Publications, 1991.

Stephens, Julie. 'Feminist Fictions: A Critique of the Category "Non-Western Woman" in Feminist Writings on India', *SS* VI:92–125.

Stokes, Eric. *The English Utilitarians and India*. Oxford: Clarendon Press, 1959; reprint edn, Delhi: Oxford India Paperbacks, 1989.

———. 'Imperialism and the Scramble for Africa: The New View', in William Roger Louis, ed., *Imperialism: The Robinson and Gallagher Controversy*. New York: New Viewpoints, 1976.

Subrahmanyam, Sanjay. 'Golden Age Hallucinations', *Outlook* (20 August 2001).

Sykes, W. H. 'Statistics of the Educational Institutions of the East India Company in India', *Journal of the Statistical Society of London* 8 (September 1845).

Thapar, Romila. *Ancient Indian Social History: Some Interpretations*. New Delhi: Orient Longman, 1978.

———. 'Somanatha: Narratives of a History', *Seminar*, no. 475 (March 1999), pp. 15–23.

Tharu, Susie. 'Response to Julie Stephens', *SS* VI:126–31.

——— and Tejaswini Niranjana, 'Problems for a Contemporary Theory of Gender', *SS* IX: 232–60.

Thompson, Edward. *The Other Side of the Medal*. London: Hogarth Press, 1925.

Udayakumar, S. P. 'Historicizing Myth and Mythologizing History: The "Ram Temple" Drama', *Social Scientist* 25, nos 7–8 (July–August 1997).

van der Veer, Peter. *Religious Nationalism: Hindus and Muslims in India*. Berkeley: University of California Press, 1994.

van Meter, Rachel R. 'Bankimcandra's View of the Role of Bengal in Indian Civilization', in David Kopf, ed., *Bengal Regional Identity*. Lansing, Michigan: Asian Studies Center, Michigan State University, 1969.

Venkatarangaiya, Mamidipudi, ed. *The Freedom Struggle in Andhra Pradesh*. Hyderabad: Andhra Pradesh Committee Appointed for the Compilation of a History of the Freedom Struggle in Andhra Pradesh, 1965–74.

Verma, Nirmal. *Word and Memory*. Bikaner: Vagdevi Prakashan, 1988.

Vishwa Hindu Parishad. *History Versus Casuistry: Evidence of the Rama-janmabhoomi Mandir Presented by the Vishwa Hindu Parishad to the*

Government of India in December–January 1990–91. New Delhi: Voice of India, 1991.

Viswanathan, Gauri. *Masks of Conquest: Literary Study and British Rule in India.* New York: Columbia University Press, 1989.

Vivekananda, Swami. 'The Future of India', in *Complete Works of Swami Vivekananda*, Vol. III. 8 vols. Mayavati, India: Advaita Ashram, 1964.

Washbrook, David. *The Emergence of Provincial Politics—The Madras Presidency, 1870–1920*. Cambridge: Cambridge University Press, 1976.

——. 'Progress and Problems: South Asian Economic and Social History, c. 1720–1860', *Modern Asian Studies* 22, no. 1 (1988).

Witzel, Michael and Steve Farmer. 'Horseplay in Harappa', *Frontline* 17, no. 20 (30 September–13 October 2000).

Younghusband, Francis. *Dawn in India: British Purpose and Indian Aspiration.* London: J. Murray, 1930

Web Sites and Web Articles

Bharatiya Janata Party: <*http://www.bjp.org*>.

Forum of the Indian Left (New York): <*http://www.foil.org/history*>.

Frawley, David. 'The Myth of the Aryan Invasion of India': <*http://www.spiritweb.org/Spirit/myth-of-invasion.html*>.

Global Hindu Electronic Network: <*http://rbhatnagar.csm.uc.edul*>.

Hindu Net: <*http://hindunet.org*>.

Hinduism Today (Hawaii): <*http:www.spiritweb.org/HinduismToday*>.

Jammu and Kashmir: <*http://jammu-kashmir.org/KIN/Atrocities/index.html*>.

'Library of Hindu History': <*http://www.vhp.org/hindu_history*>.

1971 War: <*http://freeindia.org/1971war*>.

Rashtriya Swayamsevak Sangh: <*http://www.rss.org*>.

Satyameva Jayate: <*http://www.flex.com/~jai/satyamevajayate*>.

Swami Chinmayananda: <*http://www.tezcat.com/~bnaik/chinmaya.html*>.

Vishwa Hindu Parishad: <*http://www.vhp.org*>.

GENERAL WORKS

Books and Articles

Appadurai, Arjun. 'Global Ethnoscapes: Notes and Queries for a Transnational Anthropology', in Richard G. Fox, ed., *Recapturing Anthropology: Working in the Present*. Santa Fe: School of American Research Publications, 1991.

Apple, Michael W. and Linda K. Christian-Smith. 'The Politics of the Textbook', in Michael W. Apple and Linda K. Christian-Smith, eds, *The Politics of the Textbook*, pp. 1–21. London: Routledge, 1991.

Arquilla, John and David Ronfeldt. *Cyberwar is Coming!* Santa Monica: RAND, 1996; reprinted from *Comparative Strategy* 12 (1993), pp. 141–65.

Bauman, Zygmunt. *Globalization: The Human Consequences*. New York: Columbia University Press, 1998.

Bernal, Martin. *Black Athena: The Afroasiatic Roots of Classical Civilization, Volume I: The Fabrication of Ancient Greece 1785–1985*. London: Free Association Books; New Brunswick, NJ: Rutgers University Press, 1987.

Bharucha, Rustom. *In the Name of the Secular: Contemporary Cultural Activism in India*. New Delhi: Oxford University Press, 1998.

Bury, J. B. *The Idea of Progress: An Inquiry into Its Growth and Origin*. New York: Dover Books, 1955 [1932].

Collini, Stefan, Donald Winch, and John Burrow. *That Noble Science of Politics: A study in nineteenth-century intellectual history*. Cambridge: Cambridge University Press, 1983.

Croce, Benedetto. *History as the Story of Liberty*. London: George Allen & Unwin, 1941 [1938].

Crosby, Christina. *The Ends of History: Victorians and the 'Woman Question'*, New York and London: Routledge, 1991.

Daniel, E. Valentine. *Charred Lullabies: Chapters in an Anthropology of Violence*. Princeton: Princeton University Press, 1996.

Deleuze, Gilles and Felix Guattari. *A Thousand Plateaus: Capitalism and Schizophrenia*, trans. Brian Massumi. Minneapolis: The University of Minnesota Press, 1987.

Dickens, Charles. *Hard Times*. Harmondsworth: Penguin Books, 1983.

Federation of Hindus-Associations. *Bhagwan's Call for Dharma Raksha* [including the publication *Hinduism Simplified*]. Diamond Bar, California: FHA, [1999?].

Foucault, Michel. *The Order of Things: An Archaeology of the Human Sciences*. New York: Vintage Books, 1973.

Fuentes, Carlos. 'Chiapas: Latin America's First Post-Communist Rebellion', *New Perspectives Quarterly* 11, no. 2 (Spring 1994).

Gandhi, M. K. *Hind Swaraj or Indian Home Rule*. Reprint edn, Ahmedabad: Navajivan Publishing House, 1962.

——. *The Collected Works of Mahatma Gandhi*. 100 vols. New Delhi: Government of India, Ministry of Information and Broadcasting, Publications Division, 1958–94.

Ghosh, Amitav. *In an Antique Land*. Delhi: Ravi Dayal, 1992.

Ginzburg, Carlo. *Ecstasies: Deciphering the Witches' Sabbath*, trans. Raymond Rosenthal. New York: Penguin Books, 1991.

Harris, Wilson. *History, Fable & Myth in the Caribbean and Guianas*. Georgetown, Guyana: The National History and Arts Council, Ministry of Information and Culture, 1970.

Hegel, Georg Wilhelm Friedrich. *The Philosophy of History*, trans. J. Sibree. New York: Dover Publications, 1956.

Iyer, Raghavan, ed. *The Moral and Political Writings of Mahatma Gandhi*. 3 vols. Oxford: Clarendon Press, 1986.

Jones, Richard Foster. 'Science and English Prose Style in the Third Quarter of the Seventeenth Century', *PMLA* 45 (1930), pp. 977–1009.

Lakha, Salim. 'Growth of Computer Software Industry in India', *Economic and Political Weekly* (6 January 1990).

Lal, Vinay. 'Nehru as a Writer', *Indian Literature*, no. 135 (January–February 1990), pp. 20–46.

——. *South Asian Cultural Studies: A Bibliography*. Delhi: Manohar, 1996.

——. 'Discipline and Authority: Some Notes on future histories and epistemologies of India', *Futures* 29, no. 10 (December 1997).

——. 'The Politics of Time at the Cusp of the Millennium', *Humanscape* 6, no. 12 (December 1999), pp. 5–12.

Lefkowitz, Mary R. and Guy MacLean Rogers, eds. *Black Athena Revisited*. Chapel Hill: University of North Carolina Press, 1996.

Leonard, Karen. *The South Asian Americans*. Westport, CT: Greenwood Press, 1997.

Levine, Philippa. *The Amateur and the Professional: Antiquarians, Historians, and Archaeologists in Victorian Britain, 1838–1886*. Cambridge: Cambridge University Press, 1986.

MacIntyre, Alisdair. *After Virtue*, 2nd edn. Notre Dame: University of Notre Dame Press, 1984.

Mathew, Biju. 'Byte-Sized Nationalism: Mapping the Hindu Right in the United States', *Rethinking Marxism* 12, no. 3 (Fall 2000), pp. 108–28.

Michaels, Alex, ed. *The Pandit: Traditional Scholarship in India*. Delhi: Manohar, 2001.

Nehru, Jawaharlal. *Glimpses of World History: Being Further Letters to his Daughter, Written in Prison, and Containing a Rambling Account of History for Young People*. London, 1934; reprint edn, Delhi: Oxford University Press, 1982.

Prasad, Monica. 'International Capital on "Silicon Plateau": Work and Control in India's Computer Industry', *Social Forces* 77, no. 2 (December 1998), pp. 429–52.

Ramanujan, A. K. *Folktales from India: A Selection of Oral Tales from Twenty-two Languages*. New York: Pantheon Books, 1991.

Rapaport, Richard. 'Bangalore: Western Technology Giants?' *Wired* 4, no. 2 (February 1996), pp. 109–14, 164–70.

Rogers, John D. 'Historical Images in the British Period', in Jonathan Spencer, ed., *Sri Lanka: History and the Roots of Conflict*. London: Routledge, 1990.

Ronfeldt, David. *Cyberocracy, Cyberspace, and Cyberology: Political Effects of the Information Revolution*. Santa Monica: RAND, 1991.

——, John Arquilla, Graham E. Fuller, and Melissa Fuller. *The Zapatista Social Netwar in Mexico*. Santa Monica: RAND, for the United States Army, 1998.

Said, Edward. 'Third World Intellectuals and Metropolitan Culture', *Raritan* 9, no. 3 (Winter 1990), pp. 27–50.

——. *Culture and Imperialism*. New York: Viking, 1993.

Sardar, Ziauddin. *Postmodernism and the Other: The New Imperialism of Western Culture*. London: Pluto Press, 1998.

—— and Jerome R. Ravetz, eds, *Cyberfutures: Culture and Politics on the Information Superhighway*. London: Pluto Press, 1996.

Sengupta, Somini. 'Hindu Nationalists Are Enrolling, and Enlisting, India's Poor', *New York Times* (13 May 2002).

Shboul, Ahmad M. H. *Al-Mas'udi and His World: A Muslim Humanist and his Interest in non-Muslims*. London: Ithaca Press, 1979.

Shenk, David. *Data Smog: Surviving the Information Glut*. New York: HarperCollins, 1997.

Sprat, Thomas. *The History of the Royal Society of London*. 1st edn, 1667; 4th edn, London: J. Knapton, J. Walthoe, etc., 1734.

Stremlau, John. 'Bangalore: India's Silicon City', *Monthly Review* (November 1996).

Takaki, Ronald. *Strangers from a Different Shore: A History of Asian Americans*. New York: Penguin Books, 1989.

Thompson, E. P. 'Eighteenth-Century English Society: Class Struggle Without Class?', *Social History* 3, no. 2 (May 1978).

Todorov, Tzvetan. *The Conquest of America: The Question of the Other* [1982], trans. Richard Howard. New York: Harper Perennial Book, 1992.

Turner, Victor. *Dramas, Fields and Metaphors: Symbolic Action in Human Society*. Ithaca, New York: Cornell University Press, 1974.

Vertovec, Steven. 'Three Meanings of "Diaspora", Exemplified among South Asian Religions', *Diaspora* 6, no. 3 (1997).

Vishwa Hindu Parishad of Chicago. *14th Anniversary 1992 Calendar*. Chicago: Vishwa Hindu Parishad, 1992.

——. *Seventeenth Annual Calendar, 1995*. Chicago: Vishwa Hindu Parishad, 1995.

Wood, Frances. *Did Marco Polo Go to China?* Boulder, Colorado: Westview Press, 1998 [1995].

Wright, Louis B. 'The Elizabethan Middle-Class Taste for History', *The Journal of Modern History* 3, no. 2 (June 1931).

Newspaper Articles

Lancaster, John. 'Activism Boosts India's Fortunes: Politically Vocal Immigrants Help Tilt Policy in Washington', *Washington Post* (9 October 1999), p. A1.

Sundaram, Viji. 'Diet, Dress Code Enrage Hindu Worshippers', *India-West* (31 March 1995), p. A1, 12.

Web Sites and Web Articles

Dominguez, Richard. 'Digital Zapatismo', 1998: <*http://www.nyu.edu/projects/wary/DigZap.html*>.

'Prophet of Terror and the Religion of Peace—Part I': <*http://www.flex.com~jai/satyamevajayate/mohwar1.html*>. Part II is available at 'mohwar2' and Part III at 'mohwar3'.

Vedic astrologer: <*http://members.aol.com/_ht_a/Jyotishi/index.html*>.

Wray, Stephen. 'Rhizomes, Nomads, and Resistant Internet Use', July 7, 1998: <*http://www.ny.edu/projects/wray/RhizNom.html*>.

Wray, Stephen. 'Transforming Luddite Resistance into Virtual Luddite Resistance: Weaving a World Wide Web of Electronic Civil Disobedience', April 7, 1998: <*http://www.nyu.edu/projects/wray/luddite.html*>.

'The X-Rated Paradise of Islam': <*http://www.flex.com/~jai/satyamevajayate/heaven.html*>.

Index